田径竞赛与技术规则

2025
汉英对照

中国田径协会　审定

人民体育出版社

图书在版编目（CIP）数据

田径竞赛与技术规则.2025：汉英对照 / 中国田径协会审定. -- 北京：人民体育出版社，2025. -- ISBN 978-7-5009-6502-2

Ⅰ.G820.4

中国国家版本馆CIP数据核字第202445YV19号

田径竞赛与技术规则.2025：汉英对照

中国田径协会　审定
出版发行：人民体育出版社
印　　装：北京新华印刷有限公司

开　本：787×960　16开本　　印　张：34.375　　字　数：649千字
版　次：2025年8月第1版　　印　次：2025年8月第1次印刷
书　号：ISBN 978-7-5009-6502-2
印　数：1—3,000册
定　价：120.00元

版权所有·侵权必究
购买本社图书，如遇有缺损页可与发行与市场营销部联系
联系电话：（010）67151482
社　　址：北京市东城区体育馆路8号（100061）
网　　址：https://books.sports.cn/

前　言

《田径竞赛与技术规则》是世界范围内田径运动规范开展和不断发展的基础。世界田联（World Athletics）作为田径规则制定者，每两年根据会员协会的提案或田径发展需要，发布新版本的规则；同时，世界田联每年适时在其官网发布经由理事会批准的最新修订内容，以满足竞赛需要。中国田径协会不定期对规则进行翻译，此次特同步出版发行规则中文版和汉英对照版，为广大从业人员和读者提供田径竞赛与技术规则最新的规范性文件。

上一次正式出版的是中文版《田径竞赛规则》2018—2019。自此，世界田联已经发布了2020版、2022版和2024版的《田径竞赛与技术规则》（Competition and Technical Rules）。与《田径竞赛规则》（Competition Rules）2018—2019版相比，世界田联从2020版开始进行了重大改版，主要包括：组织名称由国际田联（IAAF）变更为世界田联（World Athletics）（2019年）；规则名称由《田径竞赛规则》改为《田径竞赛与技术规则》，规则内容首次划分为竞赛规则和技术规则两部分，条目和顺序也随之重新编排。竞赛规则现包括三个部分：第一部分通则（General）、第二部分官员（Officials）和第三部分世界纪录（World Records）。技术规则包括：第一部分通则（General）、第二部分径赛项目（Track Events）、第三部分田赛项目（Field Events）、第四部分全能项目比赛（Combined Events Competitions）、第五部分200米标准椭圆形跑道体育场（短道）比赛[200m Standard Oval Track Stadium（Short Track）Competitions]、第六部分竞走项目（Race Walking Events）、第七部分路跑比赛（Road Races）和第八部分越野跑、山地跑和野外跑（Cross Country, Mountain and Trail Races）。

经世界田联授权，中国田径协会组织翻译并出版本书。本书包含世界田联《田径竞赛与技术规则》2024版的全部章节和说明内容，并纳入世界田联2024年全年更新发布的修订内容，且增加了"运动鞋规程""译者注"，便于读者全面、准确理解规则原版精神。为区别于2024年1月发布的英文原版，本书定版为2025版。此版以英文和中文译文对照的形式呈现，以方便读者阅读、理解和学习。

中国田径协会始终致力于提升规则翻译和中文表述的规范性、严肃性和逻辑性，不断调整完善原有竞赛规则的用词用语。本版也对前版语言描述的统一性和准确性进行了进一步的完善和修正。由于该版本变化较大，且世界田联发布修订频繁，在翻译及整合内容时难免出现错误或不尽如人意之处，希望大家提出宝贵意见和建议（如有，请以电子邮件形式发送至中国田径协会竞赛部邮箱jingsaibu@athletics.org.cn），以便再版时予以修正和完善。如果出现异议或不同的理解，则以世界田联颁布的最新英文版规则为准。

本次规则由谭进、刘后振、刘志强、吕季东、李继辉翻译，杨烽、杨中民、张苏审校，审定过程中听取了国际、国内诸多一线裁判专家的宝贵意见与建议。

中国田径协会

2025年6月

TABLE OF CONTENTS

RULES OF INTERPRETATION ································ (1)

DEFINITIONS ··· (7)

COMPETITION RULES ······································ (12)

    PART I GENERAL ···································· (13)

    PART II OFFICIALS ·································· (16)

    PART III WORLD RECORDS ························ (48)

TECHNICAL RULES ·· (62)

    PART I GENERAL ···································· (63)

    PART II TRACK EVENTS ·························· (89)

    PART III FIELD EVENTS ·························· (136)
        Vertical Jumps ···································· (147)
        Horizontal Jumps ································· (164)
        Throwing Events ································· (173)

    PART IV COMBINED EVENTS COMPETITIONS ············ (209)

    PART V 200M STANDARD OVAL TRACK STADIUM (SHORT
        TRACK) COMPETITIONS ························ (213)

    PART VI RACE WALKING EVENTS ·················· (223)

    PART VII ROAD RACES ···························· (231)

    PART VIII CROSS COUNTRY, MOUNTAIN AND TRAIL RACES ··· (237)

ATHLETIC SHOE REGULATION ·························· (248)

目　录

规则解释 …………………………………………………… （ 1 ）

定义 ………………………………………………………… （ 7 ）

田径竞赛规则 ……………………………………………… （ 12 ）

　　第一部分　通则 ……………………………………… （ 13 ）

　　第二部分　官员 ……………………………………… （ 16 ）

　　第三部分　世界纪录 ………………………………… （ 48 ）

田径技术规则 ……………………………………………… （ 62 ）

　　第一部分　通则 ……………………………………… （ 63 ）

　　第二部分　径赛项目 ………………………………… （ 89 ）

　　第三部分　田赛项目 ………………………………… （ 136 ）

　　　　高度跳跃项目 …………………………………… （ 147 ）

　　　　水平跳跃项目 …………………………………… （ 164 ）

　　　　投掷项目 ………………………………………… （ 173 ）

　　第四部分　全能项目比赛 …………………………… （ 209 ）

　　第五部分　200米标准椭圆形跑道体育场（短道）比赛 …… （ 213 ）

　　第六部分　竞走项目 ………………………………… （ 223 ）

　　第七部分　路跑比赛 ………………………………… （ 231 ）

　　第八部分　越野跑、山地跑和野外跑 ……………… （ 237 ）

运动鞋规程 ………………………………………………… （ 248 ）

WORLD ATHLETICS

RULES OF INTERPRETATION

WORLD ATHLETICS

规则解释

These Rules of Interpretation, set out principles of interpretation, other general provisions, and definitions, that apply to all Rules and Regulations (whether issued before or after these Rules of Interpretation come into effect), unless specifically stated otherwise in a specific Rule or Regulation.

1. General Principles of Interpretation

1.1　In the event of any inconsistency between the Constitution and any other Rules or Regulations, the Constitution shall prevail.

1.2　The Constitution, Rules, and Regulations will be published in English and French, and any other language decided by the Chief Executive Officer. In the event of any inconsistency between the English version and any other version, the English version shall prevail.

1.3　Rules and Regulations are to be interpreted and applied in a manner that protects and advances their respective purposes. In the event that a matter arises that is not foreseen in the Rules or Regulations in issue, it shall be addressed in the same manner.

1.4　In the event of a question arising at any time on a matter not provided for in, or as to the meaning or proper interpretation or application of any Rules or Regulations, Council may determine the same, by reference to the purpose(s) of the Rules or Regulations in issue.

1.5　In all Rules and Regulations, unless expressly specified otherwise:

　　1.5.1　words importing one gender include the other genders;

　　1.5.2　words in the singular include the plural, and words in the plural include the singular;

　　1.5.3　references to Clauses, Paragraphs, Schedules and Appendices are, unless otherwise stated, references to clauses, paragraphs, schedules, and appendices to those Rules or Regulations (as applicable);

　　1.5.4　any reference to a provision in a Rule or Regulation includes any modifications or successor provisions made or issued from time to time;

除非具体规则或规程另有明确规定，本解释规则规定了适用于所有规则和规程（无论是在本解释规则生效之前还是之后发布的）的解释原则、其他一般规定和定义。

1. **解释的一般原则**

1.1　世界田联章程与其他规则与规程不一致之处，以世界田联章程为准。

1.2　世界田联章程、规则及规程将以英文及法文出版，并以首席执行官决定的任何其他语言出版。如果其他版本与英文版本不一致，要以英文版本为准。

1.3　规则和规程应以保护和促进其各自目的的方式进行解释和适用。如果在比赛中出现相关规则或规程未预见的问题，应以同样的方式处理。

1.4　任何时候，如对比赛中任何规则或规程未予规定的事项，或者对其含义、适当解释或适用产生疑问，世界田联理事会可参照有关规则或规程的宗旨作出决定。

1.5　在所有规则和规程中，除非另有明确规定：

　　1.5.1　表示一种性别的词包括其他性别；

　　1.5.2　单数词包括复数，复数词包括单数；

　　1.5.3　除非另有说明，否则对条款、段落、附表和附录的引用是对这些规则或规程（如适用）的条款、段落、附表和附录的引用；

　　1.5.4　对规则或规程中任何条款的引用包括不时制定或发布的任何修改或后续条款；

1.5.5	any reference to the International Athletics Association Federation (or IAAF) shall mean World Athletics, formerly the International Athletics Association Federation (or IAAF);
1.5.6	any reference to legislation includes any modification or re-enactment of legislation enacted in substitution of that legislation, and any regulation, order-in-council or other instrument from time to time issued or made under that legislation;
1.5.7	any reference to an agreement includes that agreement as modified, supplemented, novated or substituted from time to time;
1.5.8	a reference to "writing" or "write" includes fax and email;
1.5.9	a reference to "may" shall mean "in the sole discretion of such person";
1.5.10	Unless otherwise defined, a reference to a person includes natural persons, corporate bodies, and unincorporated bodies (whether or not having separate legal personality), and also includes the legal personal representatives, successors and permitted assigns of such person;
1.5.11	a reference to a "day" means any day of the week and is not limited to working days;
1.5.12	an expression of time refers to Central European Standard Time;
1.5.13	headings and tables of content are for reference only and shall not affect the proper interpretation and application of the Rules or Regulations in question;
1.5.14	schedules and appendices form an integral part of the Rules or Regulations to which they are scheduled/appended, but if there is any inconsistency between any provisions in the main body of the Rules or Regulations and the content of the schedules or appendices, the provisions in the main body of the Rules or Regulations shall prevail;
1.5.15	where commentary is provided, it is to be used as an aid to the proper interpretation of the provision(s) on which it is commenting; and
1.5.16	any words following the terms "including", "include", "in particular", "such as", "for example", or any similar expression, shall be construed as illustrative and shall not limit the sense of the words, description, definition, phrase or term preceding those terms.

1.5.5 凡提及国际田径协会联合会（或国际田联），均指世界田联，前身为国际田径协会联合会（或国际田联）；

1.5.6 关于立法，包括为取代该立法而修改或重新执行的其他立法，以及依据该立法由世界田联理事会或其他机构修订并公布的任何规程；

1.5.7 对协议的任何引用包括经不时修改、补充、更新或替换的协议；

1.5.8 "书面"或"书写"包括传真和电子邮件；

1.5.9 "可以"一词应指"由该人全权决定"；

1.5.10 除非另有定义，人包括自然人、法人团体和非法人团体（无论是否具有单独的法人资格），还包括该人的法人代表、继承人和许可受让人；

1.5.11 "天"是指一周中的任何一天，不仅限于工作日；

1.5.12 关于时间的表达是指欧洲中部标准时间；

1.5.13 标题和目录仅供参考，不得影响有关规则或规程出现疑问时的正确解释和适用；

1.5.14 附表及附录是所附表/附录的规则或规程的组成部分，但如规则或规程主体内的任何条文与附表或附录的内容不一致，要以规则或规程主体内的条文为准；

1.5.15 若提供评注，则应用于帮助正确解释所评注的条款；和

1.5.16 术语"包括""特别""例如"，或任何类似表达之后的任何词语要解释为说明性词语，且不得限制这些术语之前的词语、说明、定义、短语或术语的含义。

2. General Provisions

2.1 Since the Rules and Regulations apply globally, insofar as possible they are to be interpreted and applied not by reference to particular national or local laws, but rather by reference to general principles of law common to most if not all legal systems. Subject thereto, the Rules and Regulations are governed by and are to be interpreted and applied in accordance with the laws of Monaco (excluding its conflict of law rules).

2.2 If any provision or part-provision of any Rules or Regulations is or becomes invalid, illegal or unenforceable, it shall be deemed deleted, but that shall not affect the validity, legality and enforceability of the rest of the Rules or Regulations.

2.3 Where a Rule or Regulation refers to a decision to be taken by World Athletics, without further specifying the decision-making body, that decision shall be made by Council, or by its chosen delegate.

2.4 Where a Rule or Regulation confers a power or imposes a duty on the holder of an office, that power shall be exercised, or the duty is to be performed, by the holder for the time being of the office, unless delegated to another person where the holder is properly authorised to delegate such powers.

2.5 Any deviation from the provisions of any Rules or Regulations by an officer or other representative of World Athletics and/or any irregularity, omission, or other defect in the procedures followed by such officer or other representative shall not invalidate any finding, procedure or decision unless it is shown to render that finding, procedure or decision unreliable.

2.6 Notifications:

    2.6.1 Save where expressly specified otherwise, any notification to be given under a Rule or Regulation to World Athletics, without further specifying the body or person to whom the notification is to be given, is only sufficiently given if it is made in writing, in English or French, and delivered by electronic mail to notices@worldathletics.org For the avoidance of doubt, this rule does not apply to the service of any process or other documents in any litigation or arbitration or other external dispute resolution proceedings of any kind.

规则解释

2. 一般规定

2.1 由于本规则和规程适用于全球，因此，在尽可能的情况下，本规则和规程的解释和适用不应参考特定的国家或地方法律，而应参考大多数（如果不是所有）法律体系共同适用的一般法律原则。但本规则和规程受摩纳哥法律管辖，并应根据摩纳哥法律进行解释和适用（除了其法律冲突规则）。

2.2 如果规则或规程的任何条款或部分条款无效、非法或不可执行，则应视为删除，但这不影响其他部分规则或规程的有效性、合法性和执行性。

2.3 凡由世界田联制定的规则或规程，而未进一步指明其他决策机构，则该决定要由世界田联理事会或其选定的代表作出。

2.4 任何规则或规程将权力或职责授予某一人，此权力或职责须由该人行使或履行，除非授权于他人，而该等权力已获适当授权。

2.5 世界田联的官员或其他代表对任何规则或规程的规定的任何偏离，和/或该官员或其他代表所遵循的程序中的任何违规、遗漏或其他缺陷，均不应使任何认定、程序或决定无效，除非有证据表明该认定、程序或决定不可靠。

2.6 通知：

2.6.1 除非另有明确规定，根据规则或规程向世界田联发出的任何通知，无须进一步指定要向哪个机构或个人发出通知，只有以书面形式，英文或法文，并通过电子邮件发送至notices@worldathletics.org，才算充分。为避免疑义，本规则不适用于任何诉讼、仲裁或任何形式的其他外部争议解决过程中任何程序或其他文件的送达。

2.6.2　Any notification to be given under a Rule or Regulation by a person (the "Notifying Party") will be deemed to have been sufficiently given to the party to whom the notice is required to be given (the "Receiving Party") if it is made in writing and signed or authorised by an authorised person of the Notifying Party and delivered by one of the following means to the Receiving Party:

2.6.2.1　by post to the last known address of the Receiving Party;

2.6.2.2　by personal delivery, including by courier, to the published physical address of the Receiving Party;

2.6.2.3　by electronic mail, to the published email address of the Receiving Party; or

2.6.2.4　by facsimile to the published facsimile number of the Receiving Party.

2.7　Deadlines and time limits:

2.7.1　Any deadline or time limit that is stated in a Rule or Regulation to run from notification shall be deemed to start running on the day on which the notification is delivered. Any deadline or time limit that is stated in a Rule or Regulation to run from the happening of another event or the doing of an act or thing shall be deemed to start running on the day after the happening of the event or the doing of the act or thing.

2.7.2　Official holidays and non-working days are included in the calculation of deadlines and time limits, save where they would be the last day of the deadline or time limit in question, in which case the last day of that deadline or time limit will be the next day that is not an official holiday or non-working day.

2.7.3　A deadline or time limit will be deemed to have been complied with if the notification is delivered or other act or thing is done before midnight Central European Standard Time on the day on which the deadline or time limit expires.

规则解释

2.6.2 任何个人（"通知方"）根据规则或规程发出的通知，如果以书面形式作出并由通知方的授权人签署或授权，并通过以下方式之一交付给接收方，则将被视为已充分发送给需要接收通知的一方（"接收方"）：

2.6.2.1 邮寄至接收方最后已知的地址；

2.6.2.2 通过专人（包括快递）递送至接收方已公布的实际地址；

2.6.2.3 通过电子邮件发送至接收方已公布的电子邮件地址；或

2.6.2.4 传真至接收方已公布的传真号码。

2.7 期限和时限：

2.7.1 任何规则或规程中规定自通知之日起计算的截止日期或时限，应当自通知发出之日起计算。任何规则或规程中规定自另一事件发生之日起计算的截止日期或时限，应当自另一行为或事情实施之日起计算。

2.7.2 法定节假日及非工作日均包括在截止日期和时限的计算中，但如果它们是该截止日期或时限的最后一天，则该截止日期或时限的最后一天将是下一个非法定节假日或工作日的日子。

2.7.3 如果在截止日期或时限到期之日的欧洲中部标准时间午夜之前发出通知、完成其他行为或事情，则视为已遵守截止日期或时限。

2.8 Transitional provisions:

    2.8.1 Rules and Regulations shall come into effect on the date specified by Council, unless specified otherwise.

    2.8.2 Council may amend, supplement, replace or revoke Rules or Regulations from time to time, as it sees fit. Such amendments and/or supplementary and/or replacement provisions shall come into effect on the date specified by Council.

    2.8.3 Unless expressly specified otherwise, Rules and Regulations (including amendments and supplementary or replacement provisions) shall apply retroactively if they are procedural, but if they are substantive they shall not apply retroactively, but rather only to matters arising after they come into effect. Instead, any matter that is pending as of the date the Rules or Regulations come into effect, and any matter that arises after that date but relates to facts occurring prior to that date, shall be governed by the substantive provisions of the Rules and Regulations in force prior to that date, unless the principle of lex mitior applies.

3. Generally Applicable Definitions

Unless a contrary intention appears, defined words and defined terms used in these Rules of Interpretation and/or in any other Rules and Regulations shall be denoted by starting with capital letters, and shall have the meaning set out in the Generally Applicable Definitions, or the meaning given to them in the Constitution.

2.8 过渡条款：

  2.8.1 除非另有规定，规则与规程应自世界田联理事会规定的日期生效。

  2.8.2 世界田联理事会可随时酌情修订、补充、替换或撤销规则或规程。这些修订和/或补充和/或替换条款应自世界田联理事会指定的日期起生效。

  2.8.3 除另有明确规定外，规则与规程（包括修订和补充或替代规定）如果是程序性的，则应追溯适用；但如果是实质性的，则不追溯适用，而只适用于生效后出现的问题。相反，规则或规程生效之日尚未解决的任何事项，以及该日期之后出现但与该日期之前发生的事实有关的任何事项，应受该日期之前有效的规则和规程的实质性规定的管辖，除非适用从宽法原则。

3. 一般适用定义

除非有相反的意图，本解释规则或规程，或者任何其他规则或规程中使用的定义词语和术语应以大写字母开头，并具有普遍适用定义中规定的含义或具有世界田联章程赋予它们的含义。

DEFINITIONS

定　义

GENERALLY APPLICABLE DEFINITIONS

These Generally Applicable Definitions are the definitions of certain commonly used terms, that apply to the Constitution and all Rules and Regulations (whether issued before or after these Generally Applicable Definitions come into effect), unless specifically stated otherwise in the Constitution or any specific Rule or Regulation.

"Anti-Doping Rules" has the same meaning as defined in the Constitution.

"Area Association" has the same meaning as defined in the Constitution.

"Athlete" means, unless specified otherwise, any Person who is entered for, or participating in, an Athletics event or competition of World Athletics, its Members or Area Associations by virtue of their agreement, membership, affiliation, authorisation, accreditation, entry or participation.

"Athlete Support Personnel" means, unless specified otherwise, any coach, trainer, manager, authorised Athlete Representative, agent, team staff, official, medical or para-medical personnel, parent or any other Person working with, treating or assisting an Athlete participating in, or preparing for, an Athletics event or competition.

"Athletics" has the same meaning as defined in the Constitution.

"Athletics Integrity Unit" has the same meaning as defined in the Constitution.

"CAS" has the same meaning as defined in the Constitution.

"Constitution" has the same meaning as defined in the Constitution.

"Country" means a self-governing geographical area of the world recognised as an independent state by international law and international governmental bodies.

"Integrity Code of Conduct" has the same meaning as defined in the Constitution.

一般适用定义

除非世界田联章程或任何具体规则或规程另有明确规定，这些普遍适用的定义是某些常用术语的定义，适用于世界田联章程及所有规则和规程（无论是在这些普遍适用的定义生效之前还是之后发布）。

"反兴奋剂规则"与世界田联章程中定义相同。

"地区联合会"与世界田联章程中定义相同。

除非另有规定，"运动员"是指任何根据协议、会员资格、隶属关系、授权、注册、报名或参与，而报名或参加世界田联及其成员协会或地区协会的田径赛事或比赛的人士。

除非另有规定，"运动员保障人员"是指任何教练员、训练员、经理、授权运动员代表、经纪人、团队工作人员、官员、医疗或辅助医疗人员、家长或任何其他与运动员共事、治疗或协助该运动员参加或准备田径赛事或比赛的人员。

"田径"与世界田联章程中定义相同。

"田径诚信机构"与世界田联章程中定义相同。

"CAS"与世界田联章程中定义相同。

"章程"与世界田联章程中定义相同。

"国家"是指世界上被国际法和国际政府机构认可为独立国家的自治地理区域。

"诚信行为准则"与世界田联章程中定义相同。

"Integrity Unit" has the same meaning as defined in the Constitution.

"International Competitions" has the same meaning as World Rankings Competitions.

"International-Level Athlete" means, unless stated otherwise, an Athlete who is entered for or is competing in an International Competition.

"IOC" has the same meaning as defined in the Constitution.

"Major Event Organisation" means any international multi-sport organisation (e.g., the IOC) that acts as the ruling body for any continental, regional or other World Rankings Competition.

"Member Federation" has the same meaning as defined in the Constitution.

"Person" means any natural person (including any Athlete or Athlete Support Personnel) or an organisation or other entity.

"Regulations" has the same meaning as defined in the Constitution.

"Rule" means a principle, instruction, direction, standard or procedure approved from time to time by Council within its powers and responsibilities, which shall not be inconsistent with the Constitution. A reference to "a" Rule (singular) means the Rule in which the reference to the Rule is made, unless stated otherwise.

"Rules" has the same meaning as defined in the Constitution.

"Territory" means a geographical area of the world which is not a Country, but which has aspects of self-government, at least to the extent of being autonomous in the control of its sport, and which is recognised as such by the World Athletics.

"WADA" has the same meaning as defined in the Constitution.

"World Athletics Global Calendar" means the calendar of competitions published on the World Athletics website from time to time.

定 义

"诚信机构"与世界田联章程中定义相同。

"国际比赛"与世界田联章程中定义相同。

除非另有说明,"国际级运动员"是指参加或正在参加国际比赛的运动员。

"国际奥委会"与世界田联章程中定义相同。

"重大赛事组织"是指作为任何洲际、地区或其他世界排名比赛的管理机构的任何国际综合运动组织(如国际奥委会)。

"会员联合会"与世界田联章程中定义相同。

"人"是指任何自然人(包括任何运动员或运动员支持人员)、组织或其他实体。

"规程"与世界田联章程中定义相同。

"规则(Rule)"是指世界田联理事会在其权力和职责范围内不时批准的原则、说明、指示、标准或程序,且不得与世界田联章程相抵触。除非另有说明,对"某项"规则(单数)的引用是指引用该规则。

"规则(Rules)"与世界田联章程中定义相同。

"地区"是指世界上不是一个国家,但具有自治需求的某一地理区域,它至少在管理当地体育运动的程度上具有自主性,且该自主性获得了世界田联的认可。

"WADA"与世界田联章程中定义相同。

"世界田联全球日历"是指世界田联网站上不时发布的比赛日历。

"World Athletics Series" or "WAS" means the competitions in World Athletics' four-yearly official competition programme such as the World Athletics Championships, World Athletics Indoor Championships, World Athletics U20 Championships, World Athletics Relays, World Athletics Road Running Championships, World Athletics Race Walking Team Championships, and World Athletics Cross Country Championships, and World Athletics Series Event or WAS Event means any one of these events.

"World Rankings Competitions" means:

1. Competitions held or sanctioned by World Athletics:

    a. World Athletics Series.

    b. Olympic Games.

    c. The athletics programme of Games and other Athletics Competitions with participants from different Areas.

    d. Invitation meetings/circuits and label road races.

    e. International Matches with participants from different Areas.

2. Competitions held or sanctioned by an Area Association:

    a. Area Championships (of all types and disciplines).

    b. Intra-Area Competitions.

    c. The athletics programme of Games and other Athletics Competitions with participants from a single Area.

    d. Invitation meetings/circuits and road races.

    e. International Matches with participants from a single Area.

定 义

"**世界田径系列赛**"或者"**WAS**"是指世界田联四年一度的正式比赛计划中的比赛，例如世界田径锦标赛、世界田联室内田径锦标赛、世界田联青年U20田径锦标赛、世界田联接力赛、世界田联路跑锦标赛、世界田联竞走团体锦标赛、世界田联越野跑锦标赛，而世界田联系列赛事或 WAS 赛事是指其中任何一项赛事。

"**世界排名赛**"是指：

1. **世界田联举办或许可的比赛：**

    a. 世界田径系列赛。

    b. 奥运会。

    c. 运动员来自不同地区的综合运动会的田径项目和其他田径比赛。

    d. 邀请赛/巡回赛和标牌路跑赛事。

    e. 运动员来自不同地区的国际比赛。

2. **由地区协会举办或许可的比赛：**

    a. 地区锦标赛（所有分组和项目）。

    b. 地区内的比赛。

    c. 运动员来自同一地区的综合运动会田径项目和其他田径比赛。

    d. 邀请赛/巡回赛和路跑赛事。

    e. 运动员来自同一地区的国际比赛。

3. Competitions held or sanctioned by a National Member Federation:

   a. National Senior Championships (in the disciplines included in the World Athletics Championships and World Athletics Indoor Championships competition programme).

   b. Other selected domestic competitions as identified by the Member Federation held in compliance with the World Athletics Competition and Technical Rules for which an application is submitted within the terms and conditions established by World Athletics and with its approval.

3. **由国家会员协会举办或许可的比赛：**

    a. 国家高级锦标赛（世界田联锦标赛和世界田联室内锦标赛比赛所涵盖的项目）。

    b. 会员联合会确定的其他选定的国内比赛，这些比赛须符合世界田联规定的条款和条件并经世界田联批准。

COMPETITION RULES

田径竞赛规则

PART I GENERAL

1. **Authorisation to Stage Competitions**

1.1 World Athletics is responsible for supervising a global competition system, which comprises all World Rankings Competitions, in cooperation with the Area Associations and Member Federations. World Athletics shall coordinate its competition calendar and those of the respective Area Associations and, in part, those of the Member Federations in order to avoid or minimise conflicts. All World Rankings Competitions must be authorised by World Athletics, an Area Association or a Member Federation in accordance with this Rule 1. Any combination or integration of Invitation Meetings into a Series / Tour or League requires a permit from World Athletics or the concerned Area Association including the necessary regulation or contractual condition for such an activity. The operation may be delegated to a third party. In the event that an Area Association fails to properly manage and control World Rankings Competitions in accordance with these Rules, World Athletics shall be entitled to intervene and take such steps as it deems necessary.

1.2 World Athletics alone shall have the right to organise the Athletics competition at the Olympic Games and the competitions that are included in the World Athletics Series.

1.3 [Intentionally left blank.]

1.4 Area Associations shall have the right to organise Area Championships and they may organise such other intra-Area events as they deem appropriate.

1.5 Competitions requiring a World Athletics Permit:

    1.5.1 A World Athletics Permit is required for all competitions listed in paragraphs 1. (c), (d) and (e) of the World Rankings Competitions definition.

    1.5.2 The Member Federation in whose Country or Territory the World Rankings Competition is to take place, together with the relevant organising body of that competition (where applicable), shall be required to notify World Athletics (using the established process where relevant) as soon as practicable.

第一部分　通则

1. 举办比赛的授权

1.1　世界田联会同地区联合会和会员协会负责管理所有排名赛事的全球竞赛体系。世界田联安排竞赛日程和计划应统筹协调各地区联合会和部分会员协会的赛事，以避免或减少冲突。根据规则1条，所有国际排名赛事需经世界田联、地区联合会或会员协会授权。任何国际邀请赛事要成为系列赛/巡回赛或联赛，需由世界田联或相关地区联合会批准，审核资料包括竞赛规程和活动的条约性条款。赛事的运行可委托第三方。地区联合会未按本规则对世界排名赛事进行适宜管控，世界田联有权干预并采取其认为必要的措施。

1.2　世界田联对奥运会田径比赛和世界田径系列赛所含赛事享有独立举办权。

1.3　［此处留空待续。］

1.4　地区联合会有权举办地区锦标赛及其认为适宜的地区内赛事。

1.5　世界田联批准的赛事：

　　1.5.1　举办世界排名比赛定义1.（c）（d）和（e）所列的全部国际赛事，需由世界田联批准。

　　1.5.2　有意愿举办世界排名赛事的国家或领地会员协会，会同相关赛事组织机构，应尽早向世界田联（采用规定程序）提出申请。

1.5.3 World Athletics will acknowledge the notification, and grant the authorisation to stage the competition with subsequent inclusion in the list of World Rankings Competitions and publication on the World Athletics Global Calendar.

1.6 Competitions requiring an Area Association Permit:

1.6.1 An Area Association Permit is required for all Competitions listed in paragraphs 2. (b), (c),(d) and (e) of the World Rankings Competitions definition.

1.6.2 The Member Federation in whose Country or Territory the World Rankings Competition is to take place, together with the relevant organising body of that competition (where applicable), shall be required to notify the Area Association (using the established process where relevant) as soon as practicable.

1.6.3 The Area Association will acknowledge the notification and grant the authorisation to stage the competition with subsequent notification to World Athletics for inclusion in the list of World Rankings Competitions and publication on the World Athletics Global Calendar.

1.7 Competitions requiring a Member Federation Permit:

1.7.1 A Member Federation Permit is required for all competitions listed in paragraph 3. (b) of the World Rankings Competitions definition.

1.7.2 Foreign athletes may participate in those Competitions subject to Rule 5 (Requirements to Compete in International Competitions) of the Eligibility Rules. No athlete may participate in any such competition if they are ineligible to participate in the sport of Athletics under the rules of World Athletics, the host Member or the Member Federation to which they are affiliated.

1.7.3 The Member Federation in whose Country or Territory the World Rankings Competition is to take place shall be required to notify World Athletics by submitting an application through the Global Calendar Platform no later than sixty days prior to the date of the Competition.

1.7.4 World Athletics will acknowledge the notification and confirm subsequent inclusion in the list of World Rankings Competitions and publication on the World Athletics Global Calendar.

1.5.3 世界田联收到赛事申办报告，同意授权举办，将其纳入世界排名赛事计划并予以公布。

1.6 地区联合会批准的赛事：

1.6.1 举办世界排名比赛定义2.(b)(c)(d)和(e)所列的全部赛事，需经地区联合会批准。

1.6.2 有意愿举办世界排名赛事的国家或领地会员协会，会同相关赛事组织机构，应尽早向地区联合会（采用规定程序）提出申请。

1.6.3 地区联合会收到赛事申办书，同意授权举办，向世界田联报告并纳入世界排名赛事计划和予以公布。

1.7 需经会员协会批准的赛事：

1.7.1 举办世界排名比赛定义中3.(b)所列的全部赛事，需经会员协会批准。

1.7.2 外籍运动员可参加规则5条（符合参加国际比赛资格要求）所述比赛。任何人不符合世界田联、主办田协和所属会员协会的规则要求，则不具备参赛资格。

1.7.3 申办世界排名比赛的国家或地区会员协会，需于比赛日期60天以前，通过全球竞赛计划平台提交申请。

1.7.4 世界田联收到赛事申办书，同意授权举办，将其纳入世界排名赛事计划并予以公布。

2. Regulations Governing the Conduct of World Rankings Competitions

2.1 The Council may produce Regulations governing the conduct of World Rankings Competitions held under the Rules and regulating the relationships of athletes, Athlete Representatives, meeting organisers and Members. These Regulations may be varied or amended by Council as it sees fit.

2.2 World Athletics and Area Associations may designate one or more representatives to attend every World Rankings Competition requiring a World Athletics or Area Association Permit, respectively, to ensure that the applicable Rules and Regulations are complied with. At the request of World Athletics or Area Association, respectively, such representative(s) shall render a compliance report within 30 days of the end of the World Rankings Competition in question.

2. 国际排名比赛规程

2.1 世界田联理事会在规则之下，制定世界排名比赛规程，管理比赛运行，并规范运动员、运动员代表、比赛组织者和会员协会之间的关系。理事会在其认为合适的情况下，可对规程进行修改和增补。

2.2 世界田联和地区联合会可指派一名或多名代表，参与所有批准的世界排名比赛，以确保适宜比赛规则和规程的执行。该代表应根据世界田联或地区联合会各自的要求，在世界排名比赛结束后30日内提交一份关于问题的报告。

PART II OFFICIALS

3. International Officials

3.1 At competitions organised under paragraphs 1. (a), (b), (c), (d) and 2. (a), (b), (c), (d) of the World Rankings Competition definition, the following officials should be appointed internationally:

    3.1.1 Organisational Delegate(s)

    3.1.2 Technical Delegate(s)

    3.1.3 Medical Delegate

    3.1.4 Anti-Doping Delegate

    3.1.5 World Athletics Referees

    3.1.6 World Athletics Race Walking Judges

    3.1.7 International Road Course Measurer

    3.1.8 World Athletics Starter

    3.1.9 World Athletics Photo Finish Judge

    3.1.10 Jury of Appeal

The number of officials appointed in each category, how, when and by whom they shall be appointed, shall be indicated in the applicable World Athletics (or Area Association) Technical Regulations.

For competitions organised under paragraphs 1. (a), (d) and (e) of the World Rankings Competition definition, Council may appoint an Advertising Commissioner. For competitions under paragraphs 2. (a), (c), (d) and (e) of the World Rankings Competition definition, any such appointments will be made by the relevant Area Association, for competitions under paragraph 1. (c) of the World Rankings Competition definition, by the relevant body, and for competitions under paragraph 3 of the World Rankings Competition definition, by the relevant Member.

第二部分　官员

3. 国际官员

3.1 举办世界排名比赛定义1.（a）（b）（c）（d）和2.（a）（b）（c）（d）所列比赛，应从国际上指派下列官员：

  3.1.1　组织代表（1人或多人）

  3.1.2　技术代表（1人或多人）

  3.1.3　医务代表

  3.1.4　反兴奋剂代表

  3.1.5　世界田联裁判长（多人）

  3.1.6　世界田联竞走裁判员（多人）

  3.1.7　国际公路赛道丈量员

  3.1.8　世界田联发令员

  3.1.9　世界田联终点摄影裁判员

  3.1.10　申诉委员会

在适用的世界田联（或地区联合会）技术规程中，应明确说明指派各类官员的数量、方式、时间以及派出机构。

举办世界排名比赛定义1.（a）（d）和（e）所述比赛，世界田联理事会可指派1名广告管理专员。举办世界排名比赛定义2.（a）（c）（d）和（e）所述比赛，应由相关地区联合会指派。举办世界排名比赛定义1.（c）所述比赛，应由相关机构指派。举办世界排名比赛定义3所述比赛，应由相关会员协会指派。

Note (i): The International Officials should wear distinctive attire or insignia.

Note (ii): The International Officials in paragraphs 3.1.5 to 3.1.9 of this Rule may be classified according to the applicable World Athletics Policy.

The travelling and accommodation expenses of each individual appointed by World Athletics or an Area Association under this Rule or under Rule 2.2 of the Competition Rules shall be paid to the individual according to the relevant regulations.

4. Organisational Delegates

The Organisational Delegates shall maintain close liaison with the Organisers at all times and report regularly to Council (or Area Association or other relevant governing body), and they shall deal as necessary with matters concerning the duties and financial responsibilities of the Organising Member and the Organisers. They shall cooperate with the Technical Delegate(s).

5. Technical Delegates

5.1 The Technical Delegate(s), in conjunction with the Organisers, which shall afford them all necessary help, are responsible for ensuring that all technical arrangements are in complete conformity with the Technical Rules and the World Athletics Track and Field Facilities Manual.

Technical Delegates appointed for competitions other than invitation meetings shall:

5.1.1 ensure the submission to the appropriate body of proposals for the timetable of events and the entry standards;

5.1.2 approve the list of implements to be used and whether athletes may use their own implements or those provided by a supplier;

5.1.3 ensure that the applicable Technical Regulations are issued to all competing Members in good time before the competition;

5.1.4 be responsible for all other technical preparations necessary for the holding of the athletics event;

5.1.5 control the entries and have the right to reject them for technical reasons or in accordance with the Rule 8.1 of the Technical Rules (rejection for reasons other than technical must result from a ruling of World Athletics or appropriate Area Association or other relevant governing body);

注（ⅰ）：国际官员应穿戴易于区别的服装或徽章。

注（ⅱ）：本规则3.1.5至3.1.9条涉及国际官员应按照世界田联相关政策分类。

由世界田联或地区联合会按照此规则或竞赛规则2.2条指派的官员的差旅和食宿费，应由赛事组织者依相关规定支付给个人。

4. 组织代表

组织代表应始终与组织者保持密切联系，定期向世界田联理事会（或地区联合会或其他相关管理机构）提交报告。必要时，还应处理承办会员协会和组织者的有关职责和财务责任问题。组织代表应与技术代表配合工作。

5. 技术代表

5.1 技术代表与组织者一起，提供一切必要的帮助，共同保证全部技术性安排完全符合《技术规则》和《世界田联田径场地设施手册》的要求。

指派邀请赛之外赛事的技术代表：

5.1.1 确保向相关组织提交竞赛日程和报名标准的建议；

5.1.2 批准比赛使用的器械清单，以及是否允许运动员使用自备器材或供应商提供的器械；

5.1.3 确保在赛前的适当时间，向所有参赛会员协会发送适用的技术规程；

5.1.4 负责举办田径比赛所有其他必要的技术准备；

5.1.5 管控报名，并有权以技术性原因或根据技术规则8.1条拒绝报名（如出现非技术性原因而拒绝报名，应由世界田联、相关地区联合会或其他相关管理机构作出裁决）；

5.1.6　　determine the qualifying standards for the Field Events, and the basis on which the rounds shall be arranged for Track Events;

5.1.7　　cause the seeding and draws for all events to be made in accordance with the Rules and any applicable Technical Regulations and approve all start lists;

5.1.8　　decide upon any matters which arise prior to the competition, and for which provision has not been made in these Rules (or any applicable regulations) or the arrangements for the competitions, where appropriate, in conjunction with the organisers;

5.1.9　　decide ［including where appropriate in conjunction, when available, with the relevant Referee(s) and the Competition Director］ upon any matters which arise during the competition and for which provision has not been made in these Rules (or any applicable regulations) or the arrangements for the competitions or which might require a deviation from them in order for the competition to continue in whole or in part or in order to ensure fairness to those taking part;

5.1.10　if requested, chair the Technical Meeting and brief the Athletics Referees; and

5.1.11　ensure the submission of written reports in advance of the competition on its preparations and after its conclusion on the execution, including recommendations for future editions.

Technical Delegates appointed for invitation meetings shall provide all necessary support and advice to the organisers and ensure the submission of written reports on the execution of the competition.

Specific information is provided in the Technical Delegates Guidelines which may be downloaded from the World Athletics website.

Rule 5 of the Competition Rules (and in a similar way Rule 6 of the Competition Rules) has been elaborated to better reflect the current practice in relation to the roles and duties of the respective delegates and international officials. These are intended to make clearer the powers that Technical and Medical Delegates (or persons delegated by them) have in relation to the conduct of competition, especially in relation to unforeseen events and, perhaps most importantly, when athlete medical care issues arise, particularly in out-of-stadium competitions. However, all matters under the Rules which are within the responsibilities and power of the Referee remain that way. These enhancements to the Rules should not be seen as changing this situation – they are to cover the situations which are not expressly provided for.

5.1.6 决定田赛项目的及格标准，以及径赛项目赛次的安排原则；

5.1.7 根据本规则和适用的技术规程，安排所有项目的抽签办法和抽签，确认所有参赛者名单；

5.1.8 在适当的情况下，与比赛组织者一起，对于在比赛前发生的任何问题，以及本规则（或任何适用的规程）中未作规定的任何事宜或竞赛安排，作出裁决；

5.1.9 对于比赛期间发生的任何事情，以及本规则（或任何适用的规程）中未作规定的任何事宜或竞赛安排，抑或是对比赛的全部或部分做必要的变动，作出裁决（包括在适当情况下，与相关裁判长和竞赛主任一起），以确保比赛全部或部分继续进行，或确保参赛者的公平参赛；

5.1.10 根据要求，主持技术会议，并简要介绍裁判长；

5.1.11 确保赛前提交比赛准备情况的书面报告，以及赛后提交比赛执行情况的总结，包括对未来赛事的建议。

邀请赛的技术代表，应向组织者提供一切必要的支持和建议，并确保提交比赛执行情况的书面报告。

《技术代表指南》的详细内容，可在世界田联网站下载。

竞赛规则5条（以及竞赛规则6条的相似表达）详尽阐述了目前裁判实践中各个代表和国际官员的任务与职责。这也使技术代表和医务代表（或他们的代表）在比赛过程中的职责范围更加明晰，尤其是对突发事件的处理，比如在外场比赛中，运动员需要医疗护理的情况。然而，规则中属于裁判长职责和权限范围的事宜，处理方法不变。规则的加强部分不应视为情形的变化——只是涵盖了没有明确表达的部分。

6. Medical Delegates

6.1 The Medical Delegate shall:

    6.1.1 have ultimate authority on all medical matters;

    6.1.2 ensure that adequate facilities for medical examination, treatment and emergency care will be available at the venue(s) of the competition, training and Warm-up Areas and that medical attention can be provided where athletes are accommodated and for provision of and compliance with the requirements of Rule 6.1 of the Technical Rules;

    6.1.3 make examinations and provide medical certificates in accordance with Rule 4.4 of the Technical Rules; and

    6.1.4 have the power to order an athlete to withdraw before, or to immediately retire from an event during, competition.

Note (i): The powers under Rules 6.1.3 and 6.1.4 of the Competition Rules may be passed by the Medical Delegate to (or where no Medical Delegate is appointed or available be exercised by) one or more medical doctors appointed and so designated by the Organisers who should normally be identified by an armband, vest or similar distinctive apparel. Where the Medical Delegate or doctor is not immediately available to the athlete, they may instruct or direct an official or other authorised person to act on their behalf.

Note (ii): Any athlete withdrawn or retired from a Running or Race Walking Event under Rule 6.1.4 of the Competition Rules shall be shown in the result as DNS and DNF, respectively. Any athlete not complying with such an order shall be disqualified from that event.

Note (iii): Any athlete withdrawn or retired from a Field Event under Rule 6.1.4 shall be shown in the result as DNS if they have not taken any trial. However, if they have taken any trials, the results of those trials shall stand and the athlete classified in the result accordingly. Any athlete not complying with such an order shall be disqualified from further participation in that event.

Note (iv): Any athlete withdrawn or retired from a Combined Event under Rule 6.1.4 shall be shown in the result as DNS if they have not attempted to start the first event. However, if they have attempted to start the first event, Rule 39.10 of the Technical Rules shall apply. Any athlete not complying with such an order shall be disqualified from further participation in that event.

6. 医务代表

6.1 医务代表应当：

    6.1.1 对所有医疗事务具有最终权威；

    6.1.2 根据技术规则6.1条，应确保在比赛场地、训练和热身场地有足够的医学检查、治疗、急救护理设施设备，并在运动员住地提供医疗看护；

    6.1.3 根据技术规则4.4条，进行医学检查和提供医学证明；以及

    6.1.4 有权要求运动员在赛前或赛中立即退出比赛。

注（i）：竞赛规则6.1.3条和6.1.4条所述权利可由医务代表（在没有指派医务代表或其不在场的情况下）交给组织者指定的1名或多名医生，该人员应佩戴明显的袖标、穿着背心或类似的服装。如果医务代表或医生无法立刻到位，其可指派1名官员或其他授权人士代为行使职权。

注（ii）：根据竞赛规则6.1.4条，未参赛或中途退赛的跑或竞走项目的运动员，成绩单上应分别记录为DNS和DNF。任何不遵守此规定的运动员，将被取消该项目的比赛资格。

注（iii）：根据竞赛规则6.1.4条，未参赛或中途退赛的田赛项目的运动员，如果退赛时尚未开始试跳（掷），成绩单上应记录为DNS。如果已经试跳（掷），则相应成绩应保留并依此排名。任何不遵守此规定的运动员，将被取消继续参加该项目比赛的资格。

注（iv）：根据竞赛规则6.1.4条，未参赛或中途退赛的全能项目的运动员，如果退赛时尚未开始首个项目，成绩单上应记录为DNS。但是，如果已经尝试开始了第一项比赛，则技术规则39.10条将适用。任何不遵守此规定的运动员，将被取消继续参加该项目比赛的资格。

The health and safety of all participants in the competition is a high priority consideration for World Athletics, other governing bodies and competition organisers. The availability of the expertise of a well- respected and qualified person in the role of Medical Delegate is essential to carry out these key tasks, especially as they (or those authorised by them or the Organisers) amongst other duties have the responsibility to withdraw an athlete from competition if deemed necessary for medical reasons. It is important to note that the power of the Medical Delegate (or a medical doctor acting at their request or in their place) applies to all events.

It is essential that there is a reliable communication system and procedures in place between the Medical Delegate (and those authorised to act in their place), the Technical Delegates and the Competition Director particularly in relation to the duties under Rules 6.1.3 and 6.1.4 of the Competition Rules as these have a direct impact on start lists, results and the management of the competition.

7. Anti-Doping Delegates

The Anti-Doping Delegate shall liaise with the Organisers to ensure that suitable facilities are provided for the conduct of doping control. They shall be responsible for all matters relating to doping control.

8. World Athletics Referees

8.1 Where World Athletics Referees are appointed, the Technical Delegates shall appoint the Chief among the appointed World Athletics Referees, if one was not appointed previously by the relevant body. Whenever possible, the Chief, in conjunction with the Technical Delegates, shall assign at least one World Athletics Referee for every event on the programme. The World Athletics Referee shall be the Referee of each event to which they are assigned.

8.2 In Cross Country, Road Running, Mountain Running and Trail Running competitions, World Athletics Referees, if appointed, shall provide all necessary support to the Organisers. They must be present at all times when an event to which they have been assigned is in progress. They should ensure that the conduct of the competition is in full conformity with the Rules, applicable Technical Regulations and relevant decisions made by the Technical Delegates. The World Athletics Referee shall be the Referee of each event to which they are assigned.

Specific information is provided in the World Athletics Referee Guidelines which may be downloaded from the World Athletics website.

世界田联、其他管理机构和赛事组织者非常关心所有参赛运动员的健康与安全。一名备受尊重和合格的拥有专业知识技能的人士担任医务代表是完成这些重要任务的关键，尤其是从医学角度考虑认为有必要的话，他（或者由组织者或他授权的人士）除其他职责外还有责任让运动员退出比赛。需要注意的是，医务代表（或者依其要求/代替其工作的医生）的权利适用于所有比赛。

至关重要的是，在医务代表（以及被授权行使其职责的人）、技术代表和竞赛主任之间应建立可靠的通信体系和程序，特别是关系到履行上述竞赛规则6.1.3条和6.1.4条的职责，这将直接影响参赛名单、成绩单和比赛的管理。

7. 反兴奋剂代表

反兴奋剂代表应与组织者建立联系，以保证有足够的设备用于兴奋剂检查。他应负责所有有关兴奋剂检查的事宜。

8. 世界田联裁判长

8.1　如果相关组织没有事先指定，技术代表应在已指派的世界田联裁判长中指定1人为世界田联裁判长组长。只要有可能，该组长必须与技术代表合作，为比赛日程中的每个项目指派至少1名世界田联裁判长。该世界田联裁判长应为指派项目的裁判长。

8.2　在越野跑、路跑、山地跑及野外跑中，如果指派了世界田联裁判长，他应为组织者提供所有必要的支持。当所负责的项目进行时，他必须始终在场，并确保比赛的实施完全符合世界田联规则和适用的技术规程，以及技术代表所做的相关决定。该世界田联裁判长应为指派项目的裁判长。

《世界田联裁判长指南》提供具体信息，可从世界田联网站下载。

9. World Athletics Race Walking Judges

Race Walking Judges appointed for all competitions falling under paragraphs 1. (a) and (b) of the World Rankings Competition definition must be World Athletics Gold Level Race Walking Judges.

Race Walking Judges appointed for competitions under paragraphs 1. (c), (d) and 2. (a), (b), (c), (d) of the World Rankings Competition definition shall be World Athletics Gold, Silver or Bronze Level Race Walking Judges.

10. International Road Course Measurers

At all World Rankings Competitions, an International Road Course Measurer shall be appointed or engaged to ensure that the courses where Road Events are held entirely or partially outside the stadium are measured and certified in accordance with World Athletics requirements.

The measurer shall be a member of the World Athletics/AIMS Panel of International Road Course Measurers (Grade "A" or "B").

The course should be measured in good time before the competition.

The measurer will check and certify the course if they find it conforms to the Rules for Road Races (see Rules 54.11, 55.2 and 55.3 of the Technical Rules and respective Notes). They shall also ensure compliance with Rules 31.20 and 31.21 of the Competition Rules in case a World Record may be made.

They shall cooperate with the Organisers in the course arrangements and witness the conduct of the race to ensure that the course run by athletes follows the same course that was measured and approved. They shall furnish an appropriate certificate to the Technical Delegate(s).

11. World Athletics Starters and Photo Finish Judges

At all competitions under paragraphs 1. (a), (b), (c) and 2. (a), (b) of the World Rankings Competition definition held in the stadium, a World Athletics Starter and a World Athletics Photo Finish Judge shall be appointed, respectively, by Council, the relevant Area Association or governing body. The World Athletics Starter shall start the races (and undertake any other duties) assigned to them by the Technical Delegate(s) and shall supervise the checking and operation of the Start Information System. The World Athletics Photo Finish Judge shall supervise all Photo Finish functions and shall be the Chief Photo Finish Judge.

9. 世界田联竞走裁判员

被指派世界排名比赛定义1.（a）和（b）所有比赛的竞走裁判员，都必须是世界田联金级竞走裁判员。

被指派为世界排名比赛定义1.（c）（d）和2.（a）（b）（c）（d）所述比赛的竞走裁判员，必须是世界田联金级、银级或铜级竞走裁判员。

10. 国际公路赛道丈量员

举办所有世界排名比赛，应指派国际公路赛道丈量员，或按照世界田联要求以确保全部或部分在体育场外举行的公路项目赛道得到丈量。

丈量员应是世界田联/国际马拉松及长跑协会（AIMS）国际公路赛道丈量员小组成员（A级或B级）。

应在比赛前的适当时间内丈量赛道。

丈量员还应检查和核实赛道，如他认为此赛道符合路跑规则（见技术规则54.11条、55.2条、55.3条和相关备注），则应予以认证。他还应确保遵守竞赛规则31.20条和31.21条，以备世界纪录产生。

他应与赛事组织者合作安排赛道，并监督比赛进行，以确保运动员所跑的赛道是他丈量和批准的赛道。他应将批准的证书提供给技术代表。

11. 世界田联发令员和世界田联终点摄影裁判员

世界排名比赛定义1.（a）（b）（c）和2.（a）（b）所述的所有在体育场内举行的比赛，世界田联理事会、相关地区联合会或主管部门应指派1名世界田联发令员和1名世界田联终点摄影裁判员。技术代表指定的项目应由世界田联发令员发令（及执行其他职责），并监控起跑信息系统的校检和操作。世界田联终点摄影裁判员应监督所有终点摄影裁判组的工作并担任终点摄影主裁判。

Specific information is provided in the Starting Guidelines and Photo Finish Guidelines, which may be downloaded from the World Athletics website.

It is noted that whilst the World Athletics Photo Finish Judge acts as the Chief Photo Finish Judge at those competitions to which they are appointed and the World Athletics Referees act as Referees, there remains a clear division in responsibilities between the World Athletics Starter and the other members of the start team. Whilst the World Athletics Starter takes on all the powers and duties of the Starter when starting any race to which they are allocated, they do not either then or at any other time replace or have the power to override the Start Referee.

12.　Jury of Appeal

At all competitions organised under paragraphs 1. (a), (b), (c) and 2. (a), (b) of the World Rankings Competition definition, a Jury of Appeal, which should normally consist of three, five or seven persons shall be appointed. One of its members shall be the Chairman and another the Secretary. If and when considered as appropriate, the Secretary may be a person not included in the Jury.

In instances where there is an appeal relating to Rule 54 of the Technical Rules, at least one member of the Jury of Appeal shall be a World Athletics Gold, Silver or Bronze Level Race Walking Judge.

Members of the Jury of Appeal shall not be present during any deliberations of the Jury concerning any Appeal that affects, directly or indirectly, an athlete affiliated to their own Member Federation. The chair of the Jury shall ask any member implicated by this Rule to withdraw, in the event the Jury member has not already done so. The Council or the relevant governing body shall appoint one or more alternate Jury members to substitute for any Jury member(s) who are not able to participate in an Appeal.

Furthermore, a Jury of Appeal should likewise be appointed at other competitions where the organisers deem it desirable or necessary in the interest of the proper conduct of the competitions.

The primary functions of the Jury of Appeal shall be to deal with all appeals under Rule 8 of the Technical Rules, and with any matters arising during the course of the competition which are referred to it for decision.

《发令指南》和《终点摄影指南》提供了具体信息，可从世界田联网站下载。

值得注意的是，虽然在某些赛事中世界田联终点摄影裁判员任终点摄影主裁判，世界田联裁判长担任裁判长，但是对于世界田联发令员和发令团队的其他成员，其职责仍然有明确的划分。虽然世界田联发令员在其所指定的项目中拥有发令员的所有权利和承担发令员的所有职责，但他们在任何时候都不能取代或推翻起点裁判长的决定。

12. 申诉委员会

举办世界排名比赛定义1.（a）（b）（c）和2.（a）（b）所述全部比赛，应指派一个申诉委员会，通常由3人、5人或7人组成。其中1人为主席，1人为秘书。如果可能及条件许可，秘书可以是申诉成员之外的一人。

当申诉涉及技术规则54条时，申诉委员会中应至少有1人为现任世界田联金级、银级或铜级竞走裁判员。

申诉成员不得出席任何与自己国家协会运动员有直接或间接影响的申诉裁决过程。在相关申诉委员会没有这样做的情况下，申诉主席应让本规则规定中所指的任何成员回避。世界田联理事会或相关管理机构应该指派1名或多名替补申诉委员来替换任何不能够参加申诉的申诉委员。

此外，其他比赛中，如组织者有意愿或认为对保证比赛的正常进行有必要时，也可设置申诉委员会。

申诉委员会的基本职责是处理技术规则8条提及的所有申诉，并对赛中需要申诉的其他事宜作出裁决。

13. Officials of the Competition

The Organisers of a competition and/or the relevant governing body shall appoint all officials, subject to the Rules of the Member in whose Country the competition is held and, in the case of competitions under paragraphs 1. (a), (b), (c) and 2. (a), (b) of the World Rankings Competition definition, subject to the Rules and procedures of the relevant governing body.

The following list comprises the officials considered important for the good conduct of the competition. The Organisers may, however, vary this according to local circumstances.

Management Officials

- Competition Director (see Rule 14 of the Competition Rules)

- Meeting Manager and an adequate number of assistants (see Rule 15 of the Competition Rules)

- Technical Manager and an adequate number of assistants (see Rule 16 of the Competition Rules)

- Event Presentation Manager (see Rule 17 of the Competition Rules)

Competition Officials

- Call Room Referee(s)

- Running and Race Walking Events Referee(s)

- Field Events Referee(s)

- Combined Events Referee(s)

- Video Referee(s)

- Chief Judge and an adequate number of Judges for Running and Race Walking Events (see Rule 19 of the Competition Rules)

- Chief Judge and an adequate number of Judges for each Field Event (see Rule 19 of the Competition Rules)

13. **赛事官员**

比赛组织者和/或相关管理机构，应根据比赛主办国会员协会规则指派全部官员。在举办世界排名比赛定义1.（a）（b）（c）和2.（a）（b）所述的比赛时，应根据规则和有关管理机构的程序指派全部官员。

设置下列官员对于较好地执行比赛具有重要意义。但是，组织者可以根据当地情况进行调整。

管理官员

——竞赛主任（见竞赛规则14条）

——赛事总管和足够数量的赛事总管助理（见竞赛规则15条）

——技术主管和足够数量的技术主管助理（见竞赛规则16条）

——项目展示主管（见竞赛规则17条）

竞赛官员

——检录裁判长（1人或多人）

——跑和竞走项目裁判长（1人或多人）

——田赛裁判长（1人或多人）

——全能裁判长（1人或多人）

——视频裁判长（1人或多人）

——跑和竞走项目主裁判1人和足够数量的跑和竞走项目裁判员（见竞赛规则19条）

——田赛主裁判每项1人和足够数量的田赛裁判员（见竞赛规则19条）

- Chief Judge, an adequate number of assistants and five Judges for each Track Race Walking Event (see Rule 54 of the Technical Rules)

- Chief Judge, an adequate number of assistants and eight Judges for each Road Race Walking Event (see Rule 54 of the Technical Rules)

- Other Race Walking Competition officials, as necessary, including Recorders, Posting Board operators, etc. (see Rule 54 of the Technical Rules)

- Chief Umpire and an adequate number of Umpires (see Rule 20 of the Competition Rules)

- Chief Timekeeper and an adequate number of Timekeepers (see Rule 21 of the Competition Rules)

- Chief Photo Finish Judge and an adequate number of assistants (see Rule 21 of these Rules and Rule 19 of the Technical Rules)

- Chief Transponder Timing Judge and an adequate number of assistants (see Rule 21 of these Rules and Rule 19 of the Technical Rules)

- Start Coordinator and an adequate number of Starters and Recallers (see Rule 22 of the Competition Rules)

- Starter's Assistants (see Rule 23 of the Competition Rules)

- Chief Lap Scorer and an adequate number of Lap Scorers (see Rule 24 of the Competition Rules)

- Competition Secretary and an adequate number of assistants (see Rule 25 of the Competition Rules)

- Technical Information Centre (TIC) Manager and an adequate number of assistants (see Rule 25.5 of the Competition Rules)

- Chief Marshal and an adequate number of Marshals (see Rule 26 of the Competition Rules)

- Wind Gauge Operators (see Rule 27 of the Competition Rules)

——场地竞走主裁判每项1人，足够数量的竞走主裁判助理以及竞走裁判员5人（见技术规则54条）

——公路竞走主裁判每项1人，足够数量的竞走主裁判助理以及竞走裁判员8人（见技术规则54条）

——必要时，可指派其他竞走比赛官员，包括记录员、犯规显示牌操作员等（见技术规则54条）

——检查主裁判1人和足够数量的检查裁判员（见竞赛规则20条）

——计时主裁判1人和足够数量的计时员（见竞赛规则21条）

——终点摄影主裁判1人和足够数量的终点摄影主裁判助理（见竞赛规则21条和技术规则19条）

——感应计时主裁判1人和足够数量的感应计时主裁判助理（见竞赛规则21条和技术规则19条）

——发令协调员1人、足够数量的发令员和召回员（见竞赛规则22条）

——助理发令员多人（见竞赛规则23条）

——记圈主裁判1人和足够数量的记圈员（见竞赛规则24条）

——竞赛秘书1人和足够数量的竞赛秘书助理（见竞赛规则25条）

——技术信息中心（TIC）主管1人和足够数量的技术信息中心（TIC）主管助理（见竞赛规则25.5条）

——场地管理主裁判1人和足够数量的场地管理裁判员（见竞赛规则26条）

——风速测量员多人（见竞赛规则27条）

- Chief Measurement Judge (Scientific) and an adequate number of assistants (see Rule 28 of the Competition Rules)

- Chief Call Room Judge and an adequate number of Call Room Judges (see Rule 29 of the Competition Rules)

- Advertising Commissioner (see Rule 30 of the Competition Rules)

Additional Officials

- Announcers

- Statisticians

- Doctors

- Stewards for Athletes, Officials and Media

Referees and Chief Judges should wear a distinctive attire or insignia. If deemed necessary, assistants may be appointed. Care should be taken to keep the Field of Play as free from officials and other persons as possible.

The number of officials appointed to a competition should be adequate to ensure the required duties are carried out both correctly and efficiently and also to ensure sufficient rest if the competition is over a long period of time on a single day or on several consecutive days. But care must also be taken not to appoint too many so that the competition area becomes cluttered or obstructed by unnecessary personnel. In more and more competitions, some tasks undertaken by on-field officials are being "replaced" by technology and unless a back-up is logically required, this needs to be taken into account when officials are appointed.

A Note on Safety

Competition officials at athletics events have many important functions, but none is more important than their roles in ensuring the safety of all concerned. The athletics arena can be a dangerous place. Heavy and sharp implements are thrown and pose a hazard to anyone in their path. Athletes running on the track or on runways at high speeds can hurt themselves and anyone with whom they collide. Those competing in jumping events often land in an unexpected or unintended manner. Weather and other conditions can make athletic competition unsafe either temporarily or for longer periods.

——测量主裁判（电子类）1人和足够数量的测量主裁判（电子类）助理（见竞赛规则28条）

——检录主裁判1人和足够数量的检录裁判员（见竞赛规则29条）

——广告管理专员1人（见竞赛规则30条）

其他工作人员

——宣告员（多人）

——统计员（多人）

——医生（多人）

——为运动员、官员和媒体服务的人员（多人）

裁判长和主裁判应穿着和佩戴易于识别的服装或徽章。必要时可指派助理，但应尽可能减少比赛场地内的官员和其他人员数量。

比赛应指派足够数量的官员，以确保相应的职责能够正确和高效地履行，且需保证官员在单日长时间比赛期间或连续数日比赛中有足够的休息时间。但也要注意不能指派太多官员，容易造成比赛区域的混乱或被不必要人员妨碍。越来越多的比赛中，科技产品正"取代"场内官员的一些职责。因此，指派官员时应考虑客观需要，合理安排后备人员。

安全提示

田径比赛中竞赛官员有许多重要的职责，但最为重要的是他们需要确保所有人员的安全。田径场馆也处处有危险。投掷出的器械沉重而尖锐，对飞行轨迹上的任何人员都会构成威胁。跑道或助跑道上高速跑进的运动员，不仅可能伤及自我，还可能伤害到任何冲撞到他的人。参加跳跃比赛的运动员往往会以意想不到的或者意外的方式落地。天气及其他条件也会使田径比赛暂时的或长时间的不安全。

There have been instances of athletes, officials, photographers and others who have been injured (sometimes fatally) in accidents in or near competition and training areas. Many of those injuries could have been prevented.

Officials must always be mindful of the dangers that are inherent in the sport. They must be alert at all times, and must not allow themselves to be distracted. Regardless of their official position, all officials have the responsibility to do what they can to make the athletics arena a safer place. All officials should think about safety whenever and wherever they are in the competition area, and should intervene when necessary to prevent an accident, when they see conditions or a situation that could lead to one. Ensuring safety is of the utmost importance – even more so than strict compliance with the Rules of competition. In the rare event when there is a conflict, the concern for safety must prevail.

14. Competition Director

The Competition Director shall, where applicable with the Technical, and other relevant, Delegate(s):

14.1 plan the technical organisation of a competition, including the integration of Event Presentation and Victory Ceremonies;

14.2 ensure that this plan is executed before and during the competition;

14.3 ensure that any technical problems are resolved or an alternate solution put in place;

14.4 direct the interaction between the participants in the competition;

14.5 through the communication system, be in contact with all key officials and other relevant stakeholders involved in the delivery and broadcast of the competition;

14.6 engage fully with the Event Presentation Manager to ensure compliance with Rule 17 of the Competition Rules;

14.7 ensure the accurate preparation and publication of the Call Room schedule in accordance with Rule 29.1.1 of the Competition Rules;

14.8 communicate with the Start Coordinator to ensure the efficient operation of Rule 22.1.3 of the Competition Rules;

14.9 be fully aware of the applicable regulations for the competition and the functioning of the planned technological and IT systems; and

14.10 manage any matters arising under Rule 7.5 of the Technical Rules.

已经有运动员、官员、摄影师和其他一些人在比赛和训练区域中或靠近这些区域而受伤（有时是致命的）的例子。其实，许多伤害是可以避免的。

官员们必须时刻警觉体育与危险共存，必须时刻警惕且绝不能分心。不管在什么岗位，所有官员都有责任尽其所能确保田径场馆更加安全。所有官员一旦进入比赛场地，应随时随地考虑安全问题，并在预见潜在危险情形时进行必要的干预以防止事故发生。确保安全至关重要，甚至比严格遵守比赛规则还重要得多。在极个别因素发生冲突的情形下，必须优先考虑安全。

14. 竞赛主任

竞赛主任要与技术代表及其他相关代表合作：

14.1　制定比赛的技术方案，包括项目展示和颁奖仪式；

14.2　确保方案在比赛前和比赛中得以实施；

14.3　确保任何技术问题得以解决或补救方案得以落实；

14.4　指挥赛事参与者的协调配合；

14.5　通过通信系统，与主要官员及参与比赛传递和广播的其他相关人员保持联系畅通；

14.6　全程与项目展示经理合作，确保竞赛规则17条的执行；

14.7　确保根据竞赛规则29.1.1条，按时准备和公布检录时间表；

14.8　与发令协调员联系，确保竞赛规则22.1.3条得以有效实施；

14.9　完全了解比赛的适用规程，以及技术和信息系统的功能；

14.10　依据技术规则7.5条，处理相关事宜。

During the competition, to ensure an efficient operation, the Competition Director should be located with an optimal view of the competition area, close to the Event Presentation team and with satisfactory and reliable availability of technological connections and supporting monitors.

15. Meeting Manager

The Meeting Manager shall be responsible for the correct conduct of the Competition. They shall check that all officials have reported for duty, appoint substitutes when necessary and have authority to remove from duty any official who is not abiding by the Rules. In cooperation with the appointed Marshal, they shall arrange that only authorised persons are allowed in the centre of the Field of Play.

Note: For competitions of longer than four hours or over more than one day, it is recommended that the Meeting Manager has an adequate number of Assistant Meeting Managers.

The Meeting Manager(s) must be responsible, under the authority of the Competition Director, and in accordance with the Technical Delegates' guidance and decisions, for everything happening in the Field of Play. In the stadium, they must place themselves so as to be able to see everything that is happening and to give necessary orders. They must have in their possession the complete list of all appointed officials and be able to communicate efficiently with the other Managers, Referees and Chief Judges.

In competitions that take place over multiple days in particular it is possible that some judges may not be able to officiate during the whole competition. The Meeting Manager shall have at their disposal a reserve of officials from which they can draw any replacement, if necessary. Even if all the officials for an event are present, the Meeting Manager should ensure that the officials fulfil their duties correctly and if they do not be ready to replace them.

They shall ensure that the Judges (and those assisting them) leave the arena as soon as their event is finished or when their subsequent work is done.

16. Technical Manager

16.1 The Technical Manager shall be responsible for ensuring that:

    16.1.1 the track, runways, circles, arcs, sectors, landing areas for Field Events and all equipment and implements are in accordance with the Rules;

    16.1.2 the placement and removal of equipment and implements are according to the technical organisational plan for the competition as approved by the Technical Delegate(s);

在比赛期间，为确保高效运行，竞赛主任应位于最佳观察位置，靠近项目展示团队，并有完善、可靠的联系方式和监控系统。

15. 赛事总管

赛事总管要对比赛的正常运行负责。他应检查所有裁判员的到岗情况，必要时可指派替补裁判员，并有权撤换任何不遵守规则的裁判员。与指派的场地管理裁判员配合，仅允许经授权的人员停留在比赛场地内。

注：如果比赛超过4小时或超过1天，建议配备足够数量的赛事总管助理。

赛事总管应在竞赛主任的领导下，按照技术代表的指示及决定，负责比赛场地内的所有事项。在体育场内，他必须处于能够看到赛场发生所有情况的位置，并作出必要的指令。赛事总管必须有所有指派官员的完整名单，并能够与其他主管、裁判长和主裁判进行高效的沟通。

在连续多日的比赛中，尤其是部分裁判员可能无法执裁整个赛事的比赛中，应有后备官员可以在赛事总管认为必要时进行补位。即使所有官员都已到位，赛事总管也应确保所有官员能够正确履职，否则，应进行替换。

赛事总管要确保所有裁判员（及其辅助人员）在其负责项目结束后或者其后续工作完成后尽快离开场地。

16. 技术主管

16.1 技术主管负责确保：

  16.1.1 径赛项目的跑道和田赛项目的助跑道、投掷圈、投掷弧、扇形区、落地区，以及所有器材和器械符合本规则要求；

  16.1.2 根据技术代表批准的比赛技术组织方案放置和移除比赛器材与器械；

16.1.3   the technical presentation of the competition areas is in accordance with such plan;

16.1.4   the checking and marking of any personal implements permitted for the competition is according to Rule 32.2 of the Technical Rules; and

16.1.5   they have received, or are aware of the existence of, the necessary certification under Rule 10.1 of the Technical Rules before the competition.

The Technical Manager acts under the authority of the Competition Director or the Meeting Manager but an experienced Technical Manager will undertake much of their role without any direction or supervision. They must be contactable at any time. If a Referee or a Field Event Chief Judge notices that the site where an event is taking place (or will take place) needs to be modified or improved, they must refer it to the Meeting Manager who will ask the Technical Manager to take the necessary action. Also, when a Referee feels that there is a need for a change of place of a competition (Rule 25.20 of the Technical Rules) they will act the same way through Meeting Manager who will request the Technical Manager to carry out, or have carried out, the wishes of the Referee. It must be remembered that neither the wind strength nor its change of direction is sufficient condition to change the place of the competition.

Once the Competition Director or the Technical Delegate(s) have approved the implements list to be used during the events, the Technical Manager shall prepare, order and receive the various implements. For the latter, they or their team must then carefully check their weight and dimensions, and any personal implements that are permitted and submitted, in order to comply with the Rules. They must also ensure that Rule 31.17.4 of the Competition Rules is followed in both a correct and efficient manner if a Record is set.

In relation to throwing implements, the information for manufacturers as to the range of equipment to be supplied to Organisers was removed from the Rules in 2017 and transferred to the documentation relating to the World Athletics certification system. Technical Managers should however apply these guidelines when accepting new equipment from suppliers but should not reject implements submitted for or used in competition because they do not comply with this range. It is the minimum weight that is critical in this regard.

16.1.3 比赛场地的技术性安排符合比赛技术组织方案；

16.1.4 根据技术规则32.2条，对允许比赛的自备器材进行检查和标记；和

16.1.5 在赛前已获得或知悉符合技术规则10.1条规定的必要认证。

技术主管在竞赛主任或赛事总管的领导下工作，但经验丰富的技术主管应无须指导或监督就能行使自己的职权。他们应随时可被联系到。如果裁判长或田赛项目主裁判注意到正在比赛（或即将比赛）的场地需要进行调整或改善，必须向赛事总管报告，并由赛事总管指示技术主管采取必要措施。此外，如果裁判长认为需要改变比赛场地（技术规则25.20条），他也同样需经赛事总管并由其要求技术主管执行裁判长的要求。必须牢记的是，无论风力还是风向变化，都不足以成为变更比赛场地的理由。

一旦竞赛主任或技术代表批准了比赛使用的器械清单，技术主管要准备、购置并接收各种器械。对于技术主管，他及其团队必须仔细检查器械的重量、尺寸，以及任何被允许和提交的自备器材，确保器械符合规则。若创造纪录时，他必须确保以正确、高效的方式执行竞赛规则31.17.4条。

对于投掷器械，"应提供给组织者的器械生产厂家及范围信息"已于2017年从规则中移除，并转移到世界田联认证体系的有关文件中。尽管如此，技术主管在接收供应商的新器械时也要遵循这些指南，但不应该因为器械超出了该范围而拒绝提交了或比赛中使用过的器械。就这点而言，最为重要的是器械重量的最小值。

17. Event Presentation Manager

The Event Presentation Manager shall plan, in conjunction with the Competition Director, the event presentation arrangements for the competition, in cooperation with the Organisational and Technical Delegate(s), as and where applicable. They shall ensure that the plan is accomplished, resolving any relevant problems together with the Competition Director and the relevant Delegate(s). They shall also direct the interaction between the members of the event presentation team, using the communication system to be in contact with each of them.

They shall ensure that, through announcements and the available technology, the public is informed of information concerning the athletes taking part in each event, including the start lists, intermediate and final results. The official result (placings, times, heights, distances and points) of each event should be conveyed at the earliest practicable moment after receipt of the information.

At competitions held under paragraphs 1. (a) and (b) of the World Rankings Competition definition, the English and French language Announcers shall be appointed by Council.

The Event Presentation Manager (EPM) not only has the responsibility of planning, leading and coordinating a production in presentation terms of all the activities that take place on the infield but also integrating them into the show to be presented to the spectators within the venue. The final aim of their work is to create an informative, entertaining, lively and attractive production of the show that is to be offered to the spectators. To succeed in this it is important to have a team and the necessary equipment to carry out the work. The EPM is the person in charge of coordinating the activities of the event presentation staff working on and off the field who are related to this role including but not limited to the Announcers, Scoreboard and Videoboard Operators, Audio and Video Technicians and Victory Ceremony officials.

For almost every competition, an announcer is essential. They must be placed so as to be able to follow the meeting properly and preferably near to or otherwise in immediate communication with the Competition Director or if appointed, the Event Presentation Manager.

18. Referees

18.1   One (or more) Referee(s), as appropriate, shall be appointed for the Call Room, for Running and Race Walking Events, for Field Events and for Combined Events. When appropriate, one (or more) Video Referee(s) shall also be appointed. A Referee appointed to oversee the starts is designated the Start Referee.

17. 项目展示主管

项目展示主管要与竞赛主任共同策划比赛项目的展示安排,必要时与组织代表和技术代表合作。项目展示主管负责展示计划的具体实施,与竞赛主任和相关代表一起解决任何相关问题。他还应指挥项目展示团队成员相互协作,并使用通信系统与团队成员保持联系。

他要确保通过宣告和其他可行技术,使公众获悉各项目参赛运动员的信息,包括参赛名单、分段成绩和最终成绩。收到信息后,尽早发送每个项目的官方成绩(名次、时间、高度、远度和得分)。

在举行世界排名比赛定义1.(a)和(b)所述比赛时,世界田联理事会要指派英语和法语宣告员。

项目展示主管不仅要负责计划、领导和协调赛场内进行的所有活动的展示制作,还应将其融入给场内观众展示的节目中。他工作的终极目标是为观众呈现一场提供有用信息的、有趣的、生动的以及有吸引力的节目。拥有一个团队及必要的设备以开展有关工作至关重要。项目展示主管负责协调场内外展示团队工作人员的活动,包括但不限于宣告员、文字显示屏与视频显示屏操作员、音频与视频技术人员以及颁奖仪式人员等。

几乎所有赛事,宣告员都是必不可少的。他必须身处能够跟进比赛进程的地方,最好是接近或者随时能够与竞赛主任或指派的项目展示主管进行沟通的地方。

18. 裁判长

18.1 根据情况,应分别指派1名(或多名)检录、跑和竞走项目、田赛和全能裁判长。如果需要,应指派1名(或多名)视频裁判长。被指派监督起点工作的裁判长则为起点裁判长。

The Video Referee(s) shall operate from a Video Review Room, should consult and shall be in communication with the other Referees.

At meetings where sufficient officials are available so that more than one Referee is appointed for the races, it is strongly recommended that one of them is appointed as the Start Referee. To be clear, the Start Referee in such circumstances should exercise all the powers of the Referee in relation to the start and is not required to report to or act through any other Running and Race Walking Events Referee when doing so.

However, if only one Referee is appointed to oversee the races of a certain competition, and considering the powers they have, it is strongly recommended that the Referee be positioned in the start area, during each start (at least for those events using a crouch start) to witness any eventual problem that may occur and to take any decision needed to solve it. This will be easier when a World Athletics certified start information system is in use.

If not, and if the Referee will not have time to place themselves in line with the finish line after the start procedure (as in 100m, 100/110m hurdles and 200m), and foreseeing the possible need for the Referee to decide placings, a good solution may be to have the Start Coordinator (who should have an extensive experience as a starter) being appointed to also act as Start Referee.

18.2   Referees shall ensure that the Rules and Regulations (and other regulations for each particular competition) are observed. They shall rule on any protest or objection regarding the conduct of the competition and shall decide upon any matters which arise during the competition (including in the Warm-up Area, Call Room and, after the competition, up to and including the Victory Ceremony) and for which provision has not been made in these Rules (or any applicable regulations), where appropriate or necessary in conjunction with the Technical Delegates.

The Referee shall not act as a Judge or Umpire but may take any action or decision according to the Rules based on their own observations and may overrule a decision of a Judge.

Note: For the purpose of this Rule and applicable regulations, including the Marketing & Advertising Regulations, the Victory Ceremony is concluded when all directly related activities (including photographs, victory laps, crowd interaction, etc.) are completed.

It should be carefully noted that it is not necessary for a Referee to have received a report from a Judge or Umpire in order to make a disqualification. They may act at all times by their own direct observation.

视频裁判长要在视频控制室内工作，并与其他项目裁判长进行商议和保持联系。

在有足够的官员可用的比赛中，为比赛任命1名以上裁判长，强烈建议裁判长中一人被任命为起点裁判长。需要明确的是，在这种情况下，起点裁判长应履行起点相关裁判长的职权，并且这样做时不需要向任何其他径赛裁判长报告或通过任何其他径赛裁判长行事。

然而，如果比赛仅有1名裁判长，考虑到他的职权，强烈建议裁判长位于起点区域，在每次发令期间（至少在使用蹲踞式起跑的比赛时），观察任何最终可能发生的问题，并作出解决问题所需的任何决定。当使用了世界田联认证的起跑信息系统时，该项工作会更容易些。

如果没有起点裁判长，或裁判长没有时间在发令程序后到终点（在100米、100/110米栏和200米比赛中），以及预见了可能需要裁判长来决定名次时，一个好的解决方法是指派发令协调员（应具有作为发令员的丰富经验）为起点裁判长。

18.2 如果适当或必要时，与技术代表一起，裁判长要确保本规则和规程（以及每个特定比赛的其他规程）得到执行，并裁决比赛中关于比赛行为的任何抗议和异议，处理发生于比赛期间（包括热身场地、检录处和赛后，直至颁奖仪式），以及本规则（或任何适用的规程）未作明文规定的任何事宜。

裁判长不能替代裁判员和检查裁判员判罚，但是可以根据自己的观察依据规则做出任何处理和裁决，而且可以否决裁判员的裁决。

注：就本规则和适用规程（包括营销和广告规程）而言，当所有直接相关的活动（包括拍照、绕场庆祝、观众互动等）全部完成时，颁奖仪式才算结束。

需要详细说明的是，裁判长没有必要在收到裁判员或者检查员的报告之后再作出取消比赛资格的决定。他可以随时根据自己的直接观察进行判罚。

The above Note should be interpreted to include all matters which are incidental to or relate to the Victory Ceremony and that the Referee for that event is responsible for them. When Victory Ceremonies are held at a different location or in a different session, common sense should be applied and if necessary another Referee may have to be substituted if it is not practical for the original Referee to manage the situation. See also green text after Rule 5 of the Competition Rules.

18.3 The Referees for Running and Race Walking Events shall have jurisdiction to decide placings in a race only when the Judges of the disputed place(s) are unable to arrive at a decision. They shall have no jurisdiction over matters within the responsibilities of the Chief Judge of Race Walking Events.

The Start Referee (or if one is not appointed, the relevant Running and Race Walking Events Referee) has jurisdiction to decide on any facts related to the starts if they do not agree with the decisions made by the start team except in the cases when it regards an apparent false start indicated by a World Athletics certified Start Information System, unless for any reason the Referee determines that the information provided by the System is obviously inaccurate. See also Rule 8.4.1 of the Technical Rules.

The Combined Events Referee shall have jurisdiction over the conduct of the Combined Events competition and over the conduct of the respective individual events within it (except in matters related to their jurisdiction when a Start Referee is appointed and available).

18.4 The appropriate Referee shall check all final results, shall deal with any disputed points and, in conjunction with the Chief Measurement Judge (Scientific) where appointed, shall supervise the measurements of Record performances. At the conclusion of each round of an event, the result card shall be completed immediately, signed (or otherwise approved) by the appropriate Referee or the Chief Photo Finish Judge and conveyed to the Competition Secretary.

18.5 The applicable Referee shall have authority to warn or exclude from competition, any athlete or relay team in accordance with Rule 7.1 of the Technical Rules.

18.6 The Referee may reconsider a decision (whether made in the first instance or in considering a protest) on the basis of any available evidence, provided the new decision is still applicable. Normally, such re-consideration may be undertaken only prior to the Victory Ceremony for the relevant event or any applicable decision by the Jury of Appeal.

上述注可解释为包括所有关于或伴随颁奖仪式的事项，该项目的裁判长都要对此负责。当颁奖仪式在不同地点或不同单元举行时，按照常规，如果原项目裁判长无法到场管控，则要指派另一裁判长代为行使职责。另见竞赛规则5条后的绿色文字注释。

18.3 只有在相关裁判员对运动员名次存在争议而无法判定时，跑和竞走项目裁判长才有权判定比赛的名次。他们无权管辖竞走主裁判职责范围内的事宜。

起点裁判长（或如果没有指派时，即为相关跑和竞走项目裁判长）如果不同意发令团队作出的决定，他有权决定发令的相关事宜，但是，使用了世界田联认证的起跑信息系统并检测到明显的起跑犯规的情况除外，除非该裁判长有理由确定该起跑信息系统提供的信息明显不准确。另见技术规则8.4.1条。

全能裁判长对全能项目比赛进程和全能项目中各单项比赛进程具有管辖权（当有一位起点裁判长可用并被指派时，他们管辖的事宜除外）。

18.4 相关裁判长要审核最终比赛成绩，处理任何有争议的问题，并与指定的测量主裁判（电子类）共同监督纪录成绩的测量。在项目每轮比赛结束后，要立即完成成绩记录单的填写，由相关裁判长或终点摄影主裁判签名（或其他认可形式），并送达竞赛秘书。

18.5 相关裁判长根据技术规则7.1条，有权对任何运动员或接力队予以警告或取消比赛资格。

18.6 只要新的决定可适用，裁判长可以根据任何可用的证据重新作出决定（无论是在一开始还是在出现抗议时）。通常，此类重新裁决可能在相关项目的颁奖仪式举行之前，或在申诉委员会作出适当的裁决之前作出。

This Rule clarifies that as with the Jury of Appeal (see Rule 8.9 of the Technical Rules) a Referee can reconsider a decision and may do so equally whether this was a decision by themselves in the first instance or one made when considering a protest made to them. This option can be considered especially when new evidence of information comes to hand quickly as it could avoid the need for a more complicated or involved appeal to the Jury of Appeal. But note the practical time limitations on such a reconsideration.

18.7 If, in the opinion of the appropriate Referee, circumstances arise at any competition such that justice demands that any event or any part of an event should be contested again, they shall have authority to declare the event or any part of an event void and that it shall be held again, either on the same day or on some future occasion, as they shall decide (see also Rules 8.4 and 17.1 of the Technical Rules).

It should be carefully noted by Referees and Juries of Appeal that, except in very special circumstances, an athlete who does not finish a race, should not be advanced to a later round or included in a re-run of an event.

18.8 Where an athlete with a physical disability is competing in a competition under these Rules, the appropriate Referee may interpret, or allow a variation from, any relevant Rule (other than Rule 6.3 of the Technical Rules) to enable the participation of the athlete provided that such variation does not provide the athlete with any advantage over another athlete competing in the same event. In the case of any doubt or if the decision is disputed, the matter shall be referred to the Jury of Appeal.

Note: This Rule is not intended to permit the participation of guide runners for visually impaired athletes, unless specifically allowed by the regulations of a particular competition.

This Rule facilitates the participation of ambulant athletes with a disability to compete in athletic competitions with able-bodied athletes. For example, an arm amputee is not able to strictly comply with Rule 16.3 of the Technical Rules during a crouch start by putting both hands on the ground. This Rule enables a Start Referee to interpret the Rules in such a way to allow the athlete to place their stump on the ground, or to place wooden blocks or the like on the ground behind the start line on which an arm stump is placed, or in the case of a high upper arm amputee who is not able to make contact with the ground in any way, to adopt a start position without any contact with the ground.

此规则阐明了与申诉委员会一样（见技术规则8.9条），裁判长可以重新作出决定，无论是在一开始作出决定时，还是在针对向他提出抗议时。特别是当收集到新的证据后，重新裁决可以避免向申诉委员会提出更为复杂的申诉需要。但要注意此类重新裁决的实际时间限制。

18.7　在任何比赛中，如果相关裁判长认为某项比赛或某项比赛的任何部分应予重赛方为公允时，有权宣布该项比赛或该项比赛的任何部分无效，并要作出在当日或其他时间进行重新比赛的决定（见技术规则8.4条和17.1条）。

裁判长及申诉委员会应特别注意的是，除非常特殊的情况外，运动员如未完成比赛，不应晋级下一轮或者进行重赛。

18.8　当残疾运动员根据本规则参加比赛时，有关裁判长可以解释或允许相关规则的不同形式（除技术规则6.3条外）出现，从而让运动员能够参加比赛，只要这种规则的改变不给运动员提供任何相对于其他同项目参赛运动员更有利的条件。如果这种决定引起争议或对这种改变有任何质疑，要提交至申诉委员会。

注：本规则并不旨在允许视障运动员的引导员参加比赛，除非特定的比赛规程明确允许。

此规则便于让有残疾的可行动的运动员与健全运动员共同参加田径比赛。例如，手臂截肢运动员无法严格遵守技术规则16.3条——在蹲踞式起跑中双手接触地面。此规则使起点裁判长能够解释有关规则并允许运动员将残肢置于地面，或者在起点线后的地面上放置木块或类似物体以便于残肢接触，或者在上臂截肢运动员残肢无法接触地面时，可采用不接触地面的起跑姿势起跑。

It should be noted however that this Rule does not allow Referees to interpret the Rules in such a way that the relevant aspects of Rule 6 of the Technical Rules are infringed – particularly the use of technologies or appliances which would give the wearer an advantage (see Rules 6.3.3 and 6.3.4 of the Technical Rules which covers specifically the use of prostheses and other aids).

In cases where athletes with a disability are competing in the same event at the same time as able-bodied athletes and they are not compliant with the Rules (either because the Rules so specifically provide or the Referee is not able to interpret the Rules sufficiently in accordance with Rule 18.8 of the Competition Rules) then a separate result should be declared for those athletes or their participation otherwise clearly indicated in the results (see also Rule 25.3 of the Competition Rules). Regardless it is always useful to indicate, in entry and start lists and in results, the IPC classification for any para-athlete who is participating.

19. Judges

General

19.1   The Chief Judge for Running and Race Walking Events and the Chief Judge for each Field Event shall co-ordinate the work of the Judges in their respective events. If the duties of the Judges have not been allocated in advance, they shall allocate the duties.

19.2   The Judges may reconsider any original decision made by them if it was made in error, provided the new decision is still applicable. Alternatively, or if a decision has subsequently been made by a Referee or the Jury of Appeal, they shall refer all available information to the Referee or to the Jury of Appeal.

Running and Race Walking Events

19.3   The Judges, who must all operate from the same side of the track or course, shall decide the order in which the athletes have finished and, in any case where they cannot arrive at a decision, shall refer the matter to the Referee, who shall decide.

Note: The Judges should be placed at least 5m from, and in line with, the finish and should be provided with an elevated platform.

值得注意的是，此规则不允许裁判长以技术规则6条有关内容来解释，特别是使用能给佩戴者获取有利条件的技术或设备（见技术规则6.3.3条和6.3.4条，特别规定了假肢和其他辅助设备的使用）。

当残疾运动员与健全运动员在同一时间参加同一比赛，且与规则不一致时（不管是因为规则有特殊规定，还是裁判长无法按照竞赛规则18.8条进行充分解释），应单独公告这些运动员的成绩，或在成绩单上明确标示出来（见竞赛规则25.3条）。不管怎样，在报名、参赛名单和成绩中，标明参加比赛的残疾运动员的IPC（国际残奥委员会）级别总是有用的。

19. 裁判员

通则

19.1　跑和竞走项目主裁判与田赛各项目主裁判要协调本组裁判员的工作。如裁判员未事先分工，主裁判要进行分工。

19.2　只要新的决定更适用，裁判员发现原先决定错误，他可以重新作出决定。或者，如果裁判长或申诉委员会随后作出决定，裁判员要向裁判长和申诉委员会提供所有可用的信息。

跑和竞走项目

19.3　裁判员必须在跑道或赛道的同一侧执行任务，要判定运动员抵达终点的名次。遇到任何无法作出决定的情况时，要将问题提交相关裁判长，由裁判长作出判定。

注：裁判员的位置应距终点至少5米，并与终点线在同一直线上。应为裁判员提供升高的平台。

Field Events

19.4　　The Judges shall judge and record each trial and measure each valid trial of athletes in all Field Events. In the High Jump and Pole Vault, precise measurements should be made when the bar is raised, particularly if Records are being attempted. At least two Judges should keep a record of all trials, checking their recordings at the end of each round of trials.

The appropriate Judge shall normally indicate the validity or non-validity of a trial by raising a white or red flag, as appropriate. Alternate visual indication may also be approved.

Unless a Judge is sure that an infringement of the Rules has occurred they will normally give the benefit of any doubt to the athlete, determine that the trial is valid and raise a white flag. However when a Video Referee is appointed and with access to footage for the Field Events, there is an option in the case of some doubt for the Judge in conjunction with the on-field Referee to delay the raising of either flag until they have sought the advice of the Video Referee - always ensuring either that the landing mark is preserved or the trial is measured in case it is valid. Alternatively, the Judge, if in real doubt, could raise the red flag, ensure the mark is preserved or that the trial is measured, and then seek advice from the Video Referee.

It is recommended that for each Field Event only one set of white and red flags is used in order to reduce the possibility of any confusion about the validity of trials. It is considered that it is never necessary to use more than one set of flags in a jumping event. Where a specific scoreboard is not available to indicate the wind reading in Horizontal Jumps, some form of indication other than a red flag should be used to indicate an excessive reading.

In the case of throwing events, with respect to:

a. indications by other circle Judges to the Judge with the flags that a failure has been made, it is recommended that an alternate form of indication to flags is used such as a small red card held in that Judge's hand;

b. the landing of an implement on or outside the sector line, it is recommended that an alternate form of indication to a flag is used - such as a Judge's outstretched arm parallel to the ground;

c. a judgment in the javelin throw that the metal head has not touched the ground before any other part of the javelin, it is recommended that an alternate form of indication to a flag is used - such as the pushing of the open hand of the Judge towards the ground.

田赛项目

19.4 在所有田赛项目中，裁判员要判定和记录运动员每次的试跳（掷），并测量运动员每次有效试跳（掷）的成绩。在跳高和撑竿跳高项目中，横杆提升时要准确测量，特别是运动员试跳纪录高度时。至少应安排两名裁判员对所有试跳（掷）进行记录，并在每轮次比赛结束后核对记录结果。

相关裁判员通常要举白旗或红旗以示意一次试跳（掷）的成功或失败。用视觉设备显示替代也可被批准。

除非裁判员确认有违反规则的情况，他们通常会作出运动员是无辜的考量，作出成功试跳（掷）的决定并举白旗示意。但如指派了视频裁判长且可以查看比赛录像时，裁判员若有疑虑，可与现场执裁的裁判长商议延迟举旗，在征求视频裁判长的意见后再作出判定——试跳（掷）有效的话要始终保护好落地点或测量距离。或者，裁判员若确实有疑虑，可以在举红旗后，确保保护好落地点或测量距离，然后征求视频裁判长的意见。

建议田赛每个项目只使用一套红白旗，以减少试跳（掷）有效判罚的混乱情况。对于跳跃项目，完全没必要使用多余一套红白旗。若在远度跳跃项目中没有可用的风速显示牌，则应使用除红旗外的其他形式来显示超风速的读数。

关于在投掷项目中的情况：

a. 投掷圈裁判员向举旗裁判员提示有犯规情况时，建议使用非旗示的另一种形式表示，如裁判员手举小红牌；

b. 投掷器械落地点在落地区角度线上或在落地区角度线以外时，建议使用非旗示的另一种形式表示，如裁判员伸展手臂并使手臂平行于地面；

c. 判定标枪的金属枪头未先于标枪的其他部位触地时，建议使用非旗示的另一种形式表示，如裁判员将张开的手推向地面。

20. Umpires (Running and Race Walking Events)

20.1 Umpires are assistants to the Referee, without authority to make final decisions.

20.2 The Umpires shall be placed by the Referee in such a position that they may observe the competition closely and, in the case of a failure or violation of the Rules (other than Rule 54.2 of the Technical Rules) by an athlete or other person, make an immediate written report of the incident to the Referee.

20.3 Any such breach of the Rules should be communicated to the relevant Referee by the raising of a yellow flag or any other reliable means approved by the Technical Delegate(s).

20.4 A sufficient number of Umpires shall also be appointed to supervise the takeover zones in Relay Races.

Note (i): When an Umpire observes that an athlete has run in a different lane from their own, or that a relay takeover has taken place outside the takeover zone, they should immediately mark on the track with suitable material the place where the infringement took place or make a similar notation on paper or by electronic means.

Note (ii): The Umpire(s) shall report to the Referee any breach of the Rules, even if the athlete (or team, for Relay Races) does not finish the race.

The Chief Umpire (see Rule 13 of the Competition Rules) is the assistant of the Running and Race Walking Events Referee and indicates the placement of and co-ordinates the work and reports of each Umpire. Charts which may be downloaded from the World Athletics website recommend the points at which the Umpires (subject always to the number available) should be placed for the various Track Events. It must be understood that the charts describe one possibility. It is up to the Meeting Manager in consultation with the Running and Race Walking Events Referee to select the appropriate number of Umpires according to the level of the meeting, the number of entries and the number of available officials.

Indication of an infringement

When the events take place on a synthetic track, it has been the practice to provide the Umpires with adhesive tape so that they can mark the track where an infringement has taken place – although the Rules [see note (i) above] now acknowledge that this may be and is often done in other ways.

20. 检查裁判员（跑和竞走项目）

20.1　检查裁判员是裁判长的助手，无权做最终裁决。

20.2　相关裁判长要指定检查裁判员站在能密切观察比赛的地点。如发现运动员或其他人员犯规或违例时（技术规则54.2条除外），应立即向有关裁判长提交书面报告。

20.3　出现违反规则的情况，应举黄旗示意或采用任何经技术代表批准的有效方法通知有关裁判长。

20.4　要指派足够数量的检查裁判员在各接力区检查接力赛跑。

注（ⅰ）：当检查裁判员观察到运动员离开自己的跑道进入其他分道或在接力区外进行交接棒时，检查裁判员应立即用适当的材料在跑道上标出犯规地点，或在纸上做类似标记，或通过电子手段记录。

注（ⅱ）：即使运动员（或接力队）没有完成比赛，检查裁判员也要将任何违反规则的情况报告给有关裁判长。

检查主裁判（见竞赛规则13条）是跑和竞走项目裁判长的助手，指定每个检查裁判员的位置以及协调工作和报告。从世界田联官方网站可下载检查裁判员（根据可用人数）在不同径赛项目中推荐位置的图表。但必须说明的是，图表只提供了一种借鉴。应由赛事总管与跑和竞走项目的裁判长商议，根据赛事等级、报名人数以及可用裁判人数来确定检查裁判员的数量。

关于犯规的标示

当比赛在塑胶跑道上进行时，通常向检查裁判员提供胶布以便其标记犯规发生的位置，尽管规则［见上述注（ⅰ）］现在明确可以使用其他方法且经常使用其他方式进行标示。

Note that the failure to report an infringement in a particular way (or at all) does not prevent a valid disqualification being made.

It is important that Umpires "report" all instances where they believe the Rules have been infringed, even when the athlete or team does not finish the race. The addition of Rule 8.4.4 of the Technical Rules is intended to standardise practice and to complement Note (ii) to Rule 20 of the Competition Rules - as there has been a clear difference of approach across the world.

The standard practice overall should be that where an athlete/relay team does not finish a race, it is generally to be denoted as DNF rather than DQ, including in hurdles races where a technical rule has been breached but the athlete obviously stopped racing even if eventually reaching the finish line. Rule 8.4.4 of the Technical Rules is in place to cover the situation where such an athlete or team makes a protest.

21. Timekeepers, Photo Finish Judges and Transponder Timing Judges

21.1　In the case of hand timing, a sufficient number of timekeepers for the number of athletes entered shall be appointed. One of them shall be designated the Chief Timekeeper. They shall allocate duties to the Timekeepers. These Timekeepers shall act as back-up Timekeepers when Fully Automatic Photo Finish or Transponder Timing Systems are in use.

21.2　Timekeepers, Photo Finish and Transponder Timing Judges shall act in accordance with Rule 19 of the Technical Rules.

21.3　When a Fully Automatic Timing and Photo Finish System is used, a Chief Photo Finish Judge and an adequate number of assistants shall be appointed.

21.4　When a Transponder Timing System is used, a Chief Transponder Timing Judge and an adequate number of assistants shall be appointed.

The Guidelines for Manual Timekeeping may be downloaded from the World Athletics website.

22. Start Coordinator, Starter and Recallers

22.1　The Start Coordinator shall:

要注意的是，若检查裁判员未能用特定方式报告犯规情况（或完全没有），也不影响作出取消比赛资格的决定。

检查裁判员"报告"所有其认为犯规的情况是非常重要的，即使运动员或运动队当时还没有完成比赛。技术规则8.4.4条的增加旨在规范实践并补充竞赛规则20.4条的注（ⅱ）——因为世界各地的做法存在明显差异。

总体的标准做法应是，如果运动员或接力队没有完成比赛，则通常标示为DNF而不是DQ，包括在跨栏比赛中，运动员违反技术规则明显停止了比赛但最终到达终点的情况。技术规则8.4.4条适用于此类运动员或代表队提出抗议的情况。

21. 计时员、终点摄影裁判员和感应计时裁判员

21.1 使用手计时计取比赛成绩时，将根据运动员的报名人数指派足够数量的计时员，指定其中1人为计时主裁判，他为计时员分配任务。当使用全自动计时和终点摄影系统或感应计时系统时，这些计时员将作为后备计时员进行工作。

21.2 计时员、终点摄影裁判员和感应计时裁判员要根据技术规则19条进行工作。

21.3 使用全自动计时和终点摄影系统时，要指派1名终点摄影主裁判和足够数量的终点摄影主裁判助理。

21.4 使用感应计时系统时，要指派1名感应计时主裁判和足够数量的感应计时主裁判助理。

《人工计时指南》可从世界田联网站下载。

22. 发令协调员、发令员和召回员

22.1 发令协调员的职责如下：

22.1.1 Allocate the duties of the start team. However, in the case of competitions under paragraphs 1. (a), (b), (c) and 2. (a), (b), (c) of the World Rankings Competitions definition, the determination of which events will be assigned to the World Athletics Starter will be the responsibility of the Technical Delegates.

22.1.2 Supervise the duties to be fulfilled by each member of the team.

22.1.3 Inform the Starter, after receiving the relevant order from the Competition Director, that everything is in order to initiate the start procedure (e.g. that the Timekeepers, the Judges and, when applicable, the Chief Photo Finish Judge, Chief Transponder Timing Judge and the Wind Gauge Operator are ready).

22.1.4 Act as an interlocutor between the technical staff of the timing equipment company and the Judges.

22.1.5 Keep all papers produced during the start procedure including all documents showing the reaction times and/or false start waveform images if available.

22.1.6 Ensure that following any ruling under Rules 16.8 or 39.8.3 of the Technical Rules, the procedure set out in Rule 16.9 of the Technical Rules is followed.

All members of the start team must be well informed about the Rules and how they should be interpreted. The team must also be clear on what procedures it will follow when implementing the Rules, so that the events can continue without delay. They must understand well the respective duties and roles of each member of the team, especially the Starter and the Start Referee.

22.2 The Starter, whose primary responsibility is to ensure a fair and equitable start for all competitors, shall have entire control of the athletes on their marks. When a Start Information System is used to assist in races using a crouch start, Rule 16.6 of the Technical Rules shall be applied.

22.3 The Starter shall position themselves so that they have full visual control over all athletes during the start procedure.

It is recommended, especially for staggered starts, that loudspeakers in the individual lanes be used for relaying the commands and the start and any recall signals to all athletes at the same time.

22.1.1　划分发令团队成员的职责。但在举办世界排名比赛定义1.（a）（b）（c）和2.（a）（b）（c）所述的比赛时，将由技术代表确定哪些项目由世界田联发令员承担发令工作。

22.1.2　监督发令团队每位成员履行职责的情况。

22.1.3　接到竞赛主任的有关命令后，确认所有计时员、相关裁判员和终点摄影主裁判、感应计时主裁判、风速测量员都已准备就绪，通知发令员开始发令程序。

22.1.4　作为计时设备公司技术人员和裁判员之间的对话者。

22.1.5　保存发令过程中产生的所有纸质文件，包括起跑反应时和/或起跑犯规波形图（如果有）。

22.1.6　确保依据技术规则16.8条或39.8.3条作出的任何裁决，按技术规则16.9条规定的程序执行。

发令团队所有成员必须通晓规则且知道如何解释规则。发令团队也必须清楚该如何按照规则执行发令程序，以确保比赛的连续及不延误。他们还必须相当清楚发令团队每个成员的职责和角色，特别是发令员和起点裁判长。

22.2　发令员的主要职责是确保所有参赛人员公平公正地起跑，发令员要完全掌控"各就位"的运动员。在蹲踞式起跑的比赛中，使用起跑信息系统帮助发令时，要适用技术规则16.6条。

22.3　在发令过程中，发令员要使自己处于能够完全看清所有起跑运动员的位置。

建议在每条分道上摆放一个扩音器，以便使口令、发令及任何召回信号同时传至所有运动员，在梯形起跑时更应如此。

Note: The Starter shall place themselves so that the whole field of athletes falls into a narrow visual angle. For races using a crouch start it is necessary that they are so placed that they can ascertain that all athletes are currently steady in their set positions before the gun is fired or the starting apparatus is activated. (All such starting apparatus is termed "gun" for the purpose of the Rules.) Where loudspeakers are not used in races with a staggered start, the Starter shall so place themselves that the distance between them and each of the athletes is approximately the same. Where, however, the Starter cannot place themselves in such a position, the gun shall be placed there and discharged by electric contact.

The Starter's commands have to be clear and heard by all athletes but, unless they are a long way from the athletes and without a speaker system, they should avoid shouting whilst giving the commands.

22.4　　One or more Recallers shall be assigned to assist the Starter.

Note: For races of 200m, 400m, 400m Hurdles, 4 × 100m, 4 × 200m, the Medley Relay and 4 × 400m Relays, there shall be at least two Recallers.

22.5　　Each Recaller shall place themselves so that they can see each athlete assigned to them.

22.6　　The Starter and/or each Recaller shall recall or abort the race if any infringement of the Rules is observed. After a recalled or aborted start the Recaller shall report their observations to the Starter, who decides whether and to which athlete(s) a warning or disqualification shall be issued (see also Rules 16.7 and 16.10 of the Technical Rules). For disciplinary infringements, the decision is made by the referee (See also Rule 16.5 of the Technical Rules).

22.7　　Warning and disqualification under Rules 16.8 and 39.8.3 of the Technical Rules may be decided only by the Starter (see also Rule 18.3 of the Competition Rules).

It is necessary to take into account Rule 18.3 of the Competition Rules when interpreting both this Rule and Rule 16 of the Technical Rules, for in effect it is both the Starter and the Referee responsible for the starts who can determine whether a start is fair. On the other hand a Recaller has no such power and whilst they may recall a start, they cannot act unilaterally thereafter and must simply report their observations to the Starter.

The Starting Guidelines may be downloaded from the World Athletics website.

注：发令员站位时，要使自己以狭窄的视角就能观察到全部运动员。运动员采用蹲踞式起跑时，在发令枪响或发令设备启动前，发令员的站位应使自己能看清运动员在鸣枪前的"预备"姿势均处于稳定状态（规则中所有发令设备均称为"发令枪"）。在采用梯形起跑的比赛中，如未使用扩音器，则发令员的位置与每名运动员之间的距离要大致相等。如发令员不能取得这种位置，要将发令枪置于该处，用电子触发装置发令。

发令员的口令必须清晰并让所有运动员听到，但应避免在发令时喊叫，除非他离运动员很远且没有扩音系统。

22.4　要指派1名或多名召回员协助发令员工作。

注：200米、400米、400米栏、4×100米接力赛、4×200米接力赛、异程接力赛和4×400米接力比赛时，至少要有2名召回员。

22.5　召回员的站位要使自己能看清所负责的每位运动员。

22.6　如果观察到任何违反规则的情况，发令员和/或每位召回员要召回或中止比赛。召回或中止发令后，召回员应向发令员报告他的观察情况，由发令员决定是否给予以及要给哪名（些）运动员警告或取消比赛资格的判罚（另见技术规则16.7条和16.10条）。对于运动员违反纪律的行为，则由裁判长作出决定（另见技术规则16.5条）。

22.7　只有发令员有权依据技术规则16.8条和39.8.3条作出警告和取消比赛资格的判罚（另见竞赛规则18.3条）。

在解释此规则及技术规则16条时，有必要考虑竞赛规则18.3条，因为实际上发令员和起点裁判长都可以判定起跑是否公允。反过来说，召回员没有此项权利，当他召回起跑后，他不能单独行事，且必须向发令员报告他的观察情况。

《发令指南》可从世界田联网站下载。

23. Starter's Assistants

23.1 The Starter's Assistants shall check that the athletes are competing in the correct heat or race and that their bibs are worn correctly.

23.2 They must place each athlete in their correct lane or position, assembling the athletes approximately 3m behind the start line (in the case of races started in echelon, similarly behind each start line). When this has been completed, they shall signal to the Starter that all is ready. If a new start is ordered, the Starter's Assistants shall assemble the athletes again.

23.3 The Starter's Assistants shall be responsible for the readiness of batons for the first athletes in a Relay Race.

23.4 When the Starter has ordered the athletes to their marks, the Starter's Assistants must ensure that Rules 16.3 and 16.4 of the Technical Rules are observed.

23.5 In case of a false start, the Starter's Assistants shall proceed in accordance with Rule 16.9 of the Technical Rules.

24. Lap Scorers

24.1 Lap Scorers shall keep a record of the laps completed by all athletes in races longer than 1500m. Specifically, for races of 5000m and longer, and for Race Walking Events, a number of Lap Scorers under the direction of the Referee shall be appointed and provided with lap scoring cards on which they shall record the times over each lap (as given to them by an official Timekeeper) of the athletes for whom they are responsible. When such a system is used, no Lap Scorer should record more than four athletes (six for Race Walking Events). Instead of manual lap scoring, a computerised system, which may involve a transponder carried or worn by each athlete, may be used.

24.2 One Lap Scorer shall be responsible for maintaining, at the finish line, a display of the laps remaining. The display shall be changed each lap when the leader enters the finish straight. In addition, manual indication shall be given, when appropriate, to athletes who have been, or are about to be, lapped.

The final lap shall be signalled to each athlete, usually by ringing a bell.

Guidelines for Lap Scoring may be downloaded from the World Athletics website.

23. 助理发令员

23.1 助理发令员要检查运动员的参赛项目、组次和佩戴号码是否正确。

23.2 助理发令员须正确安排每名运动员的道次或站位，使运动员在起跑线后约3米处（如为梯形起跑，则站在各自分道起跑线后大约3米处）集合。完成这项工作后，要向发令员示意一切准备就绪。当下令重新起跑时，助理发令员要重新召集运动员。

23.3 接力赛跑时，助理发令员要负责为第一棒运动员准备接力棒。

23.4 发令员对运动员发出"各就位"的口令时，助理发令员必须保证技术规则16.3条和16.4条得到遵守。

23.5 当发生起跑犯规时，助理发令员要根据技术规则16.9条执行。

24. 记圈裁判员

24.1 1500米以上各项比赛，记圈裁判员要记录所有运动员完成的圈数。特别是5000米及以上各项目和竞走项目比赛时，要指定若干记圈裁判员，在相关裁判长的指挥下工作。记圈裁判员要在记圈表上记录其负责的运动员每圈时间（由1名正式计时员提供）。当采用这种记圈方法时，每位记圈裁判员负责记录的运动员不得超过4人（竞走项目不得超过6人）。也可以使用计算机记圈系统替代人工记圈，让每位运动员携带或佩戴一个传感器。

24.2 要指派1名记圈裁判员负责在终点线处显示剩余圈数。当领先运动员每次进入终点直道时，要变换显示的圈数。此外，在适当时候，要以人工提示的方式通知已被套圈或将被套圈的运动员。

最后一圈时，要以一定的信号通知每位运动员，通常以铃声作为信号。

《记圈指南》可以从世界田联网站下载。

25. Competition Secretary, Technical Information Centre (TIC)

25.1 The Competition Secretary shall collect the full results of each event, details of which shall be provided by the Referee, the Chief Timekeeper, Chief Photo Finish Judge or Chief Transponder Judge and the Wind Gauge Operator. They shall immediately relay these details to the Announcer, record the results and convey the result card to the Competition Director.

Where a computerised results system is used, the computer recorder at each Field Event shall ensure that the full results of each event are entered into the computer system. The track results shall be input under the direction of the Chief Photo Finish Judge. The Announcer and the Competition Director shall have access to the results via a computer.

25.2 In events in which athletes are competing with different specifications (such as implement weights or hurdle heights), the relevant differences should be clearly indicated in the results or a separate result shown for each category.

25.3 Where the applicable regulations for a competition other than under paragraphs 1. (a) and (b) of the World Rankings Competition definition permit the simultaneous participation of athletes:

25.3.1 competing with the assistance of another person, i.e. a guide runner; or

25.3.2 using a mechanical aid which is not authorised under Rule 6.3.4 of the Technical Rules;

their results shall be listed separately and, where applicable, their para classification shown.

25.4 The following standard abbreviations and symbols should be used in the preparation of start lists and results where applicable:

Did not start	DNS
Did not finish (Running or Race Walking or Combined Events)	DNF
No valid trial recorded	NM

25. 竞赛秘书和技术信息中心（TIC）

25.1 竞赛秘书要收集各项目比赛的全部成绩以及由裁判长、计时主裁判、终点摄影主裁判或感应计时主裁判与风速测量员等提供的详细资料。他要立刻将这些资料发送给宣告员，还应记录这些比赛成绩，并将成绩记录单上报竞赛主任。

当使用计算机成绩管理系统时，田赛各项目比赛场地的计算机记录人员要确保将全部成绩录入计算机系统。录入径赛成绩要在终点摄影主裁判的指挥下进行。宣告员和竞赛主任要通过计算机系统查询比赛成绩。

25.2 运动员参加不同规格（如器材重量或栏架高度）的比赛时，这些不同之处应在成绩记录单上明确标示或每一种类别的成绩应分别标注。

25.3 当举行世界排名比赛定义1.（a）和（b）之外的比赛时，适用的规程若允许，下列运动员可以同时参赛：

25.3.1 在他人协助下进行比赛，如1名引导员；或

25.3.2 使用技术规则6.3.4条未授权的机械性辅助设备；

他们的成绩要分别列出，且情况允许时，要标注运动员的残奥分级。

25.4 下列的标准缩写及符号，应在相应的参赛名单和成绩记录单上使用：

未参加比赛	DNS
未完成比赛（跑、竞走或全能项目）	DNF
没有记录有效试跳（掷）	NM

Disqualified (followed by the applicable Rule number)	DQ
Valid trial in High Jump and Pole Vault	"O"
Failed trial	"X"
Passed trial	"—"
Retired from competition (Field Events)	r
Qualified by place in Track Events	Q
Qualified by time in Track Events	q
Qualified by standard in Field Events	Q
Qualified by performance in Field Events	q
Advanced to next round by Referee	qR
Advanced to next round by Jury of Appeal	qJ
Advanced to next round by draw	qD
Bent knee (Race Walking Events)	">"
Loss of contact (Race Walking Events)	"~"
Yellow Card (followed by the applicable Rule number)	YC
Second Yellow Card (followed by the applicable Rule number)	YRC
Red Card (followed by the applicable Rule number)	RC
Lane infringement (Rules 17.3.3 and 17.3.4 of the Technical Rules)	L
Competing under protest	P

If an athlete is warned or disqualified in an event for an infringement of any Rule, reference shall be made in the official results to the Rule which has been infringed.

If an athlete is disqualified from an event for acting in an unsporting or improper manner, reference shall be made in the official results giving reasons for such disqualification.

取消参赛资格（并注明适用的规则条款）	DQ
跳高及撑竿跳高成功的试跳	"O"
失败的试跳（掷）	"X"
免跳（掷）	"–"
退出比赛（在田赛比赛中）	r
径赛项目中以名次晋级	Q
径赛项目中以成绩晋级	q
田赛项目达到及格标准晋级	Q
田赛项目以成绩晋级	q
由裁判长裁决晋级到下一轮	qR
由申诉委员会裁定晋级到下一轮	qJ
由抽签晋级到下一轮	qD
屈膝（竞走项目）	">"
腾空（竞走项目）	"~"
黄牌（注明适用的规则条款）	YC
第二张黄牌（注明适用的规则条款）	YRC
红牌（注明适用的规则条款）	RC
分道跑犯规（技术规则17.3.3条和17.3.4条）	L
抗议下比赛	P

如果运动员在比赛中因违反规则而被警告或取消参赛资格，要在正式成绩单上引用违反规则的条款。

如果运动员因违反体育道德或有不当行为被取消参赛资格，要在正式成绩单上给出取消参赛资格的原因。

Rules 25.2-4 of the Competition Rules as from 2015 are designed to standardise procedures and the use of terminology in common situations in start lists and results. Rules 25.2 and 25.3 of the Competition Rules acknowledge the not uncommon situation in many competitions below the top level (and even in some high level competitions) where athletes of different age or who have para classifications are competing in the same competitions. This Rule confirms that this is acceptable - including as a means of meeting minimum competitor number requirements, even for the purposes of Rule 31.1 of the Competition Rules as well as setting out how the results should be presented.

Given that disqualifications can be made for both technical and disciplinary reasons, it is very important that the reason for a disqualification is always indicated in the results. This is achieved by always stating the Rule under which the athlete was warned or disqualified next to the symbol.

The use of "r" is designed to cover situations in which an athlete decides not to continue in a Field Event because of injury (or any other reason as it is not necessary for them to provide one). Most commonly, this will be in High Jump or Pole Vault and here it is important to note that this has implications for the further conduct of the competition, including the application of time for trials under Rule 25.17 of the Technical Rules, as a retirement may reduce the remaining athletes in the competition to 1 or, 2 or 3 and the application of a longer time for trials will be required.

In other Field Events, an alternate method would be to show all remaining trials as a pass, but the use of "r" provides a clear indication that the athlete is no longer intending to compete in that event – whereas showing passes still leaves the possibility that the athlete could later change their mind.

See also the green text with respect to Rule 6 of the Competition Rules.

An athlete shall be regarded as DNS if:

a. after their name having been included on the start list for any event, they do not report to the Call Room for that event; or

从2015年开始，竞赛规则25.2至25.4条旨在使参赛名单及成绩单上一般情况下的程序和使用术语标准化。竞赛规则25.2条和25.3条认可许多非顶级赛事中并不罕见的情况（甚至在一些高水平比赛中），如不同年龄或不同残奥分级的运动员参加同一比赛。本规则确认这是可以接受的——包括为执行竞赛规则31.1条，作为达到最少参赛人数要求的一种手段，以及规定成绩该如何呈现。

由于取消参赛资格可以出于技术或者纪律原因，因此在成绩单上注明取消资格的原因尤为重要。这是通过始终在符号旁边说明运动员被警告或者被取消资格的规则条款实现的。

符号"r"是在一名运动员因受伤（或任何其他原因，因为运动员们没有必要提供原因）而决定不继续参加田赛项目的情况下使用。最常见的是在跳高或撑竿跳高中，此情况尤其重要，因为牵涉到该项目比赛后续的进行，包括根据技术规则25.17条——试跳的可用时限，因为运动员退赛可能使比赛中剩余的运动员数量减少至1人、2人或3人，这时就需要更长的试跳时限。

在其他田赛项目中，另一种方法是将所有剩余的试跳（掷）显示为免跳，但使用符号"r"则清楚地表明运动员不再打算参加该项目，而显示免跳则仍然保留运动员以后改变他们的想法的可能性。

另见竞赛规则6条绿色文字部分。

以下情况，则运动员被认为是未参加比赛（DNS）：

a.在他们的名字被列入任何项目的参赛名单后，未能在检录处报到；或

b. having passed through the Call Room, they do not make any attempt in a Field Event or do not attempt to make a start in a Running or Race Walking Event; or

c. Rule 39.10 of the Technical Rules applies.

25.5　A Technical Information Centre (TIC) will be established for competitions held under paragraphs 1.(a), (b), (c) and 2. (a), (b), (c) of the World Rankings Competition definition and is recommended for other competitions held over more than one day. It may be a virtual or physical operation, or a combination of both. The main function of the TIC is to ensure smooth communication between each team delegation, the organisers, the Technical Delegates and the competition administration regarding technical and other matters relating to the competition.

An effectively managed Technical Information Centre will significantly assist in the delivery of a high quality competition organisation. The TIC Manager should have excellent knowledge of the Rules and equally importantly of the specific Regulations for the particular competition.

The hours of operation of the TIC should reflect the hours of the competition plus some periods of time before and after when there will need to be interaction between the various parties, particularly between the team delegations and the Organisers. It is common, although not essential, for larger events to have "branches" of the TIC (sometimes called Sport Information Desks) in the main athlete accommodation locations. If this is the case, there must be excellent communication between the SID(s) and the TIC.

Because the hours of operation of the TIC and SID(s) may be long, it will be necessary for the TIC Manager to have several assistants and for them to work in shifts. Where a virtual TIC is fully or partially in operation, the hours of operation may more easily be extended, but it is important to make clear the hours during which the virtual operation will be monitored.

Whilst some duties of the TIC are covered in the Rules (see for example Rule 25 of the Competition Rules, and Rules 8.3 and 8.7 of the Technical Rules), others will be set out in the Regulations for each competition and in competition documents such as team handbooks etc.

b. 运动员经过检录处，而在田赛项目比赛中未进行任何试跳（掷）或在跑和竞走项目比赛中未起跑；或

c. 出现技术规则39.10条的情况。

25.5　举行世界排名比赛定义1.（a）（b）（c）和2.（a）（b）（c）所述比赛，应设立技术信息中心（TIC），建议在其他超过1天的比赛中也设立技术信息中心。技术信息中心可以采用线上或线下运行，或者两者结合起来运行。技术信息中心的主要功能是确保在每个代表队、组织者、技术代表和竞赛管理部门之间，有关技术和其他涉及比赛的信息可以顺畅交流。

有效管理的技术信息中心对于举办一场高质量比赛至关重要。技术信息中心主管应熟练掌握规则以及同等重要的特定比赛的特定规程。

TIC的运行时间应在比赛时间的基础上，加上赛前和赛后的一段时间，这段时间中各方需要沟通，特别是运动队和组织者之间进行沟通。通常情况下，尽管不是绝对的，大型赛事在运动员主要住地会设TIC的"分支机构"（有时称为体育信息台，SID）。如果是这种情况，SID（s）和TIC之间必须沟通顺畅。

由于TIC和SID（s）的运行时间可能较长，有必要为技术信息中心主管配备若干技术信息中心助理，并安排他们轮班工作。如果采用线上 TIC 全部或部分运行，则可以更容易地延长运行时间，但当采用线上运行时，明确监控线上运行时间是很重要的。

虽然竞赛规则中规定了TIC的部分职责（见竞赛规则25条、技术规则8.3条和8.7条），其他职责应在每个赛事规程和赛事文件中明确，如参赛队手册等。

26. Marshal

The Marshal shall have control of the Field of Play and shall not allow any persons other than the officials and athletes assembled to compete or other authorised persons with valid accreditation to enter and remain therein.

The Marshal's role is to regulate entry to the Field of Play during preparations immediately beforehand and while the event is in progress. They operate generally in accordance with the plan established by the Competition Director and, in relation to more immediate matters, receive their orders directly from the Meeting Manager. Accordingly, they will:

a. manage the control for the entrances into the arena of the athletes, the officials and on-field volunteers, service staff, accredited press photographers and the TV crews. At each competition, the number of such in-field accreditations is agreed beforehand and all these persons must wear a special bib;

b. manage the control at the point where the athletes leave the arena (usually for larger events into the Mixed Zone and/or the Post Event Control Area) when they have finished their event;

c. ensure that, at all times, the sight lines to the competition sites are as clear as possible for the spectators' benefit as well as for television.

They are directly answerable to the Meeting Manager who must be able to contact them at any time if the need arises.

To assist the Marshal and their team in their work, it is usual that those persons permitted to enter the arena, other than the athletes, are clearly distinguishable by means of the special bib or accreditation card or distinctive uniform.

27. Wind Gauge Operator

The Wind Gauge Operator shall ascertain the velocity of the wind in the running direction in events to which they are appointed and shall then record and sign the results obtained and communicate them to the Competition Secretary.

Whilst in practice it may be that the Wind Gauge Operator, the Technical Manager or a Photo Finish Judge actually puts the gauge in the correct place ultimately it is the responsibility of the relevant Referee to check that this is done and in accordance with the Rules (see Rules 17.10 and 29.11 of the Technical Rules).

26. 场地管理裁判员

场地管理裁判员要对比赛区域有控制权，除有关当值裁判和被召集参赛的运动员，或其他有相应注册权限授权的人员外，不允许其余任何人员进入或停留在比赛场内。

场地管理裁判员的角色是在比赛即将开始或比赛进行时规范比赛场地的人员进入。他主要根据竞赛主任的计划工作，更多的是直接从赛事总管处接收指令行事。他相应地开展以下工作：

a. 管理控制运动员、裁判以及现场志愿者、服务人员、注册的摄影及电视媒体进入场地。每场比赛的这些场内注册证件数量应事先批准，且所有上述人员应佩戴特殊号码（服装）；

b. 管理控制运动员在完成比赛后离开比赛场地的通道（通常大型赛事是进入混合采访区和/或赛后控制区域）；

c. 始终确保现场观众及电视观众观看比赛场地的视线中尽可能干净。

他们直接向赛事总管负责，赛事总管如有需要可随时联系到场地管理裁判员。

为了便于场地管理裁判员及其团队工作，通常允许进入比赛场地的人员，除运动员之外，都应清晰佩戴特殊号码、注册证件或者身穿明显的制服。

27. 风速测量员

风速测量员要测定相关项目跑进方向上的风速，要记录测量结果，在风速记录表上签名并提交给竞赛秘书。

然而在实际情况中，可能是风速测量员、技术主管或终点摄影裁判员将风速仪放置于正确位置，并由相关裁判长最终负责确认此项工作按照规则完成（见技术规则17.10条和29.11条）。

It is noted that particularly for the Track Events the wind gauge can be operated remotely. In such cases it is almost always connected to the Photo Finish and results "system", so that a Wind Gauge Operator will not be required, and their duties are filled, for example, by someone in the Photo Finish team.

28. Measurement Judge (Scientific)

One Chief Measurement Judge (Scientific) and one or more assistants shall be appointed when Electronic or Video Distance Measurement or other scientific measurement device is to be used.

Before the start of the competition, they will meet the technical staff involved and familiarise themselves with the equipment.

Before each event, they will supervise the positioning of the measuring instruments, taking account of the technical requirements given by the manufacturer and the instrument calibrating laboratory.

To ensure that the equipment is operating correctly, they shall, before the event, supervise a set of measurements in conjunction with the Judges and under the supervision of the Referee, to confirm agreement with results achieved using a calibrated and verified steel tape. A form of conformity shall be issued and signed by all those involved in the test and attached to the results card.

During the competition they shall remain in overall charge of the operation. They will report to the Referee to certify that the equipment is accurate.

Note: A set of check measurements should be made after, and if circumstances justify it during, the event usually without reference to the steel tape.

When electronic or video distance measuring equipment is used, a Chief Judge is placed as the official in charge in a similar way as is the case with Photo Finish or Transponder Timing. In the case of video measurement, the Chief Measurement Judge will be expected to take a more active and hands-on role during the events, than would be the case with fully on-field electronic distance measurement.

In particular, this should involve ensuring that an appropriate communication system is in place between the on-field Judges and the Judges undertaking the video reading to ensure that each measurement is correctly made and that in the case of the Horizontal Jumps, the landing mark is not raked out until an image has been confirmed.

Whether it is the Chief Measurement Judge or another Judge who is responsible for ensuring the video reading is correct, they must be especially careful to ensure that the current, and not a previous, trial is the one that is measured.

需要注意的是，特别是径赛项目，风速仪可以远程操控。在此类情况下，风速仪与终点摄影及成绩系统相连，所以不需要风速测量员，其职责由其他人员来履行，如终点摄影团队成员。

28. 测量裁判员（电子类）

当使用电子、视频测距设备或其他电子测量仪器时，要指派1名测量主裁判（电子类）和1名或多名助理裁判员。

比赛开始以前，他将与有关技术人员见面，熟悉器材设备。

各项目比赛开始前，需根据制造商和仪器校准实验室的技术要求，监督或指导测量仪的位置摆放。

为确保测量设备精确运行，项目比赛前，在裁判长的监督下，测量员要和裁判员一起，检测一组电子测量成绩与经过校准和验证的钢尺测量所得结果的一致性。出具一张一致性检测表，由所有参与测试人员签名，并将它附在该项成绩单后面。

比赛进行中，他要继续全面负责仪器的操作，并向裁判长报告，证明该仪器的准确性。

注：应在比赛结束后，以及如果情况合理也可在比赛期间，进行一组测量检查，通常不参考钢尺。

当使用电子或视频测距仪时，应像终点摄影或感应计时一样，指派一名主裁判负责。相对于电子测距仪测量，使用视频测距仪时，测量主裁判在比赛中要更为主动并直接上手操作。

特别需要确保场内裁判员和视频判读裁判员之间的顺畅沟通，以保证每次测量准确，以及在远度跳跃项目中图像确认后才能扫平落地点。

不管是测量主裁判还是其他负责裁判员负责视频判读的正确性，他都应尤其认真地确保他测量的是当前试跳而不是之前试跳的成绩。

田径竞赛与技术规则（2025）

29. Call Room Judges

29.1 The Call Room Chief Judge shall:

 29.1.1 in conjunction with the Competition Director, prepare and publish a Call Room schedule setting out for each event at least the first and final entry times for each Call Room in use and the time at which the athletes will depart for the competition area from the (final) Call Room;

 29.1.2 supervise the transit between the Warm-up Area and the competition area to ensure that the athletes, after being checked in the Call Room, be present and ready at the competition area for the scheduled start of their event.

The Call Room Judges shall ensure that athletes are wearing the national or Club uniform clothing officially approved by their national governing body, that the bibs are worn correctly and correspond with start lists, that shoes, number and dimension of spikes, advertising on clothing and athletes' bags comply with the Rules and applicable Regulations and that unauthorised material is not taken into the Field of Play.

The Judges shall refer any unresolved issues or matters arising to the Call Room Referee.

A well planned and efficiently managed Call Room is fundamental to the success of a competition. Planning to ensure sufficient space at the point when the Call Room will be at its fullest capacity, how many call rooms (and sections within each) are required and a reliable communication system with the other officials and to notify the athletes when to report from the Warm-up Area are always important. Other considerations will vary according to the type of competition and the number of checks which it is decided will be undertaken in the Call Room. For example at most school meets it is unlikely that checking advertising on uniforms will be an issue, whereas checking spike lengths to protect the track surface may be. It is important that in the planning process it is determined which checks will be made and preferably these should be communicated to the athletes and teams in advance to avoid stress or confusion immediately before competition. The Call Room Judges must ensure the athletes are in the correct heat, race or group and that they leave for the competition area in a timely manner in accordance with the Call Room schedule. Where possible, the schedule should be made available to the athletes and teams prior to the commencement of each day of competition.

29. 检录裁判员

29.1 检录主裁判的职责如下：

    29.1.1 会同竞赛主任，准备并公布检录时间表，该时间表至少应包括各项目比赛运动员进入各检录处的第一次和最后一次检录通知时间，以及运动员离开（最终）检录处进入比赛场地的时间。

    29.1.2 监督运动员从热身场地到比赛场地之间的转场，确保在检录处完成检录后，运动员根据项目预定的开赛时间到达比赛场地并做好准备。

检录裁判员要确保运动员穿着其国家主管部门正式批准的国家或俱乐部比赛服。正确佩戴号码布，号码与参赛名单一致，运动员的鞋、鞋钉的数量和规格、服装和运动员包上的广告应符合本规则和适用的规程规定。未经批准的物品不得带入比赛场地。

检录裁判员要将发生在检录过程中未能解决的问题或事宜提交检录裁判长。

周密计划和有效管理的检录处是比赛成功举办的基础。计划要确保及明确检录处在人员最多的情况下有足够空间、需要多少检录室（以及每个多少分区）、与其他官员沟通的可靠的联络系统、通知运动员何时从热身场地来报到，这些都很重要。其他方面的考虑应根据比赛类型及检录处的检查内容而有所不同。例如，在学校比赛中不大可能检查服装上的广告，但是可能检查鞋钉长度以保护跑道。在计划阶段确定检查内容很重要，而且最好提前与运动员和代表队沟通，以避免赛前紧张和混乱。检录处裁判员须确保运动员处于正确的组别、比赛或分组，以及根据检录时间表按照时间抵达比赛场地。如果可能，检录时间表应在每天开始比赛前告知运动员和代表队。

30. Advertising Commissioner

The Advertising Commissioner (when appointed) will supervise and apply the current Marketing & Advertising Rules and Regulations and shall determine any unresolved advertising issues or matters arising in the Call Room in conjunction with the Call Room Referee.

30. 广告管理专员

广告管理专员（如指派）应监督并执行现行营销和广告的规则和规程，并要与检录裁判长共同确定发生在检录处的任何没有解决或有关广告的未尽事宜。

PART III WORLD RECORDS

31. World Records

Submission and Ratification

31.1 A World Record shall be made in a bona fide competition which has been duly arranged, advertised and authorised before the day of the event by the Member in whose Country or Territory the event takes place and which has been conducted under and in compliance with the Rules. For individual events, at least three athletes and for relay events, at least two teams must be bona fide competitors in the event. Except for Field Events conducted as provided in Rule 9 of the Technical Rules and competitions held outside the stadium under Rules 54 and 55 of the Technical Rules, no performance set by an athlete will be ratified if it has been accomplished during a mixed competition.

Note: Women only Road Race records are subject to the conditions set out in Rule 32 of the Competition Rules.

31.2 The following categories of World Records are accepted by World Athletics:

  31.2.1 World Records;

  31.2.2 World U20 Records.

Note (i): For the purposes of these Rules, unless the context dictates otherwise, World Records refers to all categories of records under this Rule.

Note (ii): World Records under Rules 31.2.1 and 31.2.2 of the Competition Rules shall recognise the best ratified performances achieved at any facility complying with Rule 31.12 or 31.13 of the Competition Rules.

31.3 An athlete (or athletes in the case of a relay event) who sets a World Record must:

  31.3.1 have been eligible to compete under the Rules;

第三部分　世界纪录

31.　世界纪录

提交申请与批准

31.1　纪录要在真诚努力的比赛中创造，该项目比赛日之前，经举办国或地区的会员协会正式安排、宣传和授权，并完全按规则进行管理和比赛。个人项目至少有3人参赛，接力项目至少有2队参赛，他们必须是真诚努力地完成比赛。除按技术规则9条举办的田赛项目和按技术规则54条、55条举办的运动场外的比赛外，运动员在男女混合比赛中所创成绩不予承认。

注：只有女性参加的公路比赛纪录应符合竞赛规则32条所列条件。

31.2　世界田联承认的世界纪录有下列几种：

31.2.1　世界纪录；

31.2.2　世界青年U20纪录。

注（ⅰ）：就本规则而言，除非上下文中另有规定，本规则中的世界纪录涉及所有的纪录种类。

注（ⅱ）：竞赛规则31.2.1条和31.2.2条规定的世界纪录，要承认在符合竞赛规则31.12条或31.13条的任何场地设施条件下达到的最好批准成绩。

31.3　创造世界纪录的运动员（或接力比赛项目中的运动员）必须：

31.3.1　符合世界田联规则规定的参赛资格；

31.3.2   have been under the jurisdiction of a Member;

31.3.3   in the case of a performance submitted under Rule 31.2.2 of the Competition Rules, unless the athlete's date of birth has been previously confirmed by the Chief Executive Officer, have their date of birth confirmed by their passport, birth certificate or similar official documentation, a copy of which, if not available to be attached to the application form, must be provided by the athlete or athlete's Member Federation to the Chief Executive Officer without delay;

31.3.4   in the case of relay events, must all be eligible to represent a single Member in accordance with Eligibility to Represent a Member Rules;

31.3.5   submit to doping control immediately after the end of the event, where the athlete has broken or equalled a World Record. No delays other than those identified in the Anti-Doping Rules and the sample(s) shall be accepted. Doping controls for the ratification of a World Record shall be conducted in accordance with the Anti-Doping Rules and the sample(s) shall be sent for analysis to a WADA accredited laboratory as soon as possible after collection. Doping control samples collected for the ratification of World Records in endurance events from 400m upwards shall be analysed for Erythropoiesis Stimulating Agents (ESA). The doping control documentation (doping control form and corresponding laboratory results) shall be sent to World Athletics as soon as it is available and, ideally, together with the World Record Application Form (see CR 31.6). The doping control documentation will be reviewed by the Athletics Integrity Unit and the performance will not be ratified in the following circumstances:

   a.   if a doping control is not conducted, or

   b.   if the doping control has not been conducted in accordance with the Competition Rules or the Anti-Doping Rules, or

   c.   if the doping control sample is not suitable for analysis or has not been analysed for ESA (for endurance events from 400m upwards only), or

31.3.2 隶属于某一个世界田联会员协会；

31.3.3 申报竞赛规则31.2.2条纪录者，除非该运动员的出生日期事先已得到首席执行官的确认，否则第一次为该运动员申报纪录时，必须提交其护照、出生证或证明其出生日期的类似正式文件的副本。如果没有随附有效申请表，必须由运动员或运动员的国家协会提交给首席执行官，不得延误；

31.3.4 在接力比赛中，按照会员代表资格规则的规定，运动员必须都有资格代表单一会员协会；

31.3.5 运动员打破或追平世界纪录，在该项目比赛结束后立即接受兴奋剂检查。除《反兴奋剂规则》中的延误要被接受外，不得接受任何延误。批准世界纪录的兴奋剂检查要按照《反兴奋剂规则》进行，样品收集后要尽快送至世界反兴奋剂机构（WADA）认可的实验室进行分析。为批准400米以上耐力项目世界纪录而采集的兴奋剂对照样本应进行红细胞生成激素刺激剂（ESA）的分析。兴奋剂检查文件（兴奋剂检查表格和对应的实验室结果）要尽快送往世界田联，理想的情况下应与填写的世界纪录申请表同步提交（见竞赛规则31.6条）。兴奋剂检查文件将由田径诚信机构审核，下列情况中的成绩将不被认可：

a. 如果没有进行兴奋剂检查，或者

b. 如果未按照《竞赛规则》或《反兴奋剂规则》进行兴奋剂检查，或者

c. 如果兴奋剂检查样本不适合进行分析或未进行ESA分析（仅适用于400米以上耐力项目），或者

d. if the doping control results in an anti-doping rule violation.

Note (i): In the case of a Relay World Record, all members of the team must be tested.

Note (ii): If an athlete has admitted that, at some time prior to achieving a World Record, they had used or taken advantage of a substance or technique prohibited at that time, then, subject to the advice of the Athletics Integrity Unit, such record will not continue to be regarded as a World Record by World Athletics.

31.4 When a performance equals or betters an existing World Record, the Member of the Country where the performance was set shall collect together, without delay, all the information required for ratification of the Record by World Athletics. No performance shall be regarded as a World Record until it has been ratified by World Athletics. The Member should immediately inform World Athletics of its intention to submit the performance.

31.5 The submitted performance shall be better than or equal to the existing World Record for that event, as accepted by World Athletics. If a World Record is equalled, it shall have the same status as the existing World Record.

31.6 The official application form of World Athletics shall be completed and dispatched to the Office within 30 days. If the application concerns a foreign athlete (or a foreign team), a duplicate of the form shall be sent within the same period to the Member of the athlete (or team).

Note: Forms are available, on request, from the World Athletics Office, or may be downloaded from the World Athletics website.

31.7 The Member of the Country where the performance was set shall send, with the official application form:

31.7.1 The printed programme of the competition (or electronic equivalent);

31.7.2 The complete results of the event, including all information required under this Rule;

31.7.3 In the case of a Track World Record where Fully Automatic Timing was in operation, the Photo Finish and zero control test images;

31.7.4 Any other information required to be submitted by this Rule, where such information is or should be in its possession.

d. 如果兴奋剂检查结果违反了反兴奋剂规则。

注（ⅰ）：如果创造了接力赛跑纪录，则全队成员均须接受检查。

注（ⅱ）：如果一名运动员承认在创造某项世界纪录前的某时，曾使用了当时禁用的物质或方法，并从中获得利益，则根据田径诚信机构的建议，世界田联将不再承认此项成绩为世界纪录。

31.4 当一项成绩平或超过现有世界纪录时，创纪录所在国/地区协会要立即收集一切必要的材料上报世界田联审批，不得延误。未经世界田联批准，任何成绩都不能被承认为世界纪录。该会员协会应立即向世界田联报告其申报成绩的意图。

31.5 申报纪录的成绩要超过或平世界田联认可的该项目的现有世界纪录。如果是平该项目的纪录，则应具备与原纪录相同的情形。

31.6 要填写世界田联的正式申请表，并在30天内寄往世界田联总部办公室。如果申请纪录涉及外国运动员（或运动队），则要将表格副本在同一期限内寄交创纪录者所属协会。

注：申请表格可向世界田联总部索取或从世界田联网站下载。

31.7 创纪录所在地的世界田联会员协会要随正式申请表附上：

31.7.1 印制好的大会秩序册（或电子版）；

31.7.2 该项目的全部比赛成绩，包括本规则要求的所有信息；

31.7.3 关于使用全自动计时的径赛项目世界纪录，则需要终点摄影图片和"零测试"图像；

31.7.4 本规则要求的任何其他信息，这些信息应该包括在内。

31.8 Performances made in Qualification Rounds, in deciding ties in High Jump and Pole Vault, in any event or part of an event which is subsequently decreed void under the provisions of Rule 18.7 of the Competition Rules or Rules 8.4.2, 17.1 or 25.20 of the Technical Rules, in Race Walking Events in which Rule 54.7.3 of the Technical Rules is applied and the athlete is not disqualified or in individual events in Combined Events competitions, regardless of whether or not the athlete completes the whole Combined Events competition, may be submitted for ratification.

31.9 The President and the Chief Executive Officer of World Athletics together are authorised to ratify World Records. If they are in any doubt whether or not the performance should be ratified, the case shall be referred to Council for decision in accordance with the Governance Rules.

31.10 When a World Record has been ratified, the Chief Executive Officer will:

31.10.1 so inform the athlete's Member, the Member applying for the World Record and the relevant Area Association;

31.10.2 supply the official World Record Plaques, for presentation to World Record holders.

31.10.3 update the official List of World Records. This list shall represent the performances regarded by World Athletics as being, from the date of the list, the best ratified performances yet set by an athlete or team of athletes in each of the recognised events listed in Rule 32 of the Competition Rules.

31.11 If the performance is not ratified, the Chief Executive Officer will give the reasons.

Specific Conditions

31.12 For World Records on 400m Standard Oval Track:

31.12.1 The performance shall be made in a World Athletics certified athletics facility or at a competition area which conforms to Rule 2 of the Technical Rules or, where applicable, Rule 11.2 or 11.3 of the Technical Rules.

31.8 在径赛晋级赛或田赛及格赛赛次中、在跳高和撑竿跳高的决名次赛中、在随后根据竞赛规则18.7条或技术规则8.4.2条、17.1条或25.20条规定而被宣布无效的比赛或部分比赛中、在适用了技术规则54.7.3条的竞走项目中，且运动员未被取消比赛资格，或在无论运动员是否完成了整个全能项目的单项比赛中，所取得的成绩均可被提交申请。

31.9 世界田联主席和首席执行官联名有权批准世界纪录。如果他们对是否承认纪录产生任何疑问，则要提交世界田联理事会依据管理规则作出裁决。

31.10 一项世界纪录获批后，首席执行官将：

  31.10.1 通知申请该纪录的会员协会、该运动员所属的会员协会和有关地区联合会；

  31.10.2 为世界纪录创造者颁发正式的世界纪录纪念牌。

  31.10.3 更新正式的世界纪录表。该表要反映自世界田联成立以来，运动员（或运动队）在竞赛规则32条承认的比赛中，创造了被世界田联承认的最好批准成绩。

31.11 如果世界纪录未被批准，首席执行官将给出原因。

特定条件

31.12 400米标准椭圆形跑道世界纪录：

  31.12.1 创造世界纪录要在世界田联认证的田径场，或在符合技术规则2条规定的比赛场，如条件适用，包括技术规则11.2条或11.3条的场地。

31.12.2　For any performance at any distance of 200m or more to be ratified, the track on which it was made shall not exceed 402.3m (440 yards) and the race shall have started on some part of the perimeter. This limitation does not apply to the Steeplechase Events where the water jump is placed outside a normal 400m track.

31.12.3　A performance in an oval Track Event shall be made in a lane where the running line radius does not exceed 50m, except where the bend is formed with two different radii, in which case the longer of the two arcs should not account for more than 60° of the 180° turn.

31.12.4　A performance in a Track Event on a 400m Standard Oval Track may be made only on a track which conforms to Rule 14 of the Technical Rules.

31.13　For World Records on 200m Standard Oval Track (Short Track):

31.13.1　The performance shall have been made in a World Athletics certified athletics facility or at a competition area, which complies with Rules 41 to 43 of the Technical Rules as applicable.

31.13.2　For races of 200m and over, the oval track may not have a nominal length of more than 201.2m (220 yards).

13.13.3　The performance may be made on an oval track with a nominal length less than 200m provided that the distance run is within permitted tolerance for the distance.

31.13.4　The performance in an oval Track Event shall be made in a lane where the projected running line radius on the constant banked bend segment does not exceed 27m and, for multiple lap events, the two straights each are at least 30m long.

31.14　For World Records in Running and Race Walking Events:

31.14.1　The performance shall be timed by official Timekeepers, by a Fully Automatic Timing and Photo Finish System (for which a zero control test has been undertaken in accordance with Rule 19.19 of the Technical Rules) or by a Transponder System (see Rule 19.24 of the Technical Rules) complying with the Rules.

31.12.2 承认200米或200米以上任何项目的纪录时，创纪录所用跑道的周长不得超过402.3米（440码），而且要在椭圆跑道上的某一部分起跑。水池位于标准400米跑道外的障碍赛跑项目不受此限制。

31.12.3 创纪录所用跑道的外侧分道的半径不得超过50米，但下列情况除外：用两个不同半径画出弯道，用较大半径画出的弧长，在180°的弯道中不超过60°。

31.12.4 只有在符合技术规则14条规定的400米标准椭圆形跑道上创造的纪录方予承认。

31.13 200米标准椭圆形跑道（短道）上创造的世界纪录：

31.13.1 纪录要在世界田联认证的田径场，或符合技术规则41至43条规定的比赛场创造。

31.13.2 承认200米或200米以上项目的纪录时，创纪录所用椭圆跑道的周长不得超过201.2米（220码）。

31.13.3 只要实际跑进距离在容差范围内，在少于200米的椭圆跑道上创造的纪录也可被承认。

31.13.4 在椭圆跑道上创造的成绩，要求坡面处跑道的投影半径不得超过27米，多圈比赛的两个直道不得短于30米。

31.14 跑和竞走项目的世界纪录必须符合以下条件：

31.14.1 纪录要根据规则由正式计时员、一台经批准的全自动计时和终点摄影系统（已根据技术规则19.19条进行"零测试"）或感应计时系统（见技术规则19.24条）计时方予承认。

31.14.2　For races up to and including 800m (including 4×200m and 4×400m), only performances timed by a Fully Automatic Timing and Photo Finish System complying with the Rules shall be ratified.

31.14.3　For performances made outdoors up to and including 200m, except for 200m races on a 200m Standard Oval Track, information concerning wind velocity, measured as indicated in Rules 17.8 to 17.13 of the Technical Rules inclusive, shall be submitted. If the wind velocity, measured in the direction of running, averages more than 2 metres per second, the performance will not be ratified.

31.14.4　No performance will be ratified where the athlete has infringed Rule 17.3 of the Technical Rules except,

a.　in cases covered in Rules 17.3.1 and 17.3.2 of the Technical Rules, or

b.　in cases covered in Rules 17.3.3 and 17.3.4 of the Technical Rules, if it is the first infringement in the event,

nor in the case of an individual event where an athlete has recorded a false start as allowed under Rule 39.8.3 of the Technical Rules.

31.14.5　For performances up to and including 400m (including 4 × 200m and 4 × 400m) under Rule 32 of the Competition Rules, starting blocks linked to a World Athletics certified Start Information System under Rule 15.3 of the Technical Rules must have been used and have functioned correctly so that reaction times were obtained and are shown on the results of the event.

Note: This Rule 31.14.5 does not apply to World U20 Records.

31.14.2 800米及800米以下的径赛项目（包括4×200米接力和4×400米接力），只有依据规则采用全自动计时和终点摄影系统所记录的成绩，方予承认。

31.14.3 批准室外200米及200米以下各项目的纪录，不包括在200米标准椭圆形跑道的200米比赛，要申报按技术规则17.8至17.13条的规定测量的有关风速数据。如果跑进方向测量的顺风平均风速超过2米/秒，所创纪录不予承认。

31.14.4 如果运动员违反了技术规则17.3条的规定，成绩将不予认可，除了

a. 技术规则17.3.1条和17.3.2条包含的情况，或

b. 但不包括根据技术规则17.3.3条和17.3.4条规定在该项目中第一次犯规，

也不包括允许运动员依据技术规则39.8.3条规定记录了一次起跑犯规的全能单项。

31.14.5 竞赛规则32条规定的承认世界纪录的项目中，400米及400米以下项目（包括4×200米接力和4×400米接力）的世界纪录，必须按照技术规则15.3条正确、有效地使用连接起跑器的世界田联认证的起跑信息系统，该系统能获得正确的起跑反应时，并能显示在比赛的成绩单上。

注：本规则31.14.5条不适用于U20世界纪录。

The amendment to Rule 17.3 of the Technical Rules means for World Record ratification that if an athlete or relay team achieves a record time and, in that race, that athlete (or any athlete in the relay team) made a single infringement under Rules 17.3.3 or 17.3.4 of the Technical Rules, and in the case of an event with more than one round, it was the first infringement in the event, the record can stand. If the athlete or relay team achieves a record time and, in that race, an infringement occurred more than once or the athlete or relay team carried over such infringement from a previous round of the same event, the record cannot be ratified.

31.15　For World Records set over multiple distances in the same race:

    31.15.1　A race shall be stated to be over one distance only.

    31.15.2　A race based on the distance covered over a given time may be combined with a race over a fixed distance (for example, 1 Hour and 10,000m - see Rule 18.3 of the Technical Rules).

    31.15.3　It is permissible for the same athlete to submit multiple performances for ratification in the same race.

    31.15.4　It is permissible for several athletes to submit performances for ratification in the same race.

    31.15.5　A performance will not be ratified at a shorter distance if the athlete did not finish the full distance of that race.

31.16　For World Records in Relay Events:

The time set by the first athlete in a relay team may not be submitted for ratification as a World Record.

31.17　For World Records in Field Events:

    31.17.1　The performances shall be measured either by three Field Judges using a calibrated and verified steel tape or bar or by a scientific measuring apparatus, the accuracy of which has been confirmed in accordance with Rule 10 of the Technical Rules.

技术规则17.3条的修改意味着，如果运动员（或接力队中的任何运动员）依据技术规则17.3.3条或17.3.4条只有一次犯规，或者在有多赛次比赛的项目中第一次犯规，那么该运动员（或接力队）在那场比赛中所达到的纪录成绩将被批准为世界纪录。如果运动员（或接力队中的任何运动员）依据技术规则17.4.3条或17.4.4条的犯规多于一次或者在相同项目不同赛次中多次犯规，那么该运动员（或接力队）在那场比赛中所达到的纪录成绩将不被批准。

31.15　同一比赛中创造多个距离的世界纪录：

  31.15.1　该赛事仅为单一距离赛事。

  31.15.2　可以把规定时间的计程比赛和规定距离的计时比赛结合（例如，1小时计程赛和10000米计时赛，见技术规则18.3条）。

  31.15.3　允许1名运动员在同一比赛中创造多项纪录。

  31.15.4　允许几名运动员在同一比赛中创造不同的纪录。

  31.15.5　运动员未完成全程比赛距离，不得取其中一段较短距离的成绩作为纪录。

31.16　接力项目世界纪录：

在接力赛跑中，第一棒运动员的成绩不能申报世界纪录。

31.17　田赛项目世界纪录：

  31.17.1　田赛各项纪录要由3名裁判员使用经过校检的钢卷尺或钢直尺进行测量，也可使用经批准的科学测量仪器进行测量，该仪器的精度应符合技术规则10条的规定。

31.17.2 In the Long Jump and Triple Jump conducted outdoors, information concerning wind velocity, measured as indicated in Rules 29.10 to 29.12 of the Technical Rules shall be submitted. If the wind velocity, measured in the direction of jumping, averages more than 2 metres per second, the performance will not be ratified.

31.17.3 World Records may be credited for more than one performance in a competition, provided that each World Record so ratified shall have been equal or superior to the best previous performance at that moment.

31.17.4 In Throwing Events, the implement used shall have been checked prior to the competition in accordance with Rule 16 of the Competition Rules. If the Referee becomes aware during an event that a World Record has been equalled or bettered, they shall immediately mark the implement used and undertake a check to ascertain whether it still complies with the Rules or if there has been any change in characteristics. Normally, such implement shall be checked again after the event in accordance with Rule 16 of the Competition Rules.

31.18 For World Records in Combined Events:

The conditions as set out in Rule 39.8 of the Technical Rules shall have been complied with in each of the individual events. In addition, for those events where wind velocity is required to be measured, the average velocity (based on the algebraic sum of the wind velocities, as measured for each individual event, divided by the number of such events) shall not exceed plus 2 metres per second.

31.19 For World Records in Race Walking Events:

At least three Judges who are either World Athletics Gold or Silver Level Race Walking Judges shall be officiating during the competition and shall sign the application form.

31.20 For World Records in Road Race Walking Events:

31.20.1 The course must be measured by an "A" or "B" grade World Athletics/AIMS approved measurer who shall ensure that the relevant measurement report and any other information required by this Rule is available to World Athletics upon request.

31.17.2 申报室外跳远和三级跳远的纪录,要提交根据技术规则29.10至29.12条的规定测量的该项目的风速数据。如果在跳跃方向上测定的顺风平均风速超过2米/秒,则所创纪录不予承认。

31.17.3 在田赛项目的一次比赛中,可承认多个成绩为世界纪录。被承认的每个纪录都要平或超过当时已有的世界最好成绩。

31.17.4 投掷项目中使用的器械要在赛前根据竞赛规则16条进行检测。如果在比赛中裁判长意识到平纪录和超纪录的情况,他应立即标记并检测所用器械是否仍然符合规则规定,或其属性是否发生变化。通常,应在比赛结束后根据竞赛规则16条再次对该器械进行检测。

31.18 全能项目世界纪录:

每项单项申报世界纪录应遵守技术规则39.8条规定的条件。另外,对于那些需要测量风速的单项平均风速不超过+2米/秒(为每个单项测量风速,以各项目测量的风速总和除以项目数量)。

31.19 竞走项目世界纪录:

比赛至少要有3名世界田联金级或银级竞走裁判员执裁,并要在申请纪录表上签名。

31.20 公路竞走项目世界纪录:

31.20.1 比赛赛道路线必须经由1名世界田联或国际路跑协会批准的A级或B级丈量员丈量。他要确认相关测量报告和本规则要求的任何其他信息能满足世界田联的要求。

31.20.2　The circuit shall be no shorter than 1km and no longer than 2km with a possible start and finish in a stadium.

31.20.3　Any course measurer who originally measured the course or other suitably qualified official designated by the measurer (after consulting the relevant body) with a copy of the documentation detailing the officially measured course must validate that the course covered by the athletes conforms to the course measured and documented by the official course measurer.

31.20.4　The course must be verified (i.e. re-measured) as late as possible before the race, on the day of the race or as soon as practical after the race, by a different "A" grade measurer from any of those who did the original measurement.

Note: If the course was originally measured by at least two "A" or one "A" and one "B" grade measurers, no verification (re-measurement) under this Rule 31.20.4 will be required.

31.20.5　World Records in Road Race Walking Events set at intermediate distances within a race must comply with the conditions set under Rule 31 of the Competition Rules. The intermediate distances must have been measured, recorded and subsequently marked as part of the course measurement and must have been verified in accordance with Rule 31.20.4 of the Competition Rules.

31.21　For World Records in Road Running Events:

31.21.1　The course must be measured by an "A" or "B" grade World Athletics/AIMS approved measurer who shall ensure that the relevant measurement report and any other information required by this Rule is available to World Athletics upon request.

31.21.2　The start and finish points of a course, measured along a theoretical straight line between them, shall not be further apart than 50% of the race distance.

31.21.3　The overall decrease in elevation between the start and finish shall not exceed 1:1000, i.e. 1m per km (0.1%).

31.20.2 环形路线不要短于1公里，也不要长于2公里，尽可能将起点和终点设在体育场内。

31.20.3 任何原来负责丈量此赛道的丈量员，或其他经丈量员指派的有资质的官员（在咨询相关机构后），应持有经正式丈量过的赛道的详细资料的副本，证实比赛中运动员所走的路线就是正式赛道丈量员所丈量并经过认证的路线。

31.20.4 必须在比赛前、比赛当天或比赛之后立即进行路线现场证实（即再次丈量），且丈量不是由原来丈量路线的A级丈量员进行。

注：如果赛道在初次丈量时，由至少2名A级丈量员或1名A级和1名B级丈量员丈量，则不需要根据规则31.20.4条对赛道进行再次丈量。

31.20.5 在一个项目的分段距离中，创造公路竞走项目世界纪录必须符合竞赛规则31条的条件。分段距离必须作为路线丈量的一部分内容，被丈量、记录并随后做出标记，并且根据竞赛规则31.20.4条的规定进行了复核。

31.21 公路项目世界纪录：

31.21.1 赛道路线必须经由1名或多名世界田联或国际路跑协会批准的A级或B级丈量员丈量。他要确认相关测量报告和本规则要求的任何其他信息能满足世界田联的要求。

31.21.2 赛道起点、终点之间的直线距离不要超过比赛距离的50%。

31.21.3 起点、终点之间的总下降坡度不要超过1∶1000，即每公里1米（0.1%）。

31.21.4　Any course measurer who originally measured the course or other suitably qualified official designated by the measurer (after consulting the relevant body) with a copy of the documentation detailing the officially measured course shall in advance of the race check that the course is laid out in conformity with the course measured and documented by the official course measurer. They shall then ride in the lead vehicle during the competition or otherwise validate that the same course is run by the athletes.

31.21.5　The course must be verified (i.e. re-measured) as late as possible before the race, on the day of the race or as soon as practical after the race, by a different "A" grade measurer from any of those who did the original measurement.

Note: If the course was originally measured by at least two "A" grade or one "A" and one "B" grade measurers, no verification (re-measurement) under this Rule 31.21.5 will be required.

31.21.6　World Records in Road Running Events set at intermediate distances within a race must comply with the conditions set under Rule 31 of the Competition Rules. The intermediate distances must have been measured, recorded and subsequently marked as part of the course measurement and must have been verified in accordance with Rule 31.21.5 of the Competition Rules.

31.21.7　For the Road Relay, the race shall be run in stages of 5km, 10km, 5km, 10km, 5km, 7.195km. The stages must have been measured, recorded and subsequently marked as part of the course measurement with a tolerance of ± 1% of the stage distance and must have been verified in accordance with Rule 31.21.5 of the Competition Rules.

Note: It is recommended that national governing bodies and Area Associations adopt similar rules to the above for the recognition of their own records.

31.21.4　任何原来负责丈量此赛道的丈量员，或其他经丈量员指派的有资质的裁判员（在咨询相关机构后），应持有经正式丈量过的赛道的详细认证资料的副本，且要坐在赛事先导车中，或以其他方式证实比赛中运动员所跑的路线就是丈量员丈量并经过认证的路线。

31.21.5　必须在比赛前、比赛当天或比赛之后立即进行路线现场证实（即再次丈量），且丈量不是由原来丈量路线的A级丈量员进行。

注：如果赛道在初次丈量时，由至少2名A级丈量员或1名A级和1名B级丈量员丈量，则不需要根据规则31.21.5条对赛道进行再次丈量。

31.21.6　在一个项目的分段距离中，创造公路项目世界纪录必须符合竞赛规则31条的条件。分段距离路线必须作为路线丈量的一部分内容，被丈量、记录并随后做出标记，并且根据竞赛规则31.21.5条的规定进行了复核。

31.21.7　公路接力项目要按5公里、10公里、5公里、10公里、5公里、7.195公里的赛段跑进。此赛段必须作为路线丈量的一部分内容，被丈量、记录并随后做出标记，在丈量赛段中允许有±1%的误差，并且必须按照竞赛规则31.21.5条的规定经过验证。

注：建议国家/地区和地区联合会采用类似上述规则承认本国或本地区的纪录。

32. Events for which World Records and World U20 Records are Recognised

	Event	Men	Women	U20 Men	U20 Women	Timing
Running Events	50m	✓	✓			FAT
	60m	✓	✓	✓	✓	FAT
	100m	✓	✓	✓	✓	FAT
	200m	✓	✓	✓	✓	FAT
	200m sh	✓	✓	✓	✓	FAT
	400m	✓	✓	✓	✓	FAT
	400m sh	✓	✓	✓	✓	FAT
	800m	✓	✓	✓	✓	FAT
	800m sh	✓	✓	✓	✓	FAT
	1000m	✓	✓	✓	✓	FAT or HT
	1000m sh	✓	✓	✓	✓	FAT or HT
	1500m	✓	✓	✓	✓	FAT or HT
	1500m sh	✓	✓	✓	✓	FAT or HT
	1 Mile	✓	✓	✓	✓	FAT or HT
	1 Mile sh	✓	✓	✓	✓	FAT or HT
	2000m	✓	✓			FAT or HT
	3000m	✓	✓	✓	✓	FAT or HT
	3000m sh	✓	✓	✓	✓	FAT or HT
	5000m	✓	✓	✓	✓	FAT or HT
	5000m sh	✓	✓	✓	✓	FAT or HT
	10000m	✓	✓	✓	✓	FAT or HT
	1 Hour	✓	✓			FAT or HT
	3000m SC	✓	✓	✓	✓	FAT or HT
Hurdle Races	50m Hurdles	✓	✓			FAT
	60m Hurdles	✓	✓	✓	✓	FAT
	100m Hurdles		✓		✓	FAT
	110m Hurdles	✓		✓		FAT
	400m Hurdles	✓	✓	✓	✓	FAT

32. 承认世界纪录和U20世界纪录的项目

	项　目	男子	女子	U20 男子	U20 女子	计时
跑	50米	✓	✓			FAT
	60米	✓	✓	✓	✓	FAT
	100米	✓	✓	✓	✓	FAT
	200米	✓	✓	✓	✓	FAT
	200米 短道	✓	✓	✓	✓	FAT
	400米	✓	✓	✓	✓	FAT
	400米 短道	✓	✓	✓	✓	FAT
	800米	✓	✓	✓	✓	FAT
	800米 短道	✓	✓	✓	✓	FAT
	1000米	✓	✓	✓	✓	FAT or HT
	1000米 短道	✓	✓	✓	✓	FAT or HT
	1500米	✓	✓	✓	✓	FAT or HT
	1500米 短道	✓	✓	✓	✓	FAT or HT
	1英里	✓	✓	✓	✓	FAT or HT
	1英里 短道	✓	✓	✓	✓	FAT or HT
	2000米	✓	✓			FAT or HT
	3000米	✓	✓	✓	✓	FAT or HT
	3000米 短道	✓	✓	✓	✓	FAT or HT
	5000米	✓	✓	✓	✓	FAT or HT
	5000米 短道	✓	✓	✓	✓	FAT or HT
	10000米	✓	✓	✓	✓	FAT or HT
	1小时	✓	✓			FAT or HT
	3000米障碍	✓	✓	✓	✓	FAT or HT
跨栏	50米栏	✓	✓			FAT
	60米栏	✓	✓	✓	✓	FAT
	100米栏		✓		✓	FAT
	110米栏	✓		✓		FAT
	400米栏	✓	✓	✓	✓	FAT

continued

Event		Men	Women	U20 Men	U20 Women	Timing
Field Events	High Jump	✓	✓	✓	✓	n/a
	Pole Vault	✓	✓	✓	✓	n/a
	Long Jump	✓	✓	✓	✓	n/a
	Triple Jump	✓	✓	✓	✓	n/a
	Shot Put	✓	✓	✓	✓	n/a
	Discus Throw	✓	✓	✓	✓	n/a
	Hammer Throw	✓	✓	✓	✓	n/a
	Javelin Throw	✓	✓	✓	✓	n/a
Combined Events	Pentathlon sh		✓		✓	FAT
	Heptathlon		✓		✓	FAT
	Heptathlon sh	✓		✓		FAT
	Decathlon	✓	✓	✓	✓	FAT
Race Walking Events	3000m sh		✓			FAT or HT
	5000m sh	✓				FAT or HT
	10000m		✓	✓	✓	FAT or HT
	10km			✓	✓	FAT or HT or TT
	20000m	✓	✓			FAT or HT
	20km	✓	✓			FAT or HT or TT
	Half Marathon(track)	✓	✓			FAT or HT
	Half Marathon(road)	✓	✓			FAT or HT or TT
	30000m	✓				FAT or HT
	35000m	✓	✓			FAT or HT
	35km	✓	✓			FAT or HT or TT
	Marathon(track)	✓	✓			FAT or HT
	Marathon(road)	✓	✓			FAT or HT or TT
	50000m	✓	✓			FAT or HT
	50km	✓	✓			FAT or HT or TT
Road Races	Road Mile	✓	✓			FAT or HT or TT
	5km	✓	✓			FAT or HT or TT
	10km	✓	✓			FAT or HT or TT
	Half Marathon	✓	✓			FAT or HT or TT
	Marathon	✓	✓			FAT or HT or TT
	50km	✓	✓			FAT or HT or TT
	100km	✓	✓			FAT or HT or TT

（续表）

项　　目		男子	女子	U20男子	U20女子	计时
田赛	跳高	✓	✓	✓	✓	n/a
	撑竿跳高	✓	✓	✓	✓	n/a
	跳远	✓	✓	✓	✓	n/a
	三级跳远	✓	✓	✓	✓	n/a
	铅球	✓	✓	✓	✓	n/a
	铁饼	✓	✓	✓	✓	n/a
	链球	✓	✓	✓	✓	n/a
	标枪	✓	✓	✓	✓	n/a
全能	五项全能 短道		✓		✓	FAT
	七项全能		✓		✓	FAT
	七项全能 短道	✓		✓		FAT
	十项全能	✓	✓	✓	✓	FAT
竞走	3000米 短道		✓			FAT or HT
	5000米 短道	✓				FAT or HT
	10000米		✓	✓	✓	FAT or HT
	10公里			✓	✓	FAT or HT or TT
	20000米	✓	✓			FAT or HT
	20公里	✓	✓			FAT or HT or TT
	半程马拉松（跑道）	✓	✓			FAT or HT
	半程马拉松（公路）	✓	✓			FAT or HT or TT
	30000米	✓				FAT or HT
	35000米	✓	✓			FAT or HT
	35公里	✓	✓			FAT or HT or TT
	马拉松（跑道）	✓	✓			FAT or HT
	马拉松（公路）	✓	✓			FAT or HT or TT
	50000米	✓				FAT or HT
	50公里	✓	✓			FAT or HT
路跑	1英里路跑	✓	✓			FAT or HT or TT
	5公里	✓	✓			FAT or HT or TT
	10公里	✓	✓			FAT or HT or TT
	半程马拉松	✓	✓			FAT or HT or TT
	马拉松	✓	✓			FAT or HT or TT
	50公里	✓	✓			FAT or HT or TT
	100公里	✓	✓			FAT or HT or TT

continued

Event		Men	Women	U20 Men	U20 Women	Timing
Road Races	Road Relay (42.195km)	✓	✓			FAT or HT or TT
Relay Races	4×100m	✓	✓	✓	✓	FAT
	4×200m	✓	✓			FAT
	4×200m sh	✓	✓			FAT
	4×400m	✓	✓	✓	✓	FAT
	4×400m sh	✓	✓			FAT
	4×400m Mixed*	✓	✓			FAT
	4×800m	✓	✓			FAT or HT
	4×800m sh	✓	✓			FAT or HT
	4×1500m	✓	✓			FAT or HT
	Distance Medley	✓	✓			FAT or HT

*Universal event

sh = Short Track (200m Standard Oval Track – Part V of the Technical Rules)

Fully Automatically Timed performances (FAT)

Hand Timed performances (HT)

Transponder Timed performances (TT)

Note (i): Except Race Walking and Road Mile competitions, World Athletics shall keep two World Records for women in Road Races: a World Record for performance achieved in mixed gender ("Mixed" or "Mx") races and a World Record for performance achieved in single gender ("Women only" or "Wo") races.

In Race Walking, only one World Record is kept, and it can be achieved either in a Mixed or Women only race. In the Road Mile, only single gender World Records are kept.

Note (ii): A women only road race can be staged by having separate women's and men's start times. The time differential should be chosen to prevent any possibility of assistance, pacing or interference, especially on courses involving more than one lap of the same section of the course.

（续表）

项 目		男子	女子	U20 男子	U20 女子	计时
路跑	公路接力赛（42.195公里）	✓	✓			FAT or HT or TT
接力	4×100米	✓	✓	✓	✓	FAT
	4×200米	✓	✓			FAT
	4×200米 短道	✓	✓			FAT
	4×400米	✓	✓	✓	✓	FAT
	4×400米 短道	✓	✓			FAT
	4×400米混合接力*	✓	✓			FAT
	4×800米	✓	✓			FAT or HT
	4×800米 短道	✓	✓			FAT or HT
	4×1500米	✓	✓			FAT or HT
	长距离异程接力	✓	✓			FAT or HT

*混合项目

sh = 短道（200米标准椭圆形跑道——第Ⅴ部分技术规则）

全自动电子计时成绩（FAT）

手计时成绩（HT）

传感器计时成绩（TT）

注（ⅰ）：除了竞走和1英里路跑比赛，世界田联将承认两种女子路跑世界纪录：一种是男女混合性别（混合）比赛世界纪录，另一种是单一性别（女子）比赛世界纪录。

竞走项目，只承认一种世界纪录，既可以是在混合性别比赛中取得的，也可以是在仅有女子比赛中取得的成绩。1英里路跑项目，只承认单一性别比赛中取得的成绩为世界纪录。

注（ⅱ）：女子路跑可允许有男子参赛，但不和女子同时起跑。起跑时间的间隔应不能出现协助、领跑或干扰的情况，尤其不能使套圈距离超过一圈。

Note (iii): For the Road Mile, either Fully Automatic Times to 0.01 second accuracy or Hand / Transponder Times to 0.1 second accuracy will be accepted.

Decathlon U20 Women: Only ratified if over 7300 points.

Half-Marathon Race Walk: Initial records to be recognised after 1 January 2026. For the purpose of recognising the first World Record, the minimum performance that needs to be beaten will be published in 2025.

The 30000m for men shall be deleted from the list upon ratification of the initial record for 35000m.

35000m Race Walk: Initial records to be recognised after 1 January 2023. The performance shall be better than 2:22:00 for men and 2:38:00 for women.

35km Race Walk Men: Initial record to be recognised after 1 January 2023. The performance shall be better than 2:22:00.

Marathon Race Walk: Initial records to be recognised after 1 January 2026. For the purpose of recognising the first World Record, the minimum performance that needs to be beaten will be published in 2025.

50000m Race Walk Women: Initial record to be recognised after 1 January 2019. The performance shall be better than 4:20:00.

33. Other Records

33.1 Games, championships, meeting and other similar records may be established by the relevant body having control over the competition or by the organisers.

33.2 The record should recognise the best performance achieved at any edition of the applicable competition in accordance with the Rules, with the exception that wind velocity readings may be ignored, if so stated in the applicable regulations for the competition.

注（iii）：1英里路跑项目，全自动电子计时成绩应精确到0.01秒，手计时成绩应精确到0.1秒。

女子U20十项全能项目：只承认7300分以上的成绩。

半程马拉松竞走：初始纪录将于2026年1月1日以后被承认。为了承认首个世界纪录，需要打破的最低成绩将于2025年公布。

男子30000米项目要在35000米的初始纪录获得批准后从名单中删除。

35000米竞走：初始纪录在2023年1月1日以后被承认。男子成绩要优于2:22:00，女子成绩要优于2:38:00。

男子35公里竞走：初始纪录在2023年1月1日以后被承认。成绩要优于2:22:00。

马拉松竞走：初始纪录将于2026年1月1日以后被承认。为了承认首个世界纪录，需要打破的最低成绩将于2025年公布。

女子50000米竞走：初始纪录在2019年1月1日以后被承认。成绩要优于4:20:00。

33. **其他纪录**

33.1 综合性运动会田径比赛纪录、锦标赛纪录、赛会纪录和其他类似的纪录可以由相关管理比赛的机构或组织者确定。

33.2 如果比赛的适用规程中有说明，纪录应标明达到最好成绩的比赛所依据规则的版本，除了可以忽略风速读数外。

WORLD ATHLETICS

TECHNICAL
RULES

田径技术规则

PART I GENERAL

1. General

World Rankings Competitions must be organised in conformity with the Competition Rules and Technical Rules and any applicable Regulations and shall be listed on the World Athletics Global Calendar.

In all competitions, events may be held in a different format from that provided under the Competition and Technical Rules, but rules giving more rights to the athletes than they would have obtained applying the actual Rules, may not be applied. These formats shall be decided or authorised by the relevant governing body having the control over the competition.

In the case of mass participation events held outside the stadium, these Rules should normally only be applied in full to those athletes, if any, who are designated as taking part in the elite or other defined section of the races such as age group categories for which there are placings for awards or prizes. Race organisers should outline in the information provided to other athletes which other rules will apply to their participation, particularly those pertaining to their safety.

Note: For non-World Rankings Competitions Members should adopt the Rules and Regulations to conduct such competitions.

Whilst these Rules already contemplate some variations from their strictest applications, it is emphasised that competition organisers may go even further in using different formats for competitions - the only restriction being that the athlete may not receive more "rights" in such circumstances. For example, it is acceptable to reduce the number of trials in a Field Event or reduce the time allowed for an athlete to take their trial but not to increase either.

With respect to mass participation Running and Race Walking Events, race organisers are advised to emphasise in the information provided to all participants the rules and procedures that will apply to the various categories, especially in relation to safety considerations, particularly when all or part of the race is not closed to traffic. This may for example allow athletes (other than those competing in the elite or other categories to whom Rule 6.3 of the Technical Rules would apply) to use head or earphones when they are running on a closed course but prohibit their use (or at least recommend against it) for the slower runners when the course is open to traffic.

田径技术规则

第一部分　通则

1. **通则**

世界排名比赛必须按照竞赛规则和技术规则及任何适用的规定进行组织，并要列入世界田联全球日历。

在所有比赛中，可采用不同于竞赛和技术规则规定的形式，但是不能采用使运动员获得比现有规则更多权益的规则。这些比赛形式将由对比赛有管控权的相关管理机构决定或授权。

如果是在场外举行的大众参与的项目中，这些规则通常只完全适用于部分运动员，即精英组或设有名次奖品、奖金的分龄组比赛的运动员。比赛组织者应将赛事概况、适用于不同组别的规则条款，尤其是有关安全的规定向全体运动员公示。

注：会员协会举行非世界排名比赛应采用本规则和规程。

虽然在严格执行规则的过程中已经考虑到它们的一些变化，需要强调的是，赛事组织者可以在比赛形式上做出更多变化，唯一的限制便是在这种情况下运动员不会获得更多的"权益"。例如，在田赛中减少试跳（掷）次数，或者减少运动员每次试跳（掷）的时限，而不是增加，这些都是可以接受的。

对于大众参与的跑和竞走赛事，建议赛事组织者在提供给所有参赛人员的信息中强调适用于不同类别比赛情况的规则和程序，特别是有关安全的，尤其是赛事全部或者部分在未封闭路面举行时。例如，可以允许运动员（非精英组或其他类别的运动员适用技术规则6.3条的情况）在交通封闭赛道跑步时使用耳机，但是对于交通不封闭的赛道要禁止（或至少不建议）较慢的跑者使用耳机。

2. The Athletics Facility

Any firm, uniform surface that conforms to the specifications in the Track and Field Facilities Manual, may be used for Track and Field Athletics.

400m Standard Oval Track Stadium competitions under paragraphs 1. (a) and (b) of the World Rankings Competition definition may be held only on facilities that hold a World Athletics Class 1 Athletics Facility Certificate. It is recommended that, when such facilities are available, 400m Standard Oval Track Stadium competitions under paragraphs 1. (c), (d), (e) and 2. of the World Rankings Competition definition should also be held on these facilities.

In any case, a World Athletics Class 2 Athletics Facility Certificate shall be required for all facilities intended for use for 400m Standard Oval Track Stadium competitions under paragraphs 1. (c) and 2. (a), (b), (c) of the World Rankings Competition definition. It is recommended that all competitions under paragraphs 1. (d), (e), 2. (d), (e) and 3. of the World Rankings Competition definition should also be held on certified facilities or, at least, the facility must conform to the Rules and Regulations, as amended from time to time. If the applicable regulations or World Rankings Competition categories so require, the facility must be certified.

Note (i): The World Athletics Track and Field Facilities Manual, which is available from the World Athletics Office, or may be downloaded from the World Athletics website, contains more detailed and defined specifications for the planning and construction of Track and Field facilities including further diagrams for track measurement and marking.

Note (ii): The current standard forms required to be used for the certification application and measurement report as well as the Certification System Procedures are available from the World Athletics Office, or may be downloaded from the World Athletics website.

Note (iii): For Road Race Walking, Road Running or Cross Country, Mountain and Trail courses, see Rules 54.11, 55.2, 55.3, 56.1 to 56.5, and 57.1 of the Technical Rules.

Note (iv): For the 200m Standard Oval Track (Short Track) Athletics Facility, see Rule 41 of the Technical Rules.

2. 田径场地

任何坚固、表面平整一致、符合《世界田联田径场地设施手册》中有关规定的面层均可用于田径运动。

凡举办世界排名比赛定义1.（a）和（b）所述的400米标准椭圆形跑道体育场比赛，只允许在获得世界田联一级场地设施证书的场地上举行。如具备这种场地条件，建议举办国际比赛定义1.（c）（d）（e）和2条所述的400米标准椭圆形跑道体育场比赛也在这种场地上举行。

在任何情况下，举办世界排名比赛定义1.（c）和2.（a）（b）（c）所述的400米标准椭圆形跑道体育场比赛所使用的田径场地设施，均需获得世界田联二级场地设施证书。建议世界排名比赛定义1.（d）（e）、2.（d）（e）和3条所述的所有比赛，其竞赛场地设施亦应获得资质证书，或至少场地设施应满足随时修改的规则和规程的要求。如果所适用的规程，或世界排名赛事的类别有要求，则场地设施必须认证。

注（i）：《世界田联田径场地设施手册》可从世界田联总部办公室获得或从世界田联官方网站下载，该手册详细制定了田径场地的设计与施工的技术要求，包括跑道测量和标记的标绘图。

注（ii）：认证申请和测量报告所使用的现行标准表格及认证系统程序，可向世界田联总部办公室索取或从世界田联官方网站下载。

注（iii）：公路竞走、路跑、越野跑、山地跑和野外跑项目，参见技术规则54.11条、55.2条、55.3条、56.1—56.5条和57.1条。

注（iv）：200米标准椭圆形跑道（短道）田径场地设施见技术规则41条。

3. Age and Sex Categories

Age Categories

3.1　Competition under these Rules may be divided into age group classifications as follows or as additionally prescribed in the relevant competition regulations or by the relevant governing body:

Under-18 (U18) Men and Women: Any athlete of 16 or 17 years on 31st December in the year of the competition.

Under-20 (U20) Men and Women: Any athlete of 18 or 19 years on 31st December in the year of the competition.

Master Men and Women: Any athlete who has reached their 35th birthday.

Note (i): All other matters concerning Masters' competitions are referred to the World Athletics/WMA Handbook approved by World Athletics and WMA.

Note (ii): Eligibility, including minimum ages for participation in Competitions, shall be subject to the applicable Technical Regulations.

3.2　An athlete shall be eligible to compete in an age group competition under these Rules if they are within the age range specified in the relevant age group classification. An athlete must be able to provide proof of their age through presentation of a valid passport or other form of evidence as permitted by the applicable regulations for the competition. An athlete who fails or refuses to provide such proof shall not be eligible to compete.

Note: See Eligibility Rules for sanctions for non-compliance with this Rule 3.

Whilst Rule 3.1 of the Technical Rules defines the age groups in a particular way, it is the regulations for each competition which determine which age groups will apply and whether, as envisaged by Note (ii), younger athletes can participate.

3. 年龄与性别分组

年龄分组

3.1 适用本规则的比赛可按以下年龄组、按相关竞赛规程规定分组或按相关的管理机构规定分组。

18岁以下少年男子和少年女子（U18）组：凡在比赛当年12月31日前满16或17周岁者。

20岁以下青年男子和青年女子（U20）组：凡在比赛当年12月31日前满18或19周岁者。

老将男子和女子组：凡年满35周岁者。

注（ⅰ）：所有有关老将比赛的其他事宜请查阅世界田联/世界老将协会批准的《世界田联/世界老将协会手册》。

注（ⅱ）：参赛资格，包括参加世界田联比赛的最小年龄需符合有关技术规程。

3.2 如果运动员属于相应的年龄分组，他就有资格参加本规则规定的该年龄组的比赛。运动员必须提供能证明其年龄的材料，如比赛适用的规程规定的有效护照或其他形式的证据。如果运动员不能或拒绝提供这些证明材料，他将没有资格参加比赛。

注：关于不遵守本规则3条的处罚，见有关参赛资格的部分条款。

尽管技术规则3.1条规定了特定的年龄组别，每个比赛的规程又规定了什么年龄组别适用。正如注（ⅱ）的说明，应当注明是否允许更年轻的运动员参赛。

Sex Categories

3.3　　Competition under these Rules is divided into men's, women's and universal classifications. When a mixed competition is conducted outside the stadium or in one of the limited cases set out in Rule 9 of the Technical Rules, separate men's and women's classification results should still be declared or otherwise indicated. When a universal event or competition is conducted a single classification result only shall be declared.

3.4　　An athlete shall be eligible to compete in men's (or universal) competition if they either were born and, throughout their life, have always been recognised as a male or comply with the applicable Regulations issued pursuant to Rule 3.6.1 of the Technical Rules and are eligible to compete under the Rules and Regulations.

3.5　　An athlete shall be eligible to compete in women's (or universal) competition if they either were born and, throughout their life, have always been recognised as a female or comply with the applicable Regulations issued pursuant to Rule 3.6.2 of the Technical Rules and are eligible to compete under the Rules and Regulations.

3.6　　The Council shall approve Regulations to determine the eligibility for:

　　　　3.6.1　　men's competition for males who are female to male Transgender;

　　　　3.6.2　　women's competition for females who are male to female Transgender; and

　　　　3.6.3　　women's competition for female classification (athletes with differences in sex development).

An athlete who fails or refuses to comply with the applicable regulations shall not be eligible to compete.

Note: See Eligibility Regulations for Transgender Athletes or Eligibility Regulations for the Female Classification, as appropriate, for sanctions for non-compliance with this Rule 3.6.

Universal competition covers events in which men and women participate together without separate classification of results as well as relay or team events in which both men and women are included in the same teams.

性别分组

3.3　使用本规则的比赛分为男子组、女子组和混同组。当举行男女混合的外场比赛或根据技术规则9条规定设定的限制性比赛，男、女比赛的成绩要分别公布或标注。当举行混同组的比赛时，只公布单一分组的成绩。

3.4　如果运动员出生时为男性，且在生活中一直被认定为男性，或遵守技术规则3.6.1条发布的适用的规程，并根据规则和规程有资格竞赛，则该运动员应有资格参加男子组（或混同组）的比赛。

3.5　如果运动员出生时为女性，且在生活中一直被认定为女性，或遵守技术规则3.6.2条发布的适用的规程，并根据规则和规程有资格竞赛，则该运动员应有资格参加女子组（或混同组）的比赛。

3.6　世界田联理事会将批准规程，以确定参赛资格：

3.6.1　从女性变为男性的运动员参加男子组比赛；

3.6.2　从男性变为女性的运动员参加女子组比赛；

3.6.3　女性分类（性别发展异常的运动员）参加女子组比赛；

如果运动员未能满足或拒绝遵守适用的规程的要求将失去参赛资格。

注：不遵守本规则3.6条的处罚，见跨性别运动员资格规程或女性分类资格规程。

混同组比赛包括男女共同参赛且未单独分类成绩的项目，也包括男女共同组队的接力赛或集体项目。

4. Entries

4.1 Competitions under the Rules are restricted to eligible athletes.

4.2 The eligibility of an athlete to compete outside of their own country is as set forth in Rule 5 of the Eligibility Rules (Requirements to Compete in International Competitions). Such eligibility shall be assumed unless an objection to their status is made to the Technical Delegate(s) (see also Rule 8.1 of the Technical Rules).

Simultaneous Entries

4.3 If an athlete is entered in both a Track Event and a Field Event, or in more than one Field Event taking place simultaneously, the appropriate Referee may, for one round of trials at a time, or for each trial in the High Jump and Pole Vault, allow an athlete to take their trial in an order different from the start list (or as determined in accordance with Rule 25.6.1 of the Technical Rules). However, if an athlete subsequently is not present for that particular trial, it shall be deemed that they are passing once the period allowed for the trial has elapsed. As this possibility exists only for that particular round / trial allowed by the Referee, if the athlete is then not present for a subsequent round / trial, when their competing order will be again according to the start list (or as determined in accordance with Rule 25.6.1 of the Technical Rules), it will be counted as a failure once the period allowed for the trial has elapsed.

Note: In Field Events, the Referee shall not allow an athlete to take a trial in a different order in the final round of trials but the Referee may allow an athlete to do so during any earlier round of trials. In Combined Events, a change may be allowed in any round of trials.

The Note clarifies that allowing an athlete to take a trial in a different order in the final round of trials (irrespective of the number of rounds of trials) because of a clash with another event is not permitted. If an athlete is not present in the final round and has not previously indicated that they will pass, then the time allowed for their trial will run and if they do not return before it expires, then they will be recorded as a failure (see also Rule 25.18 of the Technical Rules where a change of order will normally not be made when a replacement trial is awarded - in any round of trials).

4. **报名**

4.1 取得参赛资格的运动员方能报名参加规则规定的比赛。

4.2 运动员出国参赛的资格由资格规则5条决定（出国参赛的要求）。除非技术代表收到对其参赛身份提出的异议，否则应假定其具有此种资格（另见技术规则8.1条）。

兼项

4.3 如果1名运动员报名的一项径赛和一项田赛，或多个田赛同时进行，相关裁判长可以允许该运动员在田赛的每一轮次，或在跳高和撑竿跳高项目的每次试跳（掷）中，以不同于检录单的顺序（或由技术规则25.6.1条决定的顺序）试跳（掷）。如果该运动员随后未能在这一特定的改变顺序的试跳（掷）时到达，一旦该次试跳（掷）的时限结束，将视其该次试跳（掷）为免跳（掷）。因为这种可能性仅存在于裁判长允许的特定轮次或试跳（掷）中，当检录单顺序（或由技术规则25.6.1条所决定的顺序）再次到来，如果运动员在后续轮次/试跳（掷）仍未到，且属于他（她）的时限结束，则该次试跳（掷）将认定为失败。

注：田赛项目比赛中，相关裁判长不得允许运动员在比赛的最后一轮中变更试跳（掷）的顺序，但在此之前的任何轮次，允许运动员变更比赛顺序。全能比赛中，任何轮次都允许变更顺序。

注释阐明了不允许运动员因为与其他项目冲突而变更最后一轮比赛的顺序（不管总共多少轮次）。如果运动员在最后一轮比赛中未能出现且未事先告知将免跳（掷），从其试跳（掷）的时间开始计时，若在时限内未能返回，则被记录为一次失败［见技术规则25.18条，在任何轮次的试跳（掷）中，当给予补试跳（掷）时，通常不得改变顺序］。

Failure to Participate

4.4 At all competitions under paragraphs 1. (a), (b), (c) and 2. (a), (b) of the World Rankings Competition definition, an athlete shall be excluded from participation in all further events (including other events in which they are simultaneously participating) in the competition, including relays, in cases where:

    4.4.1 final confirmation was given that the athlete would start in an event but then failed to participate;

    Note: A fixed time for the final confirmation of participation shall be published in advance.

    4.4.2 an athlete qualified in any Qualification Round of an event for further participation in that event but then failed to participate further;

    Note: If the applicable regulations require a Repechage Round, failure to participate in that round is not an infringement of this Rule.

    4.4.3 an athlete failed to compete honestly with bona fide effort. The relevant Referee will decide on this and the corresponding reference must be made in the official results.

    Note: The situation foreseen in Rule 4.4.3 of the Technical Rules will not apply to individual events within Combined Events.

However, a medical certificate, provided by and based on an examination of the athlete by the Medical Delegate appointed under Rule 6 of the Competition Rules or, if no Medical Delegate has been so appointed, by a medical doctor so designated by the Organisers, may be accepted as sufficient reason to accept that the athlete became unable to compete after confirmations closed or after competing in a previous round but will be able to compete in further events (except Combined Events individual events) on a subsequent day of the competition. Other justifiable reasons (e.g. factors independent of the athlete's own actions, such as problems with the official transport system) may, after confirmation, also be accepted by the Technical Delegate(s).

放弃比赛

4.4 在举办世界排名比赛定义1.（a）（b）（c）和2.（a）（b）所述的比赛中，如发生下列情况，有关运动员将被取消参加本次比赛所有后续项目（包括其参赛的其他兼项项目）的参赛资格，包括接力比赛的参赛资格：

    4.4.1 经过最后确认，运动员将参加某项目比赛，但后来没有参加此项目比赛；

    注：须提前公布参赛项目的最后确认时间。

    4.4.2 运动员在某项目的任何径赛晋级赛或者田赛及格赛中获得后续比赛的参赛资格，但后来没有继续参加比赛；

    注：如果适用的规程要求进行复活赛，则未能参加该轮比赛并不违反本条款。

    4.4.3 运动员未能真诚努力地完成比赛。相关裁判长会就此作出裁决，并必须在正式成绩单上做出相应的注释。

    注：技术规则4.4.3条的情况不适用于全能项目的各单项比赛。

但是，由根据竞赛规则6条指派的医务代表对运动员进行医学检查后，或者如果没有指定的医务代表则由组织者指定的医生代替，他们所签发的医疗证明可作为接受该运动员在最后确认结束后或者在上一赛次后不能参加比赛的充分理由，但其可以参加以后几天的比赛（全能项目的单项比赛除外）。其他合理的理由（例如，不是运动员自身的原因，而是官方交通系统的问题）经确认后，也可被技术代表接受。

The relevant Referee, once aware of such a situation and is satisfied that the athlete who abandoned the race was not competing with a bona fide effort, must make a reference to this in the relevant results as "DNF TR4.4.3". Either in the process of the Technical Delegate(s) making such a decision or the Jury of the Appeal considering any appeal arising from it, reasons for the withdrawal or non-participation proposed by or on behalf of the athlete can be considered. The Rule sets out the process that should explicitly be followed in the case of a medical reason.

Failure to Report to the Call Room(s)

4.5 Subject always to any additional sanction under Rule 4.4 of the Technical Rules, and except as provided below, an athlete shall be excluded from participation in any event in which they are not present in the Call Room(s) at the relevant time as published in the Call Room schedule (see Rule 29 of the Competition Rules). They shall be shown in the results as DNS.

The relevant Referee will decide on this (including whether the athlete may compete under protest if a decision cannot be made immediately) and the corresponding reference must be made in the official results.

Justifiable reasons (e.g. factors independent of the athlete's own actions, such as problems with the official transport system or an error in the published Call Room schedule) may, after confirmation, be accepted by the Referee and the athlete may then be allowed to take part.

5. **Clothing, Shoes and Athlete Bibs**

Clothing

5.1 In all events, athletes must wear clothing which is clean, and designed and worn so as not to be objectionable. The clothing must be made of a material which is non-transparent even if wet. Athletes must not wear clothing which could impede the view of the Judges.

At all competitions under paragraphs 1. (a), (b), (c) and 2. (a), (b), (c) of the World Rankings Competition definition, and when representing their Member Federation under paragraphs 1. (e) and 2. (e) of the World Rankings Competition definition, athletes shall participate in the uniform clothing approved by their Member Federation. The Victory Ceremony and any lap of honour are considered part of the competition for this purpose.

相关裁判长在得知此类情况后，若运动员放弃比赛之前没有真诚努力地完成比赛，裁判长必须在相应成绩单上注明"DNF TR4.4.3"。不管是在技术代表作出此类决定的过程中，还是申诉委员会在事后审议与此有关的申诉时，都应考虑由运动员本人或其代表作出的退赛或者放弃比赛决定的理由。本规则规定，若为医疗原因，应完全按照规则的程序执行。

检录未到

4.5 根据技术规则4.4条，可能会导致追加处罚，除以下情况外，如果在公布的检录时间表（见竞赛规则29条）规定的检录时间内，某运动员没到检录处，将被取消该项目的参赛资格。成绩单中记录为"DNS"。

相关裁判长将对此作出裁决（包括没有立即作出裁决时，运动员是否可以"在抗议下"参加比赛），并必须在正式成绩单上做出相应的注释。

正当理由（例如，不受运动员自身行为支配的因素，如官方的交通系统问题或公布的检录时间表错误等）经确认后，可能被裁判长接受，运动员可被允许参赛。

5. **服装、鞋与运动员号码**

服装

5.1 各项目参赛运动员必须穿着干净的服装，其设计式样和穿着方式应无碍观瞻。服装的材料如果浸湿时不得透明。运动员不得穿有碍裁判员观察的服装。

运动员在参加世界排名比赛定义1.（a）（b）（c）和2.（a）（b）（c）所述的比赛，以及代表他们的会员协会参加世界排名比赛定义1.（e）和2.（e）所述的比赛，应穿着其会员协会正式批准的统一服装。颁奖仪式和运动员获胜后的绕场庆贺均被视为比赛的一部分，也应执行本规则的规定。

Note: Rule 5.1 of the Technical Rules should be interpreted widely in terms of what "could impede the view of the judges", including athletes wearing their hair in a particular way.

Shoes

5.2   Athletes may compete either barefoot or in Athletic Shoes on one or both feet. Athletes must comply with all Regulations relating to the wearing of Athletic Shoes approved by the Council.

5.3   [Intentionally left blank.]

5.4   [Intentionally left blank.]

5.5   [Intentionally left blank.]

5.6   [Intentionally left blank.]

See also the Athletic Shoe Regulations in the "Book of Rules Book C: Competition", published separately on the website.

Athlete Bibs

5.7   Every athlete shall be provided with two bibs which, during the competition, shall be worn visibly on the front of the torso and on the back, except in the Jumping Events, where one bib may be worn on the front of the torso or on the back only. Either the athletes' names or other suitable identification will be allowed instead of numbers on any or all of the bibs. If numbers are used, they shall correspond with the number allocated to the athlete on the start list or in the programme. If track suits are worn during the competition, bibs shall be worn on the track suit in a similar manner.

5.8   No athlete shall be allowed to take part in any competition without displaying the appropriate bib(s) and/or identification.

5.9   These bibs must be worn as issued and may not be cut, folded or obscured in any way. In running or walking events of 10000 metres and longer, the bibs may be perforated to assist the circulation of air, but the perforation must not be made on any of the lettering or numerals which appear on them.

5.10   Where a Photo Finish System is in operation, the Organisers may require athletes to wear additional number identification of an adhesive type on the side of their shorts or lower body.

注：技术规则5.1条应按照"阻碍裁判员的观察"进行更为广泛的解释，包括运动员以特殊方式佩戴假发等。

鞋

5.2　运动员可以赤脚、单脚或双脚穿鞋参加比赛。如果穿比赛用鞋，则该比赛用鞋必须符合经世界田联理事会批准的所有规定。

5.3　［此处留空待续。］

5.4　［此处留空待续。］

5.5　［此处留空待续。］

5.6　［此处留空待续。］

另请参见网站上单独发布的"规则手册C：竞赛"中的运动鞋规程。

运动员号码

5.7　在比赛中要为每名运动员提供2块号码布，将其分别佩戴在胸前和背后的显著位置，跳跃项目比赛除外，跳跃项目运动员可在胸前或背后只佩戴1块号码布。允许使用运动员的姓名或者其他适宜的身份标识取代数字号码印在1块或所有号码布上。如果使用数字号码，运动员的号码必须与检录单或秩序册中的号码一致。如在比赛时穿运动服，则必须按相同的方式佩戴号码布。

5.8　不按规定佩戴号码布和（或）身份标识者不得参加比赛。

5.9　号码布须依其原样佩戴，不得以任何形式剪裁、折叠或遮挡。在10000米及更长距离的跑和竞走项目中，可在号码布上打孔以利于空气流动，但不得在号码布的文字或数字上穿孔。

5.10　凡采用终点摄影计时系统，组织者可要求运动员在短裤或者大腿的侧面佩戴有黏性的附加编号标识。

5.11　　　If an athlete does not follow any part of this Rule 5 and:

    5.11.1　　refuses the direction of the relevant Referee to comply; or

    5.11.2　　participates in the competition,

they shall be disqualified.

Rule 5.11 of the Technical Rules prescribes the sanction if any aspect of Rule 5 of the Technical Rules is not followed. It is expected however that where possible the relevant officials should request and encourage the athlete to comply and to advise them of the consequence if they do not. But where an athlete does not follow an aspect of the Rule during competition and it is not practical for an official to request compliance, athletes should note that disqualification may follow.

It is a responsibility of the Starters Assistants and Umpires (for Track and Out of Stadium Events) and the Judges (for Field Events) to be vigilant on these matters and report any apparent breaches to the relevant Referee.

6.　　Assistance to Athletes

Medical Examination and Assistance

6.1　　Medical examination/treatment and/or physiotherapy may be provided either on the competition area itself by the official medical staff appointed by the Organisers and identified by armbands, vests or similar distinctive apparel or in designated medical treatment areas outside the competition area by accredited team medical personnel specifically approved by the Medical or Technical Delegate(s) for the purpose. In neither case shall the intervention delay the conduct of the competition or an athlete's trial in the designated order. Such attendance or assistance by any other person, whether immediately before competition, once athletes have left the Call Room or during competition, is assistance.

Note: The competition area, which normally also has a physical barrier, is defined for this purpose as the area where the competition is being staged and which has an access restricted to the competing athletes and personnel authorised in accordance with the relevant Rules and Regulations.

5.11 如果运动员不遵守技术规则5条中任何条款，并：

    5.11.1 拒绝服从相关裁判长的指示；或

    5.11.2 参加了比赛，

他们将被取消比赛资格。

技术规则5.11条描述了没有遵守技术规则5条任何条款的处罚。尽管如此，希望相关裁判员还是要尽可能要求和鼓励运动员遵守规则，并告知不遵守规则的后果。但是，如果运动员在比赛中不遵守规则的规定，而裁判员又无法要求其遵守，运动员应注意，随后可能被取消比赛资格。

助理发令员和检查裁判员（径赛和外场项目）以及裁判员（田赛项目）要对此类事情保持警惕，并向相关裁判长报告任何明显的违规情况。

6. 为运动员提供帮助

医学检查与协助

6.1 可在比赛区域内对运动员进行必要的医学检查、治疗和（或）物理治疗，以使运动员能够参加和继续参加比赛。此类医学检查、治疗和（或）物理治疗由组织者指定的佩戴袖标、穿背心或身着其他明显标识服装的医务人员在比赛区域内进行，也可由注册随队医疗人员经医务代表或技术代表特批，在比赛区域外指定的治疗区域内进行。但这两种情况都不得使比赛的正常进程或该运动员既定的试跳（掷）顺序延误。不论是在比赛前，还是在运动员离开检录处时或者是在比赛中，任何其他人的帮助和协助均被认为是为运动员提供帮助。

注：比赛场地通常设有硬隔离，定义为进行比赛的场地，并且只有参赛运动员或相关规则和规程授权的工作人员能够进入。

6.2　　　Any athlete giving or receiving assistance from within the competition area during an event (including under Rules 17.14, 17.15.4, 54.10.8 and 55.8.8 of the Technical Rules) shall be warned by the Referee and advised that, if there is any repetition, they will be disqualified from that event.

Note: In cases under Rules 6.3.1 or 6.3.6 of the Technical Rules, disqualification may be made without warning.

Assistance not Allowed

6.3　　　For the purpose of this Rule, the following examples shall be considered assistance, and are therefore not allowed:

　　　6.3.1　　Pacing in races by persons not participating in the same race, by athletes lapped or about to be lapped or by any kind of technical device (other than those permitted under Rules 6.4.4 and 6.4.8 of the Technical Rules).

　　　6.3.2　　Possession or use of video recorders, radios, CD, radio transmitters, mobile phone or similar devices in the competition area.

　　　6.3.3　　Except for shoes complying with Rule 5 of the Technical Rules, the use of any technology or appliance that provides the user with an advantage which they would not have obtained using the equipment specified in, or permitted by, the Rules.

　　　6.3.4　　The use of any mechanical aid, except by an athlete with an impairment as authorised or permitted in accordance with the Mechanical Aids Regulations.

　　　See also the Mechanical Aids Regulations in the "Book of Rules Book C: Competition", published separately on the website.

　　　6.3.5　　Provision of advice or other support by any official of the competition not related to or required by their specific role in the competition at the time (e.g. coaching advice, indication of the take-off point in a jumping event except to indicate a failure in Horizontal Jumps, time or distance gaps in a race etc.).

6.2　任何运动员在某项目（包括技术规则17.14条、17.15.4条、54.10.8条、55.8.8条）的比赛区域中提供或接受帮助都将受到裁判长的警告，并被告诫如果再犯，将被取消该项目的比赛资格。

注：在技术规则6.3.1条或6.3.6条的情况下，可不经警告取消比赛资格。

不允许的帮助

6.3　根据本规则，下列情况应被认为是为运动员提供帮助，应予禁止：

6.3.1　比赛中，由不是同场比赛者、已被超圈者、将被超圈者，或使用其他任何技术设备（除技术规则6.4.4条和6.4.8条允许的）为运动员提供速度分配。

6.3.2　运动员在比赛场内持有或使用录像机、收音机、CD机、无线电广播通信机、移动电话或类似装置。

6.3.3　除了使用符合技术规则5条的比赛用鞋外，运动员所使用规则限定的设备中不能有可以获取有利条件的任何技术或设备。

6.3.4　使用任何辅助设备，除非从可能性上看，使用辅助器械不会为运动员提供比不使用此类辅助设备的运动员更好的整体竞争优势。

另请参阅网站上单独发布的"规则手册C：比赛"中的辅助设备规程。

6.3.5　由该比赛项目不相关的裁判员，或在该比赛中有特定岗位要求的人员提供建议或其他支持（例如，指导建议、指示跳跃项目中的起跳点，但在水平跳跃项目中指示犯规的起跳点、比赛中的时间或距离差距等除外）。

6.3.6　Receiving physical support from another athlete (other than helping to recover to a standing position) that assists in making forward progression in a race.

Assistance Allowed

6.4　For the purpose of this Rule, the following shall not be considered assistance, and are therefore allowed:

6.4.1　Communication between the athletes and their coaches not placed in the competition area.

In order to facilitate this communication and not to disturb the staging of the competition, a place in the stands, close to the competition area of each Field Event, should be reserved to the athletes' coaches.

Note: Coaches and other persons otherwise complying with Rules 54.10 and 55.8 of the Technical Rules may communicate with their athlete(s).

6.4.2　Medical examination/treatment and/or physiotherapy under Rule 6.1 of the Technical Rules necessary to enable an athlete to participate or continue participation once on the competition area.

6.4.3　Any kind of personal safeguard (e.g. bandage, tape, belt, support, wrist cooler, breathing aid etc.) for protection and/or medical purposes. The Referee, in conjunction with the Medical Delegate, shall have the authority to verify any case should the Referee judge that to be desirable. (see also Rules 32.4 and 32.5 of the Technical Rules)

6.4.4　Heart rate or speed distance monitors or stride sensors or similar devices carried or worn personally by athletes during an event, provided that such device cannot be used to communicate with any other person.

6.4.5　Viewing by athletes competing in Field Events, of images of previous trial(s), recorded on their behalf by persons not placed in the competition area (see Note to Rule 6.1 of the Technical Rules). The viewing device or images taken from it must not be taken into the competition area beyond the immediate area in which those providing the recording are placed. To ensure a better view of the images, the athlete may hold the device whilst communicating with the persons who have taken the images.

6.3.6 接受来自另一运动员有助于其在比赛中继续行进的行为支持（不包括帮助其恢复到站立位置）。

允许的帮助

6.4 根据本规则的规定，下列情况不认为是提供帮助，应予允许：

6.4.1 运动员与不在比赛区域内的教练员进行交流。

为便于这种交流，且不干扰比赛进行，在靠近每一项田赛比赛场地最近的看台上，应为参赛运动员的教练员保留座席。

注：教练员和其他人员依据技术规则54.10条和55.8条，可以和他的运动员进行交流。

6.4.2 在比赛区域内，依据技术规则6.1条，对运动员进行必要的医学检查、治疗和（或）物理治疗，以使运动员能够参加或继续参加比赛。

6.4.3 出于保护或医疗目的的各类个人防护品（如绷带、胶带、护腰、支持物、手腕冷却器、呼吸辅助设备等）。裁判长与医务代表一起，有权核实使用上述物品是否合理。（另见技术规则32.4条和32.5条）

6.4.4 如果不用于与其他人取得联系，在比赛中运动员可以携带或佩戴个人设备，如心率仪、速度距离检测仪、步幅传感器或其他类似设备。

6.4.5 参加田赛项目的运动员，可观看由在比赛区域（见技术规则6.1条的注释）外人员代为拍摄的先前的试跳（掷）影像，但观看设备或影像资料不得带入拍摄区域以外的比赛区域。为了确保更好地观看影像，运动员可边手持设备，边与拍摄人员交流。

6.4.6　　Hats, gloves, shoes, items of clothing provided to athletes at official stations or when otherwise approved by the relevant Referee.

6.4.7　　Receiving physical support from an official or other person designated by the organisers to recover to a standing position or to access medical assistance.

6.4.8　　Electronic lights or similar appliance indicating progressive times during a race, including of a relevant record.

Rule 6 of the Technical Rules has been the subject of constant change in recent years to reflect the way in which athletics is conducted, to respect the role of coaches, to manage innovation and new products, etc. World Athletics will continue to respond to new products and trends as soon as they become common place during events and competitions.

Changes to these rules are designed to facilitate the athletes' participation in the competition as much as possible and to reduce unnecessary conflict between athletes/coaches and the officials. Each of these rules should be interpreted in this light whilst always ensuring the competition is conducted fairly to all.

Rule 6.3.5 of the Technical Rules however makes it clear that the officials should not assist any athlete beyond what is required of their role – and specifically states as an example that officials should not provide details of the take-off position in jumping events, other than for the purpose of indicating the point of "impact" in a foul jump in Horizontal Jumps.

7.　　Warnings and Disqualification

Bona Fide Participation, Unsporting and Improper Conduct

7.1　　Athletes and relay teams shall participate in athletics competitions in a bona fide manner and shall not engage in unsporting or improper conduct. Any athlete or relay team failing to comply with this Rule may be warned or disqualified.

The applicable Referee shall have authority to warn or exclude from competition, any athlete or relay team guilty of breaches of this Rule or Rule 6.1 Note (ii), (iii) or (iv) of the Competition Rules or Rules 6, 16.5, 17.14, 17.15.4, 25.5, 25.19, 54.7.6, 54.10.8 or 55.8.8 of the Technical Rules. Warnings may be indicated to the athlete by showing a yellow card, exclusion by showing a red card. Warnings and exclusions shall be entered on the result card and communicated to the Competition Secretary and to the other Referees.

6.4.6 在官方指定的站点或经相关裁判长同意向运动员提供的帽子、手套、鞋、衣服等。

6.4.7 接受来自裁判员或组织者指定的其他人员的物理援助，以恢复站立姿势或获取医疗帮助。

6.4.8 电子灯或类似设备显示比赛中行进时间，包括相关纪录。

技术规则6条在近些年不断更改以反映田径运动的开展方式、尊重教练员这一角色、管理创新以及新产品等。一旦新产品和趋势在比赛中经常见到，世界田联会持续对此作出回应。

此规则的修改是为了尽可能地便于运动员参赛，减少运动员或教练员与裁判员之间不必要的冲突。此规则的每一条款均应从这个角度解释，但还要随时确保比赛公平进行。

然而，技术规则6.3.5条明确规定，裁判员不应超出其职责范围帮助任何运动员，并特别举例说明，裁判员不应在跳跃项目中提供起跳位置的信息，除非在水平跳跃项目中裁判员为了指示犯规试跳的"接触"点。

7. 警告和取消比赛资格

真诚参赛，违反体育道德和不正当行为

7.1 运动员和接力队要真诚地参加比赛，不得有违反体育道德或不正当的行为。任何不遵守本规则的运动员或接力队都可被警告或取消比赛资格。

任何运动员或接力队在比赛中违反了此条规则，或依据竞赛规则6.1条注（ⅱ）（ⅲ）或（ⅳ），或依据技术规则6条、16.5条、17.14条、17.15.4条、25.5条、25.19条、54.7.6条、54.10.8条或55.8.8条，相关裁判长有权予以警告或取消比赛资格。给予运动员警告，应向运动员出示黄牌；取消其比赛资格，应出示红牌。这两种处罚均要填入成绩记录单，并告知竞赛秘书和其他裁判长。

In disciplinary matters, the Call Room Referee has authority starting from the Warm-up Area up to the competition area. In all other instances, the Referee applicable to the event in which the athlete is or was competing, shall have authority.

The applicable Referee (where practicable after consulting the Competition Director) may warn or remove any other person from the competition area (or other area related to the competition including the Warm-up Area, Call Room and coaches seating) who is acting in an unsporting or improper manner or who is providing assistance to athletes that is not permitted by the Rules.

Note (i): The Referee may, where the circumstances justify it, exclude an athlete or relay team without a warning having been given. (see also Note to Rule 6.2 of the Technical Rules)

Note (ii): For events outside the stadium, the Running and Race Walking Events Referee shall, wherever practicable (e.g. under Rules 6, 54.10 or 55.8 of the Technical Rules), give a warning prior to disqualification. If the Referee's action is contested, Rule 8 of the Technical Rules will apply.

Note (iii): When excluding an athlete or relay team from competition under this Rule, if the Referee is aware that a yellow card has already been given, they should show a second yellow card followed immediately by a red card.

Note (iv): If a yellow card is given and the Referee is not aware that there is a previous yellow card, it shall, once this is known, have the same consequence as if it was given in association with a red card. The relevant Referee shall take immediate action to inform the athlete or relay team or their team of their exclusion.

The below key points are made to provide guidance and clarity in relation to the way in which cards are shown and recorded:

a. Yellow and red cards can be given either for disciplinary reasons (refer mostly to this Rule) or for certain technical infringements that are disciplinary in nature.

b. Whilst it is normal and usually expected that a yellow card would have been given before a red card, it is envisaged that in the cases of particularly bad unsporting or improper behaviour or failing to participate in a bona fide manner, a red card can be given immediately. It should be noted that the athlete or relay team has in any case the opportunity to appeal such a decision to the Jury of Appeal.

检录裁判长有权处理从热身场地开始直至比赛场地涉及纪律方面的事宜。其他情况下，相关项目裁判长有权对参赛运动员比赛中或比赛后的行为进行判罚。

任何其他人有违反体育道德或不正当行为，或向运动员提供规则不允许的帮助的情况，相关裁判长（如果可能，征求竞赛主任意见后）可予以警告或将其驱离比赛场地（或比赛相关区域，包括热身场地、检录处、教练员席）。

注（ⅰ）：裁判长在必要时不需警告，可以直接取消运动员或接力队的比赛资格。（另见技术规则6.2条的注）

注（ⅱ）：在体育场外的比赛，在任何可行的情况下（如依据技术规则6条、54.10条或55.8条），跑和竞走项目裁判长在取消运动员比赛资格之前要予以其警告。如果裁判长的判罚出现争议，将执行技术规则8条。

注（ⅲ）：根据本规则取消运动员或接力队的比赛资格时，如果裁判长知道运动员已有1张黄牌，他应在出示第2张黄牌后紧接着出示红牌。

注（ⅳ）：如果运动员已有1张黄牌，而裁判长并不知道他已有1张黄牌，一经发现，具有与一起出示红牌相同的后果。相关裁判长要立即采取行动，通知运动员、接力队或已被取消比赛的运动队。

以下要点旨在为红黄牌出示与记录给予指导和进一步明确：

a. 黄牌、红牌可以就纪律方面的原因出示（主要参考此条规则），也可以是一些本质上是纪律性的技术犯规。

b. 通常情况下，出示红牌之前应出示黄牌，然而在极其恶劣违反体育道德或有不正当行为或未能真诚参赛的情况下，可以直接出示红牌。值得注意的是，不管怎样，运动员或接力队都有向申诉委员会提出申诉的权利。

c. There will be also some cases in which it is not practical or even logical for a yellow card to have been issued. For example the Note to Rule 6.2 of the Technical Rules specifically allows for an immediate red card if justified in cases covered by Rule 6.3.1 of the Technical Rules such as pacing in races.

d. A similar situation might also follow when a Referee issues a yellow card and the athlete or relay team responds in such an inappropriate manner that it is justified to then immediately give a red card. It is not essential for there to be two completely different and distinct in time instances of inappropriate behaviour.

e. As per Note (iii), in cases where a Referee is aware that the athlete or relay team in question has already received a yellow card during the competition and they propose to issue a red card, the Referee should first show a second yellow card and then the red card. However if a Referee does not show the second yellow card, it will not invalidate the issuing of the red card.

f. In cases where a Referee is not aware of a pre-existing yellow card, and they show only a yellow card, once this becomes known, the appropriate steps should be taken to disqualify the athlete as soon as possible. Normally, this would be done by the Referee advising the athlete directly or through their team.

g. In cases of relay events, cards received by one or more members of the team during any round of the event shall count against the team. Therefore, if one athlete receives two yellow cards or two different athletes receive a yellow card in any round of the particular event, the team shall be regarded as having received a red card and shall be disqualified.

Disqualification resulting from an infringement of a Technical Rule (other than Rule 7.1 of the Technical Rules)

7.2 If an athlete is disqualified from an event for an infringement of a Technical Rule (except under Rule 7.1 of the Technical Rules) any performance accomplished in the same round of that event up to the time of the disqualification shall not be valid. However, performances accomplished in a previous round of that event, other previous events or previous individual events of a Combined Event shall remain valid. Such disqualification from an event shall not prevent an athlete from taking part in any further event in that competition.

c. 某些情况下，出示黄牌不实际或不合理。例如，技术规则6.2条注中特别允许了依据技术规则6.3.1条直接出示红牌的情况，比如在比赛中领跑。

d. 类似情况也可能随之而来，当裁判长出示了黄牌，而运动员或接力队以不当行为作出回应时，裁判长有理由立即出示红牌。对于不当行为的事例，并非必须是两个完全不同或发生在不同时间的行为。

e. 根据注（iii），当裁判长得知当事运动员或接力队在比赛中已经有1张黄牌，并且打算出示1张红牌时，应首先出示第二张黄牌，然后再出示红牌。但是，如果裁判长没有出示第二张黄牌，也并不会影响出示红牌的有效性。

f. 当裁判长不知道运动员已经有1张黄牌时，他们只出示了1张黄牌，一旦知情，应尽快采取合理的措施取消该运动员的比赛资格。通常情况下，由该裁判长直接告知该运动员或通过其代表队告知。

g. 在接力项目中，1名或多名运动员在任何一轮比赛中有的牌均计入该队。因此，如果在该项目的任何一轮比赛中，1名运动员有2张黄牌或者2名不同的运动员有1张黄牌，则该队要被视为有1张红牌并要被取消比赛资格。

因违反技术规则而被取消比赛资格（除技术规则7.1条外）

7.2 如果运动员因违反技术规则而被取消比赛资格（除了技术规则7.1条），那么他在该项目该赛次中取得的成绩无效。然而在此项目之前的赛次，以及前面参加的其他项目取得的成绩或全能项目中前面的单项成绩则有效。这种取消资格不影响该运动员参加其他所有后续项目的比赛。

Disqualification resulting from exclusion under Rule 7.1 of the Technical Rules

7.3　　If an athlete is excluded from competition under Rule 7.1 of the Technical Rules, they shall be disqualified from that event. If the athlete's second warning occurs in a different event, they shall be disqualified only from the second event. Any performance accomplished in the same round of that event up to the time of the disqualification shall not be valid. However, performances accomplished in a previous round of that event, other previous events or previous individual events of a Combined Event shall remain valid. Such disqualification shall prevent an athlete from taking part in all further events or rounds of events (including individual events of a Combined Event, other events in which they are simultaneously participating and relays) in that competition.

7.4　　When a relay team is excluded from competition under Rule 7.1 of the Technical Rules, it shall be disqualified from that event. Performances accomplished in a previous round of that event shall remain valid. If the disqualification of the relay team was the consequence of an athlete(s) acting in a manner that would lead to a disqualification under Rule 7.1 if competing in an individual event, Rule 7.3 of this Rule will be applicable to such athlete(s). Otherwise, such disqualification shall not prevent any athlete of that team taking part in any other event(s) in that competition.

However, if the behaviour of one or more such individual athletes is considered serious enough, Rule 7.1 of the Technical Rules may be applied to them with the applicable consequences.

7.5　　If the offence is considered serious, the Competition Director shall report it to the relevant governing body for consideration of further disciplinary action.

Rule 7.3 shall also be applied to an athlete whose second warning in the competition incurred in the relay race, or who had a direct exclusion in the relay race that led to the disqualification of the team.

8.　　Protests and Appeals

8.1　　Protests concerning the status of an athlete to participate in a competition must be made, prior to the commencement of such competition, to the Technical Delegate(s). Once the Technical Delegate(s) make(s) a decision, there shall be a right of appeal to the Jury of Appeal. If the matter cannot be settled satisfactorily prior to the competition, the athlete shall be allowed to compete "under protest" and the matter be referred to the relevant governing body.

因违反技术规则7.1条而被取消比赛资格

7.3 运动员在比赛中违反技术规则7.1条，他将被取消该项目的比赛资格。如果运动员的第二次警告出现在另外的比赛项目中，他将被取消第二次警告所在项目的比赛资格。他在该项目该赛次比赛中取得的成绩无效。但在此项之前的赛次以及前面参加的其他项目取得的成绩或全能项目中前面的单项成绩有效。受到这种取消资格的判罚，运动员将不能继续参加本次赛会所有后续项目或赛次（包括全能项目的单项、兼项参加的其他项目及接力项目）的比赛。

7.4 接力队在比赛中违反技术规则7.1条，接力队将被取消该项目的参赛资格。但在该项目前面赛次比赛中取得的成绩有效。如果接力队被取消比赛资格是由于运动员在个人项目比赛中根据规则技术7.1条被取消比赛资格的行为方式导致的，则本规则7.3条将适用于该运动员（们）。否则，这种取消资格并不妨碍该队任何运动员或接力队继续参加本次赛会任何其他项目的比赛。

然而，如果运动员个人1次或多次的犯规行为性质严重，则依据技术规则7.1条进行相应的判罚。

7.5 如果认为该次犯规性质严重，竞赛主任须向相关管理机构报告以考虑进一步的纪律处罚。

技术规则7.3条也适用于在接力赛中受到第二次警告的运动员，或在接力赛中直接被取消比赛资格而导致该接力队被取消比赛资格的运动员。

8. **抗议与申诉**

8.1 对运动员的参赛资格提出抗议，必须在比赛开始前向技术代表提出。技术代表作出裁定后，相关人员有权向申诉委员会提出申诉。如果在赛前未能圆满解决该申诉，则须允许该运动员"在抗议下"参加比赛，并将此申诉提交给相关管理机构。

8.2　　　Protests concerning the result or conduct of (a round of) an event shall be made within 30 minutes of the official announcement of the result of that (round of the) event.

The Organisers of the competition shall be responsible for ensuring that the time of the announcement of all results is recorded.

8.3　　　Any protest shall be made orally to the Referee by an athlete, by someone acting on their behalf or by an official representative of a team. Such person or team may protest only if they are competing in the same round of the event to which the protest (or subsequent appeal) relates (or are competing in a competition in which a team points score is being conducted). To arrive at a fair decision, the Referee should consider any available evidence which they think necessary, including a film or picture produced by an official video recorder, or any other available video evidence. The Referee may decide on the protest or may refer the matter to the Jury of Appeal. If the Referee makes a decision, there shall be a right of appeal to the Jury. Where the Referee is not accessible or available, the protest should be made to them through the Technical Information Centre.

Note: The World Athletics Photo Finish Judge, where appointed, should act on behalf of the Running and Race Walking Events Referee regarding protests about the placing of athletes.

8.4　　　In a Running or Race Walking Event,

　　　　　8.4.1　　if an athlete makes an immediate oral protest against having been charged with a false start, the Start Referee (or if one is not appointed, the relevant Running and Race Walking Events Referee) may, if they are in any doubt, allow the athlete to compete "under protest" in order to preserve the rights of all concerned. Competing "under protest" should not be allowed if the false start was indicated by a World Athletics certified Start Information System, unless for any reason the Referee determines that the information provided by the System is obviously inaccurate. If an athlete is allowed to compete under protest, a red and white (diagonally halved) card shall be raised in front of the athlete.

8.2 如抗议涉及某项（赛次）比赛的成绩或进程，则要在该项（赛次）比赛成绩正式公告后30分钟内提出。

比赛组织者要确保记录下所有比赛成绩的公告时间。

8.3 所有抗议均须由运动员本人、运动员代表或运动队代表向有关裁判长口头提出。运动员或运动队所提抗议（以及随后的申诉）必须与其正在参加的同一项目的同一赛（轮）次的比赛（或正在参加进行团体积分的比赛）相关。为了作出公正裁决，裁判长应考虑任何有效的证据，包括由大会正式摄像机拍摄的视频、照片或其他视频证据。裁判长可就抗议作出裁决，也可将该问题提交申诉委员会。裁判长作出裁决后，运动员仍有向申诉委员会提请申诉的权益。当裁判长不在或无法联系时，抗议应由技术信息中心向裁判长提出。

注：如果指派了世界田联终点摄影裁判员，在涉及运动员名次的抗议时，其应作为跑和竞走项目裁判长。

8.4 在跑和竞走项目中，

8.4.1 如果运动员对起跑犯规的判罚提出即时的口头抗议，起点裁判长（或如果没有指派起点裁判长，相关跑和竞走项目裁判长）对此存在疑问，可以让该运动员"在抗议下"比赛，以便保留所有相关的权益。如果起跑犯规是由世界田联批准的起跑信息系统检测到的，则不允许其"在抗议下"比赛，除非裁判长认定该起跑信息系统提供的信息明显不准确。如果运动员被允许"在抗议下"比赛，要在该运动员面前出示红白牌（用对角线分为红白两半）。

8.4.2　a protest may be based on the failure of the Starter to recall a false start or, under Rule 16.5 of the Technical Rules, to abort a start. The protest may be made only by, or on behalf of, an athlete who should normally have completed the race with bona fide effort. If the protest is upheld, any athlete who committed the false start or whose conduct should have led to the start being aborted, and who was subject to warning or disqualification according to Rules 16.5, 16.8 or 39.8.3 of the Technical Rules, shall be warned or disqualified. Whether or not there may be any warning or disqualification, the Referee shall have the authority to declare the event or part of the event void and that it or part of it shall be held again if in their opinion justice demands it.

Note: The right of protest and appeal in Rule 8.4.2 of the Technical Rules shall apply whether or not a Start Information System is used.

8.4.3　if a protest or appeal is based on an athlete's incorrect exclusion from an event due to a false start and it is upheld after the completion of the race, then the athlete should be afforded the opportunity to run on their own to record a time in the event and consequently, if applicable, to be advanced to subsequent rounds. No athlete should be advanced to a subsequent round without competing in all rounds unless the Referee or Jury of Appeal determines otherwise in the particular circumstances of the case, e.g. the shortness of time before the next round or the length of the race.

Note: This Rule may also be applied by the Referee, the Jury of Appeal in other circumstances where it is deemed appropriate (see Rule 17.1 of the Technical Rules).

8.4.4　when a protest is made by or on behalf of an athlete or team which did not finish a race, the Referee must first ascertain whether the athlete or team was or should have been disqualified for a breach of the Rules unrelated to the matter raised in the protest. Should that be the case, the protest shall be dismissed.

8.4.2　对发令员未能召回的起跑犯规,以及根据技术规则16.5条的规定,对未能中止的起跑进行抗议。抗议通常应只能由通过真诚努力地完成了该项比赛的运动员或其代表提出。如果抗议成立,则任何在本项比赛中负有起跑犯规责任或做出一定行为导致起跑中止的运动员,以及根据技术规则16.5条、16.8条或39.8.3条的规定应给予警告或取消比赛资格的运动员,将被警告或取消比赛资格。无论是否有运动员被警告或取消比赛资格,出于公正目的,裁判长有权宣布比赛或比赛的一部分无效,该比赛或比赛的一部分应重新进行。

注:无论是否使用起跑信息系统,运动员都可以引用技术规则8.4.2条提出抗议和申诉。

8.4.3　如果运动员由于起跑犯规的错误判罚而被取消比赛资格,他提出抗议或申诉,比赛结束后,如果抗议或申诉成立,则应给予运动员单独比赛的机会并且记录成绩,如果该成绩符合晋级标准,运动员应晋级下一赛次。任何运动员未参加比赛,则不得晋级后续赛次的比赛,除非裁判长或申诉委员会在特殊情况下作出决定,如下一赛次之前的时间很短或比赛的时长很短等。

注:裁判长或申诉委员会也可在其他认为合适的情况下运用这条规则(见技术规则17.1条)。

8.4.4　当抗议由未完成比赛的运动员或运动队的代表提出时,裁判长必须首先确定,该运动员或运动队是否因违反与抗议中提及的事项无关的规则而被取消资格。如果是这种情况,则抗议要被驳回。

When the Start Referee decides on an immediate oral protest made by an athlete for being charged with a false start, they have to consider all the available data and in case of a reasonable possibility that the athlete's protest may be valid, they should allow the athlete to compete under protest. After the race, a final decision must be taken by the Referee, a decision that may be subject of an appeal to the Jury. The Referee should not normally allow an athlete to compete under protest if the false start has been detected by a Start Information System that appears to be working properly or in cases where it is very clear by visual observation that the athlete has committed a false start and there is no valid reason to allow the protest. However, it is acknowledged that when the reaction time is close to the allowed limit, any movement could be hardly visible. In this case if, in the opinion of the Start Referee, it would require further study of the technological evidence, the Start Referee may decide to allow the athlete run under protest to preserve the rights of all concerned.

These rules not only apply where a Starter failed to recall a false start but where also a Starter failed to correctly "abort" a start. In both cases the Referee must consider all factors involved in the particular case and must decide if the race (or part of it) has to be re-held.

Giving two examples of extreme situations, it will not be logical or necessary to re-run a Marathon race in a case where an athlete who finishes was responsible for a non-recalled false start. But the same will probably not be the case in a sprint event where an athlete was responsible for a non-recalled false start as this may have affected the start and subsequent race of other athletes.

On the other hand, if for example in a preliminary round, or perhaps even more so in a race within a Combined Event, it was clear that only one or some athletes were disadvantaged by a failure to recall a false start or to abort a start, a Referee could decide that only those athletes be given the opportunity to run again – and if so under what conditions.

Rule 8.4.3 of the Technical Rules covers the situation in which an athlete is wrongly given a false start and excluded from a race.

8.5　　In a Field Event, if an athlete makes an immediate oral protest against having a trial judged as a failure, the Referee of the event may, if they are in any doubt, order that the trial be measured and the result recorded, in order to preserve the rights of all concerned.

If the protested trial occurred:

起点裁判长在裁决起跑犯规的口头抗议时，应考虑所有可用数据，当发现抗议有可能成立时，他应允许运动员"在抗议下"参赛。比赛后，裁判长应作出最后决定，该决定可能会被提交到申诉委员会。若起跑犯规是由明显工作正常的起跑信息系统检测到的，或者明显观察到运动员起跑犯规了，且无有效理由支持抗议时，裁判长不应允许运动员"在抗议下"参赛。但是，通常当反应时非常接近极限时，运动员的移动是很难用肉眼捕捉到的。在这种情况下，起点裁判长通常会需要进一步研究技术证据，因此，裁判长会允许运动员"在抗议下"参赛，以便维护相关各方的权益。

此规则不仅适用于发令员无法召回的起跑犯规的比赛，也适用于发令员未能正确地"中止"发令的比赛。在这两种情况下，裁判长必须考虑特殊情况下的所有因素，并决定比赛（或者部分比赛）重新进行。

举两个极端情况的例子，在马拉松比赛中完赛运动员对没有召回的抢跑负有责任则不需要重跑，重赛是不合理也是不必要的。同样的情况，在短跑项目中运动员对未能召回的抢跑负有责任可能也不需要重赛，因为这可能已经影响到其他运动员的起跑以及后续赛事。

另外，例如在初选晋级赛中，或者在全能项目的径赛比赛中，当很明显只有1名或部分运动员因未能召回起跑犯规的赛事或中止起跑而处于不利地位时，裁判长可以决定只有这部分运动员进行重赛，以及在什么样的条件下重赛。

技术规则8.4.3条涵盖了运动员因为被误判为起跑犯规并取消比赛资格的情形。

8.5　在田赛项目中，如果运动员对试跳（掷）失败的判罚提出即时口头抗议，该项目的裁判长对此也存有疑虑，可以下令测量并记录该次试跳（掷）的成绩，以便保留所有相关各方的权益。

　　如果发生对试跳（掷）判罚的抗议：

8.5.1 during the first three rounds of trials of a horizontal Field Event in which more than eight athletes are competing, and the athlete would advance to any subsequent rounds of trials only if the protest or subsequent appeal was upheld; or

8.5.2 in a vertical Field Event, where the athlete would advance to a higher height only if the protest or subsequent appeal is upheld,

the Referee may, if they are in any doubt, allow the athlete to continue competing "under protest" to preserve the rights of all concerned.

In cases where the Referee is sure that the decision of the Judges is correct, particularly by their own observation or advice received from a Video Referee, the athlete should not be allowed to continue.

But when considering whether to order the measurement of a trial which is the subject of an immediate oral protest the Referee should:

a. not do so in cases where there was a clear breach of the Rules, for example in the long jump a clear mark made in the plasticine by the athlete in question or in a throwing event where the implement has clearly landed outside the sector;

b. always do so (and immediately so as to not delay the competition) in cases where there is any doubt.

The good operation of this Rule means that the Judge with the spike or prism should always mark the point of landing (except in throwing events where the implement clearly lands outside the sector) even when they see a red flag. Apart from the possibility that the athlete may make an immediate oral protest, it is also possible that the Judge with the flags may have incorrectly or accidentally raised the wrong one.

8.6 The protested performance of the athlete and any other performance achieved by them while competing "under protest" will become valid only if a subsequent decision to that effect is made by the Referee or an appeal to the Jury of Appeal is made and it is upheld.

In Field Events where, as a result of an athlete competing "under protest", another athlete is allowed to continue in the competition when they would otherwise not have done so, such athlete's performances and eventual results will remain valid irrespective of whether the "under protest" athlete's immediate oral protest is successful.

8.5.1　在远度项目的前3轮中，有8名以上运动员参赛，如果抗议或随后的申诉成立，运动员将晋级下一轮次的比赛；或

8.5.2　在高度项目中，只有抗议或随后的申诉成立，运动员才能进入下一高度的比赛，

裁判长如存有疑虑，可以允许运动员"在抗议下"继续比赛，以保留所有相关方的权益。

当裁判长确信裁判员的判罚是正确的，特别是通过其自身观察或根据视频裁判长的意见，运动员则不应被允许继续比赛。

但在考虑是否下令测量已被提出即时口头抗议的试跳（掷）时，裁判长应该：

a. 当有明显的违反规则的情况，例如，在跳远比赛中运动员在橡皮泥上留下了明显痕迹，或在投掷项目中器械明显落于扇形落地区外时，则不应测量；

b. 若有任何疑虑，则都要测量（并立即执行，以确保不延误比赛）。

此规则的良好运用在于落点裁判员应随时标记器械落地点（投掷项目中器械明显落于扇形落地区外的情况除外），即便是他们看到了红旗示意。除了运动员即时口头抗议的可能，也有可能是裁判员举旗错误或意外地举错了旗。

8.6　只有当裁判长的裁决或申诉委员会裁决申诉成立时，该运动员有争议的成绩和其"在抗议下"比赛所取得的成绩才将成为有效成绩。

在田赛项目中，由于有运动员"在抗议下"比赛，因此另外1名本不能继续比赛的运动员被允许继续比赛，不管"在抗议下"比赛的运动员的即时口头抗议是否成功，另外这名运动员的成绩和最终成绩均为有效。

The first paragraph of Rule 8.6 of the Technical Rules applies to all events, not only to Field Events.

8.7 An appeal to the Jury of Appeal must be made within 30 minutes:

    8.7.1 of the official announcement of the amended result of an event arising from the decision made by the Referee; or

    8.7.2 of the advice being given to those making the protest, where there is no amendment of any result.

It shall be in writing, signed by the athlete, by someone acting on their behalf or by an official representative of a team and shall be accompanied by a deposit of USD 100, or its equivalent, which will be forfeited if the appeal is not allowed. Such athlete or team may appeal only if they are competing in the same round of the event to which the appeal relates (or are competing in a competition on which a team points score is being conducted).

Note: The relevant Referee shall, after their decision on a protest, immediately inform the TIC of the time of the communication of the decision. If the Referee was unable to communicate the decision orally to the relevant team(s) / athlete(s), the official time of the announcement will be that of posting of the amended result or of the decision at the TIC.

8.8 The Jury of Appeal shall consult all relevant persons, including the relevant Referee (except when their decision is to be fully maintained by the Jury of Appeal). If the Jury of Appeal is in doubt, other available evidence may be considered. If such evidence, including any available video evidence, is not conclusive, the decision of the Referee or the Chief Race Walking Judge shall be upheld.

8.9 The Jury of Appeal may reconsider a decision if new conclusive evidence is presented, provided the new decision is still applicable. Normally, such re-consideration may be undertaken only prior to the Victory Ceremony for the applicable event, unless the relevant governing body determines that circumstances justify otherwise.

In certain circumstances, the Judges (Rule 19.2 of the Competition Rules), the Referee (Rule 18.6 of the Competition Rules) and the Jury (Rule 8.9 of the Technical Rules) can each reconsider a decision made by them – if it is still applicable and practical to do so.

技术规则8.6条第一段不仅适用于田赛项目，而且适用于所有项目。

8.7 提交申诉委员会的申诉必须在30分钟以内提出：

  8.7.1 裁判长作出裁决、比赛成绩更正正式公告后；或

  8.7.2 通知抗议者比赛成绩没有任何改动后。

申诉必须以书面形式提交，由运动员本人、其代表或者运动队的代表签名，并附上100美元或其他等值货币的申诉费。如果该申诉被驳回，则申诉费不予退还。运动员或运动队提出的申诉必须与他们正在参加项目同一赛（轮）次的比赛有关（或正在参加的进行团体积分的比赛）。

注：有关裁判长在对抗议作出决定后，要立即通知技术信息中心通报决定的时间。如裁判长无法口头向有关运动队或运动员传达决定，则以技术信息中心张贴裁决结果的时间或技术信息中心更正成绩的时间为官方公告时间。

8.8 申诉委员会应向所有有关人员问询，包括相关裁判长（除非申诉委员会全力维护裁判长的裁决）。如果申诉委员会存有疑虑，则可以考虑其他有效的证据。如果根据此类证据，包括任何有效的视频证据，仍无法得出结论，则申诉委员须认可有关裁判长或竞走主裁判的裁决。

8.9 如果出现新的确凿的证据，而且条件允许，申诉委员会可以重新作出裁决。通常情况下，这些重新裁决应在有关项目颁奖仪式开始之前作出，除非相关管理机构认为有其他正当理由。

在某些情况下，如果切实可行且有实际意义的话，裁判员（竞赛规则19.2条）、裁判长（竞赛规则18.6条）以及申诉委员会（技术规则8.9条）都可以重新作出决定。

8.10　Decisions involving points which are not covered by the Rules shall be reported subsequently by the Chairman of the Jury of Appeal to the Chief Executive Officer of World Athletics.

8.11　The decision of the Jury of Appeal (or of the Referee in the absence of a Jury of Appeal or if no appeal to the Jury is made) shall be final and there shall be no further right of appeal, including to CAS.

9.　Mixed Competition

9.1　Universal competitions such as relays or other team events in which men and women compete together or events in which men and women compete for a single classification are permitted in accordance with the applicable regulations of the relevant body.

9.2　Other than under Rule 9.1, for all other competitions held completely in the stadium, mixed events between male and female participants shall not normally be permitted.

However, the following may be permitted:

- in competitions under paragraphs 1.(a), (b), (c) and 2.(a), (b), (c) of the World Rankings Competition definition in Field Events if permitted by the applicable regulations,

- in competitions under paragraphs 1.(d), (e) and 2.(d), (e) of the World Rankings Competitior definition always in Field Events and if specifically permitted by the relevant Area Association in events per Rule 9.2.1 of the Technical Rules,

- in competitions under paragraph 3 of the World Rankings Competition definition always in Field Events and if specifically permitted by the relevant National Member Federation in events per Rule 9.2.1 of the Technical Rules:

　　9.2.1　mixed stadium competition in races of 5000m or longer but it is permitted only when there are insufficient athletes of one or both sexes competing to justify the conduct of separate races. The sex of each athlete shall be shown in the result. Such races shall not, in any case, be conducted so as to allow athletes of one sex to be paced or assisted by athletes of another sex.

8.10 当裁决涉及规则以外的问题时，将由申诉委员会主席稍后向世界田联首席执行官汇报。

8.11 申诉委员会的裁决（当没有申诉委员会或者没有提交申诉给申诉委员会时，则裁判长的裁决）为最终决定，不得提出进一步的申诉，包括向体育仲裁法庭申诉。

9. **混合比赛**

9.1 根据相关管理机构适用的规程，允许男女混合一起参加如接力跑或其他集体项目的混同组比赛，即男女一起进行的比赛，或者男女为单一组别的比赛。

9.2 除技术规则9.1条规定的比赛外，其他完全在体育场内举行的所有比赛，一般不允许有男女混合参赛的项目。

但是，以下情况可被允许：

- 适用的规程允许，在世界排名比赛定义1.（a）（b）（c）和2.（a）（b）（c）所述的田赛项目比赛中，

- 在世界排名比赛定义1.（d）（e）和2.（d）（e）所述的田赛项目比赛中，以及经相关地区联合会特别许可在技术规则9.2.1条所述的项目中，

- 在世界排名比赛定义3条所述的田赛项目比赛中，以及经相关国家会员协会特别许可在技术规则9.2.1条所述的项目中：

    9.2.1 只有当1个或2个性别的运动员人数不足，合组比赛比分组比赛在组织上更合理时，才允许在体育场进行5000米或以上项目的混合比赛。每位运动员的性别必须标注在成绩单上。在任何情况下，混合比赛中不允许某一性别的运动员为另一性别的运动员提供配速或帮助。

9.2.2　　Field Events for men and women may be conducted simultaneously at one or more event sites. Separate result cards shall be used and results declared for each sex. Each round of trials of such events may be conducted either by calling all athletes of one sex followed by the other or by alternating them. For the purposes of Rule 25.17 of the Technical Rules, all athletes shall be regarded as if they were of the same sex. Where Vertical Jumps are conducted on a single event site, Rules 26 to 28 of the Technical Rules must be strictly applied, including that the bar must continue to be raised in accordance with a single set of previously announced increments for the entire competition.

The intent of Rule 9.2.1 of the Technical Rules is to facilitate the conduct of races of 5000m or longer, when small numbers of athletes of one or both sexes are entered. The intent of the Rule is not to provide opportunity for women to compete in races against men to achieve potentially better performance conditions.

To be clear, mixed competition is:

a. permitted in all national competitions in Field Events and if specifically permitted by the relevant National Member Federation in races of 5000m or longer according to Rule 9.2.1 of the Technical Rules (No additional permission from an Area Association is required);

b. permitted in competitions held under paragraphs 1.(d),(e) and 2.(d),(e) of the World Rankings Competition definition in Field Events and if specifically permitted by the relevant Area Association in races of 5000m or longer according to Rule 9.2.1 of the Technical Rules;

c. not permitted in a competition held under paragraphs 1.(a),(b),(c) and 2.(a),(b),(c) of the World Rankings Competition definition unless in the case of Field Events the applicable regulations for the competition so provide.

There are also restrictions on the recognition of World Records in mixed competitions – see Rules 31.1 (with reference to track races of 5000m and longer) and 32 (with reference to women's road races) of the Competition Rules. Rule 32 of the Competition Rules Note (ii) provides guidance on how a women only race can be achieved (enabling a women only record to be set) in a situation where both men and women are or might be competing.

(See also Rules 25.2 and 25.3 of the Competition Rules.)

9.2.2　混合比赛的田赛项目可在1个或多个比赛场地同时进行。应使用单独的成绩单，并按性别公布比赛成绩。此类赛事的每一轮试跳（掷）可以召集某一性别的运动员，随后是另一性别的运动员，或者交替进行。在执行技术规则25.17条时，所有运动员应被视为同性。当在一个比赛场地进行高度跳跃项目时，必须严格执行技术规则26至28条，包括在整场比赛中横杆必须按照一套赛前宣布的升高计划递升。

技术规则9.2.1条是为5000米及以上项目，报名参赛的单一或者两种性别的运动员人数很少时提供便利。此规则的意图不是让女性运动员在与男性运动员同场比赛中获得潜在提高成绩的机会。

要明确的是，混合比赛：

a. 在所有全国性比赛田赛项目中，以及依据技术规则9.2.1条的规定经相关国家会员协会特别许可在5000米及以上项目比赛中（无须地区联合会额外许可）；

b. 在举办世界排名比赛定义1.（d）（e）和2.（d）（e）所述比赛的田赛项目中，以及经相关地区联合会依据技术规则9.2.1条特别许可的5000米及以上项目比赛中；

c. 不允许在举办世界排名比赛定义1.（a）（b）（c）和2.（a）（b）（c）所述的比赛中举行，除非在田赛项目中适用的规程已作规定。

在男女混合比赛中，对世界纪录的承认有严格的限制条款——见竞赛规则31.1条（涉及5000米及以上径赛项目）和竞赛规则32条（涉及女子路跑项目）。竞赛规则32条注（ⅱ）提供指导，在男女共同参赛或可能共同参赛的情况下如何实现单一女子组比赛（以便能够承认女子纪录）。

（另见竞赛规则25.2条及25.3条。）

10. Surveying and Measurements

10.1 The accuracy of the markings and installations for athletics facilities under Rules 2, 11.2, 11.3 and 41 of the Technical Rules shall be checked by an appropriately qualified surveyor who shall furnish appropriate certificates together with details of any check measurements made to the relevant body and/or the facility owner or operator. They shall be given full access to stadium plans and drawings and the latest measurement report for the purpose of this verification.

10.2 For Track and Field Events in competitions under paragraphs 1. (a), (b), (c) and 2. (a), (b) of the World Rankings Competition definition, all measurements shall be made with a calibrated steel tape or bar or with a scientific measuring device. The steel tape, bar or scientific measuring device shall be manufactured and calibrated according to international standards. The accuracy of the measuring equipment used in the competition shall have been verified by an appropriate organisation accredited by the national measurement authority.

At competitions other than those held under paragraphs 1. (a), (b), (c) and 2. (a), (b) of the World Rankings Competition definition, fibreglass tapes may also be used.

Note: Concerning acceptance of Records, see Rule 31.17.1 of the Competition Rules.

11. Validity of Performances

11.1 Only Athlete performances accomplished during World Rankings Competitions are valid.

11.2 Performances in events normally conducted in the stadium, made outside traditional athletics facilities (such as those held on a temporary facility in town squares, other sporting facilities, beaches, etc.) or on a temporary facility built within a stadium shall be valid and recognised for all purposes, if they are made subject to all of the following conditions:

    11.2.1 the relevant governing body as provided in Rule 1 of the Competition Rules has issued a permit for the event;

    11.2.2 a qualified panel of National Athletics Referee are appointed to and officiate at the event;

    11.2.3 where applicable, equipment and implements in conformity with the Rules are used; and

10. **检验和测量**

10.1 技术规则2条、11.2条、11.3条和41条涉及的体育设施的标记和安装的准确性，应由合格的测量员检验和测量，他要向相关组织和（或）场地设施所有者或经营者提供检验证书和详细测量资料。需为测量员提供进入体育场的计划和图纸，以及以认证为目的的最近的测量报告。

10.2 举办世界排名比赛定义1.（a）（b）（c）和2.（a）（b）所述的径赛和田赛项目比赛，所有测量都要使用经过校验的钢卷尺、棍尺或科学测量仪器。它们均应依据国际标准生产和校准。比赛中使用的测量仪器的精准度应由国家测量部门认定的有关机构验证。

在举办世界排名比赛定义1.（a）（b）（c）和2.（a）（b）所述比赛之外的其他比赛中，测量时可以使用玻璃纤维卷尺。

注：关于承认纪录，见竞赛规则31.17.1条。

11. **有效成绩**

11.1 运动员只有在世界排名的比赛中创造的成绩方为有效。

11.2 如果符合以下所有的条件，通常在体育场内、传统田径场地以外（如在城市广场的临时设施、其他运动场地、海滩等举行）或体育场内搭建的临时场地所创造的成绩，须被认为是有效的：

  11.2.1 竞赛规则1条规定的相关管理机构签发了赛事许可；

  11.2.2 指派一批具有资格的国家田径裁判长在比赛中执裁；

  11.2.3 情况允许时，使用符合规则要求的设备和器械；和

11.2.4 the event is conducted in a competition area or facility in conformity with the Rules and in respect of which a survey has been made in accordance with Rule 10 of the Technical Rules before the event and, where possible, on the day of the event.

When a competition described in Rule 11.2 of the Technical Rules is held over more than one day, the survey should be made on the day of the first event. In either case if the surveyor can be satisfied that there will be no movement or alteration to the facilities being surveyed, the survey may be completed up to two days prior to the day of the first event.

11.3 Performances in events conducted in a fully or partly covered venue where the length or other specifications of the facility do not comply with the rules for Short Track competitions shall be valid and recognised as if they were achieved on a 400m Standard Oval Track, if they are made subject to all of the following conditions:

11.3.1 the relevant governing body as provided in Rule 1 of the Competition Rules has issued a permit for the event;

11.3.2 a qualified panel of National Athletics Referee are appointed to and officiate at the event;

11.3.3 where applicable, equipment and implements in conformity with the Rules are used;

11.3.4 in the case of an oval track, its length is greater than 201.2m (220 yards) but no greater than 400m; and

11.3.5 the event is conducted in a competition area or facility in conformity with the Rules and in respect of which, if held on a temporary facility, a survey has been made in accordance with Rule 10 of the Technical Rules.

Note: The current standard forms required to be used for reporting on the conformity of the competition area or facility are available from the World Athletics Office, or may be downloaded from the World Athletics website or the Global Calendar platform, as appropriate.

When a result is achieved on a complying facility with no advantage gained and all related rules observed, the fact that it happened at a covered competition site does not prevent a result being listed among the outdoor equivalent distances and used for any statistical purpose (performances, e.g. on covered 400m tracks and straights). The current practice that results made in tracks shorter than 200m count towards the Short Track results does not change.

11.2.4 比赛须在符合规则要求的场地、设施上举行。根据技术规则10条，必须在赛前对其进行检测，若可能，在比赛当天进行检测。

若技术规则11.2条所述的比赛超过1天，检测应在第一项比赛当天进行。或者如果测量员可以确认场地设施在其测量后不会有任何移动变化，则测量最多可以提前至赛前两天完成。

11.3 在完全或部分有顶的场地举行的比赛中，如果场馆设施的长度或其他规格不符合短道比赛规则，则在满足以下所有条件的情况下，比赛成绩应视为在400米标准椭圆赛道上取得的成绩，并予以承认：

11.3.1 竞赛规则1条规定的相关管理机构签发了赛事许可；

11.3.2 指派一批具有资格的国家田径裁判长技术官员在比赛中执裁；

11.3.3 情况允许时，使用符合规则要求的设备和器械；

11.3.4 如为椭圆形跑道，其长度大于201.2米（220码），但不大于400米；和

11.3.5 如涉及在临时场地上举行，比赛须在符合规则要求的场地或设施上进行，关于这点已按照技术规则10条进行了检测。

注：比赛场地设施合格报告所使用的现行标准表格可从世界田联办公室获取，也可以从世界田联网站或者视情况从全球赛历平台下载。

在没有获得任何利益且没有违反相关规则的合规场地设施上所取得的成绩，可作为与该项目相等距离的室外比赛的成绩，并可用于任何目的的统计（成绩，例如在带顶棚的400米跑道和直道上所取得的）。目前将在200米以下室内跑道上取得的成绩计入在200米室内跑道上取得的成绩的做法没有改变。

11.4　　Performances made in accordance with these Rules in Qualification Rounds, in deciding ties in High Jump and Pole Vault, in any event or part of an event which is subsequently decreed void under the provisions of Rule 18.7 of the Competition Rules, or Rules 8.4.2, 17.1 or 25.20 of the Technical Rules, in Race Walking Events in which Rule 54.7.3 of the Technical Rules is applied and the athlete is not disqualified or in individual events in Combined Events competitions, regardless of whether or not the athlete completes the whole Combined Events competition, will normally be regarded as valid for purposes such as statistics, records, rankings and the achievement of entry standards.

World Athletics has exceptionally determined that solely for the purpose of determining whether an athlete has achieved the entry standard for a Combined Events competition:

"The conditions shall have been complied with in each of the individual events, except that, in events where wind velocity is measured, at least one of the following conditions shall be satisfied:

a. The velocity in any individual event shall not exceed plus 4 metres per second.

b. The average velocity (based on the algebraic sum of the wind velocities, as measured for each individual event, divided by the number of such events) shall not exceed plus 2 metres per second."

12.　　Video Recording

In competitions held under paragraphs 1. (a), (b) and (c) of the World Rankings Competition definition and, whenever possible, in other competitions, an official video recording of all events to the satisfaction of the Technical Delegate(s) shall be made. It should be sufficient to support the role of the Video Referee when appointed and in other situations to demonstrate the accuracy of performances and any violation of the Rules.

Specific information is provided in the Video Recording and Video Referee Guidelines, which may be downloaded from the World Athletics website.

The appointment at any competition of a Video Referee will significantly affect the practical oversight of many aspects of those competitions at which sufficient video collection and replay systems are available.

11.4　在径赛晋级赛或田赛及格赛赛次中、在跳高和撑竿跳高的决名次赛中、在随后根据竞赛规则18.7条或技术规则8.4.2条、17.1条或25.20条规定而被宣布无效的比赛或部分比赛中、在适用了技术规则54.7.3条的竞走项目中，且运动员未被取消比赛资格，或在无论运动员是否完成了整个全能项目的单项比赛中，按照相关规则规定所取得的成绩，在用于统计、纪录、排名和达到报名标准时通常将被当作有效成绩。

世界田联已特别明确，仅为确定运动员是否已达到可参加全能项目比赛的参赛标准：

"条件都应符合每个单项比赛要求，除了在测量风速的项目中，至少需满足以下一个条件：

a. 在任何单项中，风速不能超过+4米/秒；

b. 平均风速（基于每个单项比赛测量的风速的代数和，除以这些项目的总数）不能超过+2米/秒。"

12.　视频录制

举办世界排名比赛定义1.（a）（b）和（c）所述的比赛，如果条件许可，在其他比赛中，要使用官方录像以满足技术代表的要求拍摄所有项目的比赛。当指派了视频裁判长时，影像录像也应足以帮助其履行其职责，还能查看成绩的准确性和是否有任何犯规情况。

世界田联提供《视频录制和视频裁判长指南》，可从世界田联网站下载。

当视频采集与回放系统可用时，应为所有比赛指派一名视频裁判长，这将对赛事许多方面的实际监督起到至关重要的作用。

The Video Referee will generally be able to act proactively in respect of the Running or Race Walking Events (e.g. the start, running inside the lane line around the curve, jostling and obstruction, breaking from lanes too early, relay changeovers). If the number of cameras and equipment is sufficient to play a similar role for some or all of the Field Events, they can undertake a similar role, but usually in a more reactive fashion when the on-field Referee requests further examination or review of a specific incident.

In the case of the Running or Race Walking Events, the Video Referee will observe the races on one or more screens in the video room and then based on either their own observations or upon referral from a Referee or Chief Umpire in the competition area, examine one or more particular issues by looking at any replayed footage that might be available. If it is clear as a result that there has been an infringement of the Rules, then they should take the appropriate decision and convey it to the Running and Race Walking Events Referee and the Chief Photo Finish Judge. Similarly, if an Umpire or Running and Race Walking Events Referee has reported a potential infringement, it should be checked by the Video Referee and the appropriate advice provided and decision taken.

In addition, official video footage will as in the past continue to be used to assist in dealing with protests and appeals.

It is becoming common for experienced companies to provide an existing service for competitions rather than Organisers setting up their own. However, either option can be used.

13. Scoring

In a match where the result is to be determined by the scoring of points, the method of scoring shall be agreed by all the competing Members or teams before the start of the match, unless provided for in the applicable regulations.

视频裁判长在跑和竞走项目比赛中通常能够主动执裁（如起跑、在弯道内侧跑进、冲撞和阻挡、提前切入内道、接力赛交接棒）。如果有足够的摄像机和设备在部分或者全部田赛项目中发挥类似作用，其也可以承担类似的职责，但是通常为被动的方式，即当场裁判长要求对特殊事件进行进一步检查和审查时。

在跑和竞走项目中，视频裁判长在录像室通过一个或多个屏幕观察比赛，然后基于其观察或者来自比赛场地裁判长或检查主裁判的问询，对一个或多个特殊事件进行回放检查。如果很明显看到了违反规则的情况，他应作出相应的裁决，并传达给跑和竞走项目裁判长以及终点摄影主裁判。类似地，如果一名检查裁判员或者跑或竞走项目裁判长报告了可能的违规情况，视频裁判长应进行检查并提供相应的建议与作出相应决定。

此外，官方录像跟过去一样将协助解决抗议与申诉。

有经验的公司为赛事提供现有服务的情况变得普遍，可以取代组织者自己布置摄像机。当然两者都可行。

13. 计分

除非在适用的规程中明确规定，在以团体总分来判定胜负的比赛中，计分方法应在赛前得到所有协会或参赛队的一致认可。

PART II TRACK EVENTS

Rules 17.1, 17.6 (except under Rules 54.12 and 55.9), 17.14, 18.2, 19 and 21.1 of the Technical Rules also apply to Parts VI, VII, and VIII of the Technical Rules.

14. Track Measurements

14.1　The nominal length of a standard running track shall be 400m ("400m Standard Oval Track"). It shall consist of two parallel straights and two bends whose radii shall be equal. The inside of the track shall be bordered by a kerb of suitable material that should be coloured white, with a height of 50mm to 65mm and a width of 50mm to 250mm. The kerb on the two straights may be omitted and a white line 50mm wide substituted.

If a section of the kerb on a bend has to be temporarily removed for Field Events, its place on the surface beneath shall be marked with a white line 50mm in width and by cones or flags, minimum height 0.15m, placed on the white line so that the edge of the base of the cone or flag pole coincides with the edge of the white line closest to the track, and placed at intervals not exceeding 4m (2m for the curved part of an inside steeplechase diversion). (flags shall be placed at an angle of 60° with the ground away from the track.) This (including also the option of temporary kerbing) shall also apply to the curved section of the steeplechase track where athletes divert from the main track to negotiate the water jump, to the outer half of the track in the case of starts according to Rule 17.5.2 of the Technical Rules and, optionally, to the straights, in this latter case, at intervals not exceeding 10m.

Note: All points on lane 1 inside lane line at which the track changes from a curve to a straight or a straight to a curve shall be marked, in a distinctive colour 50mm × 50mm on the white line, by the surveyor and a cone placed at such points during a race.

第二部分　径赛项目

技术规则17.1条、17.6条（除技术规则54.12条及55.9条外）、17.14条、18.2条、19条及21.1条也适用于技术规则第六、第七和第八部分。

14. 跑道数据

14.1　标准跑道的长度为400米（"400米标准椭圆形跑道"）。标准跑道由两条平行的直道和两条半径相等的弯道组成。跑道内侧以适宜材料制成的突沿加以分界，并漆成白色。突沿高为55至65毫米，宽为50至250毫米。两条直道上可以不设突沿，用50毫米宽的白线代替。

如因举行田赛项目比赛而需临时移除弯道突沿的一部分，则应用50毫米宽的白线在突沿下方原有位置标出，并在白线上放置锥形物或小旗，其高度至少为0.15米，锥形物的底座边沿或小旗的旗杆应与白线外沿重合，间隔不超过4米（水池设在跑道内侧的弯道部分间隔为2米）。（标志旗应朝向跑道内侧与跑道地面成60°角。）本条款（包括设置临时的突沿）也适用于障碍跑中运动员从主跑道转向跨越水池所跑的那部分跑道，也适用于依据技术规则17.5.2条进行起跑的外侧跑道，也可选择在直道上放置标志物，间隔不超过10米。

注：关于直曲段分界点，不管是从直道转至弯道，还是从弯道转至直道，都必须由测量员做标记，用50毫米×50毫米的明显的颜色标记在白线上，比赛时，在这些点上放置锥形物。

14.2　　The measurement shall be taken 0.30m outward from the kerb or, where no kerb exists on a bend (or the diversion from the track for the steeplechase water jump), 0.20m from the line marking the inside of the track.

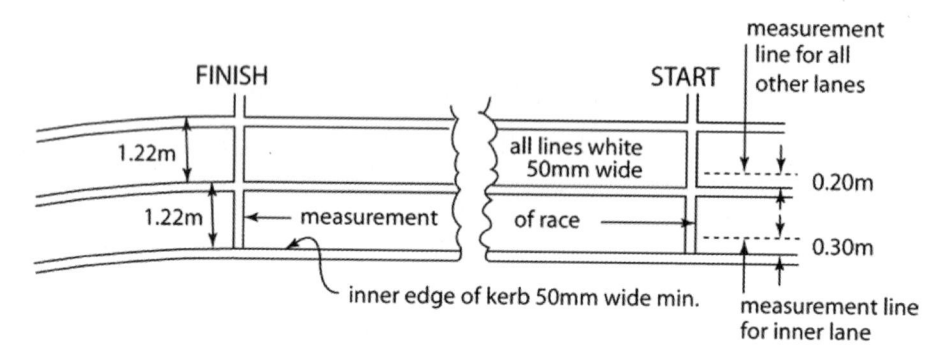

Figure TR14 – Track measurements (infield view)

14.3　　The distance of the race shall be measured from the edge of the start line farther from the finish to the edge of the finish line nearer to the start.

14.4　　In all races up to and including 400m, each athlete shall have a separate lane, with a width of 1.22m ± 0.01m, including the lane line on the right, marked by white lines 50mm in width. All lanes shall be of the same nominal width. The inner lane shall be measured as stated in Rule 14.2, but the remaining lanes shall be measured 0.20m from the outer edges of the lines.

Note: For all tracks constructed before 1 January 2004 for all such races, the lane may have a width of maximum 1.25m. However, when such a track is fully resurfaced, the lane width shall comply with this Rule.

14.5　　In competitions under paragraphs 1. (a), (b), (c) and 2. (a), (b) of the World Rankings Competition definition, the track should allow for eight lanes minimum.

14.6　　The lateral inclination of tracks towards the inside edge should not exceed 1:100 (1%) unless special circumstances exist which justify World Athletics providing an exemption, and the overall downward inclination in the running direction shall not exceed 1:1000 (0.1%) between any start and finish line.

14.2 应在跑道突沿外沿以外30厘米处测量跑道长度，如没有突沿的弯道（或从主跑道转向障碍水池段），则应在距内侧分道线外沿20厘米处进行测量。

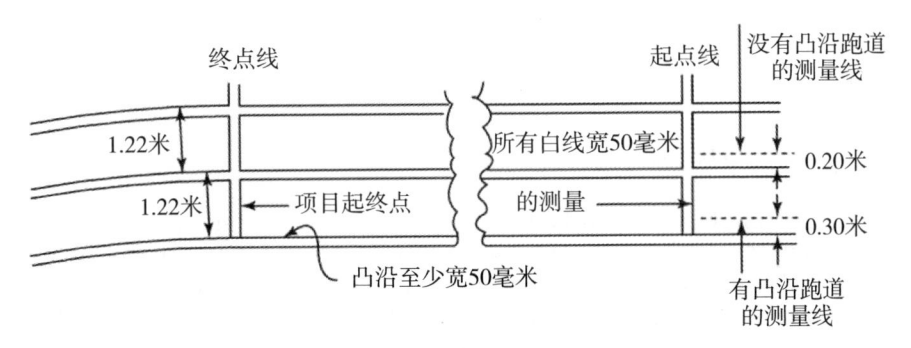

技术规则14条图　跑道测量（内场视角）

14.3 比赛距离为从起点线后沿（离终点线较远的边沿）量至终点线后沿（离起跑线较近的边沿）。

14.4 400米及400米以下各项径赛，每位运动员应占有一条分道，分道宽应为1.22米±0.01米，包括右侧的分道线，分道线为宽50毫米的白线。所有分道宽应相同。按技术规则14.2条的规定测量第1分道，其他分道应在其内侧分道线外沿以外0.20米处进行测量。

注：在2004年1月1日以前建设的场地，其分道宽最大可为1.25米。但是，当这样的场地重新铺设时，跑道宽须符合本规则要求。

14.5 举办世界排名比赛定义1.（a）（b）（c）和2.（a）（b）所述的比赛，径赛跑道至少要设8条分道。

14.6 跑道的横向倾斜度不得超过1∶100（1%），除由世界田联提供豁免证明的特殊情况外，并且在任何起点线与终点线之间在跑进方向上的向下倾斜度不得超过1∶1000（0.1%）。

14.7　　Full technical information on track construction, layout and marking is contained in the World Athletics Track and Field Facilities Manual. This Rule gives basic principles, which must be followed.

When any section of the kerb is temporarily removed this should be kept to a minimum, sufficient to enable the Field Events to function fairly and efficiently.

Colours to use for marking the track are indicated on the Track Marking Plan included in the World Athletics Track and Field Facilities Manual.

15.　Starting Blocks

15.1　　Starting blocks shall be used for all races up to and including 400m (including the first leg of the 4 × 200m, the Medley Relay and 4 × 400m) and shall not be used for any other race. When in position on the track, no part of the starting block shall overlap the start line or extend into another lane, with the exception that, provided there is no obstruction to any other athlete, the rear part of the frame may extend beyond the outer lane line.

15.2　　Starting blocks shall comply with the following general specifications:

15.2.1　　The starting blocks shall consist of two foot plates, against which the athlete's feet are pressed in the starting position and which shall be mounted on a rigid frame. They shall be entirely rigid in construction and shall give no unfair advantage to the athlete. The frame shall in no way obstruct the athlete's feet as they leave the blocks.

15.2.2　　The foot plates shall be sloped to suit the starting position of the athlete, and may be flat or slightly concave. The surface of the foot plates shall accommodate the spikes in the athlete's shoes, either by using slots or recesses in the face of the foot plate or by covering the surface of the foot plate with suitable material permitting the use of spiked shoes.

15.2.3　　The mounting of the foot plates on the frame may be adjustable, but it shall allow no movement during the actual start. In all cases, the foot plates shall be adjustable forward or backward in relation to each other. The adjustments shall be secured by firm clamps or a locking mechanism, which can be easily and quickly operated by the athlete.

14.7 《世界田联田径场地设施手册》中包含全部有关跑道结构、设计和标记的技术信息。本规则给出的基本原则必须遵守。

当突沿的任何部分临时被移开时,应尽可能减少移除的长度,以使田赛项目公平、有效地进行。

《世界田联田径场地设施手册》中指明了场地标记所使用的颜色。

15. 起跑器

15.1 400米及以下(包括4×200米、异程接力和4×400米接力的第一棒)各项径赛的起跑必须使用起跑器,其他项目不得使用起跑器。在跑道上安装起跑器时,起跑器的任何部分不得触及起跑线或延伸到其他分道,除非没有阻碍其他运动员,起跑器框架的后部可以延伸到外侧分道线以外。

15.2 起跑器应符合以下技术规范:

15.2.1 起跑器由两块抵脚板组成,供运动员起跑时两脚蹬踏,并被安装在刚性框架上。起跑器的结构必须十分坚固,不得给予运动员不公正的利益。刚性框架不得妨碍运动员双脚蹬离起跑器。

15.2.2 抵脚板须倾斜,以适应运动员的起跑姿势。板面可以是平面,也可稍呈凹形。板面上可有凹槽和沟穴,也可覆盖适宜材料,便于运动员使用钉鞋。

15.2.3 框架上抵脚板的角度可以进行调整,但在运动员起跑时不允许移动。无论何种情况,抵脚板的相对位置应可以前后调整。调整后,应使用坚固的夹具或锁扣进行固定,便于运动员简单、快速操作。

15.2.4 They shall be fixed to the track by a number of pins or spikes, arranged to cause the minimum possible damage to the track. The arrangement shall permit the starting blocks to be quickly and easily removed. The number, thickness and length of pins or spikes depend on the track construction. The anchorage shall permit no movement during the actual start.

15.2.5 When an athlete uses their own starting blocks, they shall comply with these Rules but otherwise may be of any design or construction, provided that they do not interfere with other athletes.

15.3 In competitions held under paragraphs 1. (a), (b), (c) and 2. (a), (b) of the World Rankings Competition definition and for any performances submitted for ratification as a World Record under Rule 32 of the Competition Rules, the starting blocks shall be linked to a World Athletics certified Start Information System. This system is strongly recommended for other competitions.

Note: In addition, an automatic recall system, within the Rules, may also be used.

15.4 In competitions held under paragraphs 1. and 2. (a), (b) of the World Rankings Competition definition, athletes shall use starting blocks provided by the Organisers of the competition. In other competitions on synthetic surfaced tracks the Organisers may insist that only starting blocks provided by them may be used.

This Rule should also be interpreted so that:

a. no part of the frame or footplates can overlap a start line;

b. the frame only (but not any part of the footplate) can extend into the outer lane provided there is no obstruction. This reflects the long standing practice of athletes at the start of races on a bend placing their blocks at an angle to run the most direct line after the start.

The use of lights, by deaf or hearing impaired athletes only, at the start of races is allowed and is not considered assistance. It should however be the obligation of the athlete or their team for the financing and supply of such equipment and its compatibility with the start system in use, unless at a particular meeting where there is an appointed technical partner who can provide it.

15.2.4 可用梢钉或钉子将起跑器固定在跑道上，把对跑道的损害降至最低限度。起跑器的安装应能使其快速固定和迅速移除。钉子的数量、粗细、长度应根据跑道的结构而定。应使起跑器在运动员起跑时不会移动。

15.2.5 运动员可使用自备起跑器，但必须符合本规则要求。起跑器的设计样式和结构不限，但不得妨碍其他运动员。

15.3 在举办世界排名比赛定义1.（a）（b）（c）和2.（a）（b）所述的比赛中，以及根据竞赛规则32条申请承认为世界纪录的成绩时，起跑器必须与世界田联批准的起跑信息系统连接。强烈建议在其他比赛中也使用这套系统。

注：此外，也可使用符合规则规定的自动召回系统。

15.4 在举办世界排名比赛定义1.和2.（a）（b）所述的比赛中，运动员必须使用比赛组织者提供的起跑器。在合成面层跑道上进行的其他比赛，组织者也可规定运动员必须使用主办方提供的起跑器。

这条规则应解释为：

a. 起跑器框架和抵脚板的任何部分都不能超过起跑线；

b. 在不干扰其他运动员的情况下，起跑器框架（但不包括抵脚板的任何部分）可以延伸至外侧跑道。这点主要体现在运动员长期以来在弯道起跑时将起跑器以一定角度放置，以便起跑后能够沿直线跑进。

对于聋人或有听力障碍的运动员，起跑可以使用灯，该方法不被认为是帮助。除非赛会指定技术供应商可以提供此种设备，否则运动员和其资助团队应负责提供此种设备，并且该设备应与现有起跑设备兼容。

16. The Start

16.1 The start of a race shall be denoted by a white line 50mm wide. In all races not run in lanes, the start line shall be curved, so that all the athletes start the same distance from the finish. Starting positions in events at all distances shall be numbered from left to right, facing the direction of running.

Note (i): In the case of events starting outside the stadium, the start line may be up to 0.30m in width and may be of any colour contrasting distinctively with the surface of the start area.

Note (ii): The 1500m start line, or any other curved start line, may be extended out from the outside lane to the extent that the same synthetic surface is available.

It is anticipated that, in order to efficiently complete the start procedures and for larger meetings to appropriately introduce the competitors in the race, the athletes, when assembled, should be standing and facing in the direction of the race.

16.2 In competitions under paragraphs 1. (a), (b), (c), (d) and 2. (d) of the World Rankings Competition definition, the commands of the Starter shall be given in English only. In all other competitions, the commands of the Starter shall be given in the local language, in English or in French.

16.2.1 In races up to and including 400m (including 4 × 200m, the Medley Relay as defined in Rule 24.1 of the Technical Rules and 4 × 400m), the commands (in English) shall be "On your marks" and "Set".

16.2.2 In races longer than 400m (except 4 × 200m, the Medley Relay and 4 × 400m), the command (in English) shall be "On your marks".

16.2.3 In any race when, under Rule 16.5 of the Technical Rules, the Starter is not satisfied that all is ready for the start to proceed after the athletes are on their marks or they otherwise abort the start, the command (in English) shall be "Stand up".

All races shall normally be started by the report of the Starter's gun held upwards.

16. 起跑

16.1 须用50毫米宽的白线标出起跑线。所有不分道跑的径赛项目，起跑线应为弧线，以使所有运动员从与终点相同的距离处开始起跑。所有项目的出发位置须面对跑进方向，从左至右编号。

注（i）：对于体育场外项目的起点，起跑线可以用0.30米宽的白线画出，也可用区别于起跑区域地面的任何颜色画出。

注（ii）：1500米项目的起跑线或其他弧形起跑线，可以向在相同面层的跑道延伸至外侧分道线以外。

为了有效地完成起跑程序，并且在大型比赛中方便介绍比赛运动员，当运动员在起跑线前集结时，应面向跑进方向站立。

16.2 在举办世界排名比赛定义1.（a）（b）（c）（d）和2.（d）所述的比赛中，发令员只能用英语发令。在所有其他比赛中，发令员应用当地语言、英语或法语发令。

  16.2.1 400米及400米以下的各个径赛项目（包括4×200米、技术规则24.1条定义的异程接力和4×400米接力），起跑时要使用"各就位"和"预备"的英文口令。

  16.2.2 400米以上的各个径赛项目（除了4×200米、异程接力和4×400米），起跑时要使用"各就位"的英文口令。

  16.2.3 任何径赛项目中，依据技术规则16.5条，发令员对运动员在各就位后准备起跑的过程不满意，或者由于其他原因而中止发令程序时，应用英语口令"Stand Up"。

通常所有径赛项目须由发令员用发令枪朝天鸣放，以枪声作为起跑信号。

The Starter must not initiate the start procedures before they are sure that the relevant timing team is ready as well as the Judges at the finish and in races up to and including 200m, the Wind Gauge Operator. The communication process between the start and the finish area and the timing team varies according to the level of the competition. In events organised under paragraphs 1. and 2. (a), (b) of the World Rankings Competition definition and many other high level meetings there is invariably a service company responsible for the electronic timing and the Start Information System. In this case, there will be technicians who are responsible for communication. In other competitions, a variety of communication systems are used – radios, phones, or by using flags or flashing lights.

16.3　　In races up to and including 400m (including the first leg of 4 × 200m, the Medley Relay and 4 × 400m), a crouch start and the use of starting blocks are compulsory. After the "On your marks" command, an athlete shall approach the start line, assume a position completely within their allocated lane and behind the start line. An athlete shall not touch either the start line or the ground in front of it with their hands or their feet when on their mark. Both hands and at least one knee shall be in contact with the ground and both feet in contact with the foot plates of the starting blocks. At the "Set" command, an athlete shall immediately rise to their final starting position retaining the contact of the hands with the ground and of the feet with the foot plates of the blocks. Once the Starter is satisfied that all athletes are steady in the "Set" position, the gun shall be fired.

In all races using a crouch start, as soon as they are steady in their blocks, the Starter shall raise their arm in which they hold the gun, then they shall say "Set". They shall wait then for all the athletes to be steady and shall then fire the gun.

The Starter must not raise their arm too early, especially when manual Timekeepers are being used. They are advised to raise their arm only when they feel they are about to give the command "Set".

There is no rule that enables to determine the time that elapses between the commands "On your marks" and "Set" on one hand, and on the other hand, between the command "Set" and the gun shot. The Starter shall let the athletes go once they are all motionless in the correct starting position. Which means that they may have, for certain starts, to fire the gun quite quickly, but on the other hand, they may also have to wait longer in order to make sure that they are all steady in their starting position.

发令员须确认相关计时团队和终点裁判员，200米及以下项目包括风速仪操作员，准备就位后方可启动发令程序。起点与终点以及计时团队的通信方式根据不同级别的比赛而有所不同。在世界排名比赛定义1.和2.（a）（b）所述的比赛及其他高水平赛事中，有专门的服务公司负责电子计时和起跑信息系统。在这种情况下，将有专门的技术人员负责通信。在其他比赛中，可以使用很多种通信方式，如对讲机、电话、旗示或闪烁的灯光等。

16.3 400米及400米以下的各径赛项目（包括4×200米、异程接力和4×400米接力的第一棒），运动员须使用起跑器进行蹲踞式起跑。在"各就位"口令之后，运动员须走向起跑线，完全在自己的分道内和起跑线后做好准备姿势。"各就位"后，运动员不应用手或脚触及起跑线或起跑线前的地面。双手和至少一个膝盖应触地，双脚应接触起跑器。发出"预备"口令时，运动员应立即抬高身体做好最后的起跑姿势，此时运动员的双手仍须与地面接触，双脚不离开抵脚板。一旦发令员认为所有运动员的"预备"姿势稳定后，即可鸣枪。

在所有采用蹲踞式起跑的比赛中，当运动员在起跑器上稳定后，发令员应举起持枪手，然后发出"预备"口令。待全部运动员停稳后鸣枪起跑。

发令员不应过早举起手臂，特别是在采用手计时的情况下。建议，仅当发令员将要发出"预备"口令时方可举起持枪手。

规则中没有规定"各就位"与"预备"口令的间隔时间，也没有规定"预备"和鸣枪的间隔时间。发令员应当在所有运动员以正确的起跑姿势准备并且"没有动作"时发令让运动员起跑出发。这意味着，在某些发令的时候，发令员可能需要很快地开枪，但在另外一些情况下，发令员须等待更长的时间，以确保运动员已处于稳定的起跑姿势。

16.4　　In races longer than 400m (except 4 × 200m, the Medley Relay and 4 × 400m), all starts shall be made from a standing position. After the "On your marks" command, an athlete shall approach the start line and assume a starting position behind the start line (completely within their allocated lane in races started in lanes). An athlete shall not touch any part of the ground with their hand or hands and/or the start line or the ground in front of it with their feet when on their mark. Once the Starter is satisfied that all athletes are steady in the correct starting position, the gun shall be fired.

16.5　　On the command "On your marks" or "Set", as the case may be, all athletes shall, at once and without delay, assume their full and final starting position. If, for any reason, the Starter is not satisfied that all is ready for the start to proceed after the athletes are on their marks, they shall order all athletes to withdraw from their marks and the Starter's Assistants shall assemble them again (see also Rule 23 of the Competition Rules).

Where an athlete in the judgement of the Starter,

16.5.1　　after the command "On your marks" or "Set", and before the report of the gun, causes the start to be aborted, for instance by raising a hand and/or standing or sitting up in the case of a crouch start, without a valid reason, (such reason to be evaluated by the relevant Referee); or

16.5.2　　fails to comply with the commands "On your marks" or "Set" as appropriate, or does not place themselves in their final starting position at once and without delay; or

16.5.3　　after the command "On your marks" or "Set" disturbs (an)other athlete(s) in the race through sound, movement or otherwise, resulting in such athlete(s) committing what would otherwise be a false start,

the Starter shall abort the start.

The Referee may warn the athlete for improper conduct (disqualify in case of a second infringement of the Rule during the same competition), according to Rules 7.1 and 7.3 of the Technical Rules. A green card shall not be shown. However, when an extraneous reason was considered to be the cause for aborting the start, or the Referee does not agree with the Starter's decision, a green card shall be shown to all the athletes to indicate that a false start was not committed by any athlete.

16.4 400米以上的径赛项目（除了4×200米、异程接力和4×400米），所有起跑均应采用站立姿势。在"各就位"口令后，运动员应走向起跑线，并在起跑线后做好起跑姿势（在分道起跑项目比赛中，应完全在各自的分道内）。"各就位"口令后，运动员不应用手接触地面，且不应用脚触及起跑线或起跑线前的地面。一旦发令员认为所有运动员的起跑姿势正确和稳定后，即可鸣枪。

16.5 在"各就位"或"预备"口令发出后，所有运动员均应立即做好最后的起跑姿势，不得延误。不管任何原因，如果发令员对运动员"各就位"后准备起跑的过程不满意，他应该命令所有的运动员从起跑线撤回，助理发令员将重新召集运动员（另见竞赛规则23条）。

根据发令员的判断，如果运动员有下列行为，发令员应中止起跑：

16.5.1 当运动员听到"各就位"或"预备"口令之后，在发令鸣枪发出信号之前，导致起跑中止：例如，在蹲踞式起跑中举手和（或）站立、坐下，无正当理由（由相关裁判长评估）；或

16.5.2 没有执行"各就位"或"预备"口令，或未能在有效的时间内做好最后的起跑姿势；或

16.5.3 发令员发出"各就位"或"预备"口令后，运动员用声音、动作或其他方式干扰比赛中的其他运动员（们），导致该运动员（们）抢跑。

发令员必须中止该次起跑。

裁判长将根据技术规则7.1条和7.3条，以不正当行为为理由对该运动员进行警告（同一比赛中出现第二次犯规即被取消比赛资格）。这种情况不会出示绿卡。但是，考虑其他外部原因导致起跑中止，或者裁判长不同意发令员的决定时，应向所有运动员出示绿卡，表示本次起跑犯规不是由运动员引起的。

The division of the start rules into disciplinary matters (under Rule 16.5 of the Technical Rules) and false starts (Rules 16.7 and 16.8 of the Technical Rules) ensures that the whole field was not penalised for the actions of a single athlete. It is important, in order to maintain the integrity of the intention of this division, that Starters and Referees are as diligent in the application of Rule 16.5 of the Technical Rules as in detecting false starts.

Such conduct, whether wilful or unintentional perhaps through nervousness, should cause Rule 16.5 of the Technical Rules to be applied although where the Starter is of the view that it was unintentional, the application of Rule 16.2.3 of the Technical Rules only may be appropriate.

Conversely, there will be instances in which an athlete is entitled to request a delay of the start for legitimate reasons. It is therefore vital that the Start Referee (in particular) pays attention to the environment and conditions surrounding the start, especially in relation to factors of which the Starter may not be aware because they are focussing on preparing themselves for the start and/or wearing headphones.

In all such cases, the Starter and Referee must act reasonably and efficiently and clearly indicate their decisions. If appropriate, the reasons for the decisions can be announced to the athletes in the race and, if possible or desirable, also to the announcers, television team etc. through the communication network.

A green card shall not be shown in any case when a yellow or red card has been issued.

False Start

16.6　When a World Athletics certified Start Information System is in use, the Starter and/or an assigned Recaller shall wear headphones in order to clearly hear the acoustic signal emitted when the System indicates a possible false start (i.e. when the reaction time is less than 0.100 second). As soon as the Starter and/or assigned Recaller hears the acoustic signal, and if the gun was fired, there shall be a recall and the Starter shall immediately examine the reaction times and other available information from the Start Information System in order to confirm which, if any, athlete(s) is/are responsible for the recall.

Note: When a World Athletics certified Start Information System is in operation, the evidence of this equipment shall be used as a resource by the relevant officials to assist in making a correct decision.

将起跑规则分为纪律部分（技术规则16.5条）和抢跑部分（技术规则16.7条和16.8条），以确保不因为1名运动员的行为而处罚所有运动员。很重要的一点是，为了保持这些规则的连续性和原意，发令员和裁判长在执行技术规则16.5条时应同发现抢跑犯规一样。

在此种情况下，不管是故意的行为还是由于紧张造成的非故意行为，都应该执行技术规则16.5条，除非发令员认为确实是非故意行为，可以执行技术规则16.2.3条。

反之，还有些情况下，运动员因正当理由有权要求推迟发令。起点裁判长应注意外部环境和起跑区周围的情况，特别是发令员关注起跑过程或者佩戴监控耳机而无法注意到的一些因素。

在以上情况下，发令员和裁判长必须作出合理、有效的反应，并且清楚地作出判决。如果可行，判决的原因应当场向比赛运动员宣布，在可能的情况下，该原因也应通过通信系统通报给播音员、电视制作团队等。

无论何种情况，当出示黄牌或红牌后，不得出示绿牌。

起跑犯规

16.6　当使用世界田联认证的起跑信息系统时，发令员和（或）指定的召回员应头戴耳机，以便清晰地听见监测系统发出的犯规提示声音信号（当反应时小于0.100秒）。发令枪响后，当发令员和（或）指定的召回员听到声音信号，应召回本次参赛运动员，并且发令员应立即检查起跑信息系统上的反应时和其他相关信息，以便确认对本次召回负责的运动员。

注：当使用世界田联认证的起跑信息系统时，该设备所提供的证据，应被用作能协助相关裁判员作出正确决定的一种信息来源。

16.7　　An athlete, after assuming a full and final starting position, shall not commence their start until after receiving the report of the gun. If, in the judgement of the Starter (including under Rule 22.6 of the Competition Rules), they do so any earlier, it shall be a false start. The commencement of the start is defined:

16.7.1　　in the case of a crouch start, as any motion by an athlete that includes or results in one or both feet losing contact with the foot plate(s) of the starting blocks or one or both hands losing contact with the ground; and

16.7.2　　In the case of a standing start, as any motion that results in one or both feet losing contact with the ground.

If the Starter determines that prior to receiving the report of the gun an athlete initiated a movement that was not stopped and continued into the commencement of their start, it shall also be a false start.

Note (i): Any other motion by an athlete shall not be considered to be the commencement of their start. Such instances may, if applicable, be subject to a disciplinary warning or disqualification.

Note (ii): As athletes starting races in a standing position are more prone to over-balance, if such a movement is considered to be accidental, the start should be regarded as "unsteady". If an athlete is pushed or jostled over the line before the start, they should not be penalised. Any athlete causing such interference may be subject to a disciplinary warning or disqualification.

Generally, no false start should be charged if the athlete has not lost contact with the ground or foot plates. For example, if an athlete moves their hips up, but then moves them down without their hands or feet losing contact with the ground or foot plates at any time, it should not result in a false start. It may be a reason to warn (or disqualify if there has been a previous warning) the athlete for improper conduct under Rule 16.5 of the Technical Rules.

However, in cases of a "rolling start" where the Starter (or Recaller) is of the opinion that an athlete has effectively anticipated the start through some continuous movement even if they did not move their hands or feet before the gun sounded, the race should be recalled. This can be done by a Starter or Recaller but it will be the Starter who is in the best situation to judge such a case as only they will know the position of their finger on the gun trigger when the athlete began their movement. In these cases where the Starter is sure that the athlete's movement began before the report of the gun, a false start should be awarded.

16.7 运动员在做好最后起跑姿势之后，只能在接收到发令枪发出的信号之后开始起跑。如果发令员判定（包括根据竞赛规则22.6条）运动员在发令枪发出信号之前起跑，应判为起跑犯规。起跑的开始定义为：

16.7.1 采用蹲踞式起跑时，运动员的任何动作导致单脚或双脚离开起跑器踏板，或单手或双手离开地面；和

16.7.2 采用站立式起跑时，运动员的任何动作导致单脚或双脚没有接触地面。

如果发令员判定运动员在鸣枪之前，已经开始不停地有动作并且持续到开始起跑，将视为起跑犯规。

注（ⅰ）：运动员的任何其他动作，不应视为其起跑的开始。如有这种情况，运动员可被纪律警告或取消比赛资格。

注（ⅱ）：当运动员采用站立式起跑即将失去平衡，如果这种情况被认为是偶然的，起跑应视为"不稳定"。在起跑前，如果运动员在起跑线上被推搡或挤，他可不被判罚。任何导致这种犯规的运动员可被纪律警告或取消比赛资格。

一般情况下，如果运动员没有与地面或者抵脚板失去接触，不应判抢跑。例如，如果运动员将臀部抬起，但是又接着落下，在此过程中他的手或脚没有失去与地面或者与抵脚板的接触，此情况不应判抢跑。这种情况可以根据技术规则16.5条，以不正当行为给予运动员警告（如果之前已经有过警告，则直接取消比赛资格）。

但是，在运动员"动态起跑"的情况下，如果发令员或者召回员认为，运动员使用连贯动作故意压枪起跑，即使他在响枪前没有移动他的手或者脚，此次起跑也应被召回。发令员或召回员都可以鸣枪召回，但只有发令员才能进行判罚，因为只有他知道他的手指扣发扳机的时机，以判断运动员是否压枪。在此种情况下，当发令员确认运动员的动作是在发令枪响前做出的，应该判抢跑。

In accordance with Note (ii) Starters and Referees should avoid being over-zealous in the application of Rule 16.7 of the Technical Rules to those events started from a standing position. Such instances are rare and usually occur unintentionally as it is easier to overbalance from a two-point start. It is not intended that same should be unduly penalised.

If such a movement was considered to be accidental, Starters and Referees are encouraged to first consider calling the start "unsteady" and proceed according to Rule 16.2.3 of the Technical Rules. However, repeat practices during the same event may entitle the Starter and/or Referee to consider applying either the false start or disciplinary procedures, as might best be applicable in the situation.

16.8 Except in Combined Events, any athlete responsible for a false start shall be disqualified by the Starter.

For Combined Events, see Rule 39.8.3 of the Technical Rules.

Note: In practice, when one or more athletes make a false start, others are inclined to follow and, strictly speaking, any athlete who does so has also made a false start. The Starter should warn or disqualify only such athlete or athletes who, in their opinion, were responsible for the false start. This may result in more than one athlete being warned or disqualified. If the recalled or aborted start is not due to any athlete, no warnings shall be given and a green card shall be shown to all the athletes.

16.9 In case of a false start, the Starter's Assistants shall proceed as follows:

Except in Combined Events, the athlete(s) responsible for the false start shall be disqualified and a red and black (diagonally halved) card shall be raised in front of them.

In Combined Events, in case of a first false start, the athlete(s) responsible for the false start shall be warned with a yellow and black (diagonally halved) card raised in front of them. At the same time, all the other athletes taking part in the race shall be warned with the yellow and black card raised in front of them by one or several Starter's Assistants in order to notify them that anyone committing further false starts will be disqualified. In case of further false starts, the athlete(s) responsible for the false start shall be disqualified and the red and black card shall be raised in front of them.

根据本条规则注（ⅱ），发令员和裁判长应该避免在采用站立式起跑的比赛中过度使用技术规则16.7条。这种情况很少发生，通常情况是由于采用两点支撑而造成的非故意失去平衡。在这种情况下通常不应判罚为犯规。

如果这种情况被认为是意外，建议发令员和裁判长首先判断为起跑"不稳定"，然后根据技术规则16.2.3条重新组织发令。然而，在同一场比赛中重复出现的违规行为可能会使发令员和/或裁判长考虑适用抢跑或纪律处分程序的相关规则，以适用当时的情况。

16.8　除全能项目外，任何对起跑犯规负有责任的运动员将被发令员取消该项目的比赛资格。

全能项目比赛，见技术规则39.8.3条。

注：实践中，当1名或多名运动员起跑犯规时，其他的运动员容易跟随，严格来讲，跟随者也属于起跑犯规。发令员可仅警告他认为对起跑犯规负有责任的1名或多名运动员。因此，受警告或被取消比赛资格的运动员可能不止1名。如果召回或者中止发令并非由任何运动员引起，则不应对运动员提出警告，并且要向所有运动员出示绿牌。

16.9　出现起跑犯规的情况后，助理发令员须按下述程序执行：

除全能比赛外，须取消对起跑犯规负有责任的1名或多名运动员的比赛资格，并在该运动员面前出示红黑牌（用对角线分为红黑两半）。

在全能比赛中，对第一次起跑犯规负有责任的1名或多名运动员须给予警告，并在该运动员面前出示黄黑牌（用对角线分为黄黑两半）。同时，由1名或多名助理发令员向所有该组比赛的其他运动员出示黄黑牌以示警告，并告知他们如果任何运动员再次起跑犯规将被取消比赛资格。如果再次发生起跑犯规，对起跑犯规负有责任的1名或多名运动员将被取消比赛资格，并在该运动员面前举起红黑牌。

If lane markers that provide for it are being used, then whenever a card is shown to the athlete(s) responsible for the false start, the corresponding indication should be shown on the lane marker(s).

It is recommended that the size of the diagonally halved cards be A5 and that they be doubled sided. Note that the corresponding indication on the lane marker(s) may remain yellow and red as previously, in order to avoid unnecessary expense in modifying existing equipment.

16.10　The Starter or any Recaller, who is of the opinion that the start was not a fair one, shall recall the athletes by firing a gun or activating a suitable audible signal.

The reference to a fair start does not relate solely to cases of a false start. This rule should also be interpreted as applying to other situations such as blocks slipping, a foreign object interfering with one or more athletes during a start etc.

17. The Race

Obstruction

17.1　If an athlete is jostled or obstructed during an event so as to impede their progress, then:

17.1.1　if the jostling or obstruction is considered unintentional or is caused otherwise than by an athlete, the Referee may, if they are of the opinion that an athlete (or their team) was seriously affected, in accordance with Rule 18.7 of the Competition Rules or Rule 8.4 of the Technical Rules, order that the race (for one, some or all of the athletes) be re-held or allow the affected athlete (or team) to compete in a subsequent round of the event;

17.1.2　if another athlete is found by the Referee to be responsible for the jostling or obstruction, such athlete (or their team) shall be liable to disqualification from that event. The Referee may, if they are of the opinion that an athlete (or their team) was seriously affected, in accordance with Rule 18.7 of the Competition Rules or Rule 8.4 of the Technical Rules, order that the race (for one, some or all of the athletes) be re-held excluding any disqualified athlete (or team) or allow any affected athlete (or team) (other than any disqualified athlete or team) to compete in a subsequent round of the event.

每当在对对起跑犯规负有责任的1名或多名运动员高举警告牌后，应在运动员各自分道的道次墩上做出相应的标记。

建议，红黑牌的尺寸为A5大小，并且为双面。为了避免改造现有设备而造成不必要的花费，道次墩上的指示标志可以沿用原有黄与红标志的设计。

16.10　发令员或任一召回员认为本次起跑不公允，须以鸣枪或启动可听得到的声音信号召回运动员。

关于起跑不公允的规则不仅限于起跑犯规，这些规则还应用在其他情况下。例如，起跑器打滑以及1名或多名运动员在起跑过程中受到外来物体干扰等。

17.　径赛

阻挡

17.1　如果运动员在比赛中被挤撞或阻挡，从而影响其行进时：

  17.1.1　如果挤撞或阻挡被认为是运动员非故意的行为，或者由其他方式引起的，裁判长认为运动员（或其所属队）因此受到严重的影响，根据竞赛规则18.7条或者技术规则8.4条，可命令比赛（1名、多名或所有运动员）重赛，或者允许受影响的运动员（或队）参加该项目下一赛次的比赛。

  17.1.2　如果裁判长发现其他运动员应该为挤撞或阻挡负责，该运动员（或其所属队）应被取消该项目的比赛资格。裁判长认为运动员（或其所属队）因此受到严重影响，根据竞赛规则18.7条或技术规则8.4条可以命令除被取消比赛资格外的运动员（1名、多名或所有运动员）重赛，或允许受到严重影响的运动员（或队）参加该项目下一赛次的比赛。

Note: In cases considered serious enough, Rules 7.1 and 7.3 of the Technical Rules may also be applied.

In both cases of Rules 17.1.1 and 17.1.2 of the Technical Rules, such athlete (or team) should normally have completed the event with bona fide effort.

Jostling should be understood as physical contact on one or more occasions with another athlete or athletes that results in an unfair advantage or causes injury or harm to them or, consequently, to another athlete or athletes.

17.2　In all races:

  17.2.1　including at least one bend, the direction of the race shall be left-hand inside. The lanes shall be numbered with the left-hand inside lane numbered 1;

  17.2.2　run entirely on the straight, the direction of the race may be either left-hand or right-hand inside, according to the available conditions;

  17.2.3　run in lanes (or any part of a race run in lanes), each athlete shall keep within their allocated lane from start to finish and, when running on a bend, shall not step or run on or inside the left-hand lane line or in the case of the inside lane, the kerb or line marking the border of the inside of the track;

  17.2.4　not run in lanes (or any part of a race not run in lanes), an athlete running on a bend, on the outer half of the track as per Rule 17.5.2 of the Technical Rules, or on any curved part of the diversion from the track for the steeplechase water jump, shall not step or run on or inside the kerb or line marking the applicable border (of the inside of the track, of the outer half of the track, or of any curved part of the diversion from the track for the steeplechase water jump).

Lane Infringement

17.3　In all races, if the Referee is satisfied, on the report of a Judge or Umpire or otherwise, that an athlete has infringed Rule 17.2.3 or 17.2.4 of the Technical Rules, they or in the case of a relay race, their team shall be disqualified unless

注：在认为是足够严重的情况下，也可应用技术规则7.1条和7.3条。

在上述技术规则17.1.1条和17.1.2条的两种情况下，相关运动员（或队）通常应真诚努力地完成该项目的比赛。

推挤应理解为与其他1名或多名运动员发生1次或多次身体接触，从而导致不公平的优势或者因此造成其他1名或多名运动员受伤或给其带来伤害。

17.2　在所有比赛中：

  17.2.1　在包括至少一个弯道的径赛项目中，比赛方向应为左手边靠内场。分道编号要以左边最内侧分道为第1分道。

  17.2.2　根据可用的条件，完全在直道上跑，比赛方向可为左手边或右手靠内场；

  17.2.3　分道跑（或部分分道跑比赛）项目，运动员要自始至终保持在分配的分道内，且在弯道跑时不得踏上或跑进左侧分道线内侧，或者在内侧分道跑时不得踏上、跑进突沿或跑道内侧的边界标志线；

  17.2.4　不分道跑项目（或部分不分道跑项目），当运动员在弯道上、根据技术规则17.5.2条规定的外侧一半跑道上，或在障碍跑道与水池间变更的弧道上跑进时，不得踏上或跑入突沿，或实际分道线上，或边界标志线上（跑道内侧、外侧的一半跑道，或者障碍赛中水池变更段的弧段的任何部分）。

分道跑犯规

17.3　在所有比赛中，如果裁判长根据裁判员、检查裁判员或其他关于某运动员违反技术规则17.2.3条或17.2.4条的情况，则该运动员或涉及接力项目的该接力队须被取消该项目的比赛资格。除非运动员：

17.3.1　is pushed or forced by another person or object to step or run outside their lane or on or inside the kerb or line marking the applicable border; or

17.3.2　steps or runs outside their lane in the straight, any straight part of the diversion from the track for the steeplechase water jump or outside the outer line of their lane on the bend; or

17.3.3　in all races run in lanes (or any part of races run in lanes), touches once the line on their left, or the kerb or line marking the border of the inside of the track on a bend; or

17.3.4　in all races not run in lanes (or any part of races not run in lanes), steps once on or completely over the kerb or line marking the applicable border (as defined in Rule 17.2.4 of the Technical Rules) on a bend;

and no other athlete being jostled or obstructed so as to impede the other athlete's progress (see Rule 17.1 of the Technical Rules) and no material advantage is gained (see Rule 17.4 of the Technical Rules).

In races with multiple rounds, any action defined in Rules 17.3.3 or 17.3.4 of the Technical Rules may be made only once during all rounds of an event by a particular athlete without the disqualification of that athlete. A second action will result in the disqualification of that athlete whether it was made in the same round or in another round of the same event.

In the case of Relay Races, any second action (as described in this Rule 17.3.3 and 17.3.4 of the Technical Rules) by an athlete who is a member of a team, regardless of whether committed by the same or different athletes, will result in the disqualification of the team whether it happens in the same round or in another round of the same event.

For the ratification of records, see Rule 31.14.4 of the Competition Rules.

17.4　If material advantage is gained by an athlete by improving their position by any means including under the exceptions in Rule 17.3 of the Technical Rules or by removing themselves from a "boxed" position in the race by having stepped or run inside the inside edge of the track at any point, the athlete (or team) shall be disqualified.

17.3.1 被他人推、挤而被迫踏或跑出自己的分道，或踏在实际分道线上或突沿线内侧；或

17.3.2 在直道上踏在分道线上或跑出自己的分道，在障碍水池变更跑道的直道上的任何部分踏在分道线上或跑出分道，或者在弯道上踏在或跑出自己分道的外侧分道线；或

17.3.3 在所有分道跑（或部分分道跑）项目的比赛中，在弯道上1次触及左侧分道线、突沿或跑道内侧的边界标记线；或

17.3.4 在所有不分道跑（或部分不分道跑）项目的比赛中，在弯道上一次踏上或跨越突沿、边界标志线（如技术规则17.2.4条规定的）；

并且没有任何运动员被挤撞或阻挡而妨碍其他运动员的行进（见技术规则17.1条）和没有获得实际利益（见技术规则17.4条）。

进行多个赛次的比赛时，在一个项目的所有赛次中某一运动员可有一次违反技术规则17.3.3条或17.3.4条规定的行为而不被取消该项目比赛资格的机会。无论该运动员在同一项目的同一赛次还是不同赛次出现第二次行为，都将被取消比赛资格。

在接力比赛中，无论是同一名运动员还是不同运动员，作为接力队成员的任何再一次的行为（如技术规则17.3.3条和17.3.4条所述），无论发生在相同赛次还是同一项目的其他赛次中，都将导致该接力队被取消比赛资格。

有关申报纪录，见竞赛规则31.14.4条。

17.4 如果运动员通过任何方式提高名次（包括技术规则17.3条例外的情况）或使自己在比赛中为摆脱"被包夹"而踏上或跑入跑道内沿以内，而获得实际利益，运动员（或运动队）将被取消比赛资格。

Rule 17.4 specifically outlaws the practice of an athlete seeking to improve their position in races by moving onto the inside of the track (whether intentionally or after being pushed or jostled there by another athlete) to get out of a boxed position by running on the inside until clear. Whilst normally running on the inside of lane 1 in the straight (as distinct from doing so on the bend) would not lead to mandatory disqualification, the Referee has the power to disqualify in their discretion if this occurs and the athlete is advantaged even if the initial reason for being there was the result of being pushed or jostled. In such cases the athlete should take immediate steps to return to the track without seeking or gaining any advantage.

Where a race is started in lanes and then continues not using separate lanes, Rules 17.2 and 17.3 of the Technical Rules apply accordingly to each such part of the race. Therefore, only one infringement according to Rules 17.3.3 or 17.3.4 is allowed. A second infringement in the same race will result in disqualification. When determining whether the exception in 17.3.3 applies in cases where some part of the shoe/foot is also to the left of the line, there is a requirement for at least some part of the outline of athlete's shoe/foot to be touching the line, i.e. some contact with the line (depicted by the outline of the relevant part of the shoe or foot) is required for this exception to apply. If this is not the case, then the exception does not apply.

All lane infringements should be tracked in the competition data systems and shown in the start lists and results (see Rule 25.4 of the Competition Rules for the symbol to be used).

The carry-forward rule only applies to the same event and not to a race of a different distance.

In Combined Events, an athlete should only be disqualified for more than one infringement, if it occurs during the same race. There is no carry-forward of the infringement to subsequent races within that Combined Event.

17.5 In competitions held under paragraphs 1. and 2. of the World Rankings Competition definition and where suitable in other competitions:

技术规则17.4条特别指出，运动员为了摆脱被包夹位置提高名次试图在跑道内侧内跑进，直至摆脱被包夹位置（不管是否是故意还是被其他运动员推挤）。通常当运动员在直道1道以内跑进（区别于在弯道上发生同样的行为），不一定会被取消比赛资格。如果这种情况发生，即使运动员是由于被推挤至此位置，只要运动员从中获利，裁判长有权按照自己的判断决定是否取消运动员的比赛资格。在此种情况下，运动员应立即回到跑道内，不能试图得到任何利益。

当部分分道跑项目比赛时，技术规则17.2条和17.3条分别适用于比赛的每个部分。因此，根据技术规则17.3.3条或17.3.4条的违规只允许一次。在同一场比赛中第二次犯规将被取消比赛资格。当运动员的鞋或脚部分超过左侧分道线，需至少满足运动员的鞋或脚的轮廓部分触及分道线，即与分道线有接触（按鞋或脚相关部分的轮廓描绘），要执行技术规则17.3.3条。如果不是这种情况，则不执行此规则。

所有违反分道规则的犯规情况都要在赛事数据系统中可追踪查询，并需要显示在检录单和成绩单上（标准缩写即符号的使用见竞赛规则25.4条）。

这种"累计式"规则仅仅适用于同一个项目，不能适用于不同距离的比赛项目。

在全能项目比赛中，运动员在同一个单项中多于1次的违规将被取消比赛资格。在全能项目中，后续项目比赛不适用"累计式"规则。

17.5　举办世界排名比赛定义1条和2条所述的比赛，以及其他适宜的比赛时：

17.5.1　　the 800m event shall be run in lanes as far as the nearer edge of the breakline where athletes may leave their respective lanes. The breakline shall be an arced line marked after the first bend, 50mm wide, across all lanes other than lane 1. To assist athletes identify the breakline, small cones, prisms or other suitable markers, preferably of different colour from the breakline and the lane lines, shall be placed on the lane lines immediately before the intersection of the lane lines and the breakline.

Note: In competitions under paragraphs 1. (e) and 2. (e) of the World Rankings Competition definition, the participating teams may agree not to use lanes.

17.5.2　　when there are more than 12 athletes in a race over 1000m, 2000m, 3000m, (optionally, 3000m Steeplechase with inside water jump), 5000m or 10,000m, they may be divided into two groups with one group of approximately two thirds of the athletes on the regular arced start line and the other group on a separate arced start line marked across the outer half of the track. The other group shall run as far as the end of the first bend of the race on the outer half of the track, which shall be marked by cones, flags or temporary kerbing as described in Rule 14.1 of the Technical Rules.

The separate arced start line shall be positioned in such a way that all the athletes shall run the same distance.

The breakline for 800m indicates where the athletes in the outer group in 2000m and 10,000m may join the athletes using regular start.

For group starts in 1000m, 3000m, (optionally 3000m Steeplechase with inside water jump) and 5000m, the track shall be marked at the beginning of the finish straight to indicate where athletes starting in the outer group may join the athletes using the regular start. This mark(breakpoint) shall be a 50mm × 50mm mark on the line between lanes 4 and 5 (lanes 3 and 4 in a six-lane track) immediately before which a cone or flag is placed until the two groups converge.

17.5.1 在800米跑比赛中，运动员应在自己的分道内跑完第一个弯道末端，越过抢道线后沿（距起跑线较近的边沿）之后，即可离开各自的分道。抢道线应为一条弧线，标记在第一个弯道末端，宽50毫米，横跨除了第1分道的所有跑道。为了帮助运动员识别抢道线，可在各分道线与抢道线交界处之前的分道线上放置锥形物、棱柱体或其他类似标志物，这些标志物最好与抢道线和分道线的颜色不同。

注：在举办世界排名比赛定义1.（e）和2.（e）所述的比赛中，参赛队可商定采用不分道跑。

17.5.2 在1000米、2000米、3000米、（可选水池在内场的3000米障碍）、5000米或10000米项目的比赛中，当运动员人数超过12人时，可将他们分成两组。大约2/3的运动员为一组，在常规弧形起跑线处起跑，其余运动员为外侧组，在另一条画在跑道外侧一半上的弧形起跑线处同时起跑。外侧组运动员应沿着外侧一半跑道跑至第一弯道末端，该段跑道将用技术规则14.1条所描述的锥形物、旗子或临时突沿标出。

设置第二弧形起跑线，须使所有运动员跑进的距离相等。

2000米和10000米外侧组的运动员在越过800米跑抢道线后即可加入常规起跑组的运动员中。

在1000米、3000米、（可选水池在内场的3000米障碍）和5000米分组起跑时，则应在进入终点直段道处标明外侧组运动员可以加入常规起跑组抢道线的运动员之中。该（抢道点）标记大小是50毫米×50毫米，须位于第4和第5分道（如有6条分道，则在第3和第4分道）间的分道线上，在该标记之前放置一个锥形物或小旗，直到两组合并。

If an athlete does not follow this Rule they, or in the case of a relay their team, shall be disqualified.

The markers used on the breakline for the 800m and applicable relays should be 50mm × 50mm and no more than 0.15m high.

For clarity, when complying with Rule 25.4 of the Competition Rules when stating the Rule under which an athlete is disqualified:

a. if an athlete steps on or inside the line, then state Rule 17.2.3 or 17.2.4 of the Technical Rules, as appropriate,

b. if an athlete leaves the assigned lane or the outer half of the track to the inside before the breakline or the breakpoint, then state Rule 17.5 of the Technical Rules.

Leaving the Track

17.6   An athlete, after voluntarily leaving the track, except in compliance with Rule 24.6 of the Technical Rules, shall not be allowed to continue in the race and shall be recorded as not finishing the event. Should the athlete attempt to re-enter the race, they shall be disqualified by the Referee.

Check–Marks

17.7   Except as stated in Rule 24.4 of the Technical Rules, when all or the first portion of a Relay Race is being run in lanes, athletes may not make check-marks or place objects on or alongside the running track for their assistance. The Umpires shall direct the relevant athlete to adapt or remove any marks or objects not complying with this Rule. If they do not, the Umpires shall remove them.

Note: Serious cases may further be dealt with under Rules 7.1 and 7.3 of the Technical Rules.

Wind Measurement

17.8   All wind gauge equipment shall be manufactured and calibrated according to international standards. The accuracy of the measuring equipment used in the competition shall have been verified by an appropriate organisation accredited by the national measurement authority.

如果运动员不遵守此规则，他或他所在的接力队将被取消比赛资格。

在800米和相应的接力项目比赛中，于抢道线摆放的标记物，应为宽50毫米×50毫米，高度不超过0.15米。

需明确指出，当遵守竞赛规则25.4条规定时，以下情况运动员将被取消比赛资格：

a. 如果运动员踏上或跑进分道线内侧，视情况而定应适用技术规则17.2.3条或17.2.4条，

b. 如果运动员在抢道线或抢道点前离开指定的分道或外侧一半的跑道切入内侧，应适用技术规则17.5条。

离开跑道

17.6　运动员自动离开跑道后将不得继续参加该项目比赛，技术规则24.6条规定的情形除外，并被记录为中途退出比赛（DNF）。如果该运动员试图重新进入比赛，裁判长应取消其比赛资格。

标记

17.7　除技术规则24.4条所述情形外，在全部或第一棒为分道跑的接力项目中，运动员不可在跑道上或跑道沿线做标记或放置对其有帮助的标志物。检查裁判员应指导相关运动员遵守规则或者移除不符合规则的任何标记或标志物。如果运动员不执行，检查裁判员应移除这些标记或标志物。

注：严重情况可根据技术规则7.1条和7.3条作进一步处理。

风速测量

17.8　凡使用的风速测量设备必须按国际标准生产制造和校准。比赛中使用的测量设备的精确度必须经过国家测量部门认可的相关机构验证。

17.9　　Non-mechanical wind gauges shall be used at all competitions under paragraphs 1. and 2. (a), (b), (c), (e) of the World Rankings Competition definition and for any performance submitted for ratification as a World Record.

A mechanical wind gauge should have appropriate protection to reduce the impact of any crosswind. Where tubes are used, their length on either side of the measuring device should be at least twice the diameter of the tube.

17.10　The Running and Race Walking Events Referee shall ensure that the wind gauge for Track Events is placed beside the straight, adjacent to lane 1, 30m (50m and 60m races) or 50m (100m, 110m and 200m races) from the finish line. The measuring plane shall be positioned 1.22m ± 0.05m high and not more than 2m away from the track.

17.11　The wind gauge may be started and stopped automatically and/or remotely, and the information conveyed directly to the competition computer.

17.12　The periods for which the wind velocity shall be measured from the flash/smoke of the Starter's gun are as follows:

	Seconds
50m	5
50m Hurdles	5
60m	5
60m Hurdles	5
100m	10
100m Hurdles	13
110m Hurdles	13

In the 200m event, except for races on a 200m Standard Oval Track, the wind velocity shall normally be measured for a period of 10 seconds commencing when the first athlete enters the straight.

17.13　The wind gauge shall be read in metres per second, rounded to the next higher tenth of a metre per second, unless the second decimal is zero, in the positive direction (that is, a reading of +2.03 metres per second shall be recorded as +2.1; a reading of -2.03 metres per second shall be recorded as -2.0). Gauges that produce digital readings expressed in tenths of metres per second shall be constructed so as to comply with this Rule.

17.9 在举办世界排名比赛定义1.和2.(a)(b)(c)(e)所述的比赛中，以及申请承认为世界纪录的任何成绩，应使用非机械式风速仪。

机械式风速仪应有适当的防护装置，以减小侧风的影响。当风速仪为圆筒状时，测速部分两端的长度应至少为圆筒直径的2倍。

17.10 跑和竞走项目裁判长应确保测量径赛项目风速时，风速仪置于直道一侧且靠近第1分道，距终点线30米（50米和60米比赛）或50米（100米、110米和200米比赛）处。风速仪的测量平面高度为1.22米±0.05米，离跑道边沿的距离不超过2米。

17.11 风速仪应能自动和（或）遥控开机、关机，并能将数据直接传送到竞赛系统。

17.12 应按下列规定时间从发令枪的闪光或枪烟开始测定风速：

	时长
50米	5秒
50米栏	5秒
60米	5秒
60米栏	5秒
100米	10秒
100米栏	13秒
110米栏	13秒

在200米比赛中，除了在200米椭圆形跑道上进行的比赛，通常应从第一名运动员进入直道时开始测量风速，测量时间为10秒。

17.13 风速的判读单位为米/秒，进位到跑进方向更高的1/10米/秒，除非小数点后第二位数字是0（即判读为+2.03米/秒，应进位并记录为+2.1米/秒，判读为-2.03米/秒，应记录为-2.0米/秒）。显示单位为1/10米/秒的数字显示式风速仪应具备自动进位的功能，以与本规则相符。

Indication of Intermediate Times

17.14　Intermediate times and preliminary winning times may be officially announced and/or displayed. Otherwise, such times must not be communicated to the athletes by persons in the competition area without the prior approval of the appropriate Referee who may authorise or appoint no more than one person to call times at each of no more than two agreed timing points.

Athletes who receive intermediate times that have been communicated in violation of this Rule shall be considered to have received assistance and shall be subject to the provisions of Rule 6.2 of the Technical Rules.

Note: The competition area, which normally also has a physical barrier, is defined for this purpose as the area where the competition is being staged and which has an access restricted to the competing athletes and personnel authorised in accordance with the relevant Rules and Regulations.

Drinking/Sponging and Refreshment Stations in Track Events

17.15　Drinking/Sponging and Refreshment Stations in Track Events, as follows:

　　17.15.1　In Running and Race Walking Events of 5000m or longer, the Organisers may provide water and sponges to athletes if weather conditions warrant such provision.

　　17.15.2　In Running and Race Walking Events longer than 10,000m, refreshments, water and sponging stations shall be provided. Refreshments may be provided either by the Organisers or the athlete and shall be placed so that they are easily accessible to, or may be put by authorised persons into the hands of, the athletes. Refreshments provided by the athletes shall be kept under the supervision of officials designated by the Organisers from the time that the refreshments are lodged by the athletes or their representatives. Those officials shall ensure that the refreshments are not altered or tampered with in any way.

　　17.15.3　An athlete may, at any time, carry water or refreshment by hand or attached to their body provided it was carried from the start or collected or received at an official station.

分段时间显示

17.14　应正式宣告和（或）显示比赛的分段时间和领先运动员完成比赛的参考时间。除此之外，未经有关裁判长事先批准，在比赛场内的任何人都不得向运动员传递此类时间信息。有关裁判长可授权，或者指派一位工作人员赛中报时，但中途报时不可多于2个协议的计时点。

运动员接受中途报时违反此规则的，将被视为得到帮助，须按技术规则6.2条规定处理。

注：比赛场地通常设有硬隔离，定义为进行比赛的场地，并且只有参赛运动员或相关规则和规程授权的工作人员能够进入。

径赛项目的饮用/用水（海绵）和补给站设置

17.15　径赛项目的饮水/用水（海绵）和补给站设置：

　　17.15.1　在5000米及以上跑和竞走项目中，根据天气情况，组织者可向运动员提供饮水和浸水的海绵块。

　　17.15.2　在10000米以上跑和竞走项目中，须设置补给、饮水和用水、浸水的海绵供应站。补给品可由组织者官方提供或运动员自备，并放置在运动员方便拿取的位置，或由授权人员递送到运动员手中。由运动员自备补给品的，自该运动员或其代表上交之时起，应始终处于组织者指定人员的监控之下。这些裁判员须确保这些补给品不会有任何变质或篡改。

　　17.15.3　运动员可以在任何时间，手持或随身携带水或补给品，但必须是从起点或在指定的官方站点上领取或得到的。

17.15.4 An athlete who receives or collects refreshment or water from a place other than the official stations, except where provided for medical reasons from or under the direction of race officials, or takes the refreshment of another athlete, should, for a first such offence, be warned by the Referee normally by showing a yellow card. For a second offence, the Referee shall disqualify the athlete, normally by showing a red card. The athlete shall then immediately leave the track.

Note: An athlete may receive from or pass to another athlete refreshment, water or sponges provided it was carried from the start or collected or received at an official station. However, any continuous support from an athlete to one or more others in such a way may be regarded as unfair assistance and warnings and/or disqualifications as outlined above may be applied.

18. The Finish

18.1 The finish of a race shall be denoted by a white line 50mm wide.

Note: In the case of events finishing outside the stadium, the finish line may be up to 0.30m in width and may be of any colour contrasting distinctively with the surface of the finish area.

18.2 The athletes shall be placed in the order in which any part of their bodies (i.e. torso, as distinguished from the head, neck, arms, legs, hands or feet) reaches the vertical plane of the nearer edge of the finish line as defined above.

18.3 In any race decided on the basis of the distance covered in a fixed period of time, the Starter shall fire the gun exactly one minute before the end of the race to warn athletes and Judges that the race is nearing its end. The Starter shall be directed by the Chief Timekeeper and, at exactly the appropriate time after the start, they shall signal the end of the race by again firing the gun. At the moment the gun is fired to signal the end of the race, the Judges appointed for that purpose shall mark the exact spot where each athlete touched the track for the last time before or simultaneously with the firing of the gun.

The distance achieved shall be measured to the nearest metre behind this mark. At least one Judge shall be assigned to each athlete before the start of the race for the purpose of marking the distance achieved.

17.15.4 运动员如果在指定官方站点以外的地方接受或获取补给品、饮用水，或者拿取了其他运动员的饮用水或补给品，除非因医学原因或在赛事工作人员的指导下，当第一次违反规则时，应由裁判长出示黄牌予以警告；第二次违反规则时，应由裁判长出示红牌，并取消该运动员的比赛资格。该运动员应立即离开赛道。

注：运动员之间可以接收或传递由起点或沿途官方供应站提供的补给品、饮水或海绵块。但由1名运动员向1名或多名运动员递送上述物品，任何持续性的支援，则被视为不公允的帮助，运动员应被警告或者取消比赛资格。

18. 终点

18.1 应用50毫米宽的白线标出终点线。

注：对终点设在体育场外的项目，终点线最多可为0.30米宽，并用任何区别于终点区域地面的颜色标记。

18.2 判定运动员的终点名次，应以其躯干（不包括头、颈和四肢）的任何部位抵达终点线的后沿垂面的顺序为准。

18.3 在规定时间的计程比赛中，发令员须在比赛结束前1分钟鸣枪，以告知运动员和裁判员比赛即将结束。发令员应在主计时员的指挥下，在规定的比赛结束时间结束的一刻，再次鸣枪结束比赛。鸣枪瞬间为比赛结束的信号，有关裁判员应标出每名运动员在鸣枪前，或鸣枪瞬间最后一次触及跑道的确切位置。

所跑距离应丈量至运动员最后足迹位置之后，以米为单位，不足1米不计。比赛开始前，应指派至少1名裁判员负责1名运动员，以便标出该运动员完成的比赛距离。

Guidelines for the conduct of the One Hour Race may be downloaded from the World Athletics website.

19. Timing

19.1 Three methods of timekeeping shall be recognised as official:

    19.1.1 Hand Timing;

    19.1.2 Fully Automatic Timing obtained from a Photo Finish System;

    19.1.3 Timing provided by a Transponder System for competitions held under Rules 54 (races not held completely in the stadium), 55, 56, and 57 of the Technical Rules only.

19.2 Under Rules 19.1.1 and 19.1.2 of the Technical Rules, the time shall be taken to the moment at which any part of the body of an athlete (i.e. torso, as distinguished from the head, neck, arms, legs, hands or feet) reaches the vertical plane of the nearer edge of the finish line.

19.3 Times for all finishers shall be recorded. In addition, whenever possible, lap times in races of 800m and over and intermediate times at every 1000m in races of 3000m and over shall be recorded.

Hand Timing

19.4 The Timekeepers shall be in line with the finish and, where possible, they should be placed at least 5m from the outside lane of the track. In order that they may all have a good view of the finish line, an elevated stand should be provided.

19.5 Timekeepers shall use manually operated electronic timers with digital readouts. All such timing devices are termed "watches" for the purpose of the Rules.

19.6 The lap and intermediate times as per Rule 19.3 of the Technical Rules shall be recorded either, by designated members of the timekeeping team using watches capable of taking more than one time, or by additional Timekeepers, or by transponders.

19.7 The time shall be taken from the flash/smoke of the gun.

《一小时计时跑赛事组织指南》可从世界田联网站下载。

19. 计时

19.1 下列3种计时方法均被承认为正式计时方法：

    19.1.1 手计时；

    19.1.2 全自动计时和终点摄影系统；

    19.1.3 技术规则54条（不是全部赛程在体育场完成的比赛项目）、55条、56条和57条规定的比赛中使用遥感感应系统提供的计时。

19.2 根据技术规则19.1.1条和19.1.2条，计时应至运动员躯干（不包括头、颈和四肢）的任何部位抵达终点线后沿垂直面的瞬间为止。

19.3 须记录所有抵达终点的运动员的时间。另外，如有可能，计取800米及以上项目的每圈时间和3000米及以上项目的每1000米的分段时间。

手计时

19.4 计时员应在跑道外侧与终点线排成一条直线。如有可能，计时员的位置应距跑道外侧至少5米远。为使所有计时员都能清楚地观察终点情况，应提供升高的计时台。

19.5 计时员应使用人工操作的具有数字显示功能的计时设备。为了保证规则的严谨性，这类设备统称为"表"。

19.6 根据技术规则19.3条中的计圈和分段计时的要求，要通过指定计时员使用可以不止一次计取分段时间的秒表计取，或通过额外的计时员计取，或通过传感器计取。

19.7 计时应从发令枪发出闪光或枪烟开始。

19.8　　Three official Timekeepers (one of whom shall be the Chief Timekeeper) and one or two additional Timekeepers shall time the winner of every event and any performances for record purposes. (For Combined Events, see Rule 39.8.2 of the Technical Rules.) The times recorded by the additional Timekeepers' watches shall not be considered unless one or more of the official Timekeepers' watches fail to record the time correctly, in which case the additional Timekeepers shall be called upon, in such order as has been decided previously, so that in all the races, three watches should have recorded the official winning time.

19.9　　Each Timekeeper shall act independently and without showing their watch to, or discussing their time with, any other person, shall enter their time on the official form and, after signing it, hand it to the Chief Timekeeper who may examine the watches to verify the reported times.

19.10　For all hand-timed races, times shall be read and recorded as follows:

19.10.1　For races on the track, unless the time is an exact 0.1 second, the time shall be converted and recorded to the next longer 0.1 second, e.g. 10.11 shall be recorded as 10.2.

19.10.2　For races partly or entirely outside the stadium, unless the time is an exact whole second, the time shall be converted and recorded to the next longer whole second, e.g. 2:09:44.3 shall be recorded as 2:09:45.

Note: For the Road Mile, the conversion shall be done to the next longer 0.1 second.

19.11　If, after converting as indicated above, two of the three watches agree and the third disagrees, the time recorded by the two shall be the official time. If all three watches disagree, the middle time shall be official. If only times from two watches are available and they disagree, the longer time shall be official.

19.12　The Chief Timekeeper, acting in accordance with the Rules mentioned above, shall decide the official time for each athlete and provide the results to the Competition Secretary for distribution.

19.8 每个项目第一名以及涉及申报纪录的成绩应由3名正式计时员（其中1人为计时主裁判）和1~2名后备计时员计取。（关于全能项目，见技术规则39.8.2条。）只有当1名或多名正式计时员的秒表不能准确地计取时间时，后备计时员的秒表所计时间才可用作替补，但事先要规定好替补的顺序，使所有径赛项目的第一名都应有3块秒表计取正式获胜成绩。

19.9 每名计时员都应独立工作，不得将所计取的成绩告诉他人或与其他人商讨所计的成绩，将成绩填写在成绩记录表内，签名后交给计时主裁判，计时主裁判可以验表以核对所报成绩。

19.10 所有采用手计时的比赛，应当按照以下方式读取和记录成绩：

19.10.1 在跑道上举行的径赛项目中，除非时间为整0.1秒，否则成绩应换算并记录为下一个较长的0.1秒，如10.11秒应记录为10.2秒。

19.10.2 部分或全部在外场举行的径赛项目，除非时间为整秒，否则成绩应换算并记录为下一个较长的整秒，如2:09:44.3应记录为2:09:45。

注：1英里路跑项目，要转换为下一个较长的0.1秒。

19.11 如果根据以上规定换算时间后，在3块正式计时的秒表中，2块秒表所计时间相同而第三块表不同时，应以这2块表所计时间为准；如3块秒表所计时间各不相同，应以中间时间为准；如只使用2块秒表计时，而所计时间不相同时，应以较长的时间为正式成绩。

19.12 计时主裁判根据上述条款要判定每名运动员的正式成绩，并将成绩单提交竞赛秘书用以发布。

Fully Automatic Timing and Photo Finish System

The System

19.13　A Fully Automatic Timing and Photo Finish System must have been tested, and have a certificate of accuracy issued within 4 years of the competition, including the following:

  19.13.1　The System must record the finish through a camera positioned in the extension of the finish line, producing a composite image.

    a.　For competitions under paragraphs 1. and 2. of the World Rankings Competition definition, this composite image must be composed of at least 1000 images per second.

    b.　For other competitions, this composite image must be composed of at least 100 images per second.

  In each case, the image must be synchronised with a uniformly marked time-scale graduated in 0.01 seconds.

  19.13.2　The System shall be started automatically by the Starter's signal, so that the overall delay between the report from the muzzle or its equivalent visual indication and the start of the timing system is constant and equal to or less than 0.001 second.

19.14　In order to confirm that the camera is correctly aligned and to facilitate the reading of the Photo Finish image, the intersection of the lane lines and the finish line shall be coloured black in a suitable design. Any such design must be solely confined to the intersection, for no more than 20mm beyond, and not extended before, the nearer edge of the finish line. Similar black marks may be placed on each side of the intersection of an appropriate lane line and the finish line to further facilitate reading.

19.15　The placing of the athletes shall be identified from the image by means of a cursor with its reading line guaranteed to be perpendicular to the time scale.

全自动计时和终点摄影系统

系统

19.13 全自动计时和终点摄影系统必须经过测试，并具备在比赛前四年内获得的精度测试合格证书，包括以下条件：

> 19.13.1 该系统通过在终点线延长线上架设的摄像机记录终点情况，并能生成用于判定成绩的合成图像。
>
> > a. 对于世界排名比赛定义1条和2条所述的比赛，合成图像必须提供至少每秒1000帧的图像。
> >
> > b. 对于其他比赛，合成图像必须提供至少每秒100帧的图像。
>
> 在任何情形下，图像必须与精确到0.01秒的时间标尺同步。
>
> 19.13.2 计时系统必须由发令员的信号自动启动开始计时，从鸣枪或类似视觉信号到计时系统启动之间的总延误时间应是恒定的，并应等于或小于0.001秒。

19.14 为了确保摄像装置对正终点线，便于判读终点拍摄的图像，分道线与终点线的交叉点应以合适的图形着成黑色。所有的这些图形必须完全限定在交叉点内，不得大于20毫米，也不得超出终点线的后沿。类似的黑色标记可以放置在适当分道线与终点线的交叉点两侧，以更便于判读。

19.15 运动员的名次须通过使用带有标线的图像读取，该标线必须与时标垂直。

19.16　The System must automatically determine and record the finish times of the athletes and must be able to produce a printed image which shows the time of any athlete. Additionally, the system shall provide a tabular overview which shows the time or other result of every athlete. Subsequent changes of automatically determined values and manual input of values (such as start time, finish time), shall be indicated by the system automatically in the time scale of the printed image and the tabular overview.

19.17　A system which operates automatically at the finish, but not at the start, shall be considered to produce Hand Times provided that the system was started in accordance with Rule 19.7 of the Technical Rules or with equivalent accuracy. The image may be used as a valid support in order to determine placings and adjust time intervals between athletes.

Note: If the timing mechanism is not started by the Starter's signal, the time-scale on the image shall indicate this fact automatically.

19.18　A system, which operates automatically at the start but not at the finish, shall be considered to produce neither Hand nor Fully Automatic Times and shall not therefore be used to obtain official times.

Operation

19.19　The Chief Photo Finish Judge shall be responsible for the functioning of the System. Before the start of the competition, they will meet the technical staff involved and familiarise themselves with the equipment, checking all applicable settings.

In cooperation with the Start Referee (or if one is not appointed, the relevant Running and Race Walking Events Referee) and the Starter, they shall initiate a zero control test, before the beginning of each session, to ensure that the equipment is started automatically by the Starter's signal within the limit identified in Rule 19.13.2 of the Technical Rules (i.e. equal to or less than 0.001 second).

They shall supervise the testing of the equipment and ensure that the camera(s) is (are) correctly aligned.

19.16 该系统必须能自动判定并记录运动员抵达终点的时间，且必须能打印出标明每名运动员抵达终点时间的图像。另外，该系统必须能够提供表格总览，标出每位运动员的时间或其他成绩信息。改变自动判读数据和手动输入的数据（如起跑开始时间、终点结束时间），可在系统打印的图像时标及表格总览中自动显示出来。

19.17 如果系统是终点自动操作，而在起跑时未能自动启动的计时装置，但只要该系统根据技术规则19.7条启动计时或具备同等精准度，应被视为手计时。该图像仍然可以作为有效证据，以判定名次和调整运动员成绩之间的间隔。

注：如果计时系统不是由发令员的信号启动，则合成的终点摄影图像上的时间标尺应能自动体现这一事实。

19.18 只能在起跑时自动启动，而不能在终点自动操作的计时装置，既不能视为手计时，也不能视为全自动计时。因此，不能视为正式时间成绩。

操作

19.19 终点摄影主裁判应负责本系统的正常运行。比赛开始前，他应与有关技术人员会面，熟悉设备的性能，检查所有可应用的设定。

在每一比赛单元开始前，终点摄影主裁判应与起点裁判长（如未指派起点裁判长，或相关跑和竞走项目裁判长）及发令员配合，进行一次零测试，以确保发令员的信号能在技术规则19.13.2条规定的时间（即小于等于0.001秒）内自动启动设备。

终点摄影主裁判还要监督设备的测试，确保所有摄影机与终点线完全对齐。

19.20　There should be at least two Photo Finish cameras in action, one from each side. Preferably, these timing systems should be technically independent, i.e. with different power supplies and recording and relaying of the Starter's signal, by separate equipment and cables.

Note: Where two or more Photo Finish cameras are used, one should be designated as official by the Technical Delegate(s) (or World Athletics Photo Finish Judge where appointed) before the start of the competition. The times and places from the images of the other camera(s) should not be considered unless there is reason to doubt the accuracy of the official camera or if there is need to use the supplementary images to resolve uncertainties in the finishing order (i.e. athletes wholly or partially obscured on the image from the official camera).

19.21　In conjunction with an adequate number of assistants, the Chief Photo Finish Judge shall determine the placing of the athletes and, as a consequence, their official times. They shall ensure that these results are correctly entered in or transferred to the competition results system and conveyed to the Competition Secretary.

At major events where the technology is available, the Photo Finish image is often immediately provided on the video board or published on the internet. It has become the practice to provide athletes, or persons on their behalf, who are considering making a protest or appeal the opportunity to see the photo, in order to avoid time being spent on any unnecessary protests or appeals.

19.22　Times from the Photo Finish System shall be regarded as official unless for any reason the appropriate official decides that they obviously must be inaccurate. If such is the case, the times of the back-up Timekeepers, if possible adjusted based on information on time intervals obtained from the Photo Finish image, shall be official. Such back-up Timekeepers must be appointed where any possibility exists of failure of the timing system.

19.23　Times shall be read and recorded from the Photo Finish image as follows:

19.23.1　For all races on the track up to and including 10,000m, unless the time is an exact 0.01 second, the time shall be converted and recorded to the next longer 0.01 second, e.g. 26:17.533 shall be recorded as 26:17.54.

19.20 至少应有两台终点摄影机分别从两侧同时拍摄。更为可取的是，这些计时系统在技术上应相对独立，如采用不同的供电电源、不同的记录系统、不同的发令信号中继设备和电缆等。

注：如使用两台或两台以上终点摄影机时，赛前应由技术代表（或被指派的世界田联终点摄影裁判员）指定其中的一台为正式摄影机。只有当有理由怀疑正式摄影机的准确性或有必要使用辅助图像来判定运动员的终点名次时（在正式摄影机拍摄的图像中，运动员的整体或部分图像被遮挡），才可使用备用摄影机记录图像的时间和名次。

19.21 在足够数量的助理裁判员的协助下，终点摄影主裁判应判定运动员的名次和成绩。他要确保这些成绩准确地录入竞赛成绩系统，并送达竞赛秘书处。

在大型比赛中，在技术条件允许的情况下，通常终点摄影照片会立刻显示在视频屏幕上或在网上发布。通过这种方式将相关信息提供给正要考虑提出申诉和抗议的运动员或其代理人，以避免他们将时间浪费在不必要的申诉和抗议上。

19.22 应以全自动计时和终点摄影系统的时间作为正式成绩，除非有关裁判员以任何理由确定该时间明显不准确。如果出现此种情况，后备计时员计取的时间可以作为正式成绩。如有可能，可以终点摄影图像上获取的时间间隔为基础进行调整。当全自动计时系统存在失误的可能性时，必须指派后备手计时员。

19.23 应按下列要求从终点图像上判读和记录时间：

19.23.1 10000米及以下各跑道上径赛项目的成绩，除非正好为0.01秒，否则应进位和记录为下一个较长的0.01秒。如26:17.533，应记录为26:17.54。

19.23.2   For all races on the track longer than 10,000m, all times not ending in two zeroes shall be converted and recorded to the next longer 0.1 second, e.g. 59:26.322 shall be recorded as 59:26.4.

19.23.3   For all races held partly or entirely outside the stadium, all times not ending in three zeroes shall be converted and recorded to the next longer whole second, e.g. 2:09:44.322 shall be recorded as 2:09:45.

Note: For the Road Mile, the conversion shall be done to the next longer 0.01 second.

Note: Events held according to Rule 11.2 of the Technical Rules shall be considered to be conducted inside the stadium for timing and recording of performance.

Transponder System

19.24   The use of Transponder Timing Systems complying with the Rules in events held under Rules 54 (races not held completely in the stadium), 55, 56, and 57 of the Technical Rules is permitted provided that:

19.24.1   None of the equipment used at the start, along the course or at the finish line constitutes a significant obstacle or barrier to the progress of an athlete.

19.24.2   The weight of the transponder and its housing carried or worn by the athlete is not significant.

19.24.3   The System is started by the Starter's gun or synchronised with the start signal.

19.24.4   The System requires no action by an athlete during the competition, at the finish or at any stage in the result processing.

19.25   For all races, all times not ending in zero shall be converted and recorded to the next longer whole second, e.g. 2:09:44.3 shall be recorded as 2:09:45.

Note (i): The official time shall be the time elapsed between the firing of the starting gun (or the synchronised start signal) and the athlete reaching the finish line. However, the time elapsed between an athlete crossing the start line and the finish line can be made known to them, but will not be considered an official time.

19.23.2 在跑道上进行的10000米以上的各径赛项目的成绩，其尾数不是2个0的，应进位和记录为下一个较长的0.1秒，如59:26.322，应记录为59:26.4。

19.23.3 部分或全部在场外举行的径赛项目的成绩，其尾数不是3个0时，应进位和记录为下一个较长的整秒，如2:09:44.322，应记为2:09:45。

注：1英里路跑项目，要转换为下一个较长的0.01秒。

注：根据技术规则11.2条举行的比赛项目，计时和记录成绩要被视作在体育场进行的比赛。

感应计时系统

19.24 举行技术规则54条（不是全部在体育场进行的比赛项目）、55条、56条和57条所述的比赛时，应使用符合世界田联规则的感应计时系统，且必须符合下列条件：

19.24.1 使用的设备不得在起点、跑进线路或终点线上给运动员的行进造成明显阻挡或障碍。

19.24.2 运动员携带或佩戴的传感器和其外壳的重量并不明显。

19.24.3 该系统须由发令员的发令枪开启，或与起跑信号同步。

19.24.4 该系统不需要运动员在比赛中、在终点或任何阶段获取成绩的过程中采取任何操作。

19.25 在所有比赛中，时间的末位数不为0时，要换算并记录到下一个较长的整秒，如2:09:44.3，应记为2:09:45。

注（ⅰ）：正式成绩为从发令枪发出信号（或同步的起跑信号）至运动员抵达终点线之间的时间。可以让运动员知道他通过起点线到终点线所用时间，但这个时间不能成为正式成绩。

Note (ii): For the Road Mile, the conversion shall be done to the next longer 0.1 second.

19.26　Whilst the determination of the finishing order and times may be considered official, Rules 18.2 and 19.2 of the Technical Rules must be applied where required.

Note: It is recommended that Judges and/or video recording(s) also be provided to assist in determining the finishing order and the identification of athletes.

It is important that when using Transponder Timing that appropriate back-up systems are put in place by the Organisers, especially to respect Rule 19.26 of the Technical Rules. The provision of back-up Timekeepers, and more importantly Finish Judges to adjudicate on close finishes (which might not be differentiated by chip timing) is strongly recommended.

19.27　The Chief Transponder Timing Judge shall be responsible for the functioning of the System. Before the start of the competition, they will meet the technical staff involved and familiarise themselves with the equipment, checking all applicable settings. They shall supervise the testing of the equipment and ensure that the passing of the transponder over the finish line will record the athlete's finish time. In conjunction with the Referee, they shall ensure that provision is made for the application, when necessary, of Rule 19.26 of the Technical Rules.

20.　Seedings, Draws and Qualification in Track Events

Rounds and Heats

20.1　Qualification Rounds shall be held in Track Events in which the number of athletes is too large to allow the competition to be conducted satisfactorily in a single round (final). Where Qualification Rounds are held, all athletes must compete in, and qualify through, all such rounds except that the relevant governing body may, for one or more events, authorise the conduct of additional qualification round(s) either at the same competition or at one or more earlier competitions to determine some or all of the athletes who shall be entitled to participate and in which round of the competition. Such procedure and any other means (such as achieving entry standards during a specified period, by specified placing in a designated competition or by specified rankings) by which an athlete is entitled to participate, and in which round of the competition, shall be set out in the regulations for each competition.

Note (i): See also Rule 8.4.3 of the Technical Rules.

注（ii）：1英里路跑项目，要转换为下一个较长的0.1秒。

19.26 当确定运动员通过终点的顺序和时间为正式成绩时，如有需要，可按技术规则18.2条和19.2条处理。

注：建议，也可采用裁判员和/或使用录像视频提供协助来判定运动员的终点名次和识别运动员。

在使用感应计时时，组织者应当使用适当的备用系统，特别是在执行技术规则19.26条的情况下。当终点判定成绩接近的名次时（这种情况下使用感应计时通常很难判定），强烈推荐使用后备手计时员。

19.27 感应计时主裁判应负责感应计时系统的工作。在比赛开始前，他应与有关技术人员会面，使自己熟悉设备，检查所有可用的设定。他应监督感应计时设备的测试，以确保通过终点线的传感器能记录下运动员到达终点的时间。需要时，他与裁判长一起，确保按照技术规则19.26条判读成绩和名次。

20. 径赛项目的排序、抽签和晋级

赛次与分组

20.1 在参赛运动员人数过多，不能用一个赛次（决赛）公平地决出名次的径赛项目中，要举行晋级赛次（决赛前的各赛次）。举行晋级赛次时，所有运动员必须参赛，并通过各赛次的比赛，以取得参加决赛的资格。除非相关管理机构同意，就1个或多个比赛项目，授权在本场或前面的1场或多场比赛中组织额外的晋级赛，来决定谁有资格参加本次比赛和参加的赛次。要求运动员以这个程序或任何其他的方法（如在特定时间内达到报名标准、通过指定比赛的名次要求或通过特定的排名等）参赛及参加比赛的赛次，都要写在比赛的规程里。

注（i）：见技术规则8.4.3条。

Note (ii): Additional qualification round(s) may include preliminary qualification round(s) and/or Repechage Round(s).

20.2 The Qualification Rounds for Track Events shall be arranged as follows by the appointed Technical Delegates. If no Technical Delegates have been appointed, they shall be arranged by the Organisers.

 20.2.1 The regulations for each competition should include tables which shall, in the absence of extraordinary circumstances, be used to determine the number of rounds, the number of heats in each round and the qualification procedure, i.e. those to advance by place and time. Such information shall also be provided for any additional qualification round(s).

 Note (i): Tables which may be used in the absence of any provision in applicable regulations or other determination by the Organisers are published on the World Athletics website.

 Note (ii): The applicable regulations may specify how vacant positions due to withdrawals in semi-finals and finals may be filled in by athletes ranked next following the previous round after those qualified.

 20.2.2 Whenever possible, athletes of each Member or team and the best performed athletes shall be placed in different heats in all Qualification Rounds of the competition. In applying this Rule after the first round, the required exchanges of athletes between heats should, to the extent possible, be made between athletes seeded in the same "group of lanes" according to Rules 20.4.3 to 20.4.5 of the Technical Rules.

 20.2.3 When Qualification Rounds are being arranged, as much information as possible about the performances of all athletes should be considered and the heats drawn so that, normally, the best performed athletes reach the final.

 This includes avoiding where possible the clashing of the best performed athletes (determined generally on performance in the qualification period but also on outstanding recent career records) in the same heats as also applies to athletes from the same Member or team.

注（ii）：额外的晋级赛可包含初选晋级赛和/或复活赛。

20.2 径赛项目的晋级赛次由技术代表安排。如未指定技术代表，则应由组织者排定。

 20.2.1 在每场比赛的竞赛规程中，若无特殊情况，应包含晋级的赛次数、每赛次的组数，以及晋级方法等信息表，例如，按名次和成绩递补各录取多少人。须为任何额外的晋级赛次提供此类信息。

 注（i）：如果在适用的竞赛规程中没有规定或者组织者没有作其他决定，可使用世界田联网站上公布的晋级表格。

 注（ii）：适用的规程可以规定，如何由晋级赛后排名靠后的运动员填补因半决赛和决赛有人退赛时而产生的空缺位置。

 20.2.2 在可能的情况下，在所有晋级赛次的比赛中，要将同一会员协会或同一参赛队的运动员，以及成绩最好的运动员编排到不同组次。第一赛次之后，通常根据技术规则20.4.3至20.4.5条，对编排在相同"道次组"中的运动员进行调整。

 20.2.3 在安排晋级赛次时，应尽可能考虑所有运动员的成绩信息，通常通过分组抽签能使成绩最好的运动员进入决赛。

 这包括尽可能避免成绩最好的运动员（通常要考虑达标成绩，也基于近期出色的职业成绩）被分到同一组，此条也适用于来自同一协会和同一参赛队的运动员。

In all such cases, adjustments of the seeding should be made after the initial allocation to the heats but before any draw is made for the lanes. After these changes are made, a final check should be made to ensure that the heats are as equal as possible.

In applying these principles, exchanges of athletes should be made:

a. in the first round, between athletes with a similar ranking on the list of best valid performances during the pre-determined period; and

b. in subsequent rounds, between athletes seeded in the same "group of lanes" according to Rules 20.4.3 to 20.4.5 of the Technical Rules.

Unless the applicable regulations provide otherwise, for major competitions, at least, the basis of the seeding should be the best times achieved by each athlete in valid conditions (including with wind readings for the relevant events) during the pre-determined period. This period may be specified in the applicable regulations or in the document setting out the entry conditions and standards for the competition. Where there is no such specification, then the "Season Best" should be used unless the Technical Delegate(s) or the Organisers decide that for one, some or all events the circumstances justify an alternate period or other criteria being applied.

Such factors as performances achieved during training or tests, even if they appeared to look like competition or notions about what an athlete might "be worth" but has never achieved, should not be taken into account in seeding.

The requirements of the Rule in relation to the "best performed athletes" does require some deviation from the strict protocol outlined above. For example, an athlete who might normally be seeded in a high position might not have any, or only a poor, valid performance in the predetermined period (through injury, illness, ineligibility or in the case of Short Track meetings only have 400m Standard Oval Track Stadium results). Whilst they would normally be placed lower or at the bottom of the seeding list, adjustment should be considered by the Technical Delegate(s). Similar principles should be applied to avoid a clash in a Qualification Round between athletes considered to be the favourites to place highly in the event if the results of the previous round would strictly dictate that they should be in the same heat. At this same time any adjustments to ensure as much as possible that athletes from the same Member or team are in different heats should also be made.

在上面所有情况中，比赛分组的调整应该在初步分组后，抽签分道前进行。进行这些更改后，应进行最终检查以确保分组尽可能均衡。

在应用上述原则时，对运动员调整应：

a. 在比赛第一轮，按照规定时段内取得的成绩对排名相近的运动员进行调整；和

b. 在后继赛次，根据技术规则20.4.3至20.4.5条，在相同"道次组"中的运动员之间进行编排调整。

除非适用的规程另有规定，对于大型比赛，分组的基础应为运动员在规定的时间内取得的有效成绩（包括风速信息）。该规定的时间通常在适用的规程或报名标准中指明。如果没有类似的说明，"赛季最佳"成绩必须使用，除非技术代表或组织者决定某1个、多个或所有项目，视情况选择替换时段或其他的适用标准。

在训练或测验中取得的成绩，即便是运动员在比赛中看似应该获得的成绩，但没有实际取得，此类成绩都不应该在编排中被考虑。

上述规则中关于"最好成绩运动员"的条款需要一些不同于条文的适当解释。例如，一名运动员通常应该按照高名次编排，但是有可能他没有在规定时段内取得任何有效成绩或成绩很差（因为受伤、生病、失去比赛资格或者参加短道比赛却只有400米标准椭圆形跑道体育场的成绩）。这样的运动员通常会被排在较后或者分组名单的后面，技术代表应考虑做出适当的调整。类似的原则应适用于避免在项目中同被认为最有希望夺冠的运动员之间的冲突，如果严格按照前一赛次的成绩，他们将被分到同一组，但是他们同被认为是比赛夺冠的热门运动员，这种情况下应该做出调整，避免他们在晋级赛次相遇。同样地，也应该尽可能避免来自同一协会或同一参赛队的运动员分在同一组。

Following these principles is more important in competitions in which the number of rounds has been reduced in some events - making accurate and well considered seeding vital to achieving both a fair and an athletically appealing outcome.

For lower level competitions, the Technical Delegate(s) or the Organisers may consider using different principles to achieve a similar final outcome.

Ranking and Composition of Heats

20.3   Ranking and Composition of Heats, as follows:

    20.3.1   For the first round, the athletes shall be ranked with the seeding determined from the relevant list of valid performances achieved during the predetermined period or in accordance with the applicable regulations.

    20.3.2   After the first round:

        a.   for events up to and including 400m, and relays up to and including 4 × 400m, seeding shall be based upon placings and times of each previous round. For this purpose, athletes shall be ranked as follows:

        Fastest heat winner

        2nd fastest heat winner

        3rd fastest heat winner, etc.

        Fastest 2nd place

        2nd fastest 2nd place

        3rd fastest 2nd place, etc.

        (Concluding with)

        Fastest time qualifier

        2nd fastest time qualifier

        3rd fastest time qualifier, etc.

根据以上原则，在一些赛次已经减少的项目比赛中，准确和经过深思熟虑的种子运动员的分组，对于保证比赛公平和运动上有吸引力显得尤其重要。

在较低水平的比赛中，技术代表或组织者可以考虑使用不同的调整原则，以取得相同的结果。

排名和分组组成

20.3 排序与分组，如下：

    20.3.1 对于第一赛次，应根据运动员在事先规定的时段内或根据适用的规程取得的有效成绩的相关名单对其进行排名。

    20.3.2 第一赛次之后：

        a. 400米及以下的各项目、4×400米及以下的各项接力，要根据运动员前一赛次的名次和成绩进行编排。根据该原则，运动员将按下列顺序排名：

        最快的第一名；

        次快的第一名；

        第三快的第一名，依次类推。

        最快的第二名；

        次快的第二名；

        第三快的第二名，依次类推。

        最后可按下列顺序补晋级：

        按成绩录取的最快者；

        按成绩录取的次快者；

        按成绩录取的第三快者，依次类推。

b. for other events, the original performance lists shall continue to be used for seeding, modified only by improvements in performances achieved during the earlier round(s).

20.3.3 In each case the athletes shall then be placed in heats in the order of seeding in a zigzag distribution, e.g. three heats will consist of the following seedings:

A	1	6	7	12	13	18	19	24
B	2	5	8	11	14	17	20	23
C	3	4	9	10	15	16	21	22

20.3.4 In each case, the order in which heats are to be run shall be determined by draw after the composition of the heats has been decided.

For the first round, in order to reduce the number of heats required, it is acceptable and normal for additional available lanes (for example a ninth lane on a straight or oval track) to be used in races up to and including 400m and to have more than one athlete in a lane at the start of an 800m race.

The random draw to determine the order in which the heats are conducted is based on fairness. In middle and long distance races the athletes running in the last heat will know as far as qualifying by times the performance they have to realise in order to qualify. Even with the shorter races there is a fairness aspect as weather conditions can change (rain suddenly falling or an alteration in wind strength or direction). Fairness dictates that order be determined by chance.

Draw for Lanes

20.4 For events up to and including 800m, and relays up to and including 4 × 400m, where there are several successive rounds of a race, lanes will be drawn as follows:

20.4.1 Unless the applicable regulations provide otherwise, for the first round and any additional qualification round as per Rule 20.1 of the Technical Rules, the lane order shall be drawn by lot.

b. 其他各项目，须继续执行运动员首轮排序成绩后分组，只有在前面赛次中提高成绩的运动员才可进行调整。

20.3.3　在任何情况下，应将运动员按排列的序号，依照蛇形分布的方法编入各组。如按下列方法将排序晋级的24名运动员编为3组。

A	1	6	7	12	13	18	19	24
B	2	5	8	11	14	17	20	23
C	3	4	9	10	15	16	21	22

20.3.4　在任何情况下，在分组确定后，应抽签排定A、B、C三组的比赛顺序。

在第一轮比赛中，为了减少组数，400米以下的项目通常可以使用额外的跑道（例如，使用直道或椭圆跑道的第9分道）；在800米项目中，1条跑道上可以安排多于1名的运动员同时起跑。

决定组次顺序的抽签应该遵循公平的原则。在中长跑比赛中，最后一组的运动员会知道晋级下一赛次的时间、成绩。在短距离比赛中，由于天气变化也存在不公平问题（突然降雨或者风速、风向发生变化），遵循公平原则就是组次顺序要随机决定。

抽签排定道次

20.4　800米及以下的各项目、4×400米及以下各项接力赛，如在一次比赛中要连续进行几个赛次时，应按下列规定抽签排定道次：

20.4.1　除非适用的规程另有规定，第一赛次和根据技术规则20.1条规定的任何额外的晋级赛，抽签排定道次；

20.4.2 For any round after the first round, athletes shall be ranked in accordance with the procedure shown in Rule 20.3.2(a) or, in the case of 800m, 20.3.2(b) of the Technical Rules.

For an eight-lane track, three draws for lanes will then be made. When there are fewer or more than eight lanes, the principles in the following system with the necessary modifications should be used.

20.4.3 For straight races:

a. one draw for the four highest ranked athletes or teams to determine placings in lanes 3, 4, 5 and 6;

b. another for the fifth and sixth ranked athletes or teams to determine placings in lanes 2 and 7, and

c. another for the two lowest ranked athletes or teams to determine placings in lanes 1 and 8.

20.4.4 For 200m races:

a. one draw for the three highest ranked athletes or teams to determine placings in lanes 5, 6 and 7;

b. another for the fourth, fifth and sixth ranked athletes or teams to determine placings in lanes 3, 4 and 8, and

c. another for the two lowest ranked athletes or teams to determine placings in lanes 1 and 2.

20.4.5 For 400m races, all relays up to and including 4×400m and 800m races started in lanes:

a. one draw for the four highest ranked athletes or teams to determine placings in lanes 4, 5, 6 and 7;

b. another for the fifth and sixth ranked athletes or teams to determine placings in lanes 3 and 8, and

20.4.2 对于第一轮之后的任何赛次，应根据技术规则20.3.2（a）条，或在800米项目中按技术规则20.3.2（b）条的程序在每一赛次之后对运动员排序。

对于具有8条可用分道的比赛，3次抽签排定1组道次。若分道数多或少于8道，抽签的原则应作出一些必要的调整。

20.4.3 直道项目：

a. 选择排列前四名的运动员或队，抽签排定3、4、5、6道；

b. 选择排列第五、六名的运动员或队，抽签排定2、7道，和

c. 选择排列在最后2名的运动员或队，抽签排定1、8道。

20.4.4 200米项目：

a. 选择排列前三名的运动员或队，抽签排定5、6、7道；

b. 选择排列第四、五、六名的运动员或队，抽签排定3、4、8道，和

c. 选择排列在最后2名的运动员或队，抽签排定1、2道。

20.4.5 400米及所有4×400米以下的接力项目和分道起跑的800米项目：

a. 选择排列前四名的运动员或队，抽签排定4、5、6、7道；

b. 选择排列第五、六名的运动员或队，抽签排定3、8道，和

c. another for the two lowest ranked athletes or teams to determine placings in lanes 1 and 2.

Note (i): The 800m event may be run with one or two athletes in each lane. However, in competitions under paragraphs 1. (a), (b), (c) and 2. (a), (b) of the World Rankings Competition definition, assigning two athletes in one lane should normally only be done in the first round, unless because of ties or advancement by the Referee or the Jury of Appeal, there are more athletes in a race of a subsequent round than lanes available. In competitions under paragraphs 1. (e), 2. (e) and 3. of the World Rankings Competition definition, 800m races may also be run without lanes using an arced start line or group starts.

Note (ii): In any 800m race, including a final, where for any reason there are more athletes competing than lanes available, the Technical Delegate(s) shall determine in which lanes more than one athlete will be drawn.

Note (iii): When there are more lanes than athletes, the inside lane(s) should always remain free.

With regard to Note (ii), there is no exact specification as to how the Technical Delegates should act as the situations which may give rise to it may vary greatly. However, this issue only affects the running of the first bend of the race and is not as important as the allocation of lanes in a shorter race. Technical Delegate(s) are advised to place the additional athlete(s) in the lane(s) where the "double-up" will cause least inconvenience - usually the outer lanes so that the athletes are not running around a tighter bend together.

As to Note (iii), where a stadium has more than eight lanes available, the Technical Delegate(s) (or if none the Organisers) should decide in advance which lanes are to be used for this purpose. For example, in the case of a nine-lane oval track, lane one would not be used in cases where less than nine athletes are taking part in a race. Consequently, for the purposes of Rule 20.4 of the Technical Rules, lane 2 is regarded as lane 1 and so on.

20.5　In competitions under paragraphs 1. (a), (b), (c) and 2. (a), (b) of the World Rankings Competition definition, for events longer than 800m, relays longer than 4×400m and any event where only a single round (final) is required, lanes/starting positions shall be drawn by lot.

c. 选择排列在最后2名的运动员或队，抽签排定1、2道。

注（ⅰ）：800米比赛每条跑道可安排1名或2名运动员。但在举办世界排名比赛定义1.（a）（b）（c）和2.（a）（b）所述的比赛中，通常应在第一轮安排2名运动员一条跑道，除非出现名次相同或者裁判长决定晋级或申诉决定晋级，导致下一赛次的运动员人数多于可用的跑道数。在举办世界排名比赛定义1.（e）2.（e）和3条所述的比赛中，800米比赛也可以不分道跑进行，采用弧形起跑或分组起跑。

注（ⅱ）：在800米比赛中，包括决赛，由于一些原因，当有超过可用分道的运动员参加比赛时，技术代表将抽签决定在哪一条分道上不止1名运动员。

注（ⅲ）：当分道多于参赛运动员人数时，不应使用内侧一条或多条分道。

关于注（ⅱ），技术代表没有特定的规范告知他们在哪些情况下如何决定，导致结果有很大差异。但是，这种情况只会影响第一弯道的跑进，并且其影响远不及短距离的分道项目。建议技术代表将额外的运动员安排在影响最小的分道上，通常为外侧跑道，这样运动员不会在弯道上过于拥挤。

关于注（ⅲ），当场地有多于8条分道时，技术代表（如没有指派技术代表，由组织者进行）将事先决定哪条分道被用于该目的。例如，在有9条椭圆形的分道上，当运动员人数少于9人时，将不使用第1分道。因为，当执行技术规则20.4条时，通常将第2分道视为第1分道使用，以此类推。

20.5 在举办世界排名比赛定义1.（a）（b）（c）和2.（a）（b）所述的比赛中，800米以上的项目和4×400米以上的接力项目，以及只进行决赛的项目，应抽签决定运动员分道或起跑位置。

20.6　　Where it is decided to conduct a series of races in an event rather than rounds and finals, the regulations for the competition shall set out all relevant considerations including seedings and draws and the method by which the final results will be determined.

20.7　　An athlete shall not be allowed to compete in a heat or lane other than the one in which their name appears, except in circumstances which, in the opinion of the Technical Delegate(s) or the Referee, justify an alteration.

Progression

20.8　　In all Qualification Rounds, the tables should, where practicable, allow at least the first and second places in each heat to qualify for the next round and it is recommended that, where possible, at least three in each heat should qualify.

Except where Rule 21 of the Technical Rules applies, any other athletes may qualify by place or by time according to Rule 20.2 of the Technical Rules, the applicable Technical Regulations, or as determined by the Technical Delegate(s). When athletes are qualified according to their times, only one system of timing may be applied.

Note: In races longer than 800 metres where rounds are conducted, it is recommended that only a small number of athletes qualify by time.

Where tables are prescribed in the regulations for a competition, it is usual that the principle set out in Rule 20.8 of the Technical Rules will have been incorporated. Where not, the Technical Delegates or Organisers should follow same when establishing the progression table to be used.

There will, however, be occasions when Rule 21 of the Technical Rules may cause a variation to be applied, particularly where there is a tie for the last qualifying position based on place. In such cases, it may be necessary for one less athlete to progress on time. In circumstances where there are sufficient additional lanes available, or in the case of the 800m (where a lane at the start may be used for more than one athlete) or a non-laned race, the Technical Delegate(s) may decide to progress an additional athlete(s).

20.6 当比赛项目决定采用举行一系列的比赛的方式，而非常规赛次及决赛，竞赛规程必须明确规定所有相关事宜，包括排序、抽签方法以及最终成绩的产生方法。

20.7 除非技术代表或裁判长认为这种更换是公平合理的，否则不允许运动员更换组别或分道参加比赛。

录取（比赛晋级）

20.8 在实践中，所有晋级赛次的晋级表应至少允许录取每组的第一、第二名运动员晋级到下一赛次，如有可能，建议每组应至少录取3人。

除出现技术规则21条所述的情况外，任何其他运动员均可根据技术规则20.2条以比赛名次或成绩晋级，或按照相应的竞赛规程、技术代表的决定，获得进入下一赛次的资格。当按时间成绩录取时，只能采用同一种计时方法。

注：800米以上项目，如进行多个赛次，建议录取时应尽量减少按成绩录取的人数。

竞赛规程如果列出了事先制定好的晋级方法，通常要包含技术规则20.8条规定的原则。当没有列出时，技术代表或组织者应遵循以上相同的原则确定晋级方法。

但在有些情况下，技术规则21条可能造成规则应用的一些变化，特别是在通过名次晋级最后1个名额出现并列时。此种情况下，可能减少1名以时间成绩晋级的运动员。在有足够额外跑道的情况下，或在800米（超过1名运动员可以使用同一条跑道起跑）或不分道跑项目中，技术代表可以决定额外的运动员晋级。

Because of the provision within Rule 20.8 of the Technical Rules that for time qualification only one system of timing may be applied it is important for back-up timing systems to be available for Qualification Rounds in case the primary system (usually Photo Finish) fails. In the event that only times from different timing systems are available for two or more heats, the Technical Delegates, in conjunction with the Running and Race Walking Events Referee, should determine, within the circumstances of the particular competition, the fairest method for determining those athletes who should proceed to the next round. Where additional lanes are available, it is recommended that this option be considered first.

Invitation Meetings

20.9 In competitions held under paragraphs 1. (d) and 2. (d) of the World Rankings Competition definition athletes may be seeded, ranked and/or allocated to lanes in accordance with the applicable regulations for the competition or any other method determined by the Organisers but, preferably, notified to the athletes and their representatives in advance.

In invitation meetings, if there is only a "final" round but with more than one race, the races should be arranged according to any applicable regulations for the meeting or the series of meetings of which it is a part. If there are none then it is usual for allocation of athletes to the various "races" to be undertaken by the Organisers or if requested by the appointed Technical Delegate(s).

Similar considerations apply to how the final ranking of the athletes in such events will be made. In some meetings the "race(s)" other than the main race are regarded as separate races and are not considered for the overall ranking but in others the results of more than one race are "combined" to give the overall ranking. It is highly advisable to ensure that whichever is to apply for the competition is also notified to the participants in advance as it may affect prizes and other considerations.

Minimum Times between Rounds

20.10 The following minimum times must be allowed, when practicable, between the last heat of any round and the first heat of a subsequent round or final:

Up to and including 200m	45 minutes
Over 200m up to and including 1000m	90 minutes
Over 1000m	Not on the same day

根据技术规则20.8条的规定，在以时间成绩晋级时，只能采用同一种计时系统计取成绩，因此在资格赛中准备备用计时系统很重要，以防主计时系统（通常为终点摄影）出现故障。当两组或多组的时间成绩来自不同的计时系统，在特定情况下，技术代表应与跑和竞走项目裁判长一起，以最公平的方式决定哪些运动员晋级下一赛次。在有额外分道的情况下，首选使用额外分道的方式。

邀请赛

20.9　在举行世界排名比赛定义1.（d）和 2.（d）所述的比赛中，可以按照相关竞赛规程或组织者确定的其他方法，对运动员进行编排、排序和/或分道，但最好事先通知运动员本人或运动员的代理人。

在邀请赛中，如果只有"决赛"一轮，但有不止一场比赛，则应按照适用于该比赛或其系列赛的任何规程来安排各场比赛。如果没有相关规程，则通常由组委会或应技术代表的要求将运动员分配到各种"比赛"中。

在决定此种比赛中运动员的最终排名时，应考虑类似的因素。在一些比赛中，除主赛外的其他比赛将不用于决定比赛的排名，但是在另外一些比赛中，多场比赛的成绩将被综合以决定整体排名。强烈建议，不管比赛使用何种方式，都要提前通知参赛运动员，因为这将影响奖金和其他一些因素。

赛次间最短间隔时间

20.10　如有可能，在任一赛次的最后一组和后续赛次的第一组或决赛之间，必须留出的最短间隔时间为：

200米及以下各项目为45分钟。

200米以上至1000米各项目为90分钟。

1000米以上各项目不在同一天举行。

21. Ties

21.1　If the Judges or the Photo Finish Judges are unable to separate the athletes for any place according to Rules 18.2, 19.17, 19.21 or 19.26 of the Technical Rules (as may be applicable), it shall be determined to be a tie and the tie shall remain.

Tie for ranking position (according to Rule 20.3.2 of the Technical Rules)

21.2　If there is a tie for any ranking position under Rule 20.3.2 of the Technical Rules, the Chief Photo Finish Judge shall consider the actual times recorded by the athletes to 0.001 second and if it is equal, the tie shall remain and lots shall be drawn to determine the higher ranking position.

Tie for last qualifying position based on place

21.3　If after the application of Rule 21.1 of the Technical Rules, there is a tie for a last qualifying position based on place, if there are lanes or positions available (including lane sharing in 800m races) the tying athletes shall be placed in the next round. If that is not practicable, lots shall be drawn to determine which athlete(s) shall be placed in the next round.

21.4　Where qualifying for the next round is based on place and time (e.g. the first three in each of two heats plus the next two fastest), and there is a tie for the last qualifying position based on place, placing the tied athletes in the next round shall reduce the number of athletes qualifying based on time.

Tie for last qualifying position based on time

21.5　If there is a tie for a last qualifying position based on time, the Chief Photo Finish Judge shall consider the actual times recorded by the athletes to 0.001 second and if it is equal, the tie shall remain. If there are lanes or positions available (including lane sharing in 800m races) the tying athletes shall be placed in the next round. If that is not practicable, lots shall be drawn to determine which athlete(s) shall be placed in the next round.

21. 成绩相等（并列）

21.1 如果裁判员或终点摄影裁判员根据技术规则18.2条、19.17条、19.21条或19.26条（可能适用）无法区分运动员的排名，则可以判定成绩相等。

成绩相等涉及排位顺序（根据技术规则20.3.2条）

21.2 如果运动员成绩相等涉及技术规则20.3.2条所述排名位置，终点摄影主裁判应考虑有关运动员的0.001秒的实际时间，如果成绩仍相等，将抽签确定较高的排名位置。

成绩相等涉及以名次决定最后一个录取资格

21.3 在应用技术规则21.1条后，成绩相等且涉及以名次决定最后一个录取资格时，如果仍有道次或起跑位置可用（包括800米比赛共享分道），成绩相等的运动员都进入下一赛次。如果实际条件不允许，将通过抽签决定进入下一赛次的运动员。

21.4 如果录取下一赛次的运动员是基于名次和成绩（例如，两组中每组的前3名，加上接下来成绩最快的2名），在以名次决定下一赛次最后一个晋级资格出现成绩相等时，将按名次录取，名次相等时应减少以成绩录取的人数。

成绩相等涉及以时间决定最后一个录取资格

21.5 如果出现最后一名在时间上成绩相等，则终点摄影主裁判要考虑运动员们被记录的0.001秒的实际时间，如果时间相同，将判定为成绩相等。如果跑道或起跑位置可用（包括800米比赛共享跑道），成绩相等的运动员都进入下一赛次。如果实际条件不允许，将通过抽签决定进入下一赛次的运动员。

22. Hurdle Races

22.1 The standard distances shall be:

Men, U20 Men and U18 Men: 110m, 400m

Women, U20 Women and U18 Women: 100m, 400m

There shall be ten flights of hurdles in each lane, set out in accordance with the following table:

Men, U20 Men and U18 Men

Distance of race	Distance from start line to first hurdle	Distance between hurdles	Distance from last hurdle to finish line
110m	13.72m	9.14m	14.02m
400m	45.00m	35.00m	40.00m

Women, U20 Women and U18 Women

Distance of race	Distance from start line to first hurdle	Distance between hurdles	Distance from last hurdle to finish line
100m	13.00m	8.50m	10.50m
400m	45.00m	35.00m	40.00m

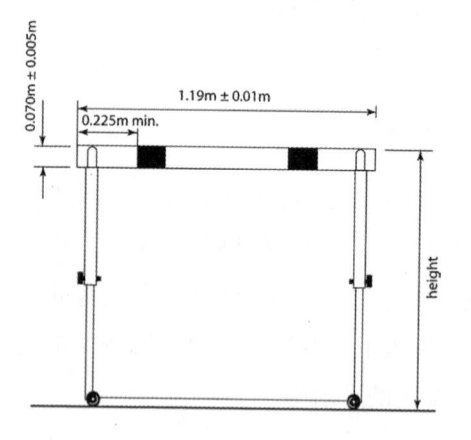

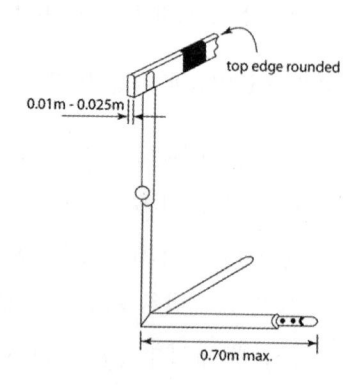

Figure TR22 – Example of a hurdle

22. 跨栏跑

22.1 标准比赛距离：

成年男子、青年男子（U20）和少年男子（U18）：110米、400米。

成年女子、青年女子（U20）和少年女子（U18）：100米、400米。

每条分道按下表设置10个栏架，各项目栏架设置（技术规则22条图）如下：

成年男子、青年男子（U20）和少年男子（U18）

全程距离	起点至第一栏	栏间距离	最后一栏至终点
110米	13.72米	9.14米	14.02米
400米	45.00米	35.00米	40.00米

成年女子、青年女子（U20）和少年女子（U18）

全程距离	起点至第一栏	栏间距离	最后一栏至终点
100米	13.00米	8.50米	10.50米
400米	45.00米	35.00米	40.00米

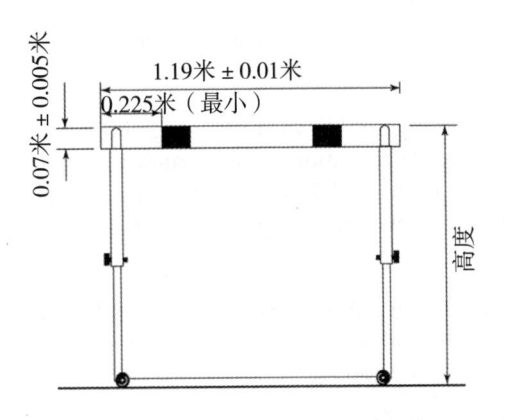

技术规则22条图　栏架

Each hurdle shall be so placed on the track that the feet shall be on the side of the approach by the athlete. The hurdle shall be so placed that the vertical plane of the side of the top bar nearer to the approaching athlete coincides with the track marking nearest the athlete.

22.2　　The hurdles shall be made of metal or some other suitable material with the top bar of wood or other non-metallic suitable material. They shall consist of two feet and two uprights supporting a rectangular frame, reinforced by one or more cross bars, the uprights to be fixed at the extreme end of each base. The hurdle shall be of such a design that a force at least equal to the weight of 3.6kg applied horizontally to the centre of the top edge of the top bar is required to tilt it. The hurdle may be adjustable in height for each event. The counterweights shall be adjustable so that at each height a force at least equal to the weight of 3.6kg and not more than 4kg is required to tilt it.

The maximum horizontal deflection of the top bar of a hurdle (including any deflection of the uprights) when subject to a centrally applied force equal to the weight of 10kg shall not exceed 35mm.

22.3　　Dimensions: The standard heights of the hurdles shall be:

Distance of race	Men	U20 Men	U18 Men	Women/U20	U18 Women
110m/100m	1.067m	0.991m	0.914m	0.838m	0.762m
400m	0.914m	0.914m	0.838m	0.762m	0.762m

Note: Due to manufacturing variations, hurdles up to 1.000m are also acceptable in the U20 110m Hurdles.

In each case, there shall be a tolerance allowance of 3mm, above and below the standard heights, to allow for variation in the manufacture. The width of the hurdles shall be from 1.18m to 1.20m. The maximum length of the base shall be 0.70m. The total weight of the hurdles shall be not less than 10kg.

22.4　　The height of the top bar shall be 70mm ± 5mm. The thickness of this bar should be between 10mm and 25mm, and the top edges should be rounded. The bar should be firmly fixed at the extremities.

放置在跑道上的栏架底座的支架指向运动员的跑来方向。放置栏架时，顶部栏板靠近运动员一侧的垂直面要与最靠近运动员的跑道上（放置栏架的）的标记重合。

（即摆放栏架时，顶部栏板后沿要与跑道上栏架标记后沿对齐）。

22.2 栏架应用金属或其他适合的材料制成，栏顶横木系木料或其他非金属材料。栏架应包括两个底座支架和用一条或数条横木加固的、用以支撑长方形框架的两根立柱，立柱固定于底座的末端。在横木顶端中央至少要在水平方向施加3.6千克的力才能使栏架翻倒，栏架的设计方为合格。栏架高度可按不同项目进行调整，并按栏架的不同高度调整栏架配重，使各种高度的栏架均需3.6千克最多不超过4千克的力方可被推倒。

当栏板中心受到相当于10千克的外力时，栏板的最大水平偏移（包括立柱的偏移）不应超过35毫米。

22.3 栏架规格——栏架的标准高度如下：

全程距离	成年男子	青年男子	少年男子	成年女子/青年女子	少年女子
110米/100米	1.067米	0.991米	0.914米	0.838米	0.762米
400米	0.914米	0.914米	0.838米	0.762米	0.762米

注：由于制造的差异，青年男子（U20）110米栏架高度最高为1.000米。

制作栏架时，栏架高度的允许误差为±3毫米。栏架宽度可为1.18～1.20米。栏架底座最长为0.70米。栏架总重量不得少于10千克。

22.4 栏顶横木高70毫米±5毫米，厚10～25毫米，上边沿应圆滑，两端应固定在支架上。

22.5　　The top bar should be painted with white and black stripes, or with other strong distinctive contrasting colours (and also in contrast with the surrounding environment), such that the lighter stripes, which should be at least 0.225m wide are on the outside. It shall be coloured so as to be visible to all sighted athletes.

22.6　　All races shall be run in lanes and each athlete shall go over each hurdle and keep to their own lane throughout. Failure to do so will result in a disqualification, unless Rule 17.3 of the Technical Rules applies.

In addition, an athlete shall be disqualified, if:

22.6.1　　their foot or leg is, at the instant of clearance, beside the hurdle (on either side) and below the horizontal plane of the top of any hurdle; or

22.6.2　　they knock down or displace any hurdle by hand, body or the front side of the lead lower limb; or

22.6.3　　they directly or indirectly knock down or displace a hurdle in their or in another lane in such a manner that there is effect or obstruction upon any other athlete(s) in the race, and/or another Rule is also infringed.

Provided that this Rule is otherwise observed and the hurdle is not displaced or its height lowered in any manner including tilting in any direction, an athlete may go over the hurdle in any manner.

The requirement to go over each hurdle should not be read as requiring the athlete to go over each hurdle in their own lane - provided always the intention of Rules 17.1 and 17.3 of the Technical Rules is followed. But if an athlete knocks down or displaces a hurdle in another lane and thereby affects the progress of another athlete they shall be disqualified.

Situations when an athlete knocks down or displaces a hurdle in another lane should be interpreted in a logical way. For example, an athlete who knocks down or displaces a hurdle in the lane of an athlete who has already gone over that hurdle, should not necessarily be disqualified unless they otherwise infringe the Rules, e.g. by moving to an inside lane on the bend or having their foot or leg, at the instant of clearance, beside the hurdle (on either side) and below the horizontal plane of the top of any hurdle. The intent of this Rule is to make it clear that an athlete who in making such action affects another athlete should be considered for disqualification.

22.5　栏顶横木应漆成黑白相间的颜色，或涂以其他强烈醒目的对比颜色（要与周围环境的颜色区分开）。位于两端的浅色条纹宽度至少为0.225米。须是所有视力正常运动员可见的颜色。

22.6　所有跨栏跑项目均为分道跑，运动员应自始至终在各自分道内跨越每个栏架完成比赛，未能做到将导致取消比赛资格，但是技术规则17.3条提及的情形除外。

此外，运动员如果有下列情况将被取消比赛资格：

22.6.1　在过栏瞬间，其脚或腿在栏架两侧以外（任意一边），且低于栏顶的水平面；或

22.6.2　用手、身体或摆动腿的正面部分撞倒或移动了栏架；或

22.6.3　直接或间接地碰倒或移动了自己分道上或其他分道上的栏架，使比赛进行中的其他运动员受到影响或阻碍了其他运动员跑进，和/或同时违反了其他的规则。

只要遵守了本规则，栏架位置没有被移动或栏架高度没有任何方式的降低（降低包括在任何方向上的倾斜），运动员可以用任何方式跨越栏架。

只要遵循了技术规则17.1条和17.3条意图的规定，跨越每个栏架的要求不应解读为运动员需要跨越自己分道内的栏架。但如果当一名运动员碰倒或者移动其他分道上的栏架而影响其他运动员跑进时，该运动员要被取消比赛资格。

应使用符合逻辑的方式解释一名运动员碰倒或移动其他分道栏架的情况。例如，当一名运动员撞倒或者移动了其他分道栏架，而该分道中的运动员已经跨越此栏架，那么不应该取消该运动员的比赛资格，除非他违反了其他规则。例如，在弯道上移动到内侧分道，或他的脚或腿在栏架两侧外（任意一边），且低于栏顶横木的水平面。此条规则在于解释清楚在何种情况下运动员将被取消比赛资格。

Referees and Umpires must nonetheless be alert and be sure that each athlete has kept to their own lane. Additionally, it is common in hurdle races that athletes stretch their arms widely while going over the hurdle, thus hitting or hampering the athlete in the next lane. This can best be noticed by Umpires standing or a video camera being placed head-on to the athletes. In this regard Rule 17.1 of the Technical Rules may be applied.

Rule 22.6.1 of the Technical Rules applies to both the athlete's "lead" and "trail" legs.

"Knocking down" a hurdle does not in itself result in disqualification. The previous reference in the Rule to deliberately knocking down a hurdle has been removed. In Rule 22.6.2, it is replaced by some more objective factors to be considered by the Referee. The most obvious example is where the athlete uses their hand but could also be for example by their chest if they "ran through" the hurdle. The front side of the lead lower limb includes all front facing parts of the leg from the top of the thigh to the end of the foot.

In relation to the Note, it will mainly be relevant to competitions at a lower level but is nonetheless applicable to all. Essentially, it permits an athlete, often one who has fallen or lost their stride pattern, to for example place their hands on the hurdle and "climb over".

22.7　Except as provided in Rules 22.6.2 and 22.6.3 of the Technical Rules, the knocking down of hurdles shall not result in disqualification nor prevent a Record being made.

23.　Steeplechase Races

23.1　The standard distances shall be: 2000m and 3000m.

23.2　For the 3000m event, there shall be 28 hurdle jumps and 7 water jumps. The distance from the start to the beginning of the first lap shall not include any jumps, those hurdles not being placed until the athletes have entered the first lap.

23.3　For the 2000m event, there shall be 18 hurdle jumps and 5 water jumps. The first jump is at the third hurdle of a lap. The previous hurdles shall be removed until the athletes have passed them for the first time.

Note: In the 2000m event, if the water jump is on the inside of the track, the finish line has to be passed twice before the first complete lap with five jumps.

因此，裁判长和检查裁判员必须注意，并确定每名运动员在各自分道内行进。此外，在跨栏比赛中，运动员在跨越栏架时摆臂幅度经常会很大，导致击打或者干扰到其他分道的运动员。这种情况通常会被检查裁判员和正对跑道的摄像机发现。在此种情况下，将执行技术规则17.1条。

技术规则22.6.1条适用于运动员的"摆动腿"和"起跨腿"。

"碰倒栏架"不一定会导致取消运动员的比赛资格。规则中先前提到的故意撞倒栏架的条款已被删除。在技术规则22.6.2条的规定下，裁判长可考虑更多的客观因素。如果他们"跑过"栏架，最明显的例子是运动员们用手推，但也可能用胸口推。"摆动腿的正面部分"意思是摆动腿的正面的任何一部分，从大腿上部到脚尖，即整条腿的前部。

关于注释中的情况，主要发生在低水平的比赛中，但仍适用于所有比赛。从本质上讲，运动员已经摔倒或者失去栏间节奏时，允许运动员将手放于栏架上，"爬越"过去。

22.7　除技术规则22.6.2条和22.6.3条所述的情形外，运动员碰倒栏架，不应被取消比赛资格，也不妨碍承认其创造的纪录。

23. 障碍跑

23.1　障碍跑的标准比赛距离为2000米和3000米。

23.2　3000米障碍跑项目，运动员须跨越28次栏架和7次水池。从起跑到第一个整圈的开始无须跨越任何障碍栏架，直到运动员进入第一圈，那些栏架才会被摆放到跑道上。

23.3　2000米障碍跑项目，运动员须跨越18次栏架和5次水池。第一个要跨越的栏架是整圈中的第三个障碍栏架。之前的两个障碍栏架须移开跑道，直至运动员第一次通过后才会被摆放到跑道上。

注：2000米障碍跑，如水池设在跑道内，则在通过终点两次后，每个整圈设5个障碍。

23.4　　For the Steeplechase Events, there shall be five jumps in a complete lap, with the water jump as the fourth. The jumps should be evenly distributed, so that the distance between the jumps shall be approximately one fifth of the nominal length of the lap.

Note: Adjustment to the hurdle spacing may be necessary to ensure that safe distances from a hurdle/start line to the next hurdle are maintained before and after the finish line, respectively, as indicated in the World Athletics Track and Field Facilities Manual.

23.5　　The hurdles shall be 0.914m ± 0.003m high for Senior and U20 Men's events, 0.838m ± 0.003m high for U18 Men's events and 0.762m ± 0.003m for Senior, U20 and U18 Women's events and shall be at least 3.94m wide.

The section of the top bar of the hurdles, and the hurdle at the water jump, shall be 0.127m ± 0.003m square.

The weight of each hurdle shall be between 80kg and 100kg. Each hurdle shall have on either side a base between 1.2m and 1.4m〔see Figure (a) TR23〕.

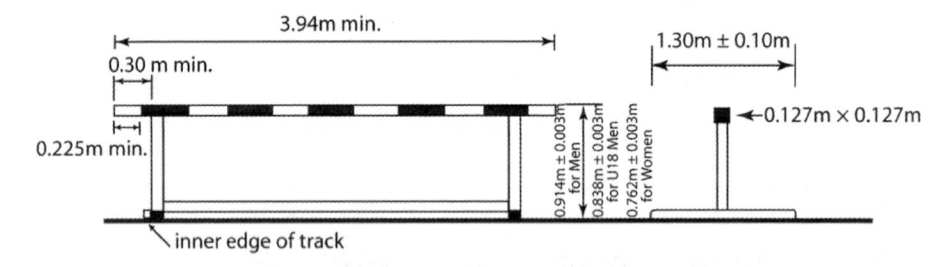

Figure (a) TR23 – Example of a steeplechase hurdle

The hurdle at the water jump shall be 3.66m ± 0.02m wide, and shall be firmly fixed in or to the pit concrete walls, so that minimal only horizontal movement is possible.

The top bars shall be made of wood or other suitable material and should be painted with white and black stripes, or with other strong distinctive contrasting colours (and also in contrast with the surrounding environment), such that the lighter stripes, which should be at least 0.225m wide, are on the outside and shall be coloured so as to be visible to all sighted athletes.

The hurdle shall be placed on the track so that at least 0.30m of the top bar will extend inside the inner edge of the track.

23.4 障碍跑项目，每个整圈须设有5个障碍，水池栏架为第四个障碍。障碍应均匀分布，各障碍之间的距离须约为1圈标准长度的1/5。

注：为了保证在终点线前后保持安全距离，栏架之间、起点至栏架的安全距离，可以根据《世界田联场地设施手册》对各自的间距作适当调整。

23.5 障碍架高度，成年男子和青年男子（U20）为0.914米±0.003米；少年男子（U18）为0.838米±0.003米；成年女子、青年女子（U20）、少年女子（U18）为0.762米±0.003米。障碍栏架宽度至少为3.94米。

所有栏架顶端横木的横截面为0.127米×0.003米。

栏架重量应为80～100千克。栏架两边各装有一个底座支架，其长度为1.20～1.40米。［技术规则23条图（a）］

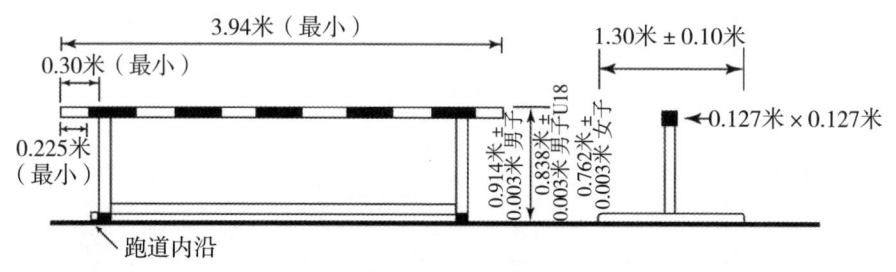

技术规则23条图（a） 障碍跑栏架

水池边栏架的宽度应为3.66米±0.02米，应牢固地固定于水池的混凝土地面，栏架不能有任何水平方向的移动。

障碍栏架的顶端横木应用木料或其他适宜的材料制成，并漆成黑白相间的条纹，或其他具有强烈对比的颜色（要与周围颜色区分开），横木两端为浅色条纹，宽度至少为0.225米，如此上色是为了具有不同视觉能力的运动员都能看见障碍栏架。

放置障碍栏架时，应使顶端横木的一端伸入跑道内沿以内最少0.30米。

Note: It is recommended that the first hurdle taken in the race should be at least 5m in width.

23.6 The water jump, including the hurdle, shall be 3.66m ± 0.02m in length and the water pit shall be 3.66m ± 0.02m in width.

The bottom of the water pit shall consist of a synthetic surface, or matting, of sufficient thickness to ensure safe landing, and allow for the spikes to grip satisfactorily. The depth of the water closest to the hurdle shall be 0.50m ± 0.05m for approximately 1.20m. From there, the bottom shall have a uniform slope of 12.4° ± 1° upwards to the level of the track at the farther end of the water pit. At the start of a race, the surface of the water shall be level with the surface of the track within a margin of 20mm.

Note: Pits to the 2018/19 specifications remain acceptable.

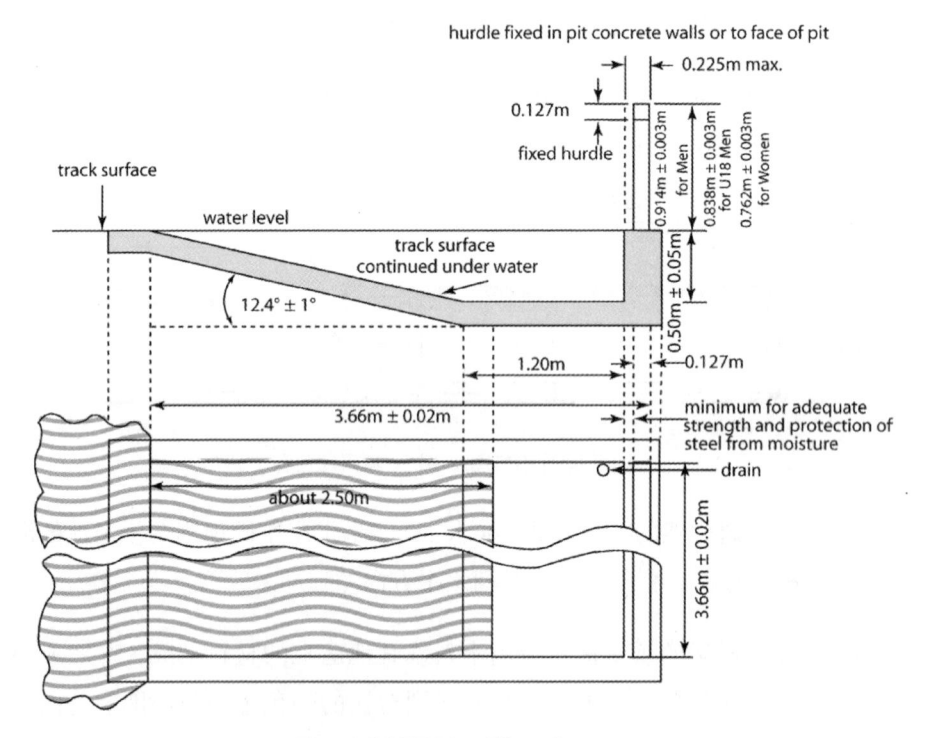

Figure (b) TR23 – Water jump

注：建议比赛中第一个障碍栏架的宽度至少为5米。

23.6　水池，包括水池边栏架，长度须为3.66米±0.02米，水池宽度须为3.66米±0.02米。

水池底部应铺设有足够厚度的人工合成材料或垫子，保证运动员落地安全，并使鞋钉能抓牢地面。靠近障碍架一侧大约1.20米范围的池底深为0.50米±0.05米。从此处起，水池底部的均匀向上倾斜度为12.4°±1°，直至与跑道水平面齐平。在比赛开始阶段，水面应与跑道水平面齐平，最多不能低于跑道20毫米。[技术规则23条图（b）]

注：2018—2019年度的水池规格依然适用。

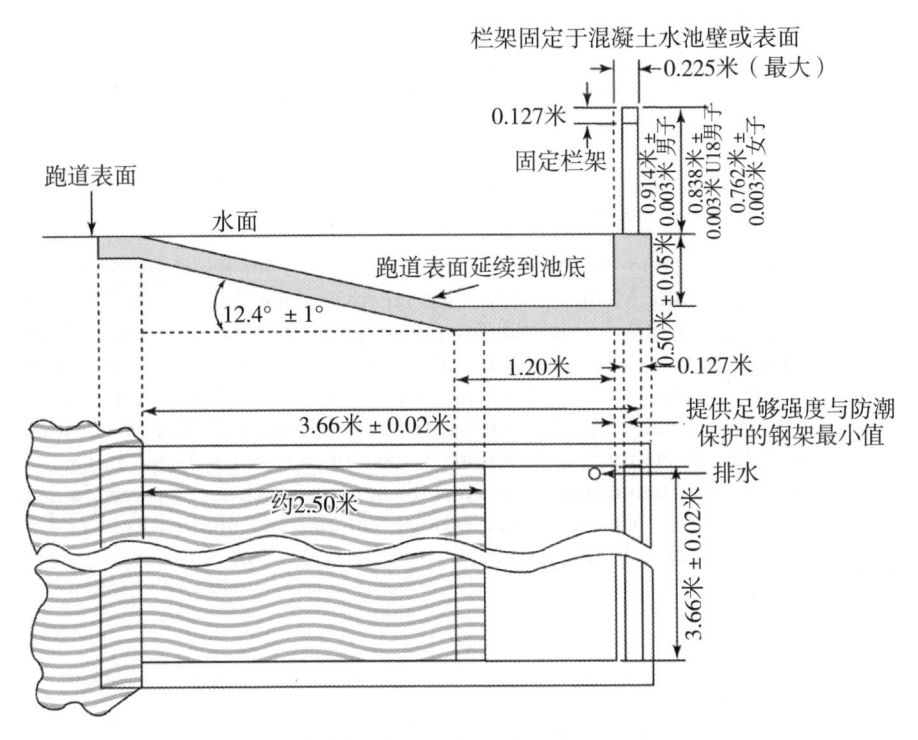

技术规则23条图（b）　障碍水池

23.7 Each athlete shall go over or through the water and shall go over each hurdle. Failure to do so will result in a disqualification.

In addition, an athlete shall be disqualified, if

23.7.1 they step to one side or other of the water jump, or

23.7.2 their foot or leg is, at the instant of clearance, beside the hurdle (on either side), and below the horizontal plane of the top of the hurdle.

Provided this Rule is observed, an athlete may go over each hurdle in any manner.

24. Relay Races

24.1 The standard distances shall be: 4 × 100m, 4 × 200m, 100m-200m-300m-400m Medley Relay (Medley Relay), 4 × 400m, 4 × 800m, 1200m-400m-800m-1600m Distance Medley Relay (Distance Medley Relay), 4 × 1500m.

Note: The Medley Relay may be run with the legs in a different order in which case the appropriate adjustments should be made to the application of Rules 24.3, 24.14 and 24.20 of the Technical Rules.

24.2 Lines 50mm wide shall be drawn across the track to mark the start of each leg distance (scratch line).

24.3 In the 4 × 100m and the 4 × 200m relays, and for the first and second changes in the Medley Relay, each takeover zone shall be 30m long, of which the scratch line is 20m from the beginning of the zone. For the third change in the Medley Relay and in the 4 × 400m and longer relays, each takeover zone shall be 20m long of which the scratch line is the centre. The zones shall start and finish at the edges of the zone lines nearest the start line in the running direction. For each takeover conducted in lanes, a designated Umpire shall ensure that the athletes are correctly placed in their takeover zone. The designated Umpire shall also ensure that Rule 24.4 of the Technical Rules is observed.

23.7 运动员必须越过或通过水面，并且跨越每一个障碍栏架，否则将被取消比赛资格。

此外，出现下列情况也将被取消比赛资格：

23.7.1 踏上水池两边的任意一边；或

23.7.2 在过栏瞬间，其脚或腿在障碍栏架侧面以外（任意一边），且低于栏顶水平面。

只要遵守本规则规定，运动员可以用任何方式跨越栏架。

24. 接力跑

24.1 标准比赛距离应为：4×100米、4×200米、100米—200米—300米—400米异程接力、4×400米、4×800米、1200米—400米—800米—1600米长距离异程接力、4×1500米。

注：异程接力赛各棒次可以不同的顺序进行比赛，在此种情况下，技术规则24.3条、24.14条和24.20条的适用应当有适当的调整。

24.2 应在分道线上画出宽50毫米的横线，标明各棒次之间的距离和接力区标志线。

24.3 在4×100米、4×200米及异程接力的第一、第二次交接棒中，各接力区的长度为30米，标志线位于距接力区开始分界线20米处。在异程接力的第三次交接棒和4×400米及更长距离的接力中，每个接力区的长度为20米，标志线位于接力区的中间。接力区的开始和结束都从接力区分界线跑进方向的后沿算起。在每次分道的交接棒过程中，专门指定1名检查裁判员以确保运动员处于各自接力区内的正确位置。这名指定的检查裁判员应确保技术规则24.4条的执行。

The Umpires must ensure that each athlete from each team takes their position in the correct lanes or position. The Starter's Assistants will be responsible for the positioning of the first runners and for ensuring that each is supplied with a baton. They may also be assigned to assist at any takeover zones which subsequently occur at the start line. Chief Umpires for each takeover zone and the umpires placed at their disposal will be responsible for the positioning of the subsequent runners. When all athletes are correctly positioned the zone Chief Umpire should advise the relevant other officials by the agreed means of communication – which for major competitions would usually be by radio.

They must also ensure that for all takeovers the receiving athletes' feet are completely inside the zone before they commence their movement which eventuates in the taking of the baton. This movement may not commence at any point outside the zone.

24.4 When all or the first portion of a Relay Race is being run in lanes, an athlete may place one check-mark on the track within their own lane, by using adhesive tape, maximum 0.05m × 0.40m, of a distinctive colour which cannot be confused with other permanent markings. No other check-mark may be used. The Umpires shall direct the relevant athlete(s) to adapt or remove any marks not complying with this Rule. If they do not, the Umpires shall remove them.

Note: Serious cases may further be dealt with under Rules 7.1 and 7.3 of the Technical Rules.

24.5 A baton shall be used for all Relay Races held in the Stadium and shall be carried by hand throughout the race. At least for competitions conducted under paragraphs 1 (a), (b), (c) and 2. (a), (b) of the World Rankings Competition definition, each baton shall be numbered and of a different colour and may include a timing transponder.

The relay baton shall be a smooth hollow tube, circular in section, made of wood, metal or any other rigid material in one piece, the length of which shall be 0.28m to 0.30m. The outside diameter shall be 40mm ± 2mm and it shall not weigh less than 50g. It should be coloured so as to be easily visible during the race.

Athletes are not permitted to wear gloves or to place material (other than those permitted by Rule 6.4.3 of the Technical Rules) or substances on their hands or on the baton in order to obtain a better grip of the baton.

If an athlete does not follow this Rule, their team shall be disqualified.

检查裁判员必须确保每个接力队的每名运动员站在正确的道次和位置。助理发令员负责安排第一棒运动员的位置，并确保每名运动员都分配到接力棒。他们也可能被指派到起点线附近的接力区协助观察随后完成的交接棒情况。每个接力区的检查主裁判和他们安排的每个检查裁判员将负责安排后继棒次运动员的位置。当每名运动员被安排好各自位置后，检查主裁判将通过事先确定好的通信方式通知其他相关裁判，通常在大赛中使用对讲机进行通信。

他们必须确保在每次交接棒过程中，在交接棒启动开始前，接棒运动员的脚要完全位于接力区内。交接棒的启动不能从接力区外开始。

24.4　当接力的全程或第一棒为分道跑时，运动员可在自己的分道内用胶布做一个标记，其最大尺寸为0.05米×0.40米，颜色应明显区别于跑道上的永久性标记。不得使用任何其他的标志物。检查裁判员须指导运动员根据规则使用标记，并移除不符合规则的标志物。如果他们不执行，检查裁判员须移除不符合规则要求的标志物。

注：情况严重的可根据技术规则7.1条和7.3条处理。

24.5　在体育场内举行的所有接力跑比赛必须使用接力棒，运动员必须手持接力棒跑完全程。至少在举办世界排名比赛定义1.（a）（b）（c）和2.（a）（b）所述的比赛中，每支接力棒必须有编号和不同的颜色，还可包括计时传感器。

接力棒应为光滑的中空圆管，外表平滑，由木料、金属或其他适宜的坚固无缝材料制成，长度为0.28～0.30米。外边框直径为40毫米±2毫米，重量不少于50克。接力棒应涂上颜色，以便在比赛中明显可见。

不允许运动员戴手套或者在手或接力棒上放置某种材料（除技术规则6.4.3条允许的外）或物质以便更好地抓握接力棒。

如果运动员不遵守此规则，其所在接力队将被取消比赛资格。

Note: *If possible, the allocation of the colour to each lane or starting order position should be shown on the start list.*

24.6 If dropped, the baton shall be recovered by the athlete who dropped it. They may leave their lane to retrieve it provided that, by doing so, they do not lessen the distance to be covered. In addition, where the baton is dropped in such a way that it moves sideways or forward in the direction of running (including beyond the finish line), the athlete who dropped it, after retrieving it, must return at least to the point where it was last in their hand, before continuing in the race. Provided these procedures are adopted where applicable and no other athlete is impeded, dropping the baton shall not result in disqualification.

But if an athlete does not follow this Rule, their team shall be disqualified.

24.7 The baton shall be passed within the takeover zone. The passing of the baton commences when it is first touched by the receiving athlete and is completed the moment it is in the hand of only the receiving athlete. In relation to the takeover zone, it is only the position of the baton which is decisive. Passing of the baton outside the takeover zone shall result in disqualification. Rule 17.3.2 of the Technical Rules shall apply when relevant.

The application of Rule 17.3.2 of the Technical Rules may be necessary when an athlete, during the takeover, steps outside the allocated lane inside the takeover zone without material advantage gained and other athletes obstructed.

In determining the position of the baton, it is the whole baton which must be considered.

Umpires must be diligent to ensure that they observe any contact with the baton prior to the baton entering the takeover zone. If the receiving athlete even touches the baton prior to the baton being inside the zone, the team will be subject to disqualification. They must also ensure that the baton is only in the hand of the receiving athlete before it "leaves" the takeover zone.

24.8 Until the moment when the baton is in the hand of only the receiving athlete, Rule 17.3 of the Technical Rules shall be applicable only to the incoming athlete. Thereafter it shall be applicable only to the receiving athlete.

注：如果可能，每个分道或出发位置的接力棒颜色应在检录单上标出。

24.6　如发生掉棒，必须由掉棒运动员拾起。允许掉棒运动员离开自己的分道拾棒，但不得因此缩短比赛距离。此外，接力棒掉在跑道两侧或跑进方向的前面时（包括越过终点线），掉棒的运动员在拾回棒后，必须至少回到他最后手持棒的位置并继续跑进。如果遵守上述程序，且没有阻碍到其他运动员，不得因掉棒取消比赛资格。

如果运动员没有遵守此条规则，则他所属的接力队将被取消比赛资格。

24.7　接力棒必须在接力区内完成交接。接力棒的交接从接力棒初次触及接棒运动员开始，到完全由接棒运动员手持才算完成。仅以接力棒的位置决定是否在接力区内完成接力。在接力区外完成交接将被取消比赛资格。发生相关情况要适用技术规则17.3.2条。

当运动员在交接棒过程中，在没有获得实质利益的情况下跑出自己分道的接力区，且阻碍了其他运动员时，可适用技术规则17.3.2条。

在决定接力棒的位置时，要考虑整个接力棒的位置。

检查裁判员必须确保他们能够观察到接棒运动员在接力棒进入接力区之前与接力棒的任何接触。如果接棒运动员在接力棒进入接力区之前接触到接力棒，该运动员所在接力队将被判取消比赛资格。他们还必须确保，在接力棒"离开"接力区之前，接力棒只在接棒运动员手中。

24.8　直到接力棒完全在接棒运动员手上的瞬间，技术规则17.3条只适用于交棒运动员，之后该规则只适用于接棒运动员。

Additionally, athletes before receiving and/or after handing over the baton, should keep in their lanes or maintain position until the course is clear to avoid obstruction to other athletes. Rules 17.2 and 17.3 of the Technical Rules shall not apply to these athletes. If, however, an athlete impedes a member of another team, including by running out of position or lane, Rule 17.1 of the Technical Rules shall be applied.

24.9 If during the race an athlete takes or picks up the baton of another team, their team shall be disqualified. The other team should not be penalised unless an advantage is obtained.

24.10 Each member of a relay team may run one leg only. Any four athletes from among those entered for the competition, whether for that or any other event, may be used in the composition of the relay team for any round. However, once a relay team has started in a competition, up to a total of four additional athletes may be used as substitutes in the composition of the team. If a team does not follow this Rule, it shall be disqualified.

24.11 The composition of a team and the order of running for a relay shall be officially declared no later than the published first call time (the time by which the athletes must be present in the Call Room) for their respective heat in each round of the competition. The team shall compete as named and in the declared order. If a team does not follow this Rule, it shall be disqualified.

24.12 The 4 × 100m race shall be run entirely in lanes.

24.13 The 4 × 200m race may be run in any of the following ways:

    24.13.1 where possible, entirely in lanes (four bends in lanes),

    24.13.2 in lanes for the first two legs, as well as that part of the third leg up to the nearer edge of the breakline described in Rule 17.5 of the Technical Rules, where athletes may leave their respective lanes (three bends in lanes),

    24.13.3 in lanes for the first leg up to the nearer edge of the breakline described in Rule 17.5 of the Technical Rules, where athletes may leave their respective lanes (one bend in lanes).

此外，运动员在接棒之前和（或）交棒之后，应留在各自分道或保持位置直到跑道畅通，以免阻挡其他运动员。技术规则17.2条和17.3条不适用于这些运动员。如果运动员阻碍了其他接力队的运动员，包括跑离所在位置或跑出分道，则按技术规则17.1条处理。

24.9 在比赛过程中，如果运动员手持或捡拾到其他接力队的接力棒，该运动员所属接力队将被取消比赛资格。其他接力队不应受罚，除非从中获得利益。

24.10 接力队的每名运动员只能参加接力赛的其中一棒。参加接力跑比赛任何赛次的4名运动员，可以是报名参加其他项目比赛的任何运动员。然而，一旦开始比赛，每队最多允许有4名替补队员参加比赛。如果违反此规定，将取消该队比赛资格。

24.11 接力队的成员组成和各棒顺序，必须在公布的每一赛次比赛各自组别检录开始时间（运动员必须到检录处报到的时间）之前正式申报。接力队必须按正式申报名单和各棒次顺序参加比赛。如不遵守此规则，将取消比赛资格。

24.12 4×100米接力比赛，应为全程分道跑。

24.13 4×200米接力比赛，可以采用以下任何一种方法进行：

24.13.1 如有可能，应为全程分道跑（4个弯道均为分道跑）。

24.13.2 前两棒是分道跑，第三棒运动员分道跑越过技术规则17.5条所述的抢道线后沿以后，可离开自己的分道（3个弯道为分道跑）。

24.13.3 第一棒运动员分道跑越过技术规则17.5条所述的抢道线后沿以后，可离开自己的分道（1个弯道为分道跑）。

Note: Where not more than four teams are competing and Rule 24.13.1 is not possible, Rule 24.13.3 should be used.

24.14 The Medley Relay race should be run in lanes for the first two legs, as well as that part of the third leg up to the nearer edge of the breakline described in Rule 17.5 of the Technical Rules, where athletes may leave their respective lanes (two bends in lanes).

24.15 The 4 × 400m race may be run in either of the following ways:

   24.15.1 in lanes for the first leg, as well as that part of the second leg up to the nearer edge of the breakline described in Rule 17.5 of the Technical Rules, where athletes may leave their respective lanes (three bends in lanes);

   24.15.2 in lanes for the first leg up to the nearer edge of the breakline described in Rule 17.5 of the Technical Rules, where athletes may leave their respective lanes (one bend in lanes).

Note: Where not more than four teams are competing, Rule 24.15.2 should be used.

24.16 The 4 × 800m race may be run in either of the following ways:

   24.16.1 in lanes for the first leg up to the nearer edge of the breakline described in Rule 17.5 of the Technical Rules, where athletes may leave their respective lanes (one bend in lanes);

   24.16.2 without the use of lanes.

24.17 If an athlete does not follow Rule 24.13, 24.14, 24.15 or 24.16.1 of the Technical Rules their team shall be disqualified.

24.18 The Distance Medley Relay race and the 4 × 1500m race shall be run without the use of lanes.

24.19 For all takeovers, athletes are not permitted to begin running outside their takeover zones, and shall start within the zone. If an athlete does not follow this Rule, their team shall be disqualified.

注：如果参赛队不多于4队，且没有条件选用本规则24.13.1条，建议按本规则24.13.3条进行比赛。

24.14 异程接力比赛，前两棒是分道跑，第三棒运动员越过技术规则17.5条所述的抢道线后沿以后，可离开自己的分道（2个弯道为分道跑）。

24.15 4×400米接力比赛，可以用以下的任何一种方法跑进：

24.15.1 第一棒是分道跑，第二棒运动员越过技术规则17.5条所述的抢道线后沿以后，可离开自己的分道（3个弯道为分道跑）；

24.15.2 第一棒运动员越过技术规则17.5条所述的抢道线后沿以后，可离开自己的分道（1个弯道为分道跑）。

注：如果参赛队不多于4队，建议使用技术规则24.15.2条所述方式进行比赛。

24.16 4×800米接力比赛，可以用以下的任何一种方法跑进：

24.16.1 第一棒运动员越过技术规则17.5条所述的抢道线后沿以后，可离开自己的分道（1个弯道为分道跑）。

24.16.2 不使用分道。

24.17 如果运动员不遵守技术规则24.13条、24.14条、24.15条或24.16.1条，该运动员所在的接力队将被取消比赛资格。

24.18 长距离异程接力及4×1500米接力比赛，采用不分道方法跑进。

24.19 运动员不允许在接力区以外起跑，必须从接力区内起跑。如果运动员不遵守本规则，该运动员所在的接力队将被取消比赛资格。

24.20　In the Medley Relay, the athletes running the final leg and in the 4 × 400m race, the athletes running the third and fourth legs (or under Rule 24.15.2 of the Technical Rules, also the second leg) shall, under the direction of a designated official, place themselves in their waiting position in the same order (inside to out) as the order of their respective team members as they enter the last bend. Once the incoming athletes have passed this point, the waiting athletes shall maintain their order, and shall not exchange positions at the beginning of the takeover zone. If an athlete does not follow this Rule, their team shall be disqualified.

Note: In the 4 × 200m race (if this event is not run entirely in lanes) where the previous leg is not run in lanes, the athletes shall line up in the order of the start list (inside to out).

24.21　In any race, when lanes are not being used, including when applicable, in 4 × 200m, the Medley Relay and 4 × 400m, waiting athletes can take an inner position on the track as incoming team members approach, provided they do not jostle or obstruct another athlete so as to impede their progress. In 4 × 200m, the Medley Relay and 4 × 400m, waiting athletes shall maintain the order in accordance with Rule 24.20 of the Technical Rules. If an athlete does not follow this Rule, their team shall be disqualified.

24.22　In the case of relay events not covered by this Rule, the relevant competition regulations should specify any particular rules that should be applied and the method by which the relay should be conducted.

Chief Umpires must remain at the zone to which they and their Umpires have been assigned. Once the athletes are correctly placed in their lanes and the race has started, zone Chief Umpires and those Umpires assigned to them are responsible for reporting any infringements of both these Rules as well as any other infringements particularly those under Rule 17 of the Technical Rules.

24.20　异程接力最后一棒运动员和4×400米比赛的第三、第四棒（或依据技术规则24.15.2条，则为第二棒）运动员应在指定裁判员的指挥下，按照同队交棒运动员进入最后一个弯道时的先后顺序（由内向外）排列各自的接棒位置。一旦交棒运动员跑过该点，接棒运动员须保持其排列顺序，不能改变其在接力区开始处的位置。如果运动员不遵守本规定，其所在的接力队将被取消比赛资格。

注：4×200米接力比赛（如不是全程分道跑时），若前一棒为不分道跑，运动员将按照检录单的顺序排列（由内向外）。

24.21　在不分道的接力比赛中，如适用，也包括4×200米、异程接力和4×400米等项目，接棒运动员在同队交棒队员即将到达时，可移向跑道内侧的位置接棒，但不得冲撞、阻挡其他运动员以致妨碍其跑进。在4×200米、异程接力和4×400米比赛中，接棒运动员须根据技术规则24.20条的规定保持他们的顺序。如果运动员没有遵守本规则，其所在的接力队将被取消比赛资格。

24.22　凡本规则未涉及的接力项目，在竞赛规程中应给出特定的规则以及执行（比赛）方案。

检查主裁判和检查裁判员必须在被分配的接力区内。当运动员被正确地安排在各自分道上，且比赛已经开始，接力区检查主裁判和检查裁判员将负责报告涉及以上规则的任何犯规情况，特别是技术规则17条中提及的犯规情况。

PART III FIELD EVENTS

25. General Conditions – Field Events

Practice Trials at the Competition Area

25.1　At the competition area and before the beginning of the event, each athlete may have practice trials. In the case of throwing events, the practice trials will be in draw order and always under the supervision of the Judges.

Whilst in the past the Rules specified that there should be two practice trials for each athlete in throwing events, there is currently no such specification. Rule 25.1 of the Technical Rules should be interpreted as allowing whatever number of practice trials that may be included in the warm-up time available. Whilst for major events, two remains a standard practice, this is regarded as a minimum and should time be available and some or all or the athletes request additional practice trials, this can be permitted.

25.2　Once a competition has begun, athletes are not permitted to use, for practice purposes, as appropriate,

　　25.2.1　the runway or take-off area;

　　25.2.2　vaulting poles;

　　25.2.3　implements;

　　25.2.4　the circle or runway or the ground within the sector with or without implements.

However, the use of implements outside the circle or runway is prohibited at any time.

The application of this Rule should not prevent an athlete from touching, preparing or taping their vaulting pole or their selected implement in readiness for their trial provided that it does not endanger, delay or obstruct another athlete or other person. It is particularly important that the Judges interpret this Rule reasonably so as to ensure the competition proceeds in an efficient manner and the athlete is able, if they so choose, to take their trial immediately their time begins.

第三部分　田赛项目

25.　田赛项目通则

在比赛区域的试跳（掷）练习

25.1　比赛开始前，每名运动员均可在比赛区域进行试跳（掷）练习。但是，投掷项目试掷练习应始终在裁判员的监控下，按抽签排定的顺序进行。

过去的规则曾明确要求投掷项目每个运动员有2次练习机会，然而现在没有具体要求。技术规则25.1条应该被理解为运动员可以在允许的热身时间内进行任意次数的练习。通常在大型赛事中，标准的练习次数为2次，这也被作为最少练习次数要求。如果热身时间充足，部分或全部运动员要求额外的练习，也应该被允许。

25.2　一旦比赛开始，运动员不得以练习为目的使用下列场地设施和器械：

  25.2.1　助跑道或起跳区；

  25.2.2　撑竿；

  25.2.3　各种投掷器械；

  25.2.4　无论徒手或持器械使用投掷圈、助跑道或落地区内地面。

  但是，任何时候都禁止在投掷圈或助跑道以外使用器械。

关于该条规则的应用：如果运动员没有造成危险，延误或阻挡其他运动员或者影响其他人，则不应该阻止运动员触碰、准备或缠绕他的撑竿，或选择投掷器械用于准备他的试跳（掷）。特别重要的是，裁判员应合理解释本规则，以确保比赛以有效的方式进行，并且运动员能够在比赛开始后立即参加试跳（掷）。

Markers

25.3 Markers, as follows:

    25.3.1 In all Field Events where a runway is used, markers shall be placed alongside it, except for High Jump where the markers can be placed on the runway. An athlete may use one or two markers (supplied or approved by the Organisers) to assist them in their run-up and take-off. If such markers are not supplied, they may use adhesive tape but not chalk or similar substance nor anything which leaves indelible marks.

    25.3.2 For throws made from a circle, an athlete may use one marker only. This marker may be placed only on the ground in the area immediately behind or adjacent to the circle but not on any lines or in the landing sector. It must be temporary, in position only for the duration of each athlete's own trial, and shall not impair the view of the Judges. No personal markers may be placed in or beside the landing area.

Note: Each marker shall be composed of a single piece only.

    25.3.3 The Judges shall direct the relevant athlete to adapt or remove any marks not complying with this Rule. If they do not, the Judges shall remove them.

Note: Serious cases may further be dealt with under Rules 7.1 and 7.3 of the Technical Rules.

    25.3.4 For Pole Vault, the Organisers should place suitable and safe distance markers beside the runway at each 0.5m between the points 2.5m to 5m from the "zero" line and at each 1.0m from the 5m to the 18m point.

If the ground is wet, the adhesive tape can be fixed to the ground by drawing pins of several colours.

标志物

25.3　标志物，具体如下：

　　25.3.1　使用助跑道的田赛项目，应沿助跑道两侧放置标志物，跳高助跑标志物可放置在助跑道上。每名运动员可放置1~2个标志物（由组织批准或提供），以帮助其助跑和起跳。如未提供此类标志物，运动员可使用胶布，但不得使用粉笔或任何不易去除痕迹的类似物质。

　　25.3.2　在投掷圈内比赛的投掷项目中，比赛中只允许运动员使用1个标志物，此标志物只能放置在投掷圈后方或紧靠投掷圈的地面上，但不能放置在任何线上或落地区内。仅限运动员在自己试掷期间临时放置，并且不能干扰裁判员的视线。落地区内及旁边不能放置任何个人标志物。

　　注：每个标志物只能由单一物体组成。

　　25.3.3　裁判员应指导相关运动员调整或移除不符合本条规则的标志物。如运动员不听从要求，裁判员将自行移除标志物。

　　注：严重情况下，可进一步按照技术规则7.1条和7.3条处理。

　　25.3.4　撑竿跳高项目，比赛组织者应在助跑道旁，距离"零线"2.5米至5米之间每间隔0.5米，以及在5米至18米之间每间隔1米处，放置适宜且安全的距离标记。

如果比赛场地湿滑，胶布可以用不同颜色的图钉固定在地上。

The requirement for each marker to be a single piece should be interpreted sensibly by the Referee. If for example the manufacturer has used two pieces connected to make a single structure which is intended to be used that way, it should be allowed. Similarly, if an athlete chooses to place both their markers in the same place or, in the case of the High Jump, an athlete who tears the tape they are given into one or more pieces to make a single marker of a different shape to stand out more clearly, these should also be acceptable.

Rule 25.3.4 of the Technical Rules is designed to assist athletes and their coaches in determining their take-off points and the progress on the runway. There is no set concept as to how they should be constructed or look – with Organisers and Referees having discretion in interpreting what is acceptable and fair within the intention of the Rule in each particular competition environment.

Performance Markers and Wind Socks

25.4 Performance Markers and Wind Socks, as follows:

    25.4.1 A distinctive flag or marker may be provided to mark the existing World Record and, when appropriate, the existing Area, National or Meeting Record.

    25.4.2 One or more wind socks should be placed in an appropriate position in all jumping events, Discus Throw and Javelin Throw, to show the athletes the approximate direction and strength of the wind.

Competing Order and Trials

25.5 Except where Rule 25.6 of the Technical Rules applies, or the applicable regulations provide otherwise, the athletes shall compete in an order drawn by lot.

If any athlete by their own decision makes a trial in an order different from that previously determined, Rules 7.1 and 7.3 of the Technical Rules shall be applied. In the case of a warning, the result of the trial (valid or failure) will stand.

If there is a Qualification Round, there shall be a fresh drawing of lot for the final.

25.6 Except for the High Jump and Pole Vault, no athlete shall have more than one trial recorded in any one round of trials of the competition.

要求每个标志物都必须由单一物体组成，裁判长对此应有合理的解读。如果制作者运用两个部件连接成一个独立结构的标志物，则应该被允许使用。类似地，如果运动员将两个标志物放在一起，或在跳高比赛中运动员将胶布撕成1片或多片，并将其组合成一个不同形状、易于看清的标志物，这些情形也应该被允许。

技术规则25.3.4条是为了帮助运动员和他们的教练员确定起跳点的位置和助跑过程。对于标志物的构造或外观没有固定的概念——在每个特定比赛环境中，组织者和裁判长可以在规则允许的范围内，自由解释什么是可接受的且公平的标志物。

成绩标志和风标

25.4 成绩标志和风标，具体如下：

    25.4.1 可放置明显的旗示或标志物以标明当前的世界纪录。如情况允许，还可放置当前地区、国家或赛会纪录标识。

    25.4.2 在所有跳跃项目、铁饼和标枪比赛中，场地适宜的位置应放置1个或多个风标，以便向运动员显示大致的风向和风力。

比赛顺序和试跳（掷）

25.5 除运用技术规则25.6条或者适用的规程另有规定外，运动员应按抽签排定的顺序进行比赛。

如果运动员自行决定不按赛前确定的顺序进行试跳（掷），按技术规则7.1条和7.3条处理。如有警告，试跳（掷）的成绩（有效或失败）将维持不变。

如果举行及格赛，决赛要重新抽签决定比赛顺序。

25.6 除跳高和撑竿跳高项目外，在任何一轮比赛中，不允许记录运动员1次以上的试跳（掷）成绩。

In all Field Events, except for the High Jump and Pole Vault, where there are more than eight athletes, each athlete shall be allowed three trials and the eight athletes with the best valid performances shall be allowed three additional trials, unless the applicable regulations provide otherwise.

In the case of the last qualifying place, if two or more athletes have the same best performances, Rule 25.22 of the Technical Rules shall be applied. If it is thus determined that there has been a tie, the tying athletes shall be allowed any additional trials, permitted by the applicable regulations.

Where there are eight athletes or fewer, each athlete shall be allowed six trials, unless the applicable regulations provide otherwise. If one or more athletes fail to achieve a valid trial during the first three rounds of trials, such athletes shall compete in subsequent rounds of trials before those with valid trials, and if more than one, in the same relative order according to the original draw.

In both cases:

25.6.1 the competing order for any subsequent rounds of trials shall be in the reverse ranking order recorded after the first three rounds of trials, unless the applicable regulations provide otherwise;

25.6.2 when the competing order is to be changed and there is a tie for any position, those tying shall compete in the same relative order according to the original draw.

Note (i): For Vertical Jumps, see Rule 26.2 of the Technical Rules.

Note (ii): If one or more athletes are permitted by the Referee to continue in a competition "under protest" in accordance with Rule 8.5 of the Technical Rules, such athletes shall compete in all subsequent rounds of trials before all others continuing in the competition and if more than one, in the same relative order according to the original draw.

Note (iii): The regulations of the relevant governing body may specify the number of trials (provided it is no more than six) and the number of athletes which may progress to each additional round of trials after the third.

除跳高和撑竿跳高外的其他田赛项目，如参赛运动员人数多于8人，则每名运动员有3次试跳（掷）机会，有效成绩最优的前8名运动员可再有3次试跳（掷）机会。除非竞赛规程另有规定。

当涉及最后1个晋级决赛轮次名额时，如果2名或多名运动员的最优成绩相等，则按照技术规则25.22条处理。如果成绩仍然相等，成绩相等的运动员应被给予规程规定的额外试跳（掷）机会。

除非竞赛规程有规定，当运动员人数为8人或少于8人时，每人均有6次试跳（掷）机会。如果1名或多名运动员在前3轮试跳（掷）时未能取得有效成绩，则该运动员应在取得有效成绩的运动员之前进行后续轮次的试跳（掷）；若有多于1名运动员，则应按照原抽签的相对顺序进行比赛。

在两种情况中：

25.6.1 　除相关竞赛规程规定外，前3轮试跳（掷）结束后，按运动员成绩进行排序，后续轮次试跳（掷）应按成绩排序的倒序进行；

25.6.2 　当比赛顺序改变，出现任何排名成绩相等时，成绩相等的运动员的试跳（掷）应按原抽签顺序进行。

注（ⅰ）：高度跳跃项目见技术规则26.2条。

注（ⅱ）：根据技术规则8.5条，如果裁判长允许1名或多名运动员"在抗议下"比赛，那么这些运动员后续轮次的试跳（掷）应排在其他继续比赛的运动员之前。如果他们超过1人，应按其原抽签的相对顺序进行比赛。

注（ⅲ）：有关管理机构可在比赛规程中明确规定，运动员试跳（掷）的次数（不能超过6次）和前三轮试跳（掷）后每轮次晋级试跳（掷）的运动员人数。

Note (iv): The regulations of the relevant governing body may specify that the competing order be changed again after any further round of trials after the third.

Note (V): In competitions held under paragraphs 1. (d) and 2. (d) of the World Rankings Competition definition, athletes may be seeded, ranked and/or allocated to competing order in accordance with the applicable regulations for the competition or any other method determined by the Organisers but preferably notified to the athletes and their representatives in advance.

When an athlete has retired from an event either by their own decision or by a decision made in accordance with Rule 6 of the Competition Rules, they may take no further part in that event, including, in the case of Vertical Jumps, in a jump-off for first place or, in the case of Combined Events, in that particular event of the Combined Events.

In situations in the horizontal Field Events where there are more than eight athletes, only the eight athletes with the best valid performances are allowed any additional trial(s). This requires an athlete to have a measured mark recorded from a fair jump or throw in at least one of their first three trials. Where less than eight athletes achieve such a valid performance it is only those athletes who are allowed any additional trial(s) even though it will mean less than eight athletes proceeding.

Recording of Trials

25.7　Except in High Jump and Pole Vault, a valid trial shall be indicated by the measurement taken.

For the standard abbreviations and symbols to be used in all other cases, see Rule 25.4 of the Competition Rules.

Completion of Trials

25.8　The Judge shall not raise a white flag to indicate a valid trial until a trial is completed. The Judge may reconsider a decision if they believe they raised the incorrect flag.

The completion of a valid trial shall be determined as follows:

25.8.1　in the case of Vertical Jumps, once the judge has determined that there is no failure according to Rules 27.2, 28.2 or 28.4 of the Technical Rules;

注（iv）：有关管理机构可在比赛规程中明确规定，可以再次改变在第三轮试跳（掷）之后的任何轮次试跳（掷）的比赛顺序。

注（v）：在世界排名比赛定义1.(d)和2.(d)所述的比赛中，运动员可以根据比赛的适用规程或组织者确定的任何其他方法进行排序、排名和/或分配比赛顺序，但最好提前通知运动员及其代表。

运动员自行决定或根据竞赛规则6条决定退出某项比赛时，不得再参加该项目比赛，包括高度跳跃项目中的决名次跳，或在全能比赛中的某个单项。

在有8名以上运动员参加的田赛远度项目中，只有取得最好有效成绩的8名运动员才能进行后续的试跳（掷）。这要求运动员至少在前三次试跳（掷）中有一次有效成绩测量并被记录。如果少于8名运动员取得有效成绩，则只有取得有效成绩的运动员才被允许进行任何后续的试跳（掷），即使这将意味着只有不足8名运动员继续进行比赛。

记录试跳（掷）

25.7　除跳高和撑竿跳高项目外，每次有效试跳（掷）测量成绩应予以显示。

应使用标准的缩写及符号记录各种出现的情形，见竞赛规则25.4条。

试跳（掷）的完成

25.8　裁判员在试跳（掷）完成后才能举白旗表示试跳（掷）成功。如果裁判员认为自己举旗错误，可以重新作出判定。

一次成功的试跳（掷）应按以下规则判定：

25.8.1　在高度跳跃项目中，裁判员判定没有违反技术规则27.2条、28.2条或28.4条的规定。

25.8.2　in the case of Horizontal Jumps, once the athlete leaves the landing area in accordance with Rule 30.2 of the Technical Rules;

25.8.3　in the case of throwing events, once the athlete leaves the circle or runway in accordance with Rule 32.17 of the Technical Rules.

Qualification Round

25.9　A Qualification Round shall be held in Field Events in which the number of athletes is too large to allow the competition to be conducted satisfactorily in a single round (final). When a Qualification Round is held, all athletes shall compete in, and qualify through, that round except that the relevant governing body may, for one or more events, authorise the conduct of additional qualification round(s) either at the same or at one or more earlier competitions to determine some or all of the athletes who shall be entitled to participate and in which round of the competition. Such procedure and any other means (such as achieving entry standards during a specified period, by specified placing in a designated competition or by specified rankings) by which an athlete is entitled to participate, and in which round of the competition, shall be set out in the regulations for each competition.

Performances accomplished in a Qualification Round or additional qualification round(s) shall not be considered as part of the final.

25.10　The athletes shall normally be divided into two or more groups such that the groups are of approximately equal strength and whenever possible so that athletes of each Member or team shall be placed in different groups. Unless there are facilities for the groups to compete at the same time and under the same conditions, each group should start its practice trials immediately after the previous group has finished.

25.11　It is recommended that, in competitions of more than three days, a rest day be provided between Qualification Rounds and the finals in the vertical jumping events.

25.12　The conditions for qualifying, the qualifying standard and the number of athletes in the final, shall be decided by the Technical Delegate(s). If no Technical Delegate(s) have been appointed, the conditions shall be decided by the Organisers. For competitions conducted under paragraphs 1. (a), (b), (c) and 2. (a), (b) of the World Rankings Competition definition, there should be at least 12 athletes in the final unless otherwise provided in the regulations for the competition.

25.8.2 在远度跳跃项目中，运动员按技术规则30.2条中的规定离开落地区。

25.8.3 在投掷项目中，运动员按技术规则32.17条的规定离开投掷圈或助跑道。

及格赛

25.9 在田赛项目中，如果参赛运动员人数较多而无法顺利地在1个赛次（决赛）完成比赛时，要举行及格赛。当举行及格赛时，所有运动员都应参加该赛次比赛，除非相关管理机构在1个或多个项目中，授权在同一场或者在1场或多场早先的比赛中进行额外的晋级赛次，以决定有权参加比赛的部分或全部运动员及参加哪个赛次的比赛。运动员获准参加比赛，以及获准进入比赛哪个赛次的程序和方法（例如，在特定时间内达到报名标准、在指定比赛中的名次或规定的排名情况），要在相关比赛的竞赛规程中说明。

及格赛或额外的晋级赛次中取得的成绩不能作为决赛成绩的一部分。

25.10 通常情况下，运动员应分为实力大致相当的两组或多组进行及格赛。如果可能，应将同一会员协会或代表队的运动员编排在不同的组。除非场地设施允许各组同时比赛，否则应在上一组比赛结束后，立即进行下一组的试跳（掷）练习。

25.11 如果比赛超过3天，建议在高度跳跃项目的及格赛与决赛之间安排1天休息。

25.12 晋级条件、及格标准和进入决赛的运动员人数须由技术代表决定，如果没有指派技术代表，则由组织者决定。举行世界排名比赛定义1.（a）（b）（c）和2.（a）（b）所述的比赛时，除非竞赛规程中有其他规定，应至少有12名运动员进入决赛。

Note: The applicable regulations may specify how vacant positions due to withdrawals in finals may be filled in by athletes ranked next following the qualification round after those qualified.

25.13　In a Qualification Round, apart from the High Jump and the Pole Vault, each athlete shall be allowed up to three trials. Once an athlete has achieved the qualifying standard, they shall not continue in the Qualification Round.

25.14　In a Qualification Round for the High Jump and the Pole Vault, the athletes, not eliminated after three consecutive failures, shall continue to compete according to Rule 26.2 of the Technical Rules (including passing a trial) until the end of the last trial at the height set as the qualifying standard, unless the number of athletes for the final has been reached as defined in Rule 25.12 of the Technical Rules. Once it is determined that an athlete will be in the final, they shall not continue in the Qualification Round.

25.15　If no athletes, or fewer than the required number of athletes, achieve the pre-set qualifying standard, the group of finalists shall be expanded to that number by adding athletes according to their performances in the Qualification Round. In the case of the last qualifying place, if two or more athletes have the same best performances in the overall results of the competition, Rule 25.22 or 26.8 of the Technical Rules as appropriate shall be applied. If it is thus determined that there has been a tie, the tying athletes shall be placed in the final.

25.16　When a Qualification Round for the High Jump and Pole Vault is held in two simultaneous groups, it is recommended that the bar be raised to each height at the same time in each group.

It is important when seeding High Jump and Pole Vault qualifying groups that the requirements of Rule 25.10 of the Technical Rules are observed. The Technical Delegates and the Referee must follow closely the progress of the Qualification Rounds of the High Jump and the Pole Vault to ensure that, on the one hand, the athletes must jump (or indicate that they are passing) as long as they are not eliminated under Rule 26.2 of the Technical Rules until the qualifying standard has been reached (unless the number of athletes for the final has been reached as defined in Rule 25.12 of the Technical Rules) and, on the other hand, any tie between athletes in the overall standings in the two groups is resolved according to Rule 26.8 of the Technical Rules. Close attention must also be kept to the application of Rule 25.14 of the Technical Rules to ensure that athletes do not unnecessarily continue in the competition once it is certain that they will be in the final regardless of what may happen to the other athletes continuing to compete in the Qualification Round.

注：适用的规程可以规定，如何由及格赛后排名紧接着的运动员填补因决赛退赛而产生的空缺位置。

25.13　在及格赛中，除跳高和撑竿跳高外，每名运动员最多有3次试跳（掷）机会。一旦运动员达到及格标准，不得继续参加及格赛。

25.14　在跳高和撑竿跳高及格赛中，运动员如果没有因连续3次试跳失败而被淘汰，则要根据技术规则26.2条（包括免跳）的规定继续比赛，直至及格高度上的最后一次试跳结束，除非根据技术规则25.12条的规定进入决赛的人数达到要求。一旦运动员确定将进入决赛，则不得继续参加及格赛。

25.15　如果运动员均未达到事先制定的及格标准或达标人数少于规定人数，则应根据运动员在及格赛中的成绩，补齐进入决赛的人数。在及格赛中决定最后一个进入决赛的名额时，如果2名或更多运动员最好成绩相等，应根据技术规则25.22条或26.8条的有关规定处理。如果运动员的成绩仍相等，那么成绩相等的运动员都进入决赛。

25.16　当跳高或撑竿跳高分两组同时进行及格赛时，建议两组同时提升横杆高度。

重要的是，在编排跳高和撑竿跳高及格赛分组时，应该遵守技术规则25.10条的规定。技术代表、裁判长必须密切关注跳高和撑竿跳高及格赛的比赛进程，一方面，直至横杆升到及格标准高度之前（除非符合技术规则25.12条的规定达到决赛人数），如果运动员没有因技术规则26.2条被淘汰，就必须试跳（或显示他们免跳）；另一方面，上述两组及格赛的总体排名中运动员的任何名次并列，应依据技术规则26.8条处理。还需密切关注技术规则25.14条的执行，不论其他继续参加及格赛的运动员情况如何，要确保进入决赛的运动员不再继续参加没有必要的比赛。

Time Allowed for Trials

25.17 The official responsible shall indicate to an athlete that all is ready for the trial to begin, and the period allowed for this trial shall commence from that moment.

For the Pole Vault, the time shall begin when the crossbar has been adjusted according to the previous wishes of the athlete.

If the time allowed elapses after an athlete has started their trial, that trial should not be disallowed.

If after the time for a trial has begun, an athlete decides not to attempt that trial, it shall be considered a failure once that period allowed for the trial has elapsed.

The following times shall not be exceeded. If the time is exceeded, unless a determination is made under Rule 25.18 of the Technical Rules, the trial shall be recorded as a failure:

Individual Events

Number of athletes remaining in the competition	High Jump	Pole Vault	Other
More than 3 athletes (or for the very first trial of each athlete)	1 min	1 min	1 min
2 or 3 athletes	1.5 min	2 min	1 min
1 athlete	3 min	5 min	—

Combined Events

Number of athletes remaining in the competition	High Jump	Pole Vault	Other
More than 3 athletes (or for the very first trial of each athlete)	1 min	1 min	1 min
2 or 3 athletes	1.5 min	2 min	1 min
1 athlete	2 min	3 min	—

试跳（掷）时限

25.17 相关裁判员须向运动员显示一切准备就绪可以试跳（掷），本次试跳（掷）时限开始计算。

在撑竿跳高中，时限从横杆按照运动员先前的意愿调整后开始计算。

如果时限结束时，运动员已经开始试跳（掷），应允许其比赛。

如果时限开始计算，运动员决定不进行试跳（掷），一旦时限结束，将视为试跳（掷）失败。

下列时限不得超过，如果超过时限，除了根据技术规则25.18条作出的决定，该试跳（掷）将记录为失败：

个人项目

剩余参加比赛的运动员人数	跳高	撑竿跳高	其他项目
多于3名运动员［或每名运动员全赛的第一次试跳（掷）］	1分钟	1分钟	1分钟
2名或3名运动员	1.5分钟	2分钟	1分钟
1名运动员	3分钟	5分钟	—

全能项目

剩余参加比赛的运动员人数	跳高	撑竿跳高	其他项目
多于3名运动员［或每名运动员全赛的第一次试跳（掷）］	1分钟	1分钟	1分钟
2名或3名运动员	1.5分钟	2分钟	1分钟
1名运动员	2分钟	3分钟	—

Consecutive Trials

	High Jump	Pole Vault	Other
Consecutive trials	2 min	3 min	2 min

Note (i): A clock which shows the remaining time allowed for a trial should be visible to an athlete. In addition, an official shall normally raise and keep raised a yellow flag during the final 15 seconds of the time allowed. Alternate visual indication may also be approved.

Note (ii): In the High Jump and Pole Vault, any change in the time period allowed for a trial, except the time specified for consecutive trials, shall not be applied until the bar is placed to a new height. In the other Field Events, except for the time specified for consecutive trials, the time limit allowed will not change.

Note (iii): When calculating the number of athletes remaining in the competition, this shall include those athletes who could be involved in a jump off for first place.

Note (iv): When only one athlete (who has won the competition) remains in High jump or Pole Vault and is attempting a World Record or other record relevant to the competition, the time limit shall be increased by one minute beyond those set out above.

Note (v): In Vertical Jumps, the number of athletes remaining in the competition is determined at the time the bar is raised to a new height.

Note (vi): The time for consecutive trials will be applied for any consecutive trial regardless of it being in the same round for a replacement trial, at the same height or consecutive heights in Vertical Jumps or when the order is changed at the end of a round of trials. The time for consecutive trials will be applied if it is longer than the time allowed for the trial based on the calculation of the number of athletes remaining in the competition. However, when an athlete, based on the calculation of the number of athletes remaining in the competition, is entitled to a longer time, then that will be applied.

连续试跳（掷）

	跳高	撑竿跳高	其他项目
连续试跳（掷）	2分钟	3分钟	2分钟

注（ⅰ）：应设置向运动员显示试跳（掷）剩余时限的时钟。此外，一名裁判员在时限尚余15秒的时间内应持续举起黄旗。替代的视觉信号也可被批准。

注（ⅱ）：在跳高和撑竿跳高比赛中，除连续试跳，直到横杆被放到一个新的高度，不允许改变试跳的时限。在田赛的其他项目中，除了连续试跳（掷）的时限可以改变，其他的时限不得改变。

注（ⅲ）：当计算仍在参赛的运动员人数时，应包括那些因成绩相等而要参加争夺第一名的决名次跳的运动员。

注（ⅳ）：在跳高和撑竿跳高比赛中，只剩下1名运动员（他已赢得比赛），他尝试破世界纪录或相关比赛纪录时，时限在上述基础上增加1分钟。

注（ⅴ）：在高度跳跃项目中，剩余运动员人数以横杆升至新高度时为准。

注（ⅵ）：连续试跳（掷）的时限适用于任何连续的试跳（掷），无论是在同一轮重新试跳（掷）、高度跳跃项目的相同高度或后继高度，还是在一轮比赛结束后改变顺序的试跳（掷）。如果连续试跳（掷）时限超过了根据剩余参赛运动员人数计算出的允许试跳（掷）时限，则将适用连续试跳（掷）时限。但是，如果根据剩余参加比赛的运动员人数计算，运动员有权获得更长的时限，则将适用这一更长的时限。

Whilst the Judges should always use a system which notifies or calls the next athlete who is to take their trial plus the one who is to follow, this is essential when the time allowed for an athlete to take their trial is one minute. They must also ensure that the competition area is completely ready for the next trial before calling the athlete and then starting the clock. The Judges, and the Referee in particular, must be fully aware of the current competition environment, including direction from Event Presentation, when deciding when to start the clock or to "time out" and call a failure.

Particular circumstances which should be taken into account are the availability of the runway for an athlete's trial in High Jump and Javelin Throw (when Running or Race Walking Events are being held simultaneously in the same competition area) and the distance for athletes to walk to and through the cage to reach the circle to take their trial in Discus Throw and Hammer Throw.

Replacement Trials

25.18   If, for any reason beyond their control, an athlete is hampered in a trial and is unable to take it, or the trial cannot be correctly recorded, the Referee shall have the authority to award them a replacement trial or to re-set the time either partially or in full.

No change in the order shall be permitted. A reasonable time shall be allowed for any replacement trial according to the particular circumstances of the case. In cases when the competition has progressed before the replacement trial is awarded, it should be taken before any other subsequent trials are then made.

There are several situations in which it may be appropriate for an athlete to be given a replacement trial including where because of procedural or technical failure a trial is not measured and it is not possible for a re-measurement to be accurately made. Whilst this should be avoided by good systems and backups, with technology being used more and more provision needs to be made for when things do go wrong. As no change in the competition order should be permitted (unless the problem is not immediately discovered and the competition has continued), the Referee must decide how long should be allowed for the replacement trial taking into account the specific circumstances of each particular case.

Absence during Competition

25.19   An athlete may not leave the immediate area of the event during the progress of the competition, unless they have the permission of, and is accompanied by, an official. If possible, a warning should be given first, but for subsequent instances or in serious cases the athlete shall be disqualified. If an athlete subsequently is not present for a particular trial, it will be counted as a failure once the period allowed for the trial has elapsed.

当试跳（掷）时限为1分钟时，裁判员有必要运用某种系统通知或提示下一名运动员准备试跳（掷）并告知随后比赛的运动员。在通知运动员试跳（掷）前，相关裁判员必须确保比赛场地准备完毕后再开始启动计时钟。裁判员，特别是裁判长，必须充分了解当前的比赛环境，包括指导项目展示，决定何时启动计时钟或因"时间结束"而记录为失败。

运动员是否能在跳高和标枪的助跑道进行试跳（掷）（当比赛区域同时进行跑或竞走项目时），以及链球和铁饼运动员要绕过护笼走到投掷圈内进行试掷所需走过的距离，这些特殊情况应该予以考虑。

重新试跳（掷）

25.18　如果由于不可控的原因，妨碍了运动员并导致不能完成试跳（掷）或成绩不能被正确记录，相关裁判长有权给予运动员一次重新试跳（掷）机会，或重新设置部分或全部的时限。

　　　运动员试跳（掷）顺序不得改变。根据赛场的具体情况，确定合理的重新试跳（掷）时间。当给予重新试跳（掷）时之前的比赛已在进行，在后续试跳（掷）开始之前应首先进行重新试跳（掷）。

有数种情形需要给予运动员重新试跳（掷）的机会，包括程序或技术上的问题导致某次成绩没测量或无法重新进行精确的测量。应运用良好的设备系统或某种形式的备份避免这样的情形，随着越来越多技术的应用，应该对可能发生的错误做好预案和准备。由于在比赛中不允许改变顺序（除非在比赛进行过程中问题没有及时发现，并已继续比赛），相关裁判长要根据每个特定案例的具体情况决定给予重新试跳（掷）所需的时间。

比赛中缺席

25.19　在比赛过程中，运动员不得离开相应比赛的场地，除非得到许可并由裁判员陪同。如果可能，第一次出现将予以警告，对于再次出现或情况严重的运动员将会被取消比赛资格。如果一名运动员没有参加某次特定的试跳（掷），则在相应的时限结束后，被视为失败。

Change of Competition Area or Time

25.20　The Technical Delegate(s) or appropriate Referee shall have the authority to change the place or time of the competition if, in their opinion, the conditions justify it. Such a change should be made only after a round of trials has been completed.

Note: Neither the wind strength nor its change of direction is sufficient condition to change the place nor time of the competition.

The phrase "round of trials" instead of "rounds" is designed to ensure a clear difference between a "round of trials" within a Field Event competition and a "round of the competition" (i.e. a Qualification Round or a Final).

If the conditions make it impossible to complete a round of trials before a change of place or time is made, the Technical Delegate (through the Referee) or Referee should normally void those trials already completed in that round of trials (always depending on and evaluating the conditions and the results of the trials up to the time of the interruption) and recommence the competition at the beginning of that round of trials. See also Rule 11.4 of the Technical Rules.

Result

25.21　Each athlete shall be credited with the best of all their trials, including, in the case of High Jump and Pole Vault, those achieved in resolving a tie for first place.

Ties

25.22　Except for the High Jump and Pole Vault, the second best performance of the athletes having the same best performances shall determine whether there has been a tie. Then, if necessary, the third best, and so on. If the athletes are still equal following the application of this Rule 25.22, it shall be determined to be a tie.

Except in Vertical Jumps, in the case of a tie for any place, including first place, the tie shall remain.

Note: For Vertical Jumps, see Rules 26.8 and 26.9 of the Technical Rules.

变更比赛场地或时间

25.20　技术代表或有关裁判长如认为情况需要，有权变更比赛场地或时间。此类变更应在一轮试跳（掷）结束之后进行。

　　　注：不得因风力和风向的变化而变更比赛场地或比赛时间。

用"试跳（掷）的轮次"代替"赛次"，目的在于明确田赛项目比赛中"试跳（掷）的轮次"与"比赛的赛次"（如及格赛或决赛）的区别。

如果无法在更改地点和时间之前结束某一轮次的试跳（掷），技术代表（通过裁判长）或裁判长通常应宣布该轮已完成的试跳（掷）无效（始终取决于对中断时试跳条件和结果的评估），并重新开始该轮次的比赛。另请参看技术规则11.4条。

成绩

25.21　每名运动员的成绩，取其所有试跳（掷）中最优成绩，包括跳高和撑竿跳高比赛中因成绩相等决定第一名的决名次跳中取得的成绩。

成绩相等

25.22　除了跳高和撑竿跳高项目，如果成绩相等，应以其次优成绩判定名次。如次优成绩仍相等，则以第三较优成绩判定，依次类推。按技术规则25.22条，如成绩依然相等，应判定运动员的比赛名次并列。

　　　除高度跳跃项目外，无论任何名次，包括第一名，成绩相等运动员的名次应并列。

　　　注：高度跳跃项目见技术规则26.8条和26.9条。

Vertical Jumps

26. General Conditions – Vertical Jumps

26.1　Before the competition begins, the Referee or the Chief Judge shall announce to the athletes the starting height and the subsequent heights to which the bar will be raised at the end of each round of trials, until there is only one athlete remaining having won the competition, or there is a tie for first place (For Combined Events, see Rule 39.8.4 of the Technical Rules).

Trials

26.2　An athlete may commence jumping/vaulting at any height previously announced by the Referee or Chief Judge and may jump/vault at their own discretion at any subsequent height. Three consecutive failures, regardless of the height at which any of such failures occur, disqualify from further jumping/vaulting except in the case of a tie for first place.

The effect of this Rule is that an athlete may pass their second or third trial at a particular height (after failing first or second time) and still jump / vault at a subsequent height.

If an athlete passes a trial at a certain height, they may not make any subsequent trial at that height, except in the case of a jump-off for first place.

In the case of the High Jump and Pole Vault, if one or more athletes are is not present when all other athletes who are present have completed the competition, the Referee shall deem that such athlete(s) have abandoned the competition, once the period for one further trial has elapsed.

Whilst Rule 26.2 of the Technical Rules provides that an athlete may not attempt the second or third trial at any particular height in Vertical Jumps if it has been deemed that they have passed an earlier trial at that height, it is suggested that in lower level competitions such as children's and school meets, the competition regulations could be adapted so as to allow an athlete to opt to take the second or third trial in such cases.

26.3　Even after all the other athletes have failed, an athlete is entitled to continue jumping until they have forfeited their right to compete further.

高度跳跃项目

26. 高度跳跃项目通则

26.1 比赛开始前，裁判长或主裁判应向运动员宣布起跳高度和每轮试跳结束后横杆的提升高度，直至比赛中只剩下一名已获胜的运动员或存在并列第一名的情形（全能项目比赛见技术规则39.8.4条）。

试跳

26.2 运动员可以在裁判长或主裁判事先宣布的横杆升高计划中的任何一个高度上开始试跳，也可在后续任何一个高度上根据自己的意愿决定是否试跳。只要运动员连续3次试跳失败，不管发生在任何高度，即失去继续比赛的资格，涉及第一名成绩相等的情况除外。

允许运动员在某一高度上第一次或第二次试跳失败后，在其第二次或第三次试跳时请求免跳，并在后续的高度上继续试跳。

运动员在某一高度上请求免跳后，不得在该高度上恢复试跳，除非出现第一名成绩相等进行决名次跳的情况。

在跳高和撑竿跳高比赛中，如果1名或多名运动员在其他运动员完成比赛后仍未出现，在又一次试跳时限结束后，相关裁判长应视该运动员（们）已放弃比赛。

虽然技术规则26.2条规定，如果运动员被认为是在某高度的试跳中免跳，那么运动员不可在高度跳跃项目中任何同一高度进行第二、三次试跳，但是建议在低水平的比赛中，如儿童或者学校运动会上，可对竞赛规程进行调整，允许运动员在这种情况下选择进行第二、三次试跳。

26.3 即使所有其他运动员均已失败，1名运动员仍有资格继续试跳，直至他放弃继续比赛的权益。

26.4　Unless there is only one athlete remaining and they have won the competition:

26.4.1　the bar shall never be raised by less than 2cm in the High Jump and 5cm in the Pole Vault after each round of trials; and

26.4.2　the increment of the raising of the bar shall never increase.

These Rules 26.4.1 and 26.4.2 of the Technical Rules shall not apply once the athletes still competing all agree to raise it to a World Record (or other record relevant to the competition) height directly.

After an athlete has won the competition, the height or heights to which the bar is raised shall be decided by the athlete, in consultation with the relevant Judge or Referee.

Note: This Rule does not apply for a Combined Events Competition.

Height Measurement

26.5　In all vertical jumping events, measurements shall be made, in whole centimetres, perpendicularly from the ground to the lowest part of the upper side of the bar.

26.6　Any measurement of a new height shall be made before athletes attempt such height. A remeasurement should be made if the bar has been substituted. In all cases of Records, the Judges shall also re-check the measurement before each subsequent Record attempt if the bar has been touched since last measured.

Crossbar

26.7　The crossbar shall be made of fibre-glass, or other suitable material but not metal, circular in crosssection except for the end pieces. It shall be coloured so as to be visible to all sighted athletes. The overall length of the crossbar shall be 4.00m ± 0.02m in the High Jump and 4.50m ± 0.02m in Pole Vault. The maximum weight of the crossbar shall be 2kg in the High Jump and 2.25kg in Pole Vault. The diameter of the circular part of the crossbar shall be 30mm ± 1mm. (see Figure TR26)

26.4 除非比赛中只剩下1名运动员，并且他已获得该项目比赛的冠军：

    26.4.1 每轮次试跳结束后，跳高项目的横杆升高不得少于2厘米，撑竿跳高项目的横杆升高不得少于5厘米；并且

    26.4.2 横杆升高的幅度不得增大。

技术规则26.4.1条和26.4.2条不适用于仍在试跳的所有运动员都同意将横杆直接升到世界纪录（或其他相关比赛的纪录）高度的情形。

当某运动员已在比赛中获胜，经与相关裁判员或裁判长协商，由该运动员决定横杆提升的高度。

注：此规定不适用于全能比赛项目。

高度测量

26.5 所有高度跳跃项目的测量均应以整数厘米为单位，从地面垂直量至横杆上沿最低点。

26.6 每次升高横杆，在运动员试跳之前，均应测量横杆高度。如果更换横杆，应重新测量横杆高度。当横杆放置在纪录高度时，有关裁判员必须进行复核测量。如果自上一次测量纪录高度后，横杆又被触及，在后续纪录高度试跳之前，裁判员必须再次测量横杆高度。

横杆

26.7 横杆应用玻璃纤维或其他适宜材料制成，不得使用金属材料。除两端外，横杆的横截面呈圆形。横杆应被涂上颜色便于不同视力水平的运动员都能够看清楚。跳高横杆全长为4.00米±0.02米，撑竿跳高横杆全长为4.50米±0.02米。跳高横杆最大重量为2千克，撑竿跳高横杆最大重量为2.25千克。横杆圆形部分直径为30毫米±1毫米。（技术规则26条图）

The crossbar shall consist of three parts - the circular bar and two end pieces, each 30mm-35mm wide and 0.15m-0.20m long for the purpose of resting on the supports of the uprights.

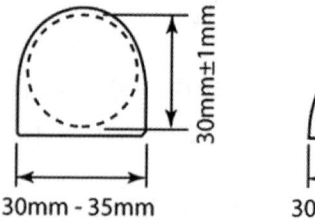

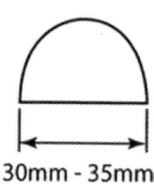

30mm - 35mm   30mm - 35mm

Figure TR26 – Alternative ends for crossbar

These end pieces shall be circular or semi-circular with one clearly defined flat surface on which the bar rests on the crossbar supports. This flat surface may not be higher than the centre of the vertical cross section of the crossbar. The end pieces shall be hard and smooth. They shall not be of, or covered with rubber or with any other material which has the effect of increasing the friction between them and the supports.

The crossbar shall have no bias and, when in place, shall sag a maximum of 20mm in the High Jump and 30mm in Pole Vault.

Control of elasticity: Hang a 3kg weight in the middle of the crossbar when in position. It may sag a maximum of 70mm in the High Jump and 0.11m in Pole Vault.

Placings

26.8   If two or more athletes clear the same final height, the procedure to decide the places will be the following:

    26.8.1   The athlete with the lowest number of jumps at the height last cleared shall be awarded the higher place.

    26.8.2   If the athletes are equal following the application of Rule 26.8.1 of the Technical Rules, the athlete with the lowest total of failures throughout the competition up to and including the height last cleared, shall be awarded the higher place.

    26.8.3   If the athletes are still equal following the application of Rule 26.8.2 of the Technical Rules, the athletes concerned shall be awarded the same place unless it concerns the first place.

横杆应由3部分组成，即圆形杆体和两端。为便于放置在横杆托上，横杆两端应宽30～35毫米，长0.15～0.20米。

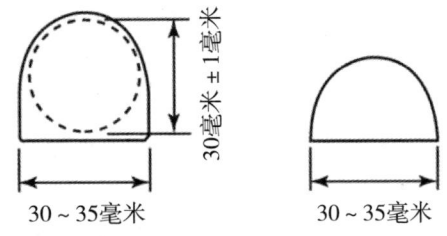

横杆两端横切面应呈圆形或半圆形，并有明确规定的平面放置在横杆托上。这个平面不能高于横杆垂直断面的中心，并要坚硬和平滑。横杆两端不得包裹橡胶或任何能增大与横杆托之间摩擦力的物质。

技术规则26条图　横杆末端（两者择其一）

横杆应无倾斜，放在横杆托上时，跳高横杆最多下垂20毫米，撑竿跳高横杆最多下垂30毫米。

横杆的弹性检查：放置横杆后，在横杆中央悬挂3千克的重物，跳高横杆最多下垂70毫米，撑竿跳高横杆最多下垂0.11米。

决定名次

26.8　如果2名或者2名以上运动员最后跳过的高度相同，将按以下程序决定名次：

26.8.1　在最后跳过的高度上，试跳次数较少者名次列前。

26.8.2　应用技术规则26.8.1条后，如成绩仍然相等，则在包括最后跳过的高度在内的全部比赛中，试跳失败总次数较少者名次列前。

26.8.3　应用技术规则26.8.2条后，如成绩仍相等，但不涉及第一名时，则运动员的名次并列。

26.8.4　If it concerns the first place, a jump-off between these athletes shall be conducted in accordance with Rule 26.9 of the Technical Rules, unless otherwise decided, either in advance according to the regulations applying to the competition, or during the competition but before the start of the event by the Technical Delegate(s) or the Referee if no Technical Delegate has been appointed. If no jump-off is carried out, including where the relevant athletes at any stage decide not to jump further, the tie for first place shall remain.

Note: This Rule 26.8.4 does not apply for a Combined Events Competition

There are a number of ways in which a jump-off may be cancelled/terminated:

a. by provision in advance of the competition set out in the regulations;

b. by decision during the competition by the Technical Delegate (or Referee if there is no Technical Delegate);

c. by decision of the athletes not to jump further prior to or at any stage of the jump-off.

Whilst any decision by the Technical Delegate or Referee not to conduct a jump-off should be made before the start of the event, there may be circumstances where this might not be possible such as where conditions at the place of competition make it impossible or undesirable to begin or continue with a jump-off. The Referee could use their powers under Rule 18 of the Competition Rules or Rule 25 of the Technical Rules to deal with this situation. It is emphasised that the athletes may make the decision not to jump further either before or at any stage during the jump-off.

Jump-off

26.9　Jump-off, as follows:

26.9.1　Athletes concerned must jump at every height until a decision is reached or until all of the athletes concerned decide not to jump further.

26.9.2　Each athlete shall have one jump at each height.

26.9.3　The jump-off shall start at the next height determined in accordance with Rule 26.1 of the Technical Rules after the height last cleared by the athletes concerned.

26.8.4　如涉及第一名时，将按技术规则26.9条的规定，在成绩相等的运动员间进行决名次跳，除非根据比赛前制定的竞赛规程作出决定，或者在赛事中该项比赛开始前由技术代表或裁判长作出决定（如没有指派技术代表，则由裁判长进行）。如果不进行决名次跳，保留并列第一名，包括相关运动员在比赛的任何阶段决定不再继续进行试跳。

注：技术26.8.4条规则不适用于全能项目。

以下为可以取消或中止决名次跳的几种情况：

a. 赛前的竞赛规程中有明确的规定；

b. 比赛中技术代表（未设技术代表时由裁判长）的决定；

c. 运动员在决名次跳之前或决名次跳过程中的任何阶段决定不再继续试跳。

虽然可能是因为赛场的环境和条件不适宜执行或继续进行决名次跳，但是技术代表或裁判长应该在该项目比赛开始前提出不执行决名次跳的决定。裁判长应按竞赛规则18条和技术规则25条的规定处理该问题。需要强调的是，运动员可在决名次跳之前或决名次跳过程中的任何阶段作出不再继续试跳的决定。

决名次跳

26.9　决名次跳，具体如下：

26.9.1　相关运动员必须在每个高度进行试跳，直到决出名次，或者所有相关运动员决定不再继续试跳。

26.9.2　每名运动员在每个高度上只有一次试跳机会。

26.9.3　运动员应在技术规则26.1条规定的最后越过高度的下一高度上开始进行决名次跳。

26.9.4　　If no decision is reached the bar shall be raised if more than one athlete concerned were successful, or lowered if all of them failed, by 2cm for the High Jump and 5cm for the Pole Vault.

26.9.5　　If an athlete is not jumping at a height, they automatically forfeit any claim to a higher place. If only one other athlete then remains, they are declared the winner regardless of whether they attempt that height.

High Jump – Example

Heights announced by the Chief Judge at the beginning of competition: 1.75m; 1.80m; 1.84m; 1.88m; 1.91m; 1.94m; 1.97m; 1.99m...

Athlete	Heights							Failures	Jump Off			Pos
	1.75m	1.80m	1.84m	1.88m	1.91m	1.94m	1.97m		1.91m	1.89m	1.91m	
A	o	xo	o	xo	x-	x x		2	x	o	x	2
B	-	xo	-	xo	-	-	x x x	2	x	o	o	1
C	-	o	xo	xo	-	x x x		2	x	x		3
D	-	xo	xo	xo	x x x			3				4

"A", "B", "C" and "D" all cleared 1.88m.

Rules 26.8 and 26.9 of the Technical Rules now come into operation; all four athletes have the same number of jumps at the height last cleared. Now, the Judges add up the total number of failures, up to and including the height last cleared, i.e. 1.88m.

"D" has more failures than "A", "B" or "C", and is therefore awarded fourth place. "A", "B" and "C" are still equal and as this concerns the first place, they shall jump at 1.91m which is the next height after the height last cleared by the athletes concerned.

As all the athletes failed, the bar is lowered to 1.89m for another jump-off. As only "C" failed to clear 1.89m, the two other athletes, "A" and "B" shall have a third jump-off at 1.91m which only "B" cleared and is therefore declared the winner.

26.9.4 如果未能决出名次，多于1名相关的运动员试跳成功则横杆要被提升，或者他们都试跳失败则横杆要降低，横杆每次升降高度：跳高为2厘米，撑竿跳高为5厘米。

26.9.5 如果一名运动员在某一高度上不进行试跳，他将自动失去争夺更高名次的资格。如果比赛中还剩下1名运动员，不管他是否试跳这一高度，他都将获得胜利。

跳高案例

比赛开始时，主裁判宣布横杆升高计划：1.75米，1.80米，1.84米，1.88米，1.91米，1.94米，1.97米，1.99米……

运动员	跳跃高度							失败次数	决名次跳			名次
	1.75米	1.80米	1.84米	1.88米	1.91米	1.94米	1.97米		1.91米	1.89米	1.91米	
A	○	×○	○	×○	×－	××		2	×	○	×	2
B	－	×○	－	×○	－	－	×××	2	×	○	○	1
C	－	○	×○	×○	－	×××		2	×	×		3
D	－	×○	×○	×○	×××			3				4

"A""B""C"和"D"都跳过1.88米。

适用技术规则26.8条和26.9条，4名运动员最后跳过的高度的试跳次数相同。这样一来，有关裁判员计算从起跳至最后跳过的高度（如1.88米）在内的每人失败的总次数。

"D"的试跳失败总次数比"A""B"或"C"多，因此获得第四名。"A""B"和"C"的名次依然相等，并涉及第一名。由于1.91米是他们最后跳过高度的下一高度，因此从1.91米开始进行决名次跳。

由于所有的运动员都未跳过，横杆降至1.89米，进行第二次决名次跳，由于只有"C"未跳过1.89米，另外两个运动员"A"和"B"需要在1.91米的高度上进行第三次决名次跳。只有"B"跳过，因而成为获胜者。

When an athlete unilaterally decides to withdraw from a jump-off, the other athlete (if only one remains) will be declared the winner in accordance with Rule 26.9.5 of the Technical Rules. It is not necessary for that athlete to attempt the applicable height. Where more than one athlete remains in the jump-off, the jump-off continues with the athletes who have not withdrawn. The athlete(s) who withdraw, shall be placed according to their then finishing place as they have forfeited any right to any higher placing (including first place) available to the remaining athletes.

Extraneous Forces

26.10　When it is clear that the bar has been displaced by a force not associated with an athlete (e.g. a gust of wind)

　　26.10.1　if such displacement occurs after an athlete has cleared the bar without touching it, then the trial shall be considered successful, or

　　26.10.2　if such displacement occurs under any other circumstance, a replacement trial shall be awarded.

27. High Jump

Competition

27.1　An athlete shall take off from one foot.

27.2　An athlete fails if:

　　27.2.1　After the jump, the bar does not remain on the supports because of the action of the athlete whilst jumping; or

　　27.2.2　They touch the ground including the landing area beyond the vertical plane through the nearer edge of the crossbar, either between or outside the uprights with any part of their body, without first clearing the bar. However, if when they jump, an athlete touches the landing area with their foot and in the opinion of the Judge, no advantage is gained, the jump for that reason shall not be considered a failure.

如果某一运动员单方面决定退出决名次跳，则其他运动员（如仅剩1名）可根据技术规则26.9.5条被宣布获胜，该运动员没有必要继续进行适用高度的试跳。如果剩余运动员超过1名，这些运动员应继续进行决名次跳。退出决名次跳的运动员将按照其当时的完成名次进行排名，因为他们已失去了与其余运动员争夺更高名次（包括第一名）的权益。

外力

26.10 当横杆明显受外力（如阵风）作用而掉落，且与运动员无关的情况：

    26.10.1 如果这种横杆掉落的情况发生在运动员越过横杆后，且身体并未触及横杆，该次试跳应视为成功，或

    26.10.2 如果在其他情况下发生横杆掉落，则运动员要获得一次重新试跳机会。

27. 跳高

比赛

27.1 运动员必须使用单脚起跳。

27.2 出现下列情况之一者，应判为试跳失败：

    27.2.1 试跳后，由于运动员的试跳动作，致使横杆未能留在两边的横杆托上；或

    27.2.2 运动员没有先越过横杆，其身体的任何部位就触及超越横杆后沿垂面，两个立柱之间或之外的地面及落地区。如果运动员在试跳中一只脚触及落地区，而裁判员认为他并未从中获得利益，则不应以此原因判该次试跳失败。

> Note: To assist in the implementation of this Rule a white line 50mm wide shall be drawn (usually by adhesive tape or similar material) between points 3m outside of each upright, the nearer edge of the line being drawn along the vertical plane through the nearer edge of the crossbar.

27.2.3　They touch the crossbar or the vertical section of the uprights when running up without jumping.

Runway and Take-off Area

27.3　The minimum width of the runway shall be 16m and the minimum length of the runway shall be 15m except in competitions held under paragraphs 1. (a), (b), (c), (d) and 2. (a), (b) of the World Rankings Competition definition, where the minimum length shall be 25m.

27.4　The maximum overall downward inclination in the last 15m of the runway and take-off area shall not exceed 1:167 (0.6%) along any radius of the minimum 16m wide rectangular area centred midway between the uprights and having the minimum radius specified in Rule 27.3 of the Technical Rules. The landing area should be placed so that the athlete's approach is up the inclination.

> Note: Runways and take-off areas to the 2018/19 specifications remain acceptable.

27.5　The take-off area shall be level or any inclination shall be in accordance with the requirements of Rule 27.4 of the Technical Rules and the World Athletics Track and Field Facilities Manual.

Apparatus

27.6　Any style of uprights or posts may be used, provided they are rigid.

They shall have supports for the crossbar firmly fixed to them.

They shall be sufficiently tall as to exceed the actual height to which the crossbar is raised by at least 0.10m.

The distance between the uprights shall be not less than 4.00m nor more than 4.04m.

27.7　The uprights or posts shall not be moved during the competition unless the Referee considers that either the take-off or landing area has become unsuitable.

注：为有助于执行上述规则，应在两个立柱之间和3米外标出一条50毫米宽的白线（通常可用胶布或类似物质），该白线后沿应与横杆后沿垂直面在一条线上，并延伸至立柱以外3米处。

27.2.3　运动员助跑未起跳，触及横杆或两侧立柱垂直面。

助跑道和起跳区

27.3　助跑道的最小宽度为16米，长度不得短于15米。在世界排名比赛定义1.（a）（b）（c）（d）和2.（a）（b）所述的比赛中，助跑道长度至少为25米。

27.4　助跑道和起跳区最后15米最大整体向下倾斜度不得超过1∶167（0.6%），任何半径最小为16米宽的长方形区域，以立柱中间为中心，最小半径见技术规则27.3条说明。落地区应放在运动员的助跑上坡的位置。

注：根据2018—2019规则建造的助跑道和起跳区仍然可以使用。

27.5　起跳区须保持水平，或任何倾斜都必须符合技术规则27.4条和《世界田联田径场地设施手册》的要求。

器材

27.6　任何类型的结构坚固的立柱或跳高架均可使用。

跳高架应有能稳定放置横杆的横杆托。

跳高架应有足够的高度，应超过横杆实际提升高度至少0.10米。

两立柱之间的距离为4.00~4.04米。

27.7　在比赛过程中不得移动立柱或跳高架，除非有关裁判长认为该起跳区或落地区已变得不适合比赛。

In such a case, the change shall be made only after a round of trials has been completed.

27.8 The crossbar supports shall be flat and rectangular, 40mm wide and 60mm long. They shall be firmly fixed to the uprights and immovable during the jump and shall each face the opposite upright. The ends of the crossbar shall rest on them in such a manner that, if the crossbar is touched by an athlete, it will easily fall to the ground, either forwards or backwards. The surface of the supports shall be smooth.

The supports shall not be of, or covered with, rubber or with any other material which has the effect of increasing the friction between them and the end pieces of the crossbar, nor may they have any kind of springs.

The supports shall be the same height above the take-off area immediately below each end of the crossbar.

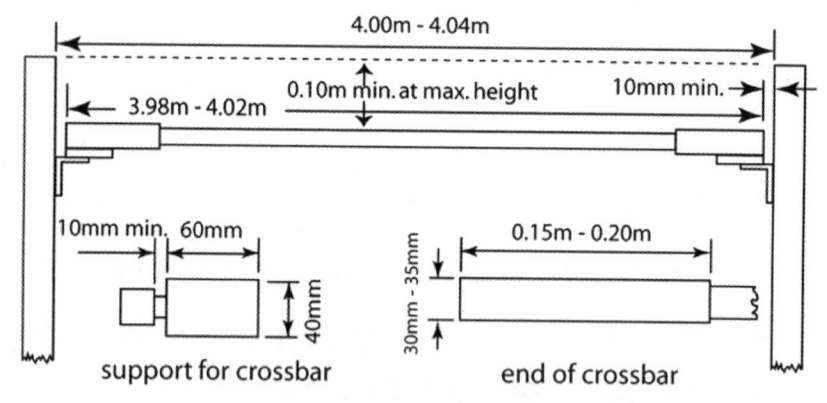

Figure TR27 – High Jump uprights and crossbar

27.9 There shall be a space of at least 10mm between the ends of the crossbar and the uprights.

Landing Area

27.10 For competitions under paragraphs 1. (a), (b), (c), (d) and 2. (a), (b) of the World Rankings Competition definition, the landing area shall be not smaller than 6m long × 4m wide × 0.7m high.

Note: Landing areas may have a cut-out in the front corners to provide clearance from the uprights. The uprights and the landing area should be designed so that there is a clearance of at least 0.1m between them when in use, to avoid displacement of the crossbar through a movement of the landing area causing contact with the uprights. The front of the landing area should be positioned about 0.1m from the vertical plane of the crossbar.

如需移动跳高架或立柱,应在一轮试跳结束后进行。

27.8　横杆托应水平放置。横杆托呈长方形,宽40毫米,长60毫米。在跳跃过程中,横杆托必须牢固地固定在立柱上且不可移动,朝向对面立柱。横杆两端放置于横杆托上,若被运动员触碰时,应易于向前或向后掉落。横杆托表面应该光滑。（技术规则27条图）

横杆托上不得包裹橡胶或其他能够增大与横杆末端之间摩擦力的任何物质,亦不得使用任何有弹性的物质。

横杆托在起跳区横杆两端的高度应该相同。

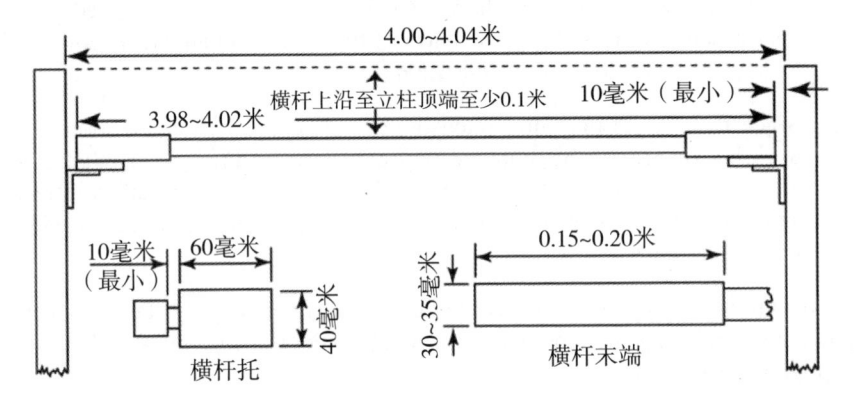

技术规则27条图　跳高架和横杆

27.9　横杆两端与立柱之间至少应有10毫米的间隙。

落地区

27.10　在世界排名比赛定义1.（a）（b）（c）（d）和2.（a）（b）所述的比赛中,落地区不能小于6米长×4米宽×0.7米高。

注：落地区前角上可以有1个切口,以提供与立柱之间的间隙。立柱和落地区的设计应确保在使用时,它们之间至少有0.1米的间隙,以避免因落地区的移动触及立柱而引起横杆移位。落地区的前部应距离横杆的垂直面约0.1米。

For other competitions, the landing area should measure not less than 5m long × 3m wide × 0.7m high.

Team of Officials

For a High Jump event, it is recommended to allocate the available officials as follows:

a. The Chief Judge will watch over the whole of the event and verify the measurements. They must be provided with two flags - white to indicate if the trial is valid and red if it is a failure. They must place themselves so as to manage two matters in particular:

  i. Frequently it happens that the crossbar having been touched by an athlete trembles on the supports. The Chief Judge, depending on the position of the crossbar, must decide when the vibrating of the bar must be stopped and the appropriate flag raised – particularly in the special situations as covered in Rule 26.10 of the Technical Rules; and

  ii. Since the athlete may not touch the crossbar, the vertical section of the uprights or ground beyond the vertical plane of the nearer edge of the crossbar, it is important to keep a watch on the position of the athlete's feet in situations where, when deciding not to complete a trial, they run to the side or go "under" the bar.

b. Two Judges, one on either side of the landing area and slightly standing back in charge of replacing the crossbar when it falls, and assisting the Chief Judge in applying the above Rules.

c. Judge - a recorder scoring the results sheet and calling each athlete (and the one who is to follow).

d. Judge in charge of the scoreboard (trial-number-result).

e. Judge in charge of the clock indicating to the athletes that they have a certain time to take their trial.

f. Judge in charge of athletes.

Note (i): This is the traditional setting-up of the officials. In major competitions, where a data system and electronic scoreboards are available, specialised personnel are certainly required. To be clear in these cases, the progress and scoring of a Field Event is followed by both the recorder and by the data system.

其他比赛，落地区应不小于5米长×3米宽×0.7米高。

裁判员团队

跳高项目比赛，建议按以下方式分配裁判员：

a. 主裁判应该全面观察本场比赛的进行并核实高度的测量。他们应该准备两面旗子，白旗标示试跳成功，红旗标示试跳失败。他们应身处合适的位置以便处置以下两种特殊情形：

　　i. 运动员触碰后，横杆在横杆托上不停颤动的情况经常发生。主裁判应依据横杆的位置，判断横杆何时停止颤动，然后合理举旗。特殊的情形在技术规则26.10条中已被提及；和

　　ii. 由于运动员可能并不触及横杆、立柱垂直面或者超越横杆后沿垂直面的地面，当运动员决定不完成试跳，跑向一边或横杆"下方"，在这种情况下观察运动员脚的位置非常重要。

b. 2名裁判员分别在落地区两端稍微靠后的位置，负责横杆掉落后的重新放置，并协助主裁判执行上述规则。

c. 记录裁判员，负责填写和记录成绩表格并通知每一名运动员（和下一名运动员）。

d. 成绩显示屏裁判员（试跳轮次—运动员号码—试跳成绩）。

e. 时限裁判员，负责向运动员显示某次试跳时限。

f. 管理裁判员，负责运动员的管理。

注（i）：这是裁判团队的常规设置。在大型比赛中，需要专业人员操作数据系统、电子显示牌。需要明确的是，记录裁判员和数据系统均要完成跟踪田赛项目的比赛进程和记录成绩。

Note (ii): Officials and equipment must be placed in such a way as not to obstruct the athlete's way nor impede the view of the spectators.

Note (iii): A space must be reserved for a wind-sock to indicate the wind direction and strength.

28. Pole Vault

Competition

28.1   Athletes may have the crossbar moved only in the direction of the landing area so that the edge of the crossbar nearest the athlete can be positioned at any point from that directly above the back end of the box to a point 80cm in the direction of the landing area.

An athlete shall, before the competition starts, inform the appropriate official of the position of the crossbar they require for their first trial and this position shall be recorded.

If subsequently an athlete wants to make any changes, they should immediately inform the appropriate official before the crossbar has been set in accordance with their initial wishes.

Once the time for the trial has started, no further change in the position of the crossbar is allowed.

Note: A line, 10mm wide and of distinguishable colour, shall be drawn at right angles to the axis of the runway, in line with the back end of the box ("zero" line). A similar line, up to 50mm wide, shall appear on the surface of the landing area and be prolonged as far as the outside edge of the uprights. The edge of the line nearer to the approaching athlete coincides with the back end of the box.

28.2   An athlete fails if:

    28.2.1   after the vault, the bar does not remain on both pegs because of the action of an athlete whilst vaulting; or

    28.2.2   they touch the ground, including the landing area, beyond the vertical plane through the back end of the box with any part of their body or with the pole, without first clearing the bar; or

注（ⅱ）：裁判员的站位和设备的摆放既不能妨碍运动员比赛，也不能阻挡观众的视线。

注（ⅲ）：须在合理位置放置风标，用于显示风向和风力。

28. 撑竿跳高

比赛

28.1　运动员可要求向落地区方向移动横杆，并使距运动员最近的横杆边沿移动至从穴斗后壁末端向落地区方向80厘米内的任一位置。

运动员应在比赛开始前将其第一次试跳所需的横杆移动距离通知有关裁判员，移动距离应被记录下来。

此后，如果运动员要求改变横杆的移动距离，应在按其原要求调整横杆位置之前及时通知有关裁判员。

一旦试跳时限开始，横杆的位置就不允许再改变。

注：需画一条10毫米宽颜色明显的线（零线），该线与穴斗前壁顶端的内沿齐平，与助跑道的中轴线垂直。一条相似的线，宽度不超过50毫米，此线也要通过落地区的表面，延伸至两立柱的外侧。此线靠近运动员助跑侧的边沿，必须与穴斗的前壁顶端相吻合。

28.2　出现下列情况之一者，应判为试跳失败：

28.2.1　试跳后，由于运动员的试跳动作，致使横杆未能留在两边的横杆托上；或

28.2.2　在越过横杆之前，运动员的身体或所用撑竿的任何部位触及穴斗前壁顶端垂直面以后的地面，包括落地区；或

28.2.3　after leaving the ground, they place their lower hand above the upper one or move the upper hand higher on the pole; or

28.2.4　during the vault, they steady or replace the bar with their hand(s).

Note (i): It is not a failure if an athlete runs outside the white lines marking the runway at any point.

Note (ii): It is not a failure if the pole touches the landing mats, in the course of trial, after properly being planted in the box.

The following should be noted in applying and interpreting Rule 28.2 of the Technical Rules:

a. the bar must be dislodged because of the action of the athlete "whilst vaulting". So, if the athlete after correctly retrieving their pole (so as not to infringe Rule 28.4 of the Technical Rules) were then to hit the crossbar or the uprights with the pole so that it was dislodged, this would not amount to a failure since it was not because of the action of the athlete whilst vaulting, unless the crossbar was still moving and, as a result, the Judge had not yet raised the white flag;

b. to take into account the effect of Note (ii) as there will be many occasions when the pole on bending will touch the landing area beyond the zero line;

c. to be aware of the possibility that the athlete can actually take off in such a way that their body or the bend of the pole will break the vertical plane through the zero line but then they return to the runway without attempting to clear the bar. Provided that they have time left for their trial and they did not touch the ground beyond the zero line, they may continue with the trial. This also applies in cases where the athlete during the time for their trial is, for any reason, placing the pole in the box or otherwise through the vertical plane of the zero line and the pole touches the ground beyond the zero line, this is a failure;

d. Judges must take particular care to detect whether any action prohibited under Rule 28.2.4 of the Technical Rules has occurred. Not only does it mean that the relevant Judge must keep an eye on the vaulter throughout the vault, but they must determine that such action was not merely incidental touching as the athlete cleared the bar. In general for Rule 28.2.4 of the Technical Rules to be applied there should be some direct action on behalf of the athlete to steady or replace the bar.

28.2.3 　　起跳离地后，将原来握在下方的手移握至上方手以上或原来握在上方的手向上移握；或

28.2.4 　　试跳时，运动员用手稳定横杆或将横杆放回横杆托上。

注（ⅰ）：运动员助跑时，在任何位置跑出助跑道白色标志线不视为试跳失败。

注（ⅱ）：运动员在试跳中，撑竿正确插入穴斗后，撑竿触及落地区垫子不视为试跳失败。

在应用和解释技术规则28.2条时，应该注意以下几种情形：

a. 横杆掉落必须是由于运动员的持竿跳跃动作导致的。因此，当运动员在合理地取回撑竿（防止违反技术规则28.4条）过程中撑竿触及横杆或立柱导致横杆掉落，则不应该视为失败，因为这不是由于运动员的持竿跳跃动作导致的，除非横杆还在晃动而且裁判员还没有举白旗。

b. 注（ⅱ）的情况应该被考虑在内，因为撑竿弯曲超过"零线"触及落地区的情形时有发生。

c. 须注意另一种可能性是运动员以正确的方式起跳，但他的身体或撑竿的弯曲触及"零线"的垂直面，但是他后续又回到助跑道而没有试图去越过横杆。如果运动员的试跳时限没过，且没有触及超越"零线"的地面，则他仍可以在其时限内进行试跳。这也适用于，运动员在他们的试跳期间，由于任何原因，把撑竿插在穴斗内或以其他任何方式通过"零线"的垂直面，并且撑竿触及超越"零线"的地面，应视为试跳失败。

d. 裁判员须特别关注技术规则28.2.4条禁止出现的动作。这不仅意味着相关裁判员在运动员起跳过程中要密切关注其持竿跳跃全程，还必须判定运动员过杆的触及动作不是偶发的。通常应用技术规则28.2.4条，运动员应有直接的动作去稳定或放回横杆。

e. there is a common practice where athletes return to the box after a trial (whether it is a clearance or failure) and place the pole in the box to check their take-off position. Provided this occurs after the trial is completed in accordance with Rule 25.8 of the Technical Rules and before the time for the next athlete's trial begins and does not otherwise delay the conduct of the competition, it is allowed.

28.3　Athletes may, during the competition, place a substance on their hands or on the pole, in order to obtain a better grip. The use of gloves is permitted.

Whilst there is no prohibition on wearing gloves or the use of permitted substances on gloves this practice should be monitored by Referees in case the practice causes concern and gives rise to possible issue of unfair assistance.

28.4　After the release of the pole, no one including the athlete shall be allowed to touch the pole unless it is falling away from the bar or uprights. If it is touched, however, and the Referee is of the opinion that, but for the intervention, the bar would have been knocked off, the vault shall be recorded as a failure.

This is one of the few rules where behaviour by an official can result in a failure being called. It is important therefore that the upright Judges are diligent in ensuring that they do not touch or catch a pole unless it is clearly falling away from the crossbar and/or uprights.

28.5　If, in making a trial, an athlete's pole is broken, it shall not be counted as a failure and they shall be awarded a replacement trial.

Runway

28.6　The minimum length of the runway, measured from the "zero" line, shall be 40m and where conditions permit, 45m. It shall have a width of 1.22m ± 0.01m and shall be marked by white lines 50mm in width.

Note: For all tracks constructed before 1 January 2004 the runway may have a width of maximum 1.25m. However, when such a runway is fully resurfaced, the lane width shall comply with this Rule.

e. 通常，运动员在试跳完成以后（无论成功还是失败）又退回来，然后把撑竿又插进穴斗检查他的起跳位置。只要是符合技术规则25.8条的规定完成试跳并在下一名运动员开始试跳之前进行，并且不会耽误比赛的正常进行，这种情况是被允许的。

28.3　比赛中，允许运动员在双手或在撑竿上用有利于抓握的物质，并允许使用手套。

允许运动员使用手套，被许可的物质也可以涂抹在手套上，但是相关裁判长应监督这种做法，以防这种做法引起关注并可能引发不公平的帮助的问题。

28.4　撑竿离开运动员的手之后，除非撑竿朝向远离横杆或立柱的方向倾倒，否则不允许有人（包括运动员）接触撑竿。如果撑竿被接触，而裁判长认为没有这种干预则横杆会被碰落，则应记录此次试跳失败。

这是由于裁判员的行为可能导致试跳失败判罚的少数情形之一。非常重要的是立柱侧的裁判员要细致地确保不要触及或抓住撑竿，除非运动员已越过横杆，且撑竿朝向远离横杆或立柱的方向倾倒。

28.5　试跳时，若撑竿折断，不应判为试跳失败，应给予该运动员一次重新试跳的机会。

助跑道

28.6　从"零"线开始测量，助跑道长度须至少长40米，条件允许时应长45米。助跑道宽度应为1.22米±0.01米。助跑道的标志线为宽50毫米的白线。

注：2004年1月1日以前建造的场地可以使用最多1.25米宽的助跑道。如果助跑道完全重新铺设面层，宽度应符合本规则要求。

28.7　The maximum lateral inclination of the runway should be 1:100 (1%) unless special circumstances exist which justify World Athletics providing an exemption and, in the last 40m of the runway, the overall downward inclination in the direction of running shall not exceed 1:1000 (0.1%).

Apparatus

28.8　The take-off for the Pole Vault shall be from a box. It shall be constructed of suitable material, with rounded or soft upper edges and shall be sunk level with the runway, with or without the synthetic surface carried over the upper edges. Any synthetic covering must be within the allowed tolerances for the height of the box. It shall be 1.00m in length, measured along the inside of the bottom of the box, 0.60m in width at the front end and tapering to 0.15m in width at the bottom of the stop board. The length of the box at runway level and the depth of the stop board are determined by the angle of 105° formed between the base and the stop board. (tolerances on dimensions and angles: ± 0.01m and − 0°/ + 1°)

The base of the box shall slope from runway level at the front end to a vertical distance below ground level of 0.20m at the point where it meets the stop board. The box should be constructed in such a manner that the sides slope outwards and end next to the stop board at an angle of approximately 120° to the base.

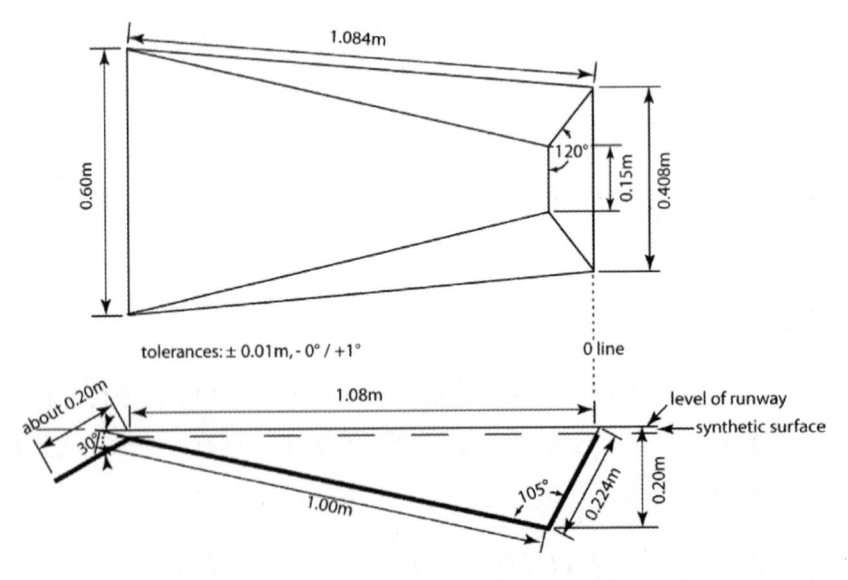

Figure (a) TR28 – Pole Vault box (top and side view)

28.7 助跑道的横向倾斜度不得超过1∶100（1%），除世界田联提供合法豁免的特殊情况外；在助跑道最后40米的跑进方向上向下总的倾斜度不得超过1∶1000（0.1%）。

器材

28.8 撑竿跳高在起跳时，撑竿必须插在穴斗内。应采用适宜的材料制作穴斗，穴斗上沿为圆弧形或软性材料，穴斗埋入地下，上沿与地面齐平，可以用也可以不用合成材料表面覆盖穴斗边缘的上沿。任何合成覆盖物都必须在穴斗高度允许的公差范围内。穴斗底部沿里边测量，它为1米长，穴斗在前面末端宽为0.60米且逐渐变小到在抵趾板底部宽为0.15米，由底部和抵趾板构成的105°角决定了在助跑水平方向上的穴斗长度和抵趾板的深度。（穴斗的尺寸和角度的容差是±0.01米和−0°/+1°）［技术规则28条图（a）］

穴斗的底部要向助跑道水平面前部末端倾斜，到抵趾板连接处是在水平地面以下0.20米的垂直距离。穴斗应由以下方式构成：两边向外倾斜且在底部末端与相邻抵趾板约成120°。

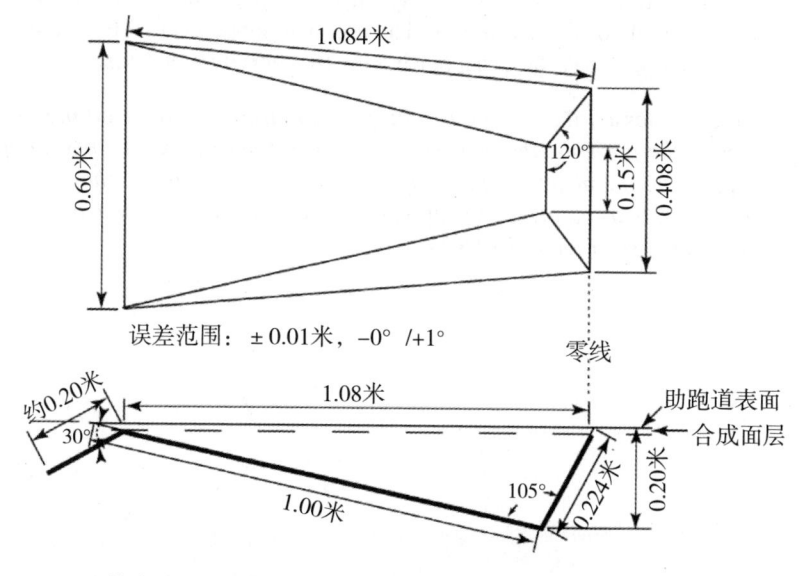

技术规则28条图（a）　撑竿跳高穴斗（俯视图和侧视图）

Note: An athlete may place padding around the box for additional protection during any of their trials. The placement of such equipment shall be done within the time allowed for the athlete's trial and shall be removed by the athlete immediately after their trial is completed. At competitions under paragraphs 1. (a), (b), (c), (d) and 2. (a), (b) of the World Rankings Competition definition this shall be provided by the organisers.

28.9 Any style of uprights or posts may be used, provided they are rigid. The metallic structure of the base and the lower part of the uprights above the landing area must be covered with padding of appropriate material in order to provide protection to the athletes and the poles.

28.10 The crossbar shall rest on horizontal pegs so that if it is touched by an athlete or their pole, it will fall easily to the ground in the direction of the landing area. The pegs shall be without notches or indentations of any kind, of uniform thickness throughout and not more than 13mm in diameter.

They shall not extend more than 55mm from the supporting members, which shall be smooth. The vertical peg backings, which shall also be smooth and be constructed in a way that the crossbar cannot rest on the top of them, shall extend 35mm-40mm above the pegs.

The distance between the pegs shall be 4.28m-4.37m. The pegs shall not be of, or covered with, rubber or with any other material which has the effect of increasing the friction between them and the end pieces of the crossbar, nor may they have any kind of springs. The pegs should support the bar in the middle of the end pieces. The crossbar supports shall be at the same height above the surfaces supporting the two upright metal bases.

Note: To lessen the chance of injury to an athlete by their falling on the feet of the uprights, the pegs supporting the crossbar may be placed upon supporting members permanently attached to the uprights, thus allowing the uprights to be placed wider apart, without increasing the length of the crossbar [see Figure (b) TR28].

注：运动员在进行每一次试跳时，可以在穴斗四周放置垫子，以便进一步保护。放置这一器材要在运动员的试跳时限内完成，并且要在他结束本次试跳后立即移除。在世界排名比赛定义1.（a）（b）（c）（d）和2.（a）（b）所述的比赛中，这种器材由组织者提供。

28.9 任何坚固的撑竿跳高架和立柱均可使用。必须用由适宜材料制作的垫子包裹撑竿跳高架底座的金属结构以及在落地区上方的立柱下部，以保护运动员和撑竿。

28.10 横杆应放置在水平方向上突出的横杆托上，以便运动员或撑竿触及横杆时，横杆易向落地区方向掉落。横杆托上不得有刻痕或缺口，横杆托应粗细均匀，直径不超过13毫米。

横杆托伸出支架的长度不超过55毫米，且必须光滑。垂直的杆托挡头也必须光滑，它的结构应使横杆不易停留在其顶部。支架应高于横杆托35~40毫米。

横杆托之间的距离为4.28~4.37米。横杆托上不得包裹橡胶或任何能够增大与横杆末端之间摩擦力的物质，亦不能有任何弹性。横杆托应支撑在横杆两端的中间部位。横杆延伸臂在支撑两个立柱的金属底座表面上方的高度须相同。

注：为了减小运动员落在立柱底座上受伤的可能性，可将横杆托置于永久性固定在立柱上的支撑件上面，以增加2个立柱之间的距离，而横杆的长度不变。[技术规则28条图（b）]

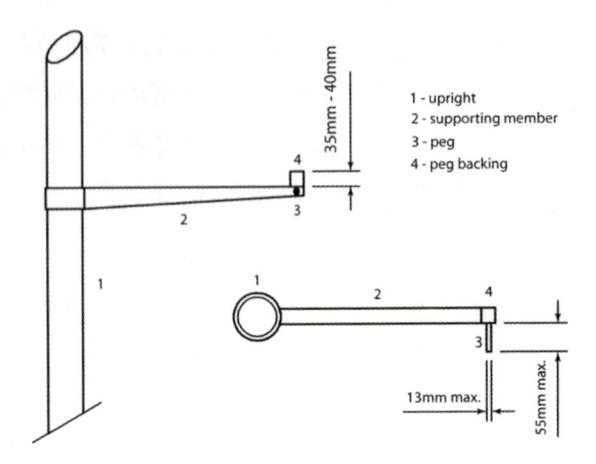

Figure (b) TR28 – Pole Vault crossbar support (view from landing area and top view)

Vaulting Poles

28.11   Athletes may use their own poles. No athlete shall use any other athlete's pole except with the consent of the owner.

Note: If the Judges are aware, they shall direct any athlete not complying with this Rule to correct the situation. If the athlete does not, such trial(s) shall be a failure. It shall also be judged as a failure, if a trial is completed before the non-compliance is noticed. In all cases considered serious enough, Rules 7.1 and 7.3 of the Technical Rules may also be applied.

The pole may be of any material or combination of materials and of any length or diameter, but the basic surface must be smooth.

The pole may have layers of tape at the grip end (to protect the hand) and of tape and/or any other suitable material at the bottom end (to protect the pole). Any tape at the grip end must be uniform except for incidental overlapping and must not result in any sudden change in diameter, such as the creation of any "ring" on the pole.

Only "regular" taping in accordance with the Rule is allowed at the grip end of the pole - rings, loops and the like are not permitted. There be any restriction on how far up or down the pole such taping extends but it should be for the purpose for which it is intended - to protect the hand. There is, however, no restriction at the bottom end of the pole and, in general, any form of taping or protection is permitted there - provided it does not give the athlete any advantage.

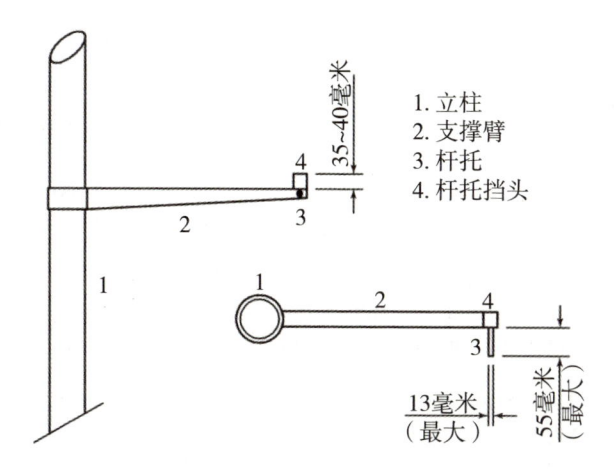

技术规则28条图（b） 撑竿跳高架横杆托和延伸臂（落地区侧视图和俯视图）

撑竿

28.11　运动员可使用自备撑竿。未经物主同意，不得使用他人的撑竿。

注：如果裁判员发现，他们要指示任何不遵守本规则的运动员纠正这种情况。如果运动员不这样做，此类试跳将视为失败。如果在发现不合规之前运动员完成了试跳，也要判定为失败。如果情况严重，也可适用技术规则7.1条和7.3条。

撑竿可用任何材料或混合材料制成，长度和直径不限，基本表面必须光滑。

可在撑竿的抓握端缠上多层保护性胶布（保护手），和（或）在撑竿下端缠上其他适当材料和胶布（保护撑竿）。任何在撑竿抓握端的胶布，除了偶尔重叠外必须一致，不能出现直径的突然改变，如在撑竿上增设任何"环状"结构。

根据规则在撑竿持握的一端进行常规的缠绕是允许的，但是环状凸起或以打结等形式缠绕是不允许的。对于向下或向上缠绕范围没有限制，但应该是出于保护手的目的。同样地，在撑竿底部末端的缠绕也没有限制，前提是出于保护撑竿的目的，而不能帮助运动员获得任何利益。

Landing Area

28.12 For competitions under paragraphs 1. (a), (b), (c), (d) and 2. (a), (b) of the World Rankings Competition definition, the landing area shall be not smaller than 6m long (behind the zero line and excluding the front pieces) × 6m wide × 0.8m high. The front pieces must be at least 2m long.

The sides of the landing area nearest to the box shall be placed 0.10m to 0.15m from the box and shall slope away from the box at an angle of at least 45° and no more than 48° [see Figure (c) TR28].

For other competitions, the landing area should measure not less than 5m long (excluding the front pieces) × 5m wide × 0.8m high.

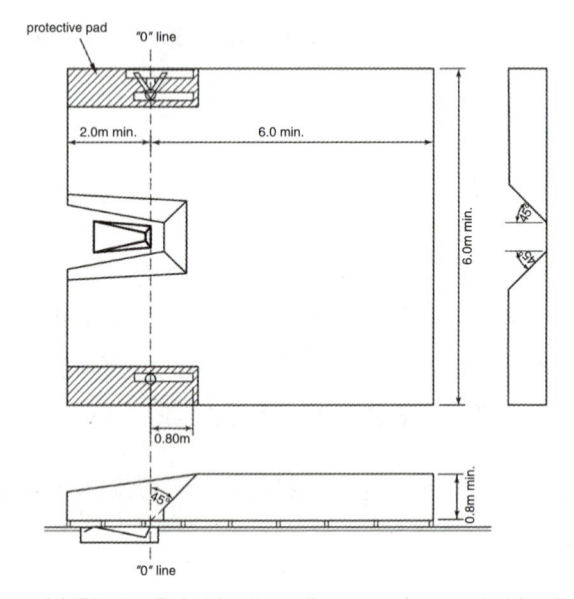

Figure (c) TR28– Pole Vault landing area (top and side views)

Team of Officials

For a Pole Vault event, it is recommended to allocate the available officials as follows:

a. The Chief Judge will watch over the whole of the event and verify the measurements. They must be provided with two flags - white to indicate if the trial is valid and red if it is a failure. They must place themselves so as to manage two matters in particular:

落地区

28.12　在世界排名比赛定义1.（a）（b）（c）（d）和2.（a）（b）条所述的比赛中，落地区不小于6米长（零线后且不包括前端部分）×6米宽×0.8米高。前端必须至少2米长。

落地区两侧边沿距离穴斗应有0.10~0.15米，从插斗方向向外倾斜至少45°但不能超过48°。［技术规则28条图（c）］

对于其他赛事，落地区的最小规格为5米长（不包括前端部分）×5米宽×0.8米高。

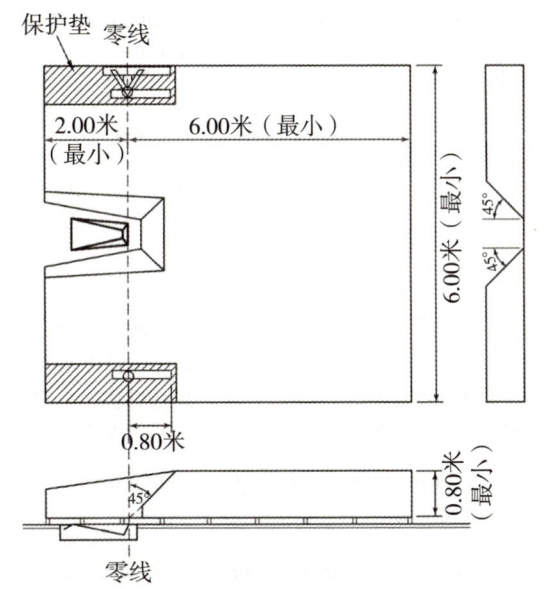

技术规则28条图（c）　撑竿跳高落地区（俯视图和侧视图）

裁判员团队

对于撑竿跳高项目，建议裁判员分配如下：

a. 主裁判应该管控比赛的全过程并且审核高度的测量。他们必须准备两面旗子，白旗标示试跳成功，红旗标示试跳失败。他们必须合理处置以下两种特殊的情形：

i. Frequently it happens that the crossbar having been touched by an athlete trembles on the supports. The Chief Judge, depending on the position of the crossbar, must decide when the vibrating of the bar must be stopped and the appropriate flag raised – particularly the special situations covered in Rules 26.10 and 28.4 of the Technical Rules; and

ii. Since before the take-off, the athlete may not touch the ground beyond the vertical plane through the back end of the box they must place themselves in such manner as to be able to determine this.

b. Two Judges, one on either side, in line with the back of the box, in charge of replacing the crossbar when it falls, and assisting the Chief Judge in applying the above Rules. They are also responsible for the correct placement of the upright as notified by the recorder according to the wishes of the athlete.

c. Judge - a recorder noting the upright positions requested by the athletes, scoring the results sheet and calling the upright position and then each athlete (and the one who is to follow).

d. Judge in charge of the scoreboard (trial-number-result).

e. Judge in charge of the clock indicating to the athletes that they have a certain time to take their trial.

f. Judge in charge of athletes.

Note (i): This is the traditional setting-up of the officials. In major competitions, where a data system and electronic scoreboards are available, specialised personnel are certainly required. To be clear in these cases, the progress and scoring of a Field Event is followed by both the recorder and by the data system.

Note (ii): Officials and equipment must be placed in such a way as not to obstruct the athlete's way nor impede the view of the spectators.

Note (iii): A space must be reserved for a wind-sock to indicate the wind direction and strength.

ⅰ. 横杆被运动员触及而在横杆托上颤动。主裁判必须根据横杆的位置和状况，作出何时举旗、何时扶停颤动的横杆的决定，遇到技术规则26.10条和28.4条所述特殊情况时更应特别注意；和

ⅱ. 由于运动员在起跳前不得触及穴斗前壁顶端垂直面之前的地面，裁判员的站位必须确保他们能对此作出清晰的判断。

b. 2名裁判员分别在穴斗前壁外侧的两边成一线，负责架设横杆和协助主裁判执行上述规则。他们还负责保证由记录员通知的运动员所需架距调整位置的准确性。

c. 记录裁判员，有一个能显示运动员所需架距的仪器，记录成绩并宣布下一名试跳运动员及其架距（和下一名运动员）。

d. 成绩显示屏裁判员（试跳轮次—运动员号码—试跳成绩）。

e. 时限裁判员，负责向运动员显示某次试跳时限。

f. 管理裁判员，负责运动员的管理。

注（ⅰ）：这是裁判团队的常规设置。在大型比赛中，需要专业人员操作数据系统、电子显示牌。需要明确的是，记录裁判员和数据系统均要完成跟踪田赛项目的比赛进程和记录成绩。

注（ⅱ）：裁判员的站位和设备的摆放既不能妨碍运动员比赛，也不能阻挡观众的视线。

注（ⅲ）：须在合理位置放置风标，用于显示风向和风力。

Horizontal Jumps

29. General Conditions – Horizontal Jumps

Runway

29.1 The minimum length of the runway, measured from the relevant take-off line shall be 40m and, where conditions permit, 45m. It shall have a width of 1.22m ± 0.01m and shall be marked by white lines 50mm in width.

Note: For all tracks constructed before 1 January 2004 the runway may have a width of maximum 1.25m. However, when such a runway is fully resurfaced, the lane width shall comply with this Rule.

29.2 The maximum lateral inclination of the runway should be 1:100 (1%) unless special circumstances exist which justify World Athletics providing an exemption and, in the last 40m of the runway, the overall downward inclination in the direction of running shall not exceed 1:1000 (0.1%).

Take-off Board

29.3 The take-off shall be marked by a board sunk level with the runway and the surface of the landing area. The edge of the board which is nearer to the landing area shall be the take-off line.

29.4 The take-off board shall be rectangular, made of wood or other suitable rigid material in which the spikes of an athlete's shoe will grip and not skid and shall measure 1.22m ± 0.01m long, 0.20m ± 0.002m wide and not more than 0.10m deep. It shall be white. In order to ensure that the take-off line is clearly distinguishable and in contrast to the take-off board, the ground immediately beyond the take-off line or any blanking board shall be in a colour other than white [see Figure (a1) TR29].

29.5 The use of video or other technology, to assist the Judges in deciding the application of Rule 30.1.1 of the Technical Rules, is strongly recommended at all levels of competition. However, if no technology is available, a plasticine indicator board placed immediately beyond the take-off line may still be used.

水平跳跃项目

29. 水平跳跃项目通则

助跑道

29.1 助跑道从起跳线开始丈量，长度不少于40米。如条件允许，为45米。助跑道宽度为1.22米±0.01米，并以50毫米宽的白线标示。

注：2004年1月1日以前建造的场地，助跑道最大宽度为1.25米。然而，如果助跑道面层全部重新铺设，宽度应符合本规则要求。

29.2 助跑道横向的最大倾斜度不得超过1∶100（1%），除非是世界田联提供了豁免（检查）证明的特殊情形。助跑道的最后40米，在跑进方向向下的整体倾斜度不得超过1∶1000（0.1%）。

起跳板

29.3 起跳板要水平埋入地下，其上平面与助跑道和落地区表面平齐。起跳板靠近落地区的边沿应为起跳线。

29.4 起跳板为长方形，用木质或其他适宜硬质材料制成，使运动员踏跳时鞋钉能够抓牢而不会打滑，起跳板长1.22米±0.01米，宽0.20米±0.002米，厚度不超过0.10米，颜色为白色。为了确保起跳线能够清晰辨识，并与起跳板颜色形成反差，紧邻起跳线以后的地面应为白色以外的颜色。［技术规则29条图（a1）］

29.5 强烈建议在各级比赛中使用视频或其他技术，以帮助裁判员运用技术规则30.1.1条进行判罚。然而，如果没有上述技术手段，仍可使用一块放在紧靠起跳线之后的橡皮泥显示板。

The plasticine indicator board shall consist of a rigid board, 0.10m ± 0.002m wide and 1.22m ± 0.01m long made of wood or any other suitable material and shall be painted in a contrasting colour to the take-off board. Where possible, the plasticine should be of a third contrasting colour. The board shall be mounted in a recess or shelf in the runway, on the side of the take-off board nearer the landing area. The surface shall rise from the level of the take-off board to a height of 7mm ± 1mm. The edges shall be cut away such that in relation to the recess, when filled with plasticine, the surface of the plasticine nearer to the take-off line shall be at an angle of 90° [see Figure (a2) TR29].

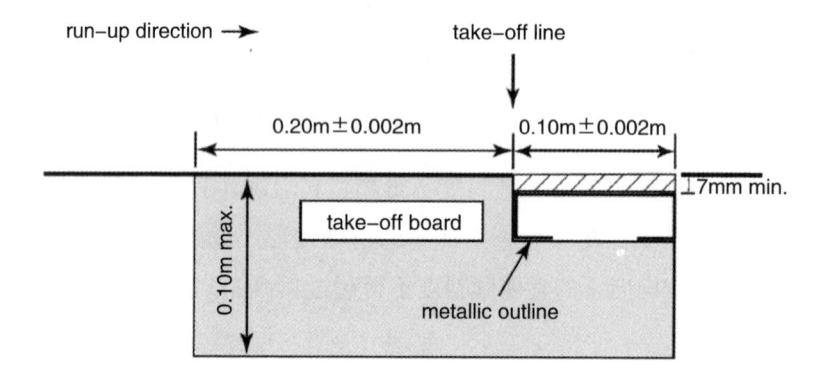

Figure (a1) TR29 – Take-off board with blanking board

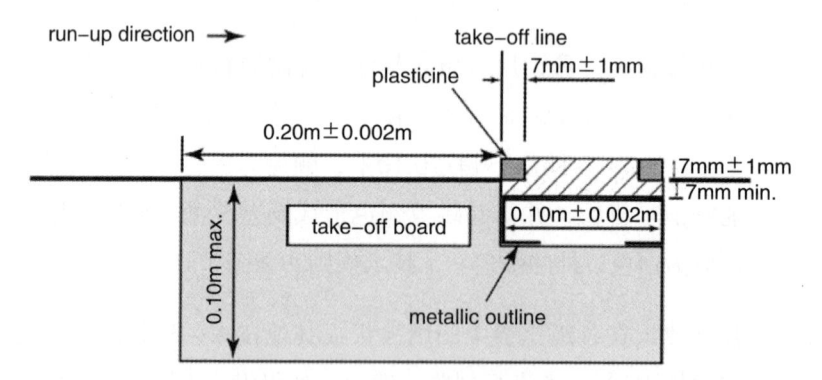

Figure (a2) TR29 – Take-off board with plasticine indicator board

橡皮泥显示板须用木质或其他适宜材料制成，质地坚硬，宽0.10米±0.002米，长1.22米±0.01米，须漆成与起跳板形成鲜明对比的颜色。如果可能，橡皮泥应采用第三种对比色。此板应安放在紧靠起跳板前端的凹槽或搁板内，表面高度超出起跳板7毫米±1毫米。显示板边沿须切掉，以便在填充橡皮泥时满足有关的凹槽靠近起跳线的橡皮泥表面应成90°。[技术规则29条图（a2）]

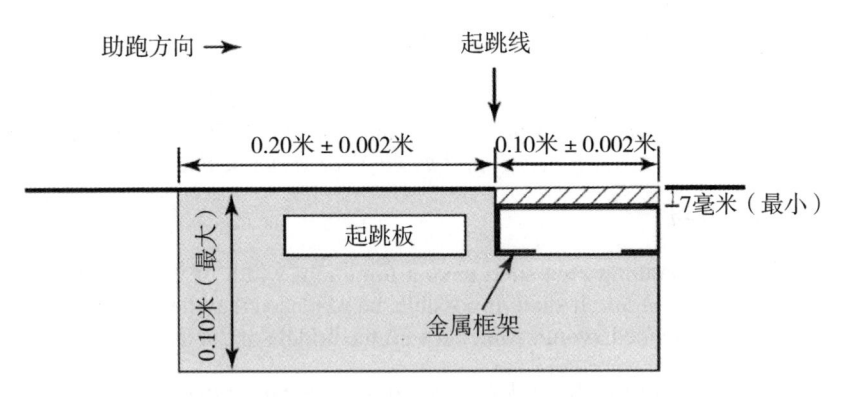

技术规则29条图（a1） 带垫板的起跳板

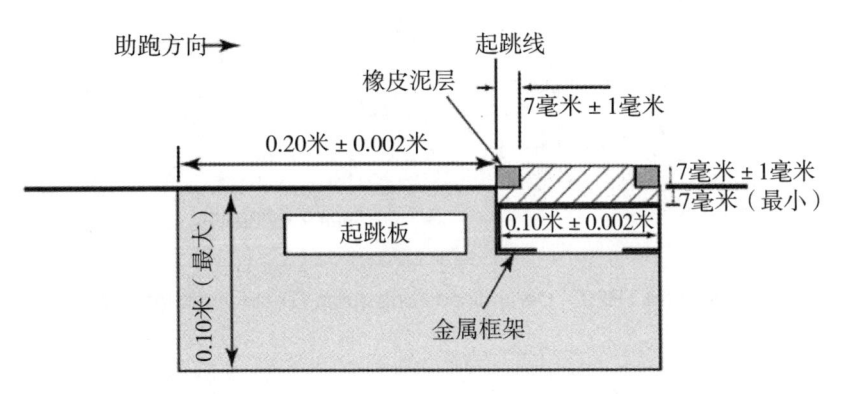

技术规则29条图（a2） 带橡皮泥显示板的起跳板

When mounted in this recess, the whole assembly shall be sufficiently rigid to accept the full force of the athlete's foot.

The surface of the board shall be of a material in which the spikes of an athlete's shoe will grip and not skid.

The plasticine can be smoothed off by means of a roller or suitably shaped scraper for the purposes of removing the footprint of an athlete.

Note (i): Where in the construction of the runway and/or take-off board there was previously provision for the placement of a plasticine indicator board and such board is not used, this recess should be filled by a blanking board flush with the take-off board.

Note (ii): The take-off board can be constructed as a single piece of board 0.30m wide with a 0.20m white section and a 0.10m in a contrasting colour, i.e. the take-off board and blanking board can be one piece.

Landing Area

29.6　The landing area shall have a minimum width of 2.75m and a maximum width of 3m. It shall, if possible, be so placed that the middle of the runway, if extended, would coincide with the middle of the landing area.

Note: When the middle of the runway is not in line with the middle of the landing area, a tape, or if necessary, two tapes, shall be placed along the landing area so that the above is achieved [see Figure (b) TR29] .

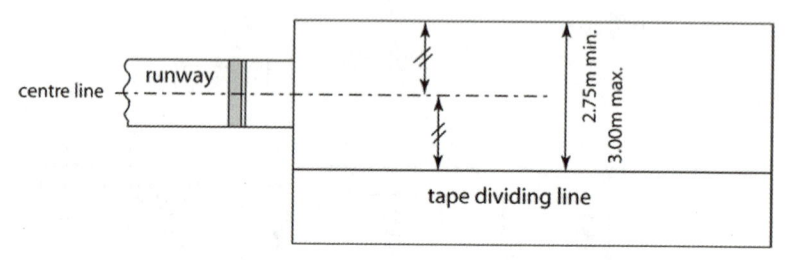

Figure (b) TR29 – Centralised Long Jump /Triple Jump landing area

Where new facilities are developed at which it is envisaged that visually impaired athletes will compete, at least one pit should be built with an increased width (3.50m instead of maximum 3.00m as in the Rules) as recommended by IPC.

显示板置于凹槽中，整套装置必须牢固，足以承受运动员起跳脚的全部力量。

板的表面须采用运动员鞋的鞋钉可以抓牢而不打滑的材料。

橡皮泥应可用滚筒或其他刮具抹平，以消除运动员的足迹。

注（ⅰ）：在修建助跑道和（或）安放起跳板时，需按前述要求放置橡皮泥显示板；不使用显示板时，应使用与起跳板平齐的垫板填平凹槽。

注（ⅱ）：起跳板为一块宽0.30米板子，其中0.20米涂成白色，0.10米为对比色，即起跳板和垫板可为一体。

落地区

29.6　落地区宽度最小2.75米，最大3米。如有可能，助跑道中心线的延长线与落地区的中心线应重合。

注：当落地区中心线与助跑道中心线不重合时，应在落地区内布置1条或2条线带，使这两条线重合，以达到上述要求。[技术规则29条图（b）]

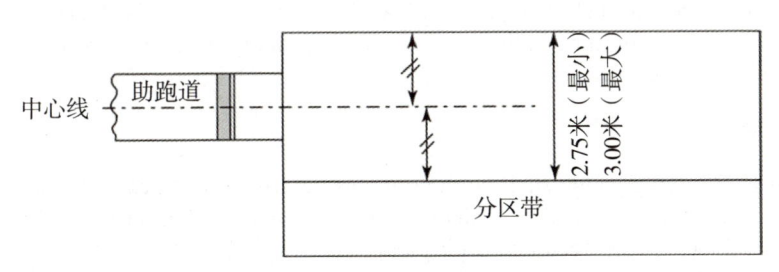

技术规则29条图（b）　跳远/三级跳远落地区形成中心线布置

建造新场地时，应考虑视力残障运动员参赛的情况，国际残奥委会建议至少应有一个沙坑的宽度应增加（最大3.50米，而不是本规则中的3.00米）。

29.7　　The landing area should be filled with soft damp sand, the top surface of which shall be level with the take-off board.

Distance Measurement

29.8　　In all horizontal jumping events, distances shall be recorded to the nearest 0.01m below the distance measured if the distance measured is not a whole centimetre.

29.9　　The measurement of each jump shall be made immediately after each valid trial (or after an immediate oral protest made under Rule 8.5 of the Technical Rules) from the nearest break in the landing area made by any part of the body, or anything that was attached to the body at the time it made a mark, to the take-off line, or take-off line extended. The measurement shall be taken perpendicular to the take-off line or its extension.

As long as no irregularity has been committed, each trial must be measured whatever the distance reached, including for the reasons that other trial measurements may become critical in determining countbacks or whether an athlete will proceed to subsequent rounds.

Except where Rule 8.5 of the Technical Rules is applied, under normal practice no trial during which an irregularity has been committed should be measured. Judges should carefully use their discretion in applying any alternate practice and usually only in special cases.

Unless video measuring is being used, for every valid trial a marker (usually metal) should be placed in a vertical position at the place of the imprint left by the athlete in the landing area nearest to the take-off line. The marker is passed through the loop at the end of the graduated steel tape so that the "zero" is on the mark. The tape should be pulled out horizontally taking care not to place it on any rise in the ground.

Wind Measurement

29.10　　The wind gauge shall be the same as described in Rules 17.8 and 17.9 of the Technical Rules. It shall be operated as described in Rules 17.11 and 29.12 of the Technical Rules and read as per Rule 17.13 of the Technical Rules.

29.11　　The relevant Field Events Referee shall ensure that the wind gauge is placed 20m from the take-off line. The measuring plane shall be positioned 1.22m ± 0.05m high and not more than 2m away from the runway.

29.7 落地区内应填充湿软的细沙，沙面须与起跳板平齐。

距离测量

29.8 所有水平跳跃项目，如测量的距离不为整数厘米时，应记录到在测量距离以下最近的0.01米。

29.9 每次有效试跳后（或根据技术规则8.5条提出即时口头抗议后），须立即测量每跳成绩，测量成绩应从运动员身体任何部位或留下痕迹瞬间附属在身体上的任何物体在落地区内的最近触及点，量至起跳线或起跳线的延长线。测量线须与起跳线或其延长线垂直。

只要没有违规行为，无论成绩如何，每次试跳都必须测量。其原因包括其他试跳成绩可能成为决定排序或运动员是否会进入后续赛次的关键。

除非应用了技术规则8.5条，通常情况下，任何发生犯规行为的试跳均不应被测量。通常只在特殊情况下，相关裁判员应审慎地适用判罚权采用任何备选的操作。

除非使用影像测距，每次有效试跳后，在落地区内运动员留下的距离起跳线的最近触及点，应垂直插上一个（通常为金属的）标志物，这个标志物穿过刻度钢卷尺末端的环，使"0"点在标志物上。水平拉紧金属卷尺，注意避免把它放在地面上的任何凸起处。

风速测量

29.10 风速仪须与技术规则17.8条和17.9条所述一致。按照技术规则17.11条和29.12条的要求操作，并按照技术规则17.13条读取数据。

29.11 相关田赛裁判长须确保风速仪置于距离起跳线20米处，测量平面高度为1.22米±0.05米，与助跑道的距离不超过2米。

29.12 The wind velocity shall be measured for a period of 5 seconds from the time an athlete passes a mark placed alongside the runway, for the Long Jump 40m from the take-off line and for the Triple Jump 35m. If an athlete runs less than 40m or 35m, as appropriate, the wind velocity shall be measured from the time they commence their run.

30. Long Jump

Competition

30.1 An athlete fails if:

    30.1.1 they while taking off (at any time prior to the instant at which they cease contact with the take-off board or ground), break the vertical plane of the take-off line with any front part of their take-off foot/shoe, whether running up without jumping or in the act of jumping; or

    Note: It will not be considered a failure, if the break of the vertical plane is made by a loose part of the shoe (e.g. shoelace).

    30.1.2 they take off from outside either end of the board, whether beyond or before the extension of the take-off line; or

    30.1.3 they employ any form of somersaulting whilst running up or in the act of jumping; or

    30.1.4 after taking off, but before their first contact with the landing area, they touch the runway or the ground outside the runway or outside the landing area; or

    30.1.5 in the course of landing (including any overbalancing), they touch the border of, or the ground outside, the landing area closer to the take-off line than the nearest break made in the sand; or

29.12 风速应从运动员经过助跑道旁的标记点时开始测量，测量时间为5秒。跳远和三级跳远风速测量标记点应分别置于距离起跳线40米和35米处。如果运动员助跑距离不足40米或35米，则须从其开始助跑时启动测量。

30. 跳远

比赛

30.1 下列情况，应判为试跳失败：

30.1.1 运动员在起跳过程中（结束与起跳板或地面接触之前任何时候），无论是在助跑后未做起跳动作的情况下还是在起跳动作中，运动员的起跳脚/鞋的任何前面部分越过起跳线的垂面；或

注：如果鞋的松散部分（如鞋带）触及了垂直面，不会判为失败。

30.1.2 运动员从起跳板任意一端以外起跳，无论是否越过起跳线的延长线或在起跳线的延长线前；或

30.1.3 运动员在助跑或跳跃时采用任何形式的空翻动作；或

30.1.4 起跳后，但在首次触及落地区之前，运动员触及了助跑道、助跑道以外地面或落地区以外地面；或

30.1.5 在落地过程中（包括失去平衡时），运动员触及落地区边沿或落地区以外地面，而这个触及点较沙坑内的最近触及点更靠近起跳线；或

30.1.6 they leave the landing area in any manner other than that described in Rule 30.2 of the Technical Rules.

Since the intent of Rule 30.1.1 focuses on the position of the front of the take-off shoe/foot, it is not relevant if the vertical plane should be broken in other ways, for example by their hands or arms or a cap or piece of jewellery falling from the athlete's body during the take-off. Similarly, a loose shoelace or the like is not relevant to the adjudication even if it breaks the plane.

30.2 When leaving the landing area, an athlete's first contact by foot with its border or the ground outside shall be further from the take-off line than the nearest break in the sand (which may be any mark made on overbalancing completely inside the landing area or when walking back, closer to the take-off line than the initial break on landing).

Note: This first contact is considered leaving.

30.3 An athlete shall not be regarded to have failed if:

30.3.1 they run outside the white lines marking the runway at any point; or

30.3.2 except as described in Rule 30.1.2 of the Technical Rules, they take off before reaching the board; or

30.3.3 under Rule 30.1.2 of the Technical Rules a part of their shoe/foot is touching the ground outside either end of the take-off board, before the take-off line; or

30.3.4 if in the course of landing, they touch, with any part of their body, or anything attached to it at that moment, the border of, or the ground outside the landing area, unless such contact contravenes Rule 30.1.4 or 30.1.5 of the Technical Rules; or

30.1.6　除技术规则30.2条所述情况外，运动员以其他方式离开落地区。

规则30.1.1条的重点在于踏跳脚/鞋的前面部分，与其他方式越过起跳线垂直面无关，如运动员的手、手臂、帽子或在起跳期间从运动员身体掉落的首饰。类似情况为，松散的鞋带等即使越过垂直面也与判罚无关。

30.2　离开落地区时，运动员脚在落地区边沿或边沿以外地面的第一触及点，要比在沙坑内的最近触及点距离起跳线更远（该最近触及点可能为因失去平衡而留下的完全在落地区内的痕迹，或者是运动员往回走时留下的距离起跳线比最初落地的触及点更近的痕迹）。

注：第一次触地过程被视为离开落地区。

30.3　下列情况，不应判为试跳失败：

30.3.1　运动员在任何位置跑出助跑道白色标志线；或

30.3.2　除技术规则30.1.2条的情况外，运动员在抵达起跳板之前起跳；或

30.3.3　按照技术规则30.1.2条的规定，运动员的鞋/脚的一部分触及起跳板任意一端以外、起跳线之前的地面；或

30.3.4　在落地过程中，运动员身体的任何部分，或落地那一刻附在身体上的任何物体，触及了落地区边沿或以外的地面。除非这一接触违反了技术规则30.1.4条或30.1.5条的规定；或

30.3.5 they walk back through the landing area after having left the landing area in the manner described in Rule 30.2 of the Technical Rules.

Take-off Line

30.4 The distance between the take-off line and the far end of the landing area shall be at least 10m and, where possible, 11m.

30.5 The take-off line shall be placed between 1m and 3m from the nearer end of the landing area.

Team of Officials

For a Long Jump or Triple Jump event, it is recommended to allocate the available officials as follows:

a. The Chief Judge will watch over the whole of the event.

b. Judge checking whether the take-off has been made correctly and measuring the trial. They must be provided with two flags - white to indicate if the trial is valid and red if it is a failure. When the jump has been measured, it is advised that the Judge stands in front of the take-off board, holding the red flag, while the landing area is levelled and, if relevant, the plasticine board is replaced. A cone may be used instead or in addition (In some competitions this position is assumed by the Chief Judge of the event).

c. Judge at the landing point determining the position of the nearest break in the landing area to the take-off line, to insert the spike/prism and then, if a tape is being used, hold the tape on the 0. When video measuring is being used, no judge will normally be required on site for this purpose. When an optic system of measuring is being used on site, two judges are needed at the landing point, one to plant the marker in the sand, the other one to read the result on the optic apparatus.

d. Judge - a recorder scoring the results sheet and calling each athlete (and the one who is to follow).

e. Judge in charge of the scoreboard (trial-number-result).

30.3.5 如果运动员按照技术规则30.2条所述的方式离开落地区后，运动员穿过落地区往回走。

起跳线

30.4 起跳线至落地区远端的距离须至少10米，如有可能，应为11米。

30.5 起跳线至落地区近端的距离须为1~3米。

裁判员团队

跳远和三级跳远比赛，建议裁判员的配置如下：

a. 主裁判，负责管控整个比赛。

b. 起跳点裁判员，判断起跳是否成功并测量成绩。起跳点裁判员须备有两面旗子——白旗标示试跳成功，红旗标示试跳失败。试跳测量完后，在平整落地区时，建议该裁判员手执红旗站在起跳板前，如果可以，在平整落地区的时候更换橡皮泥板。锥桶可被替代或增加（在某些比赛中，该职责由项目主裁判承担）。

c. 落点裁判员，判断运动员在落地区内距离起跳线最近的触及点，插上铁钎/棱镜，如果使用钢尺丈量，将钢尺零点对准铁钎。使用视频测距时，无须裁判员完成此项工作。使用光学测距仪时，需要有2名裁判员，一人在沙坑落点插上标志，另一人在光学仪器上读取成绩。

d. 记录裁判员，记录成绩单，并通知每名运动员（和下一名运动员）试跳。

e. 成绩显示屏裁判员（试跳轮次—运动员号码—试跳成绩）。

f. Judge in charge of the wind-gauge positioned at a point 20 metres from the take-off line.

g. One or more Judges or assistants in charge of levelling the landing area after each trial.

h. Judge or an assistant in charge of replacing the plasticine.

i. Judge in charge of the clock indicating to the athletes that they have a certain time to take their trial.

j. Judge in charge of athletes.

Note (i): This is the traditional setting-up of the officials. In major competitions, where a data system and electronic scoreboards are available, specialised personnel are certainly required. To be clear in these cases, the progress and scoring of a Field Event is followed by both the recorder and by the data system.

Note (ii): Officials and equipment must be placed in such a way as not to obstruct the athlete's way nor impede the view of the spectators.

Note (iii): A space must be reserved for a wind-sock to indicate the wind direction and strength.

31. Triple Jump

Rules 29 and 30 of the Technical Rules apply to Triple Jump with the following variations:

Competition

31.1　The Triple Jump shall consist of a hop, a step and a jump in that order.

31.2　The hop shall be made so that an athlete lands first on the same foot as that from which they have taken off; in the step they shall land on the other foot, from which, subsequently, the jump is performed.

　　　It shall not be considered a failure if an athlete, during a trial, touches the ground with the "sleeping" leg.

f. 风速测量裁判员，负责测量风速，风速仪置于距离起跳线20米处。

g. 1名或多名平沙裁判员或助理，每次试跳后负责平整落地区。

h. 橡皮泥板裁判员或1名助理，负责更换橡皮泥显示板。

i. 时限裁判员，负责向运动员显示某次试跳时限。

j. 管理裁判员，负责运动员的管理。

注（i）：这是裁判团队的常规设置。在大型比赛中，需要专业人员操作数据系统、电子显示牌。需要明确的是，记录裁判员和数据系统均要完成跟踪田赛项目的比赛进程和记录成绩。

注（ii）：裁判员的站位和设备的摆放既不能妨碍运动员比赛，也不能阻挡观众的视线。

注（iii）：须在合理位置放置风标，用于显示风向和风力。

31. 三级跳远

技术规则29条和30条同样适用于三级跳远项目，并增加以下变化内容：

比赛

31.1　三级跳远的"三跳"顺序是一次单足跳、一次跨步跳和一次跳跃。

31.2　单足跳应以起跳腿落地，跨步跳以另一腿（摆动腿）落地，随后，由此腿起跳，完成跳跃动作。

运动员在试跳过程中摆动腿触及地面不应视为试跳失败。

Note: Rule 30.1.4 of the Technical Rules does not apply to the normal landings from the hop and step phases.

It should be noted that it is not a failure (for that reason alone) if the athlete:

a. touches the white lines or the ground outside between the take-off line and the landing area; or

b. lands in the pit in the step phase through no fault of their own (i.e. if the Judge incorrectly indicated the take-off board) - in which such case the Referee would normally offer the athlete a replacement trial.

It is, however, a failure if the landing of the jump is not within the landing area.

Take-off Line / Take-off Area

31.3 The distance between the take-off line for men and the far end of the landing area shall be at least 21m.

31.4 Where necessary for the level of the competition, there should be a separate take-off board for men and women. The take-off line shall not be less than 13m for men and 11m for women from the nearer end of the landing area. For any other competition, this distance shall be appropriate for the level of competition.

31.5 Between the take-off board and the landing area there shall, for the step and jump phases, be a take-off area of 1.22m ± 0.01m wide providing firm and uniform footing.

Note: For all tracks constructed before 1 January 2004, this take-off area may have a width of maximum 1.25m. However, when such a runway is fully resurfaced, the lane width shall comply with this Rule.

注：技术规则30.1.4条不适用于单足跳和跨步跳时的正常落地动作。

需要注意的是，运动员出现下列情形（仅因这个原因），不应判为失败：

a. 触及在起跳线和落地区之间的白线或线外地面；或

b. 运动员自身没有犯规情形，但在跨步跳阶段落入沙坑（如裁判员错误标识起跳板位置），在这种情况下，相关裁判长通常应给予运动员一次重新试跳机会。

然而，如果运动员跳跃的落点在落地区之外，应判为失败。

起跳线/起跳区

31.3　男子起跳线至落地区远端的距离须至少21米。

31.4　根据不同比赛水平的需要，应分别设置男子和女子起跳板，起跳线至落地区近端的距离：男子不少于13米，女子不少于11米。其他比赛中，此距离应与参赛运动员的水平相适应。

31.5　在起跳板和落地区之间，对于跨步跳和跳跃阶段，应有一个1.22米±0.01米宽的坚实、匀质的起跳区。

注：2004年1月1日以前建造的场地，起跳区最大宽度可为1.25米。但是，当这种助跑道全部重新铺设时，跑道宽度应遵守本规则的规定。

Throwing Events

32. General Conditions – Throwing Events

Official Implements

32.1　In all World Rankings Competitions, the implements used shall comply with current World Athletics specifications. Only World Athletics certified implements may be used. The following table shows the implement to be used by each age group:

Implement	Women U18	Women U20/Senior	Men U18	Men U20	Men Senior
Shot	3.000kg	4.000kg	5.000kg	6.000kg	7.260kg
Discus	1.000kg	1.000kg	1.500kg	1.750kg	2.000kg
Hammer	3.000kg	4.000kg	5.000kg	6.000kg	7.260kg
Javelin	500g	600g	700g	800g	800g

Note (i): The current standard forms required to be used for the certification and renewal application as well as the Certification System Procedures are available from the World Athletics Office, or may be downloaded from the World Athletics website.

Note (ii): Recommended weights and specifications for other implements commonly used in underage, para or master competition will be listed on the World Athletics website.

32.2　Except as provided below, all such implements shall be provided by the Organisers. The Technical Delegate(s) may, based on the applicable regulations of each competition, allow athletes to use their own personal implements or those provided by a supplier, provided that such implements are World Athletics certified, checked and marked as approved by the Organisers before the competition and made available to all athletes. Unless the Technical Delegate decides otherwise, not more than two implements may be submitted by any athlete for any throwing event in which they are competing.

投掷项目

32. 投掷项目通则

正式比赛器械

32.1　在所有世界排名比赛中，应使用符合世界田联现行有关规定的器械。只有世界田联认证合格的器械方可使用。下表是各年龄组使用的器械重量：

器械	少年女子（U18）	青年女子（U20）/成年女子	少年男子（U18）	青年男子（U20）	成年男子
铅球	3.000千克	4.000千克	5.000千克	6.000千克	7.260千克
铁饼	1.000千克	1.000千克	1.500千克	1.750千克	2.000千克
链球	3.000千克	4.000千克	5.000千克	6.000千克	7.260千克
标枪	500克	600克	700克	800克	800克

注（ⅰ）：认证申请和测量报告所使用的现行标准表格及认证系统程序，可向世界田联办公室索取或从世界田联官方网站下载。

注（ⅱ）：未成年人比赛、残疾人比赛或老将赛中常用的其他器械的推荐重量和规格将列在世界田联网站上。

32.2　所有投掷器械应由组织者提供，下列情况例外：根据各项比赛的相关规程，技术代表可以允许运动员使用自备投掷器械，或者使用供货商提供的器械，但是这些器械须经过世界田联认证，并在比赛前经过组织者的检查和标记，比赛时所有运动员均可使用。除非技术代表另有决定，任何运动员在其参加的任何投掷项目中不得提交2件以上的器械。

Note: "World Athletics certified" implements may include older models that previously held a certificate but are not in production any longer.

It is becoming increasingly common for Organisers to provide a lesser range of implements than in the past (largely due to the cost of purchases). This increases the responsibility of Technical Managers and their assistants to closely check all personal implements presented for competitions - to ensure that they comply with the Rules as well as being on the World Athletics list of certified products. Implements which do not currently have but have previously had a World Athletics certificate may be accepted for competition if they comply with the Rules.

32.3 No modification shall be made to any implements during the competition. No spitting or application by other means of human body fluids on any implement, is permitted.

Assistance

32.4 The following shall be considered assistance and are therefore not allowed:

32.4.1 The taping of two or more fingers together. If taping is used on the hands and fingers, it may be continuous provided that as a result no two or more fingers are taped together in such a way that the fingers cannot move individually. The taping should be shown to the Chief Judge before the event starts.

32.4.2 The use of any device of any kind, including weights attached to the body, which in any way provides assistance when making a trial.

32.4.3 The use of gloves except in the Hammer Throw. In this case, the gloves shall be smooth on the back and on the front and the tips of the glove fingers, other than the thumb, shall be open.

32.4.4 The spraying or spreading by an athlete of any substance in the circle or on their shoes nor the roughening of the surface of the circle.

注："世界田联认证"的投掷器械可能包括以前持有证书的旧型号，但已不再生产。

与过去相比，现在组织者提供器材的情况越来越少（主要是为了降低采购成本）。这也相应地增加了技术主管及其助手的责任，他们需要仔细地核查所有用于比赛的自备器材，以保证它们符合竞赛规则并与世界田联审定的器械目录相一致。如果投掷器械目前不在世界田联审定的器械目录中，但是以前曾被审定过，在符合规则的情况下也应该被接受。

32.3　比赛中不得对任何投掷器械做任何改变。不允许在任何器具上吐痰或以其他方式使用人体体液。

帮助

32.4　下列情况应视为帮助，因此不允许：

32.4.1　使用胶带将2个或更多的手指捆在一起。如果用胶带捆绑手和手指，则可连续捆绑，但前提是不能将2根或多根手指绑在一起，这种捆绑方式使手指不能单独活动。使用胶带应在比赛开始前向有关主裁判展示。

32.4.2　当运动员试掷时，可使用任何类型的装置提供帮助，包括在身上附着重物。

32.4.3　除链球外，运动员不得在比赛中使用手套。链球手套的手掌和手背及戴手套手指的指尖是光滑的。除拇指外，其余手指应露出指尖。

32.4.4　不允许运动员向投掷圈内或鞋底喷洒任何物质，或使圈内地面粗糙。

Note: If the Judges are aware, they shall direct any athlete not complying with this Rule to correct the situation. If the athlete does not, such trial(s) shall be a failure. It shall also be judged as a failure, if a trial is completed before the non-compliance is noticed. In all cases considered serious enough, Rules 7.1 and 7.3 of the Technical Rules may also be applied.

32.5　The following shall not be considered assistance and are therefore allowed:

　　32.5.1　The use by an athlete, in order to obtain a better grip, of a suitable substance on their hands only or in the case of a hammer thrower on their gloves. A shot putter may use such substances on their neck.

　　32.5.2　The placement by an athlete, in the Shot Put and Discus Throw, on the implement, of chalk or a similar substance.

All substances used on the hands, gloves and on the implements shall be easily removable from the implement using a wet cloth and shall not leave any residue. If this is not followed, the Note to Rule 32.4 of the Technical Rules shall be applied.

　　32.5.3　The use of taping on the hands and fingers that is not in contravention of Rule 32.4.1 of the Technical Rules.

Throwing Circle

32.6　The rim of the circle shall be made of band iron, steel or other suitable material, the top of which shall be flush with the ground outside. It shall be at least 6mm thick. The inside and top of the rim shall be white. The ground surrounding the circle may be concrete, synthetic, asphalt, wood or any other suitable material.

The interior of the circle may be constructed of concrete, asphalt or some other firm but not slippery material. The surface of this interior generally shall be level and 20mm ± 6mm lower than the upper edge of the rim of the circle.

In the Shot Put, a portable circle meeting these specifications is permissible.

注：如果裁判员发现这些情况，他应命令不遵守规则的运动员进行改正。如果运动员拒不执行，这次试掷判为失败。如果一次这类试掷在被发现之前就已完成，也应被判为失败。如果情况严重，也可适用技术规则7.1条和7.3条。

32.5 下列情况不视为帮助，允许在比赛中出现：

  32.5.1 为了更好地抓握器械，运动员可在双手上使用某种适宜物质，或链球运动员可在手套上使用。铅球运动员可在其颈部涂抹此类物质。

  32.5.2 在铅球和铁饼项目中，运动员在器械上放置白垩粉或类似物质。

所有用到手上、手套上、器械上的这类物质都应可以用湿布轻松去除，且不应留下任何污渍。如果不能实现，按技术规则32.4条处理。

  32.5.3 在不违反技术规则32.4.1条的情况下，可在手或手指上使用胶带。

投掷圈

32.6 投掷圈边沿应使用扁铁、钢板或其他适宜材料制成，其上沿应与圈外地面齐平，其厚度至少为6毫米，圈的内沿和顶部应漆成白色。圈的周围地面可以为混凝土、合成材料、沥青、木材或其他材料。

圈内地面应用混凝土、沥青或其他坚硬而不滑的材料修建。圈内地面须保持水平，低于铁圈上沿20毫米±6毫米。

铅球项目可使用符合上述规定的可移动式投掷圈。

32.7　The inside diameter of the circle shall be 2.135m ± 0.005m in the Shot Put and the Hammer Throw and 2.50m ± 0.005m in the Discus Throw.

The hammer may be thrown from the discus circle provided the diameter of this circle is reduced from 2.50m to 2.135m by placing a circular ring inside.

Note: The circular ring should preferably be coloured other than white so that the white lines required by Rule 32.8 of the Technical Rules be clearly visible.

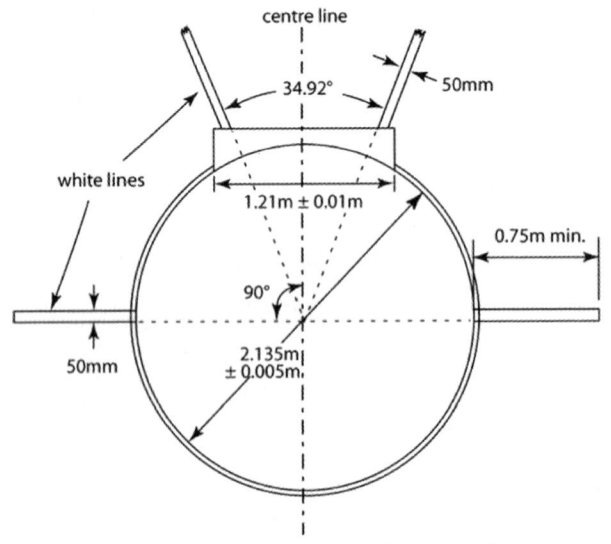

Figure (a) TR32 – Layout of Shot Put circle

32.8　A white line 50mm wide shall be drawn from the top of the rim extending for at least 0.75m on either side of the circle. The white line may be painted or made of wood or other suitable material. The rear edge of the white line shall form a prolongation of a theoretical line through the centre of the circle at right angles to the centre line of the landing sector.

32.7 铅球和链球项目，圈的内径应为2.135米±0.005米。铁饼项目，圈的内径应为2.50米±0.005米。［技术规则32条图（a）（b）（c）（d）］

可在铁饼投掷圈内放置一个圆形环，将直径从2.50米减小为2.135米，用于链球投掷。

注：该圆形环应漆成除白色外的其他颜色，以便能清楚看见技术规则32.8条规定的白线。

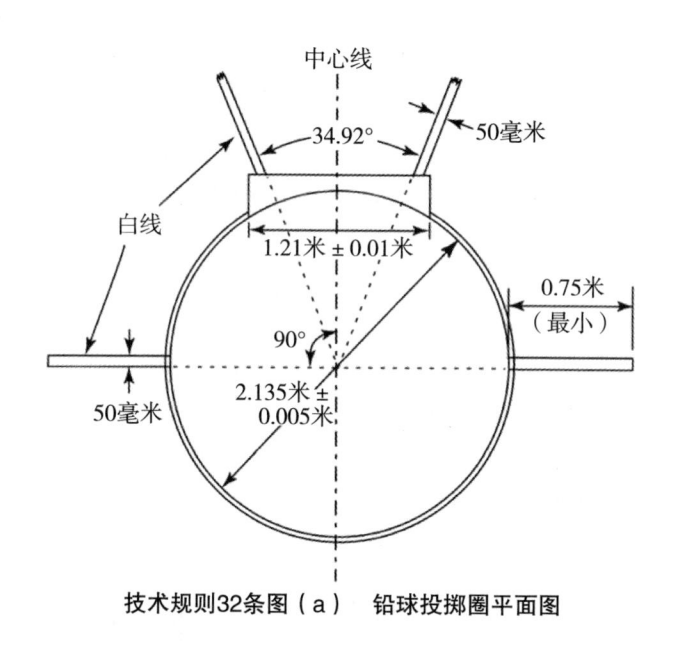

技术规则32条图（a）　铅球投掷圈平面图

32.8 从金属圈顶两侧向外各画一条宽50毫米、长至少为0.75米的白线。此线可以画出，也可用木料或其他适宜材料制成。白线后沿的延长线应能通过圆心，并与落地区中心线垂直。

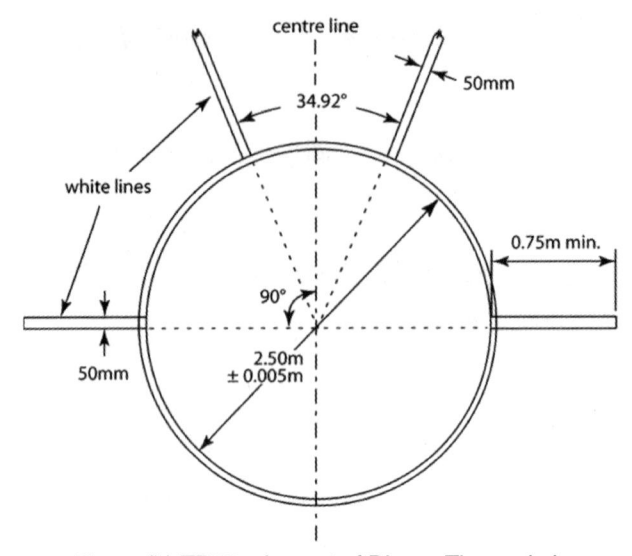

Figure (b) TR32 – Layout of Discus Throw circle

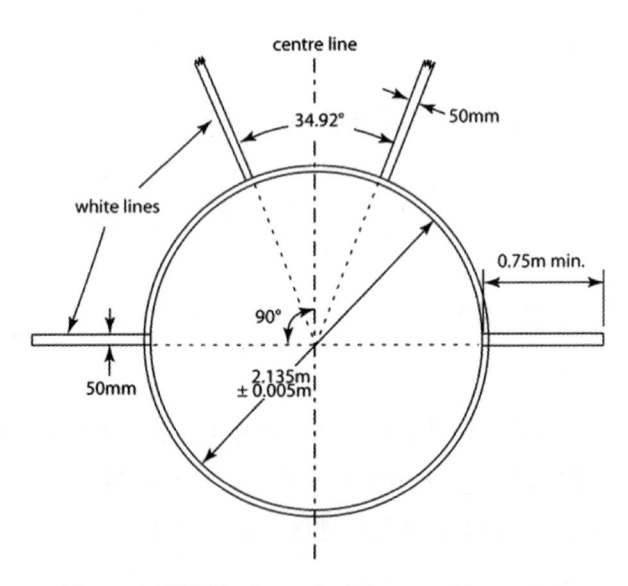

Figure (c) TR32 – Layout of Hammer Throw circle

技术规则32条图（b） 铁饼投掷圈平面图

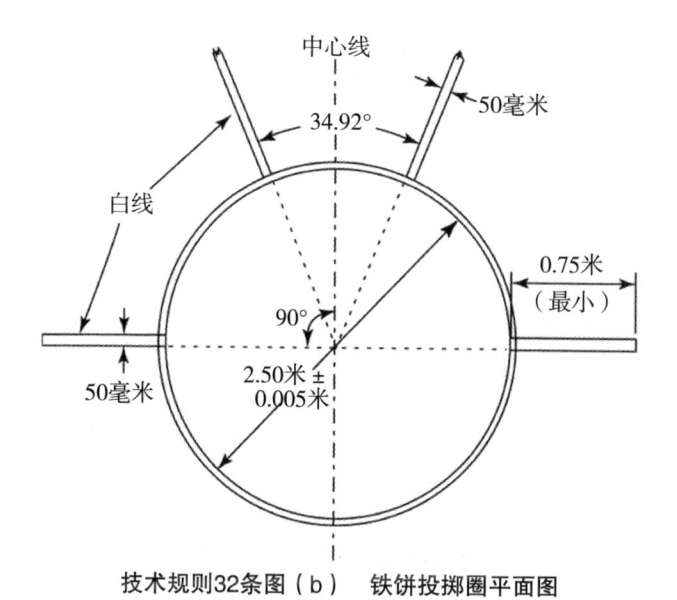

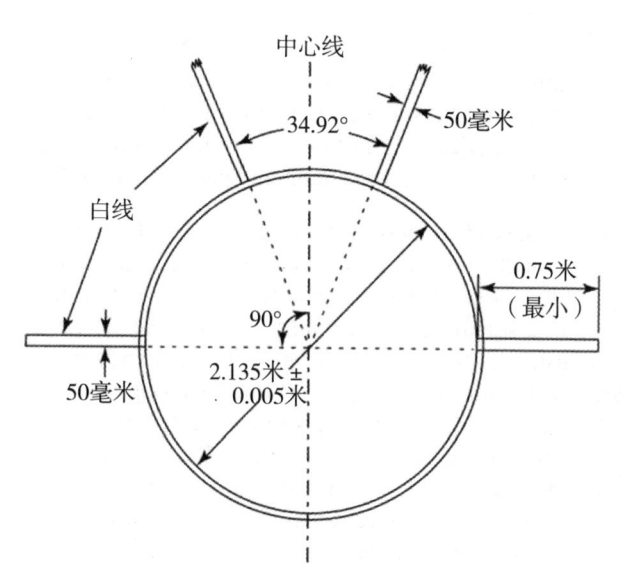

技术规则32条图（c） 链球投掷圈平面图

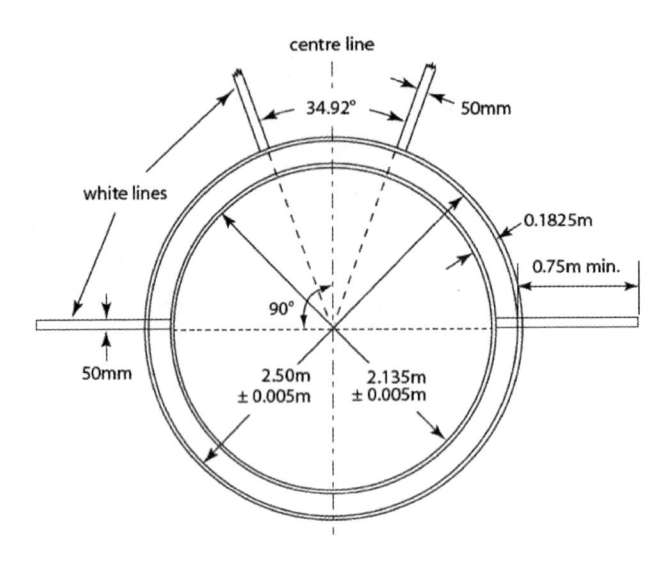

Figure (d) TR32 – Layout of concentric circles for Discus and Hammer Throw circle

Javelin Throw Runway

32.9　The minimum length of the runway shall be 30m except in competitions held under paragraphs 1. (a), (b), (c), (d) and 2. (a), (b) of the World Rankings Competition definition, where the minimum shall be 33.50m. Where conditions permit, the minimum length should be 36.50m.

It shall be marked by two parallel white lines 50mm wide and 4m apart. The throw shall be made from behind an arc of a circle drawn with a radius of 8m. The arc shall consist of an at least 70mm wide strip painted or made of wood or a suitable non-corrodible material like plastic. It shall be white and be flush with the ground. Lines shall be drawn from the extremities of the arc at right angles to the parallel lines marking the runway. These lines shall be white, at least 0.75m long and at least 70mm wide. The maximum lateral inclination of the runway should be 1 : 100 (1%) unless special circumstances exist which justify World Athletics providing an exemption and, in the last 20m of the runway, the overall downward inclination in the direction of running shall not exceed 1 : 1000 (0.1%).

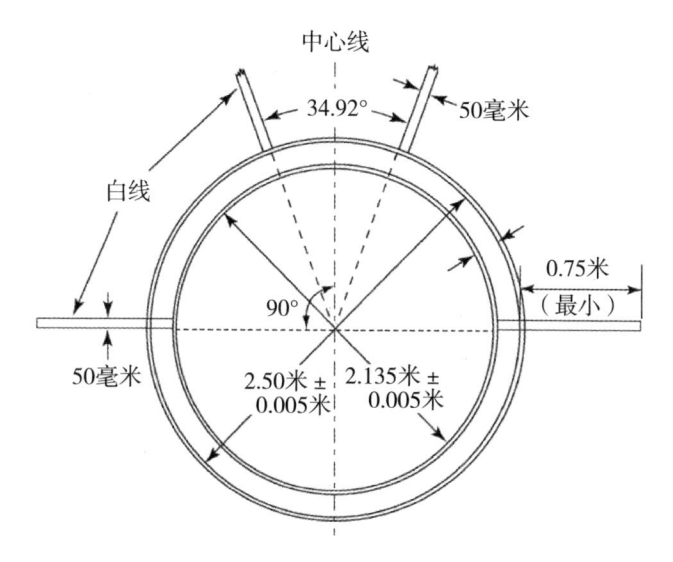

技术规则32条图（d） 铁饼、链球同心圆投掷圈平面图

标枪助跑道

32.9　助跑道的长度不短于30米，在世界排名比赛定义1.（a）（b）（c）（d）和2.（a）（b）所述的比赛中，助跑道不短于33.50米，条件允许时，最短应为36.50米。［技术规则32条图（e）］

助跑道应用两条相距4米、宽为50毫米的平行白线标出。助跑道前端是半径为8米的一条弧线，运动员应在投掷弧后面试掷。投掷弧可以画出，也可以用木料或类似塑料的且抗腐蚀的适宜材料制成，弧线至少宽70毫米，涂成白色，与地面齐平。投掷弧两端向外各画一条白色直线，与助跑道标志线垂直，线宽至少70毫米，长至少0.75米。助跑道横向的最大倾斜度为1∶100（1%），世界田联批准的合法豁免的特殊情形除外。助跑道跑进方向最后20米向下的整体倾斜度不得超过1∶1000（0.1%）。

田径竞赛与技术规则（2025）

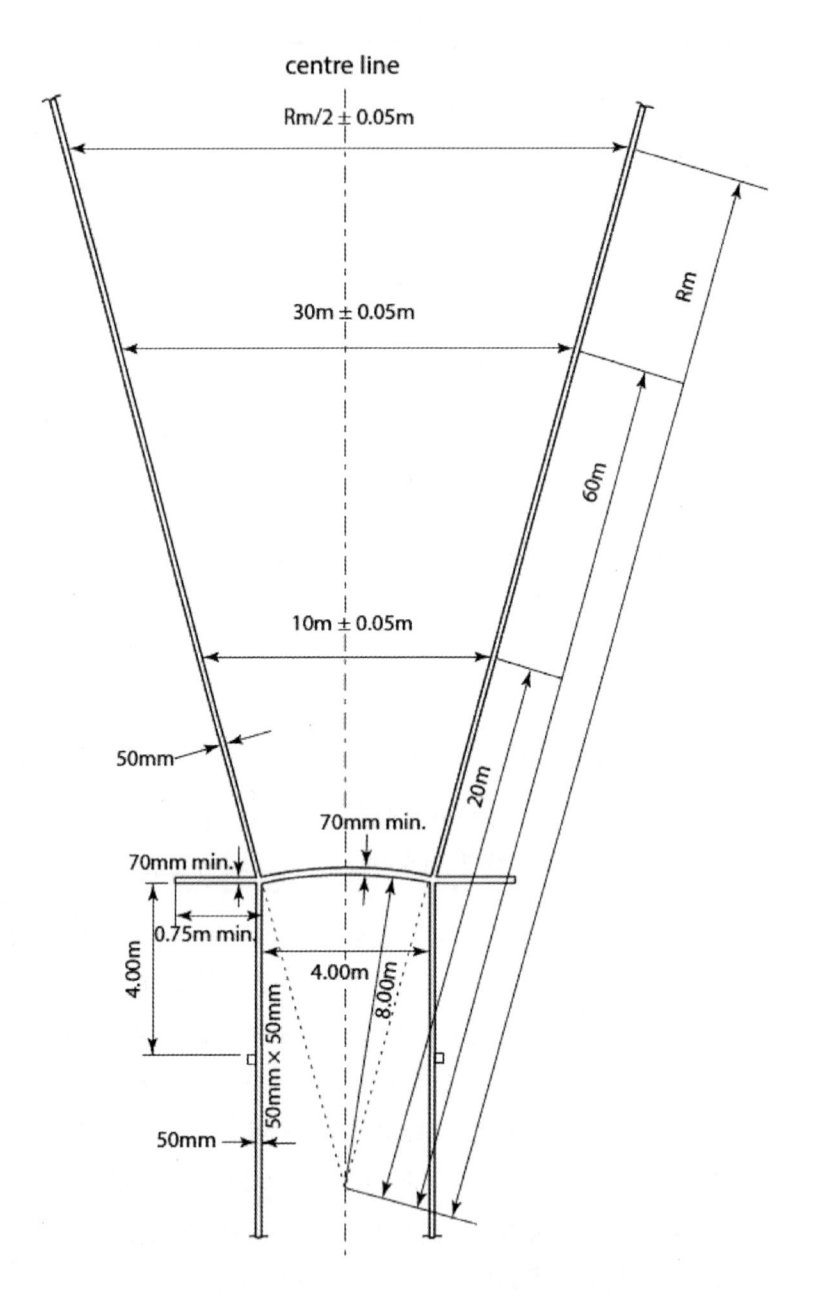

Figure (e) TR32 – Javelin Throw runway and landing sector (not to scale)

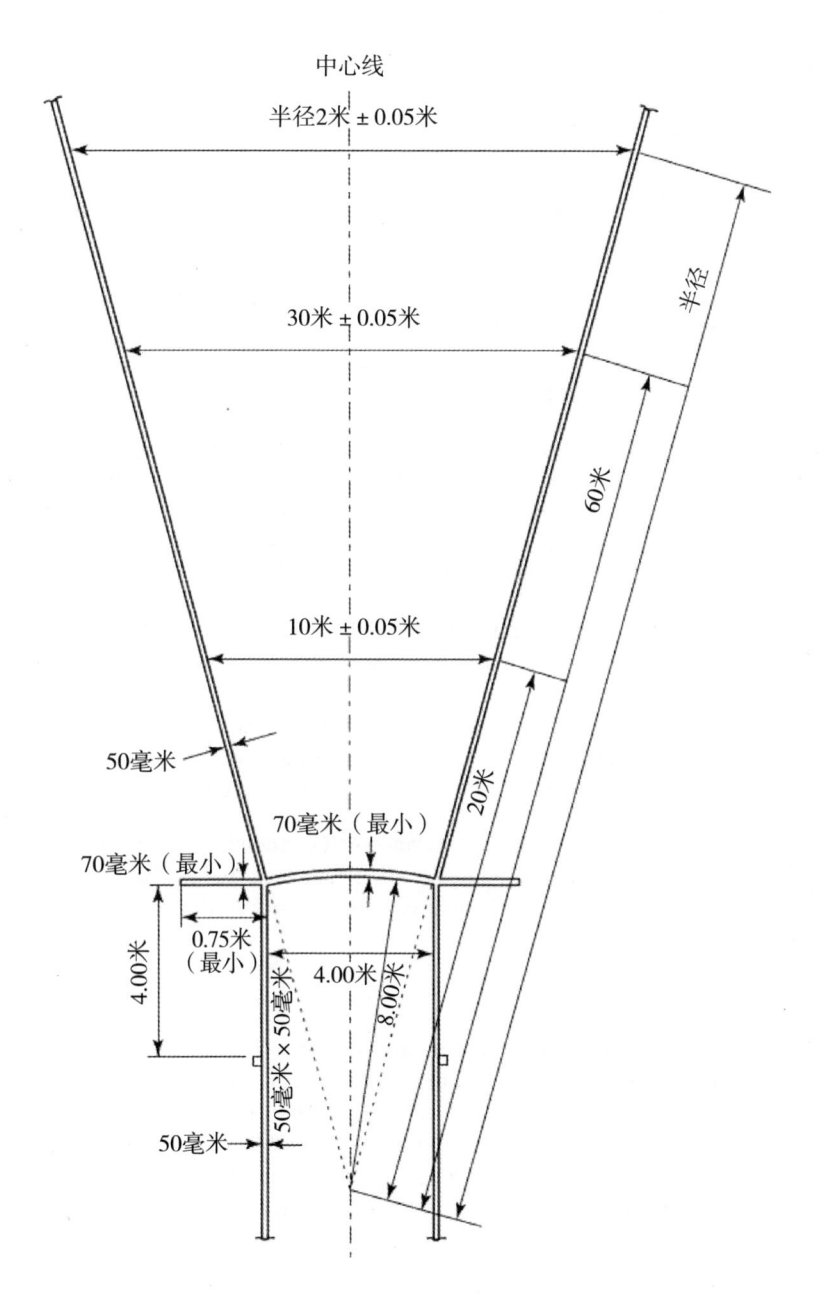

技术规则32条图（e） 标枪助跑道和落地区（非比例）

Landing Sector

32.10　The landing sector shall consist of cinders or grass or other suitable material on which the implement makes an imprint.

32.11　The maximum overall downward inclination of the landing sector, in the throwing direction, shall not exceed 1∶1000 (0.1%).

32.12　Landing Sector markings:

　　32.12.1　Except for the Javelin Throw, the landing sector shall be marked with white lines 50mm wide at an angle of 34.92° such that the inner edge of lines, if extended, would pass through the centre of the circle.

　　Note: The 34.92° sector may be laid out accurately by making the distance between the two points on the sector lines 20m from the centre of the circle 12m ± 0.05m (20 × 0.60m) apart. Thus, for every 1m from the centre of the circle, the distance across shall be increased by 0.60m.

　　32.12.2　In the Javelin Throw, the landing sector shall be marked with white lines 50mm wide such that the inner edge of the lines, if extended, would pass through the two intersections of the inner edges of the arc and the parallel lines marking the runway, and intersect at the centre of the circle of which the arc is part ［see Figure (e) TR32］. The sector angle is thus 28.96°.

The landing sector shall be of an even surface soft enough to ensure that the place of the initial fall of the implement can be clearly established by the Judges. The landing surface should not allow the implement bounce backwards thus creating a risk that the measuring point is obliterated.

Trials

32.13　In the Shot Put, Discus Throw and Hammer Throw, implements shall be thrown from a circle, and in the Javelin Throw, from a runway. In the case of trials made from a circle, an athlete shall commence their trial from a stationary position inside the circle. An athlete is allowed to touch the inside of the rim. In the Shot Put, they are also allowed to touch the inside of the stop board described in Rule 33.2 of the Technical Rules.

落地区

32.10　落地扇形区应用煤渣、草地或其他适宜材料铺设,器械落地时应能留下痕迹。

32.11　落地区在投掷方向上向下的最大整体倾斜度不得超过1∶1000（0.1%）。

32.12　扇形落地区标记:

> 32.12.1　除标枪项目外,落地区用两条夹角为34.92°的50毫米宽的白线标出,其内沿的延长线应通过投掷圈圆心。
>
> *注:可用下列方法精确设置34.92°扇形落地区:在离投掷圈圆心20米处,两条落地区标志线间的距离是12米±0.05米（20×0.6米）,即每离开圆心1米,落地区标志线间的距离增加0.6米。*
>
> 32.12.2　在标枪项目中,落地区须用两条50毫米宽的白线标出,其内沿的延长线必须通过投掷弧内沿与助跑道标志线内沿的交点并相交于投掷弧的圆心［见技术规则32条图（e）］。落地区扇形的夹角约为28.96°。

落地区表面应该平坦、柔软,保证投掷器械在最初落地时留下痕迹,以便裁判员确定落点。落地区表面应确保器械不至于反弹造成危险或导致丈量点痕迹受到破坏。

试掷

32.13　铅球、铁饼或链球的器械应从投掷圈内掷出,标枪在助跑道内完成掷出。在圈内进行试掷时,运动员应在圈内从静止姿势开始。允许运动员触及铁圈内沿。铅球比赛时,允许运动员触及技术规则33.2条所述的抵趾板内侧。

There is no restriction on how, or from which direction, an athlete may enter the circle nor in the case of the shot put is there any restriction on making contact with the stop board during this process. The relevant requirement is that once inside, they must adopt a stationary position before commencing their trial.

A stationary position means that an athlete having entered the circle to make their trial and before doing so adopts a stance in which both feet are simultaneously in firm contact with the ground inside the circle and with no contact with the top of the rim or the ground outside. Such contact to be sufficiently long in time to be visible to the judges. There is no requirement for the arms or hands or other parts of the athlete's body to be stationary.

32.14   It shall be a failure if an athlete in the course of a trial:

    32.14.1   releases the shot or the javelin other than as permitted under Rules 33.1 and 38.1 of the Technical Rules;

    32.14.2   after they have stepped into the circle and begun to make a throw, touches with any part of their body the top (or the top inside edge) of the rim or the ground outside the circle;

    Note: It will not be considered a failure if the touch occurs during any first rotation at a point completely behind the white line which is drawn outside the circle running, theoretically, through the centre of the circle.

    32.14.3   in the Shot Put, touches with any part of their body any part of the stop board other than its inner side (excluding its top edge which is considered to be part of the top);

    32.14.4   in the Javelin Throw, touches with any part of their body the lines which mark the runway or the ground outside.

Note (i): It will not be considered a failure at any time, if the touch, including of the top of the stop board, or, in the case of Javelin Throw, the throwing arc or lines marking the runway, is made by a loose part of the shoe (e.g. shoelace) or clothing, or if the touch is made by any other item (e.g. cap) which was attached to the body at the time of the start of throw and became detached during or after the throw.

运动员如何或从哪个方向进入投掷圈没有限制，或者铅球比赛时在这个过程中与抵趾板接触也都没有任何限制。相应的要求是，一旦进入投掷圈内，他们必须从静止姿势开始试掷。

静止的姿势是运动员进入投掷圈进行试掷之前，双脚同时与圈内的地面紧密接触，而不与投掷圈顶部或外部地面接触的姿势。这种接触应有足够长的时间，以便裁判员能够观察到。运动员的手臂、手或身体其他部位不要求静止。

32.14　如果运动员在试掷中出现下列情况，判为试掷失败：

32.14.1　铅球或标枪出手姿势不符合技术规则33.1条和38.1条的规定；

32.14.2　在进入投掷圈内并开始投掷动作之后，身体的任何部分触及铁圈上沿（或上沿内侧）或圈外地面；

注：但是，若触碰出现在旋转的第一圈，触碰点完全位于投掷圈外两条白线后方（理论上此两条白线后沿通过圆心），不应判为失败。

32.14.3　铅球比赛时，身体的任何部分触及除抵趾板内侧（不包括内侧上沿，这部分也视为上沿的一部分）的任何部分。

32.14.4　标枪比赛时，身体的任何部分触及助跑道标志线或线外地面。

注（i）：如果此触碰（包括抵趾板顶部的触碰，或者在标枪投掷的情况下，投掷弧或助跑道的标记线）是由鞋或衣服的松动部分（如鞋带）造成的，或者由投掷开始时附着在身体上但在投掷期间或投掷后脱落的任何其他物品（如帽子）造成的，则在任何时候都不会被视为失败。

Note (ii): It shall be considered a failure if the discus or the head of the hammer strikes the far side of the cage (left side for a right-handed thrower when facing the landing sector or the right side for a left-handed thrower when facing the landing sector) after the release of the implement.

Note (iii): It will not be considered a failure if the discus or any part of the hammer strikes the near side of the cage (right side for a right-handed thrower when facing the landing sector or the left side for a left-handed thrower when facing the landing sector) after the release of the implement, then lands within the landing sector outside the limits of the cage, provided that no other Rule is infringed, including Rule 32.10 of the Technical Rules.

It is clarified that the top inside edges of the rim of the circle and of the stop board are considered to be part of the top of the rim and stop board, respectively. This means that should an athlete make contact with the top inside edge of either the rim or the stop board then they will be considered thereby to have made a failure.

The addition of the Note to Rule 32.14.2 of the Technical Rules about the first rotation applies to rotational techniques used by athletes in Shot Put, Discus Throw or Hammer Throw. It should be interpreted that any "incidental" touch of the top of the rim or the ground outside in respect of the back half of the circle during the first rotation should not, of itself, be regarded as a failure. The addition of Note(i) to Rule 32.14 of the Technical Rules confirms that the intent of Rules 32.14.2 to 32.14.4 is to respect the purpose of the circle's or runway's limits so that the athlete complies by remaining in the circle or runway until they exit correctly. It is, unless they overbalance, only the position of their feet/shoes which is critical. It is not relevant, if the top of the rim or, in the case of Javelin Throw, the throwing arc or lines marking the runway, the ground outside or the top of the stop board is touched by a loose shoelace or the like or for example a cap or piece of jewellery falling from the athlete's body during the trial.

The limits of the cage shall be defined as the boundary formed by the cage and the gates, when in position, completed by an imaginary straight line drawn between the ends of the cage/gates closest to the landing sector.

32.15 Provided that, in the course of a trial, the Rules relative to each throwing event have not been infringed, an athlete may interrupt a trial once started, may lay the implement down inside or outside the circle or runway and may leave the circle or runway.

Note: All the moves permitted by this Rule shall be included in the maximum time for a trial given in Rule 25.17 of the Technical Rules.

注（ⅱ）：器械出手后，如果铁饼或链球的球体撞击护笼的远侧（右手投掷者面向落地区时为左侧，左手投掷者面向落地区时为右侧），则视为失败。

注（ⅲ）：出手后的铁饼或链球的任何部分撞击到护笼的近侧（右手投掷者面向落地区时为右侧，左手投掷者面向落地区时为左侧），在没有违反其他规则的情况下，包括技术规则32.10条，落在护笼限制线以外的落地区内，均不视为试掷失败。

需要说明的是，投掷圈和抵趾板的上沿内侧均被视为投掷圈和抵趾板各自上沿的一部分。这就意味着运动员如果触及上述部分将被判罚失败。

技术规则32.14.2条关于旋转第一圈的注解，适用于在铅球、铁饼或链球项目中运动员应用旋转技术。应理解为运动员在第一圈旋转时任何"偶然性的"触及投掷圈上沿或投掷圈后半部分之外的地面，仅此一项，则不应被判罚失败。技术规则32.14条注（ⅰ）的增加确认了规则32.14.2至32.14.4条的目的是尊重投掷圈或助跑道限制的目的，以便运动员遵守规定留在投掷圈或助跑道内，直到他们正确退出。除非他们失去平衡，否则只有脚/鞋子的位置才是关键。如果金属圈的顶部，或者在掷标枪时投掷弧或助跑道标志线，圈外面的地面或抵趾板的顶部在试掷过程中被松散的鞋带或类似物或者从运动员身上掉下来的物品如帽子或珠宝接触，这是没关系的。

护笼的限制线应定义为护笼和闸门就位时形成的分界线，并在离扇形落地区最近的护笼/闸门两端之间，画一条假设的直线来完成。

32.15　在试掷过程中，运动员没有违反上述各投掷项目的相关规则，运动员可中止已开始的试掷动作，可将器械放在投掷圈或助跑道内外，也可离开投掷圈或助跑道。

注：此条规则允许的所有行动均应计入技术规则25.17条规定的最大时限之内。

In these circumstances, there is no restriction on how, or from which direction, an athlete may leave the circle or runway if they choose to do. The relevant requirement is that no other Rule is or has already been infringed.

32.16 It shall be a failure if the shot, the discus, the hammer head or the head of the javelin in contacting the ground when it first lands touches the sector line or the ground outside the sector line. Moreover, it shall be a failure if the shot, the discus, the hammer head or the head of the javelin after the release but before contacting the ground touches any object [other than the cage as provided in Note (ii) to Rule 32.14 of the Technical Rules] outside the sector line.

It should be noted that for the purposes of this Rule, the position of the hammer wire or handle is not relevant. For example, the wire could land or be laying on or outside the sector line and it would not matter, provided that the head had landed correctly. The same applies in respective of determining the point from which the measurement is taken under Rule 32.20.1 of the Technical Rules.

32.17 It shall be a failure:

    32.17.1 if the athlete leaves the circle or runway before the implement has touched the ground, or

    32.17.2 for throws made from a circle, if when leaving the circle, the athlete's first contact with the top of the rim or the ground outside the circle is not completely behind the white line which is drawn outside the circle running, theoretically, through the centre of the circle;

    Note: The first contact with the top of the rim or the ground outside the circle is considered leaving.

    32.17.3 in the case of the Javelin Throw, if, when leaving the runway, the athlete's first contact with the parallel lines or the ground outside the runway is not completely behind the white line of the arc or the lines drawn from the extremities of the arc at right angles to the parallel lines. Once the implement has touched the ground, an athlete will also be considered to have left the runway correctly, upon making contact with or behind a line (painted, or theoretical and indicated by markers beside the runway) drawn across the runway, four metres back from the end points of the throwing arc. Should an athlete be behind that line and inside the runway at the moment the implement touches the ground, they shall be considered to have left the runway correctly.

在这些情形中，对运动员选择以何种方式或从何方向离开投掷圈或助跑道并没有限制。相关的要求是没有违反任何其他规则。

32.16　铅球、铁饼、链球的球体或标枪枪头第一次接触地面时，触及了落地区角度线或落在落地区角度线以外的地面，应判为失败。此外，铅球、铁饼、链球的球体或标枪枪头在投掷后落地前，触及了落地区角度线外的任何物体［技术规则32.14条注（ⅱ）所述的护笼除外］，应判为失败。

应该指出本规则实际的意思是，链球的链子或把手的位置是不包括在其中的。比如链球的链子可能在角度线上或线外，这些都无关紧要，关键是链球的球体必须正确落地。同样适用于根据技术规则32.20.1条确定从哪里开始丈量成绩。

32.17　这应判为失败：

  32.17.1　运动员在器械落地前离开投掷圈或助跑道，或

  32.17.2　在投掷圈内完成试掷，离开投掷圈时运动员首先触及的投掷圈上沿或投掷圈外地面并非完全在圈外白线的后面。该线后沿理论上要通过投掷圈的圆心；

  注：运动员第一次触及投掷圈上沿或投掷圈外地面即被认为离开。

  32.17.3　标枪比赛时，当运动员离开助跑道，首先触及的助跑道标志线或助跑道外地面不完全在投掷弧或两端白色延长线的后面，该线与助跑道标志线垂直。标枪触及地面时，当运动员触及与助跑道标志线垂直，距离投掷弧底端4米的直线或已经在该线后（该线可以画出或理论上在助跑道旁边用标志物实际标出），则被认为已经正确离开助跑道。如果在标枪触及地面时，运动员在该线后且还在助跑道内，他也将被认为已经正确离开助跑道。

The second and third sentences in Rule 32.17.3 of the Technical Rules are designed to speed up the judging process and not to create an additional method of calling a failure on the athlete. The purpose of the "4m marks" is solely to enable the Judges to raise the white flag and begin measuring the trial once the athlete retreats behind this point (in the same way as they would do if they had otherwise correctly left the runway). The only requirement is that there is no other reason for calling a failure and that the implement has touched the ground before the white flag is raised. Necessarily, if the athlete for whatever reason never progresses past the "4m marks" when making their throw then the flag can be raised once the implement has landed.

32.18　After each throw, implements shall be carried back to the area next to the circle or runway and never thrown back.

Distance Measurement

32.19　In all throwing events, distances shall be recorded to the nearest 0.01m below the distance measured if the distance measured is not a whole centimetre.

32.20　The measurement of each throw shall be made immediately after each valid trial (or after an immediate oral protest made under Rule 8.5 of the Technical Rules) from the nearest mark made in contacting the ground when it first lands by:

　　32.20.1　the shot, discus and hammer head, to the inside of the circumference of the circle along a line to the centre of the circle; or

　　32.20.2　the head of the javelin to the inside edge of the arc, along a line to the centre of the circle of which the arc is part.

As long as no irregularity has been committed, each trial must be measured whatever the distance reached, including for the reasons that other trial measurements may become critical in determining countbacks or whether an athlete will proceed to subsequent rounds.

Except where Rule 8.5 of the Technical Rules is applied, under normal practice no trial during which an irregularity has been committed should be measured. Judges should carefully use their discretion in applying any alternate practice and usually only in special cases.

技术规则32.17.3条中的第二和第三句话,是为了帮助裁判员加快判罚的程序,而不是增加判罚运动员失败的方法。"4米标志线"的作用仅仅是让裁判员可以在运动员退至该线之后举起白旗,然后开始丈量成绩(就像运动员以其他正确方式离开助跑道后所做的)。唯一的要求是,没有可被判罚失败的其他情形,并在白旗举起前,器械已经落地。必要时,在运动员投掷后,不论何种原因没有越过"4米标志线",当器械落地后,应举旗示意。

32.18　在每次试掷后,应将器械运回投掷圈或助跑道附近的区域,不得掷回。

距离测量

32.19　在所有投掷项目中,记录测量距离的最小单位为0.01米,不足1厘米不计。

32.20　每次有效投掷后(或根据技术规则8.5条提出即时口头抗议之后)应立即从器械与地面第一次触及的最近标记处进行成绩测量:

　　32.20.1　从铅球、铁饼和链球球体取直线量至投掷圈内沿,测量线应通过投掷圈的圆心;或者

　　32.20.2　从标枪枪头取直线量至投掷弧内沿,测量线应通过投掷弧的圆心。

只要没有违规行为,无论成绩如何,每次试掷都必须测量。其原因包括其他试掷成绩可能成为决定排序或运动员是否进入后续赛次的关键。

除非应用了技术规则8.5条,通常情况下没有任何犯规情形的试投(掷)均应测量成绩。只有在特殊情况下,相关裁判员应审慎地适用判罚权采用任何备选的实际操作。

Unless video measuring is being used, for every valid trial a marker (usually metal) should be placed in a vertical position at the place of the imprint left by the implement in the landing area nearest to the circle/arc. The marker is passed through the loop at the end of the graduated steel tape so that the "zero" is on the mark. The tape should be pulled out horizontally taking care not to place it on any rise in the ground.

33. Shot Put

Competition

33.1　The shot shall be put from the shoulder with one hand only. At the time an athlete takes a stance in the circle to commence a put, the shot shall touch or be in close proximity to the neck or the chin and the hand shall not be dropped below this position during the action of putting. The shot shall not be taken behind the line of the shoulders.

Note: Cartwheeling techniques are not permitted.

Stop Board

33.2　The stop board shall be white and made of wood or other suitable material in the shape of an arc so that the inner surface aligns with the inner edge of the rim of the circle and is perpendicular to the surface of the circle. It shall be placed so that its centre coincides with the centre line of the landing sector(see Figure TR33), and shall be firmly fixed to the ground or to the concrete surrounding the circle.

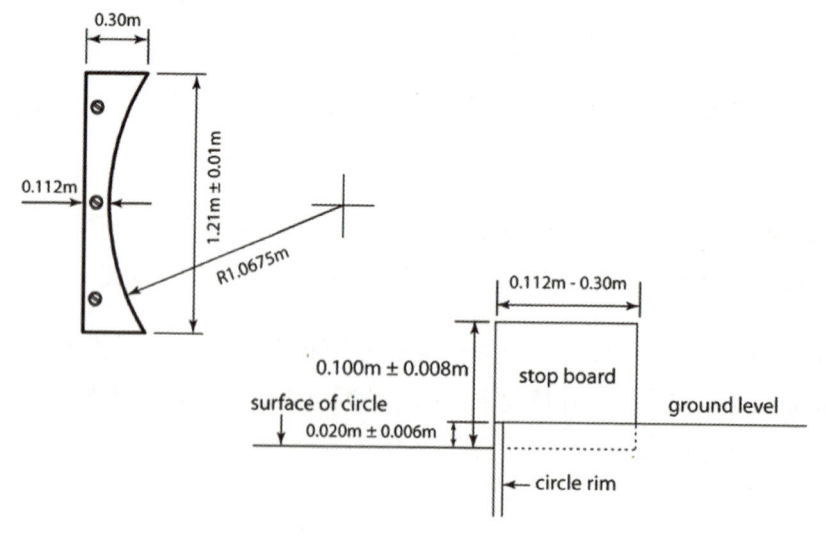

Figure TR33 – Shot Put stop board (top and side view)

除非使用影像测距,每次有效试投(掷)后,在落地区内器械留下的触地点上,距投掷圈/投掷弧线的最近处,应垂直插上一个(通常为金属的)标志物,使这个标志物穿过刻度钢卷尺末端的环,"0"点在标志物上。水平拉紧金属卷尺,注意避免把它放在地面上的任何凸起处。

33. 铅球

比赛

33.1 铅球只能用单手从肩部推出。当运动员在投掷圈内开始试掷时,铅球要抵住或靠近颈部或者下颌,在推球过程中持球手不得降到此部位以下。不得将铅球置于肩轴线后方。

注:不允许使用侧手翻式投掷技术。

抵趾板

33.2 抵趾板用木料或其他适宜材料制成,漆成白色,其形状为弧形,以使其内侧面与投掷圈内沿重合,并与投掷圈地平面垂直。抵趾板的中心应与落地区的中心线重合(技术规则33条图),并且牢固固定于地面或投掷圈外的水泥地面。

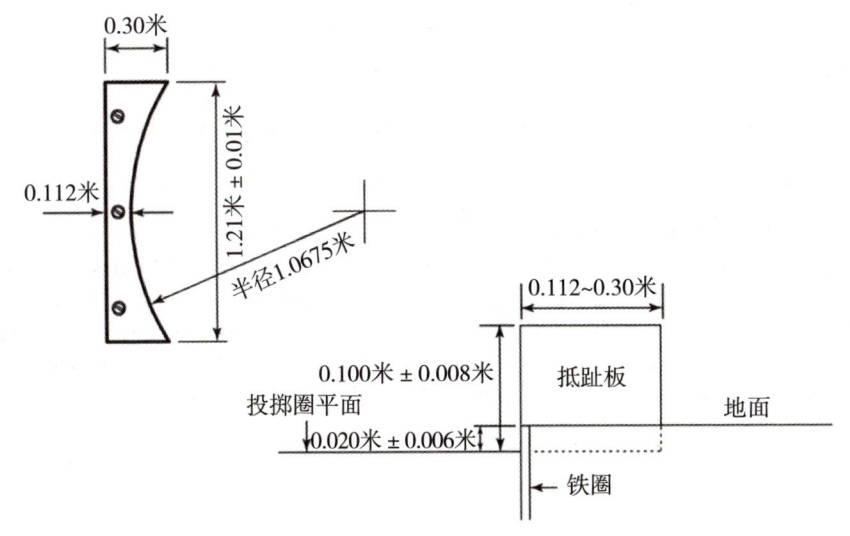

技术规则33条图　铅球抵趾板(俯视图和侧视图)

Note: Stop boards to the 1983/84 specifications remain acceptable.

33.3　　The stop board shall measure 0.112m to 0.30m wide, with a chord of 1.21m ± 0.01m for an arc of the same radius as the circle and 0.10m ± 0.008m high in relation to the level of the inside of the circle adjacent to the stop board.

Shot

33.4　　The shot shall be of solid iron, brass or any metal not softer than brass, or a shell of such metal filled with lead or other solid material. It shall be spherical in shape and its surface finish shall be smooth. If a filling is used, this shall be inserted in such manner that it is immovable and complies with the requirement for the centre of gravity as defined in Rule 36.5 of the Technical Rules.

Information for manufacturers: to be smooth, the surface average height must be less than or equal to 1.6μm, i.e., a roughness number N7 or less.

33.5　　The shot shall conform to the following specifications:

Minimum weight and diameter limits for admission to competition and acceptance of a Record					
Diameter	3.000kg	4.000kg	5.000kg	6.000kg	7.260kg
Minimum	85mm	95mm	100mm	105mm	110mm
Maximum	110mm	110mm	120mm	125mm	130mm

Team of Officials

For a Shot Put event, it is recommended to allocate the available officials as follows:

a. The Chief Judge will watch over the whole of the event.

b. Two Judges checking whether the put has been made correctly and measuring the trial. One must be provided with two flags - white to indicate if the trial is valid and red if it is a failure. When the put has been measured, it is advised that the Judge stands in the circle holding the red flag, while the implement is returned and the landing area is cleared. A cone may be placed in the circle instead (In some competitions this position is assumed by the Chief Judge of the event).

注：1983—1984年规定的抵趾板标准仍可使用。

33.3　抵趾板宽度为0.112~0.30米，弦长1.21米±0.01米，弧线的半径与投掷圈的半径相同。抵趾板高出投掷圈内相邻地面0.10米±0.008米。

铅球

33.4　铅球应用实心铁、铜或其他硬度不低于铜的固体金属制成，或由此类金属制成外壳，中心灌以铅或其他固体材料。铅球的外形必须为球形，表面结点处应光滑。如果使用填充物，要以不可移动的方式填入，并符合技术规则36.5条规定的重心要求。

制造商信息：为使表面光滑，球体表层平均高度应小于或等于1.6微米，即粗糙度为N7或更小。

33.5　铅球应符合下列规格：

允许比赛使用和承认纪录的最小重量和直径范围					
直径	3.000千克	4.000千克	5.000千克	6.000千克	7.260千克
最小	85毫米	95毫米	100毫米	105毫米	110毫米
最大	110毫米	110毫米	120毫米	125毫米	130毫米

裁判员团队

铅球比赛，建议裁判员的配置如下：

a. 主裁判，负责管控整个比赛。

b. 旗示和落点裁判员，判断试掷是否有效并对成绩进行测量。旗示裁判必须携带两面旗子——白旗标示试掷成功，红旗标示试掷失败。测量成绩后，在铅球回送和整理落地区时，建议裁判手握红旗站在投掷圈内。也可以将圆锥筒放在投掷圈内替代（在某些比赛中，该职责由该项目主裁判承担）。

Where EDM is not in use, the second Judge should pull through and hold the measuring tape in such a way that it passes through the centre of the circle.

c. Judge immediately after the throw placing a marker indicating the point from which the trial is to be measured.

d. Judge positioning the spike/prism at the point where the marker has been placed ensuring the tape is on the zero mark.

e. Judge in charge of retrieving the implements and returning them to the implement stand or placing them in the return chute.

f. Judge - a recorder scoring the results sheet and calling each athlete (and the one who is to follow).

g. Judge in charge of the scoreboard (trial-number-result).

h. Judge in charge of the clock indicating to the athletes that they have a certain time to take their trial.

i. Judge in charge of athletes.

j. Judge in charge of the implement stand.

Note (i): This is the traditional setting-up of the officials. In major competitions, where a data system and electronic scoreboards are available, specialised personnel are certainly required. To be clear in these cases, the progress and scoring of a Field Event is followed by both the recorder and by the data system.

Note (ii): Officials and equipment must be placed in such a way as not to obstruct the athlete's way nor impede the view of the spectators.

如果不使用电子测距，另一名裁判应协助使用钢尺丈量，并保持尺子通过投掷圈的圆心。

c. 落点裁判员，在试掷后立即插放一个标志，指示从该点进行测量。

d. 丈量裁判员，将铁钎/棱镜插在以上标志的位置，确保零点对正标志。

e. 器械回送裁判员，取回器械，将其回送到器械架或把器械放到斜槽送回。

f. 记录裁判员，记录成绩单，并通知每名运动员（和下一名运动员）试掷。

g. 成绩显示屏裁判员（试掷轮次—运动员号码—试掷成绩）。

h. 时限裁判员，负责向运动员显示某次试掷时限。

i. 管理裁判员，负责运动员的管理。

j. 器械管理裁判，负责投掷器械的放置与管理。

注（i）：这是裁判团队的常规设置。在大型比赛中，需要专业人员操作数据系统、电子显示牌。需要明确的是，记录裁判员和数据系统均要完成跟踪田赛项目的比赛进程和记录成绩。

注（ii）：裁判员的站位和设备的摆放既不能妨碍运动员比赛，也不能阻挡观众的视线。

34. Discus Throw

Discus

34.1 The body of the discus may be solid or hollow and shall be made of wood, or other suitable material, with a metal rim, the edge of which shall be circular. The cross section of the edge shall be rounded in a true circle having a radius of approximately 6mm. There may be circular plates set flush into the centre of the sides. The plates shall be tightly fixed and not able to be rotated. Alternatively, the discus may be made without metal plates, provided that the equivalent area is flat and the measurements and total weight of the implement correspond to the specifications. There shall be no loose parts.

Each side of the discus shall be identical and shall be made without indentations, projections or sharp edges. The sides shall taper in a straight line from any point on a circle of a radius of 25mm to 28.5mm from the centre of the discus to the beginning of the curve of the rim.

The profile of the discus shall be designed as follows. From the beginning of the curve of the rim the thickness of the discus increases regularly up to the value D. This maximum value is achieved at a distance of 25 mm to 28.5mm from the axis of the discus Y. From this point up to the axis Y, the thickness of the discus is constant. The upper and lower side of the discus must be identical. Also, the discus has to be symmetrical concerning rotation around the axis Y.

The discus, including the surface of the rim, shall have no roughness and the finish shall be smooth (see Rule 33.4 of the Technical Rules) and uniform throughout.

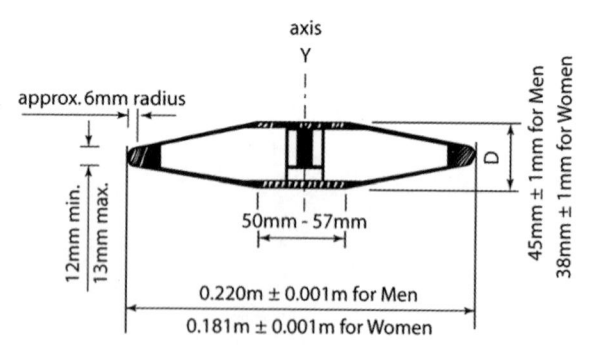

Figure TR34 – Discus

34. 铁饼

铁饼

34.1 铁饼的饼体可为实心或空心结构，应用木料或其他适宜的材料制成，周围镶以金属圈，金属圈边沿应呈圆形。外沿横断面应为标准圆形，半径约为6毫米。铁饼两面中央可镶有与饼体齐平的圆片，板材应牢固固定，不得转动。或者，铁饼也可以不安装金属圆片，只要等效面积是平的，且器械的尺寸和总重量符合规定。不得有松动的部分。（技术规则34条图）

铁饼的两面必须相同，制造时不得带有凹陷、凸起或尖锐边沿。以铁饼中心为圆心，半径为25～28.5毫米的圆上的任何点到金属圈曲线的开始处连线形成的面应呈逐步变窄的直线。

须按下列规格设计铁饼剖面。从铁圈弯曲开始，铁饼的厚度应均匀地增加至D值。铁饼中轴Y至25～28.5毫米处达到铁饼的最大厚度。从D点至Y轴的厚度应该相同。铁饼的两面必须一致，铁饼在绕Y轴旋转时必须对称。

铁饼及整个铁圈不得粗糙，结点处应光滑（见技术规则33.4条），铁饼各处应均匀一致。

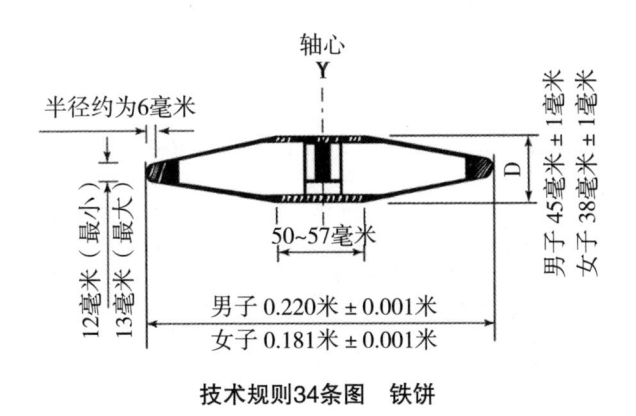

技术规则34条图　铁饼

34.2   The discus shall conform to the following specifications:

Minimum weight and diameter limits for admission to competition and acceptance of a Record:				
	1.000kg	1.500kg	1.750kg	2.000kg
Outside diameter of metal rim:				
Minimum	180mm	200mm	210mm	219mm
Maximum	182mm	202mm	212mm	221mm
Diameter of metal plate or flat centre area:				
Minimum	50mm	50mm	50mm	50mm
Maximum	57mm	57mm	57mm	57mm
Thickness of metal plate or flat centre area:				
Minimum	37mm	38mm	41mm	44mm
Maximum	39mm	40mm	43mm	46mm
Thickness of metal rim (6mm from edge) :				
Minimum	12mm	12mm	12mm	12mm
Maximum	13mm	13mm	13mm	13mm

Team of Officials

For a Discus Throw event, it is recommended to allocate the available officials as follows:

a. The Chief Judge will watch over the whole of the event.

b. Two Judges checking whether the throw has been made correctly and measuring the trial. One must be provided with two flags - white to indicate if the trial is valid and red if it is a failure. When the throw has been measured, it is advised that the Judge stands at the entrance to the cage holding the red flag, while the implement is returned and the landing area is cleared. A cone may be placed at this point instead. (In some competitions this position is assumed by the Chief Judge of the event)

34.2 铁饼应符合下列规格：

允许比赛使用和承认纪录的最小重量和直径范围：				
	1.000千克	1.500千克	1.750千克	2.000千克
金属圈外径：				
最小	180毫米	200毫米	210毫米	219毫米
最大	182毫米	202毫米	212毫米	221毫米
饼心的直径：				
最小	50毫米	50毫米	50毫米	50毫米
最大	57毫米	57毫米	57毫米	57毫米
饼心的厚度：				
最小	37毫米	38毫米	41毫米	44毫米
最大	39毫米	40毫米	43毫米	46毫米
金属圈的厚度（距边沿6毫米处）：				
最小	12毫米	12毫米	12毫米	12毫米
最大	13毫米	13毫米	13毫米	13毫米

裁判员团队

铁饼比赛，建议裁判员的配置如下：

a. 主裁判，负责管控整个比赛。

b. 旗示和落点裁判员，判断试掷是否有效并对成绩进行测量。旗示裁判员必须携带两面旗子——白旗标示试掷成功，红旗标示试掷失败。测量成绩后，在铁饼回送和整理落地区时，建议裁判手握红旗站在护笼入口处。也可以将圆锥筒放在这个点来替代。（在某些比赛中，该职责由该项目主裁判承担）

Where EDM is not in use the second Judge should pull through and hold the measuring tape in such a way that it passes through the centre of the circle.

c. Judge immediately after the throw placing a marker indicating the point from which the trial is to be measured. If the implement lands outside the sector either this Judge or the one with the spike/prism (whichever is closer to the line) should indicate this by holding their arm outstretched. No indication is required for a valid trial.

d. Judge positioning the spike/prism at the point where the marker has been placed ensuring the tape is on the zero mark.

e. one or more Judges or assistants in charge of retrieving the implements and returning them to the implement stand or placing them in the return device. Where a tape is used for measurement, one of these Judges or assistants should ensure that the tape measure is taut in order to ensure a correct measurement.

f. Judge - a recorder scoring the results sheet and calling each athlete (and the one who is to follow).

g. Judge in charge of the scoreboard (trial-number-result).

h. Judge in charge of the clock indicating to the athletes that they have a certain time to take their trial.

i. Judge in charge of athletes.

j. Judge in charge of the implement stand.

Note (i): This is the traditional setting-up of the officials. In major competitions, where a data system and electronic scoreboards are available, specialised personnel are certainly required. To be clear in these cases, the progress and scoring of a Field Event is followed by both the recorder and by the data system.

Note (ii): Officials and equipment must be placed in such a way as not to obstruct the athlete's way nor impede the view of the spectators.

Note (iii): A space must be reserved for a wind-sock to indicate the wind direction and strength.

如果不使用电子测距，另一名裁判员协助使用钢尺丈量，并保持尺子通过投掷圈的圆心。

c. 落点裁判员，在试掷后立即插放一个标志，指示从该点进行测量。如果铁饼落在落地区外，落点裁判员或负责插放铁钎/棱镜的裁判员（靠近铁饼落点一侧边线者）应举手指向界外。成功的投掷不必再做提示。

d. 丈量裁判员，将铁钎/棱镜插在以上标志的位置，确保零点对正标志。

e. 1名或多名器械回送裁判员或助手，取回器械，将其回送到器械架或通过回送设备送回。如果使用钢尺测量，落点裁判员或助手应确保卷尺拉紧，以保证准确测量。

f. 记录裁判员，记录成绩，并通知每名运动员（和下一名运动员）试掷。

g. 成绩显示屏裁判员（试掷轮次—运动员号码—试掷成绩）。

h. 时限裁判员，负责向运动员显示某次试跳时限。

i. 管理裁判员，负责运动员的管理。

j. 器械管理裁判，负责投掷器械的放置与管理。

注（ⅰ）：这是裁判团队的常规设置。在大型比赛中，需要专业人员操作数据系统、电子显示牌。需要明确的是，记录裁判员和数据系统均要完成跟踪田赛项目的比赛进程和记录成绩。

注（ⅱ）：裁判员的站位和设备的摆放既不能妨碍运动员比赛，也不能阻挡观众的视线。

注（ⅲ）：须在合理位置放置风标，用于显示风向和风力。

35. Discus Cage

35.1 All discus throws shall be made from an enclosure or cage to ensure the safety of spectators, officials and athletes. The cage specified in this Rule is intended for use when the event takes place in the Field of Play with other events taking place at the same time or when the event takes place outside the Field of Play with spectators present. Where this does not apply, and especially in training areas, a much simpler construction may be satisfactory. Advice is available, on request, from Members or from the World Athletics Office.

Note (i): The hammer cage specified in Rule 37 of the Technical Rules may also be used for Discus Throw, either by installing 2.135/2.50m concentric circles, or by using the extension of the gates of that cage with a separate discus circle installed in front of the hammer circle.

Note (ii): The hammer cage movable panels may be used when the cage is being used for discus throw to limit the danger zone.

35.2 The cage should be designed, manufactured and maintained so as to be capable of stopping a 2kg discus moving at a speed of up to 25 metres per second. The arrangement should be such that there is no danger of ricocheting or rebounding back towards the athlete or over the top of the cage. Provided that it satisfies all the requirements of this Rule, any form of cage design and construction can be used.

35.3 The cage should be U-shaped in plan as shown in Figure TR35. The width of the mouth should be 6m, positioned 7m in front of the centre of the throwing circle. The end points of the 6m wide mouth shall be the inner edge of the cage netting. The height of the netting panels or draped netting at their lowest point should be at least 4m and it should be at least 6m for the 3m nearest the front of the cage on each side.

Provision should be made in the design and construction of the cage to prevent a discus forcing its way through any joints in the cage or the netting or underneath the netting panels or draped netting.

Note (i): The arrangement of the rear panels/netting is not important provided the netting is a minimum of 3.00m away from the centre of the circle.

35. 铁饼护笼

35.1 所有的铁饼必须从挡网或护笼内掷出，以确保观众、裁判员和运动员的安全。本规则中规定的防护笼，适用于比赛场地内有其他项目同时比赛，或者在比赛场地外举行并且周围有观众存在的比赛。如果做不到这点，特别是在训练场地，结构更为简单的装置也可满足需要。如有需要，可向会员协会或世界田联办公室咨询，将得到合理的建议。

注（ⅰ）：技术规则37条中链球的防护笼也可用于铁饼投掷。既可安装一个直径分别为2.135米和2.50米的同心圆，也可将护笼的开口延长，在链球投掷圈前安装一个铁饼投掷圈。

注（ⅱ）：当链球的防护笼用于铁饼投掷，需使用护笼的可移动挡网来限制危险区域。

35.2 在设计、制造和维护铁饼护笼时，必须使其能够阻挡重量为2千克、以速度25米/秒飞行的铁饼。护笼的安放应使其消除铁饼弹出护笼、向运动员反弹或从护笼顶部飞出的危险。凡符合本条款所有要求的护笼，不论设计和结构如何均可使用。

35.3 护笼应按技术规则35条图所示设计成U字形。护笼开口的宽度为6米，位于投掷圈圆心前方7米处。护笼开口宽度6米需以挡网最前端内沿之间的距离为准。挡网或挂网最低点的高度应至少为4米，且两侧最前端3米内的挡网高度应为6米。

应在护笼的设计与施工中作出规定，防止铁饼从护笼或挡网连接处、挡网或挂网下方冲出。

注（ⅰ）：如果挂网距离投掷圈圆心的距离最小为3米，后面的挡网/挂网安放就不重要。

Note (ii): Innovative designs that provide the same or better degree of protection and do not increase the danger zone compared with conventional designs may be World Athletics certified.

Note (iii): The cage side, particularly alongside the track, may be lengthened, and/or provided with (a) movable panel(s), and/or increased in height so as to provide greater protection to athletes competing on the adjoining track during a discus competition.

The netting must be fixed in a way that the width of the mouth is the same at each height of the netting. This applies also for the panels when put into a position according to Rule 37.4 of the Technical Rules Note (ii).

35.4　The netting for the cage can be made from suitable natural or synthetic fibre cord or, alternatively, from mild or high tensile steel wire. The distance of adjacent mesh cord centres shall be a maximum of 45mm for cord netting and 50mm for steel wire netting.

Note: Further specifications for the netting and safety inspection procedures are set out in the World Athletics Track and Field Facilities Manual.

35.5　The maximum danger sector for discus throws from this cage is approximately 69°, when used by both right and left handed throwers in the same competition (calculated by assuming that the discus is released from a circumscribed circle of 1.5m radius). The position and alignment of the cage in the Field of Play is, therefore, critical for its safe use.

Note (i): The method used to determine the danger zone is illustrated in Figure TR35.

Note (ii): At each competition site, a danger zone plan for display at the venue should be prepared that plots the danger zone for the location of each throwing cage considering its configuration and orientation.

注（ⅱ）：如能提供同样或更佳角度的保护而不增大危险区，与常规设计相比具有革新式样的设计也可能得到世界田联的认证。

注（ⅲ）：为了更好地保护在铁饼比赛时临近跑道上比赛的运动员，特别是靠近跑道一边的护笼侧面可加长，和（或）配备一块（或多块）移动的挡板，和（或）增加高度。

挡网应固定牢，并确保在网的任何高度开口宽度都是相同的。这也适用于按技术规则37.4条注（ⅱ）设置挡网。

35.4　护笼挡网可采用适宜的天然材料或合成纤维，也可使用低碳钢丝或高抗张力钢丝。相邻的绳网最大中心距离为45毫米，相邻的钢丝网最大中心距离为50毫米。

注：对于护网的规格和安全检查程序在《世界田联场地设施手册》中有详细规定。

35.5　在同一场比赛中，运动员用左手或右手从护笼中掷出铁饼的最大危险扇形区大约为69°（通过假设铁饼是从半径为1.5米的外接圆中掷出计算得出），因此，护笼在比赛场地中的位置和方向对于安全使用极为重要。（技术规则35条图）

注（ⅰ）：对危险区域的确定方法在技术规则35条图中进行了展示。

注（ⅱ）：每个比赛场地，都应准备一份用于展示场馆危险区的平面图，根据每个投掷护笼的配置和方向，绘制每个投掷护笼位置的危险区域。

田径竞赛与技术规则（2025）

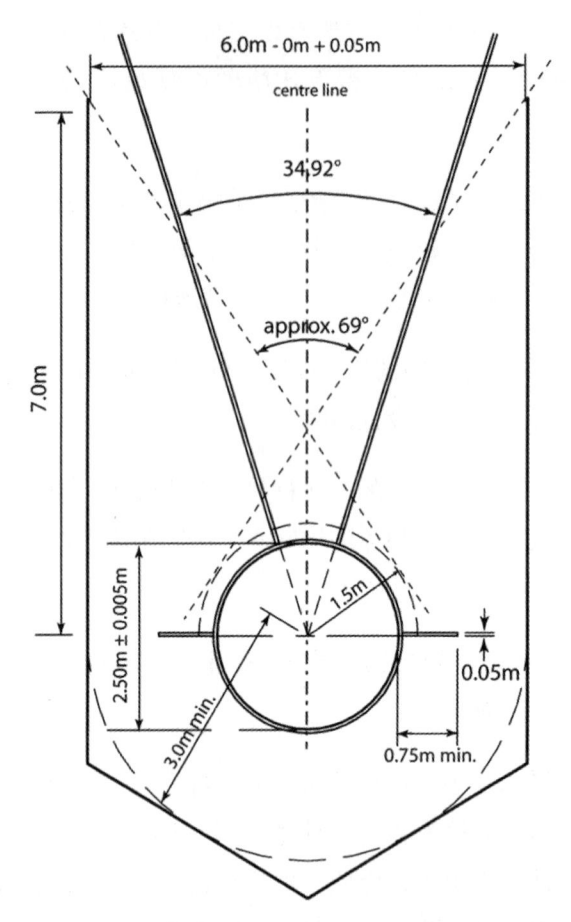

Figure TR35 – Cage for Discus Throw only (with cage dimensions to netting)

36. Hammer Throw

Competition

36.1 An athlete, in their starting position prior to the preliminary swings or turns, is allowed to put the head of the hammer on the ground inside or outside the circle.

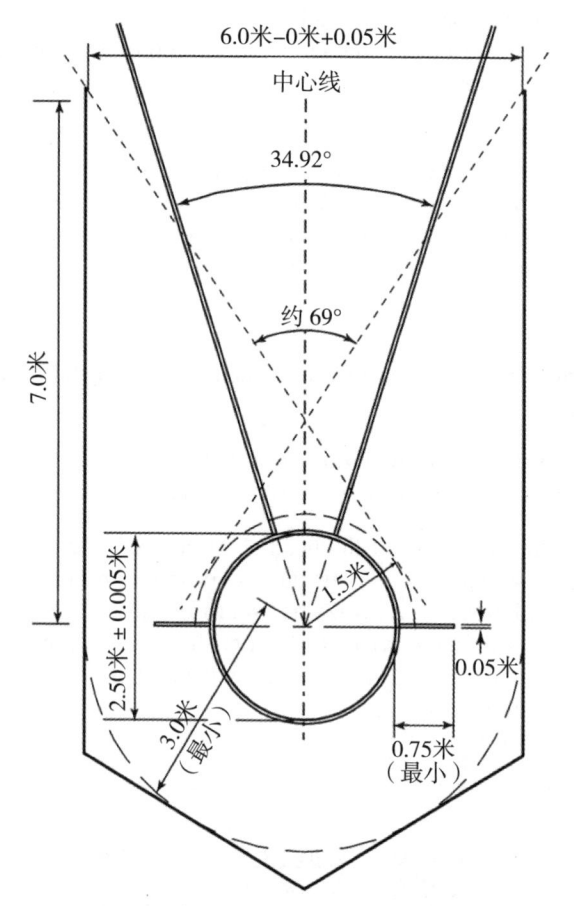

技术规则35条图　铁饼专用护笼（包含护笼尺寸和到挡网距离）

36. 链球

比赛

36.1　运动员准备进行预摆或处于旋转前的开始姿势中，允许将链球球体放在投掷圈内或圈外的地面。

36.2　It shall not be considered a failure if the head of the hammer touches the ground inside or outside the circle, or the top of the rim. The athlete may stop and begin the throw again, provided no other Rule has been breached.

36.3　If the hammer breaks during a throw or while in the air, it shall not count as a failure, provided the trial was otherwise made in accordance with this Rule. Nor shall it count as a failure if an athlete thereby loses their balance and as a result contravenes any part of this Rule. In both cases the athlete shall be awarded a replacement trial.

Hammer

36.4　The hammer shall consist of three main parts: a metal head, a wire and a handle.

36.5　The head shall be of solid iron, brass or other metal not softer than brass or a shell of such metal filled with lead or other solid material.

The centre of gravity of the head shall be not more than 6mm from the centre of the sphere, i.e. - it must be possible to balance the head, less handle and wire, on a horizontal sharp-edged circular orifice 12mm in diameter [see Figure (a) TR36]. If a filling is used, this shall be inserted in such manner that it is immovable and complies with the requirement for the centre of gravity.

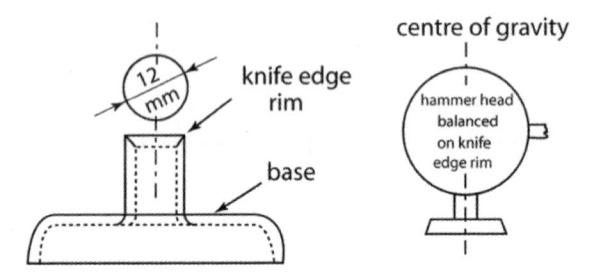

Figure (a) TR36 – Suggested apparatus for testing centre of gravity of hammer head

36.6　The wire shall be a single unbroken and straight length of spring steel wire not less than 3mm in diameter and shall be such that it cannot stretch appreciably while the hammer is being thrown.

36.2 链球球体触及投掷圈内或投掷圈外的地面，或者投掷圈上沿，不应判为试掷失败。如果运动员未违反其他规则，可停止并重新开始投掷动作。

36.3 如链球在试掷时或在空中断脱，只要试掷符合规则，不应判为一次试掷失败。如果运动员因此失去平衡而违反本规则的任何规定，也不应判作一次试掷失败。以上两种情况，应允许运动员重新进行一次试掷。

链球

36.4 链球由3个主要部分组成，即一个金属球体、一条链子和一个把手。

36.5 链球球体应用实心铁、铜或硬度不低于铜的其他金属制成，或用此类金属制成外壳，中心灌铅或其他固体材料。不得有松动的部分。

球体重心至球中心的距离不超过6毫米，即将去掉把手和链子的球体放在一个水平方向、直径为12毫米的圆形口刃上，球体能够保持平衡［技术规则36条图（a）］。如果使用填充物，应使其不能移动，并符合对重心的要求。

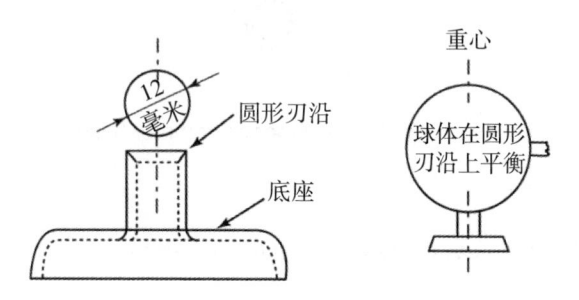

技术规则36条图（a） 建议使用的链球球体重心测量器

36.6 链子要用一根不易折断且直的有弹性的长钢丝制成。钢丝直径不小于3毫米，投掷时链子应无明显延长。

The wire may be looped at one or both ends as a means of attachment. The wire shall be connected to the head by means of a swivel, which may be either plain or ball bearing.

Note: A small section of clear vinyl tubing 50mm long with an internal diameter of 5mm may be placed over the twisted ends of the hammer wire.

36.7 The handle shall be rigid and without hinging joints of any kind. The total deformation of the handle under a tension load of 3.8kN shall not exceed 3mm. It shall be attached to the wire in such a manner that it cannot be turned within the loop of the wire to increase the overall length of the hammer. The handle shall be connected to the wire by means of a loop. A swivel may not be used.

The handle shall have a symmetric design and may have a curved or straight grip and/or brace. The minimum handle breaking strength shall be 8kN.

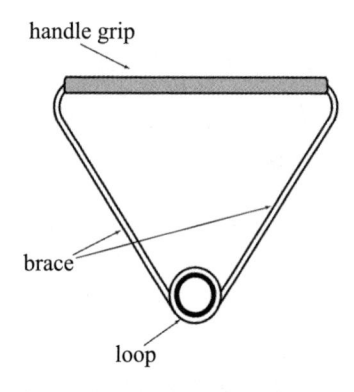

Figure (b) TR36– Generic hammer handle

Note: Other designs complying with the specifications are acceptable.

钢丝的一端或两端可弯成环状以便连接。链子应借助转动轴承与球体连接，转动轴承可为滑动轴承或滚球轴承。

注：可将一小段50毫米长、内径为5毫米的透明乙烯基管放置在钢丝扭曲部分的顶端。

36.7 把手必须质地坚硬，没有任何种类的铰链连接。当受到3.8千牛顿（kN）拉伸负荷时，把手的变形程度不超过3毫米。把手与链子的连接必须做到把手在链环中转动时，链球的总长度不得增加。把手与链子的连接应为环状连接，不得使用转动轴承。

把手应为对称设计，握把可为弧形或直柄和（或）环型。把手能承受的最小抗拉强度应为8千牛顿（kN）。［技术规则36条图（b）］

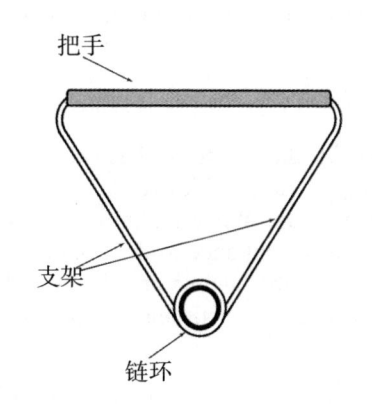

技术规则36条图（b） 一般链球把手

注：其他符合规则的设计也可使用。

36.8　The hammer shall conform to the following specifications:

Minimum weight and diameter limits for admission to competition and acceptance of a Record:					
	3.000kg	4.000kg	5.000kg	6.000kg	7.260kg
Length of hammer measured from inside of handle:					
Maximum	1195mm	1195mm	1200mm	1215mm	1215mm
Diameter of head:					
Minimum	85mm	95mm	100mm	105mm	110mm
Maximum	100mm	110mm	120mm	125mm	130mm

Note: The weight of the implement includes the totality of the hammer head, wire and handle.

Team of Officials

For a Hammer Throw event, it is recommended to allocate the available officials as follows:

a. The Chief Judge will watch over the whole of the event.

b. Two Judges checking whether the throw has been made correctly and measuring the trial. One must be provided with two flags - white to indicate if the trial is valid and red if it is a failure. When the throw has been measured, it is advised that the Judge stands at the entrance to the cage holding the red flag, while the implement is returned and the landing area is cleared. A cone may be placed at this point instead (In some competitions this position is assumed by the Chief Judge of the event).

Where EDM is not in use, the second Judge should pull through and hold the measuring tape in such a way that it passes through the centre of the circle.

c. Judge immediately after the throw placing a marker indicating the point from which the trial is to be measured. If the implement lands outside the sector either this Judge or the one with the spike/prism (whichever is closer to the line) should indicate this by holding their arm outstretched. No indication is required for a valid trial.

36.8　链球应符合下列规范：

允许比赛和承认纪录的最小重量和直径范围：					
	3.000千克	4.000千克	5.000千克	6.000千克	7.260千克
从把手内沿起算链球的全长：					
最大	1195毫米	1195毫米	1200毫米	1215毫米	1215毫米
球体的直径：					
最小	85毫米	95毫米	100毫米	105毫米	110毫米
最大	100毫米	110毫米	120毫米	125毫米	130毫米

注：器械的重量为链球球体、链子和把手的总重量。

裁判员团队

链球比赛，建议裁判员的配置如下：

a. 主裁判，负责管控整个比赛。

b. 旗示和落点裁判员，判断试掷是否有效并对成绩进行测量。旗示裁判员必须携带两面旗子——白旗标示试掷成功，红旗标示试掷失败。测量成绩后，在铁饼回送和整理落地区时，建议裁判手握红旗站在护笼入口处。也可以将圆锥筒放在这个点来替代（在某些比赛中，该职责由该项目主裁判承担）。

如果不使用电子测距，另一名裁判应协助使用钢尺丈量，并保持尺子通过投掷圈的圆心。

c. 落点裁判员，在试掷后立即插放一个标志，指示从该点进行测量。如果链球落在落地区外，落点裁判员或负责插放铁钎/棱镜的裁判（靠近链球落点一侧边线者）应举手指向界外。成功的投掷不必再做提示。

d. Judge positioning the spike/prism at the point where the marker has been placed ensuring the tape is on the zero mark.

e. one or more Judges or assistants in charge of retrieving the implements and returning them to the implement stand or placing them in the return device. Where a tape is used for measurement, one of these Judges or assistants should ensure that the tape measure is taut in order to ensure a correct measurement.

f. Judge - a recorder scoring the results sheet and calling each athlete (and the one who is to follow).

g. Judge in charge of the scoreboard (trial-number-result).

h. Judge in charge of the clock indicating to the athletes that they have a certain time to take their trial.

i. Judge in charge of athletes.

j. Judge in charge of the implement stand.

Note (i): This is the traditional setting-up of the officials. In major competitions, where a data system and electronic scoreboards are available, specialised personnel are certainly required. To be clear in these cases, the progress and scoring of a Field Event is followed by both the recorder and by the data system.

Note (ii): Officials and equipment must be placed in such a way as not to obstruct the athlete's way nor impede the view of the spectators.

37. Hammer Cage

37.1 All hammer throws shall be made from an enclosure or cage to ensure the safety of spectators, officials and athletes. The cage specified in this Rule is intended for use when the event takes place in the Field of Play with other events taking place at the same time or when the event takes place outside the Field of Play with spectators present. Where this does not apply, and especially in training areas, a much simpler construction may be satisfactory. Advice is available on request from Members or from the World Athletics Office.

d. 丈量裁判员，将铁钎/棱镜插在以上标志的位置，确保零点对正标志。

e. 1名或多名器械回送裁判员或助手，取回器械，将其回送到器械架或通过回送设备送回。如果使用钢尺测量，落点裁判员或助手应确保卷尺拉紧，以保证准确测量。

f. 记录裁判员，记录成绩单，并通知每名运动员（和下一名运动员）试掷。

g. 成绩显示屏裁判员（试掷轮次—运动员号码—试掷成绩）。

h. 时限裁判员，负责向运动员显示某次试跳时限。

i. 管理裁判员，负责运动员的管理。

j. 器械管理裁判，负责投掷器械的放置与管理。

注（ⅰ）：这是裁判团队的常规设置。在大型比赛中，需要专业人员操作数据系统、电子显示牌。需要明确的是，记录裁判员和数据系统均要完成跟踪田赛项目的比赛进程和记录成绩。

注（ⅱ）：裁判员的站位和设备的摆放既不能妨碍运动员比赛，也不能阻挡观众的视线。

37. 链球护笼

37.1 必须从挡网或护笼内将链球掷出，以确保观众、裁判员和运动员的安全。本规则中规定的防护笼，适用于比赛场地内有其他项目同时比赛，或者在比赛场地外举行并且周围有观众的比赛。如果做不到这点，特别是在训练场地，结构更为简单的装置也可满足需要。如有需要，可向会员协会或世界田联办公室咨询，将得到合理的建议。

37.2　The cage should be designed, manufactured and maintained so as to be capable of stopping a 7.260kg hammer head moving at a speed of up to 32 metres per second. The arrangement should be such that there is no danger of ricocheting or rebounding back towards the athlete or over the top of the cage. Provided that it satisfies all the requirements of this Rule, any form of cage design and construction can be used.

37.3　The cage should be U-shaped in plan as shown in Figure (a) TR37. The width of the mouth should be 6m, positioned 7m in front of the centre of the throwing circle. The end points of the 6m wide mouth shall be the inner edge of the pivoted netting. The height of the netting panels or draped netting at their lowest point shall be at least 7m for the panels/netting at the rear of the cage and at least 10m for the last 2.80m panels to the gate netting pivot points.

Provisions should be made in the design and construction of the cage to prevent a hammer forcing its way through any joints in the cage or the netting or underneath the netting panels or draped netting.

Note (i): The arrangement of the rear panels/netting is not important provided the netting is a minimum of 3.50m away from the centre of the circle.

Note (ii): Any number of posts may be used to support the netting in the position shown in Figures TR37.

37.4　Two movable netting panels 2m wide shall be provided at the front of the cage, only one of which will be operative at a time. The minimum height of the panels shall be 10m.

Note (i): The left hand panel is used for throwers turning anti clockwise, and the right hand panel for throwers turning clockwise. In view of the possible need to change over from one panel to the other during the competition, when both left and right-handed throwers are present, it is essential that this changeover should require little labour and be carried out in the minimum of time.

Note (ii): The end position of both panels is shown in the plan even though only one panel will be closed at any one time during competition.

Note (iii): When in operation, the movable panel shall be exactly in the position shown. Provision shall therefore, be made in the design of the movable panels to lock them in the operative position. It is recommended to mark (either temporarily or permanently) the operative positions of the panels on the ground.

37.2　在设计、制造、维护链球护笼时，应使其能够阻挡重量为7.260千克、以32米/秒的最大速度飞行的链球。护笼的安装应使其消除链球弹出护笼、向运动员反弹或从护笼顶部飞出的危险。凡符合本规则的要求，各种设计和结构的护笼均可使用。

37.3　护笼应按技术规则37条图（a）所示设计成U字形。护笼开口宽度应为6米，位于投掷圈圆心前方7米处。6米宽的开口的终点以活动挡网内沿为准。护笼后部挡网或挂网的最低点高度至少应为7米。至开口处的转轴前2.8米的挡网的高度至少应为10米。

应在护笼的设计与施工中作出规定，防止链球从护笼或挡网连接处、挡网或挂网下方冲出。

注（i）：投掷圈后方如何安装挡网及挂网并不重要，但挂网离投掷圈圆心距离至少要有3.50米。

注（ii）：可使用任意数量的支柱支撑技术规则37条图所示位置的网。

37.4　护笼前端应放置两块活动挡网，每块宽2米，高至少应为10米，每次只能使用其中一块。

注（i）：左侧活动挡网适用于逆时针方向旋转的运动员（右手投掷者），右侧活动挡网适用于顺时针方向旋转的运动员（左手投掷者）。左手和右手投掷者同场比赛时需要交替变动两侧挡网，因此，以最短的时间和最少的人力进行交替变动极为重要。

注（ii）：设计中显示了比赛期间任何时候只有一块活动挡网关闭时的两块活动挡网的最终位置。

注（iii）：操作时，活动挡网必须严格处于图例所示的位置。因此，设计活动挡网时必须带有将活动挡网固定在转动位置上的装置。建议在地面上设立一个操作活动挡网位置的标记（临时的或永久的）。

Note (iv): *The construction of these panels and their operation depends on the overall design of the cage and can be sliding, hinging on a vertical or horizontal axis or dismounting. The only firm requirements are that the panel in operation shall be fully able to stop any hammer striking it and there shall be no danger of a hammer being able to force its way between the fixed and movable panels.*

Note (v): *Innovative designs that provide the same or better degree of protection and do not increase the danger zone compared with conventional designs may be World Athletics certified.*

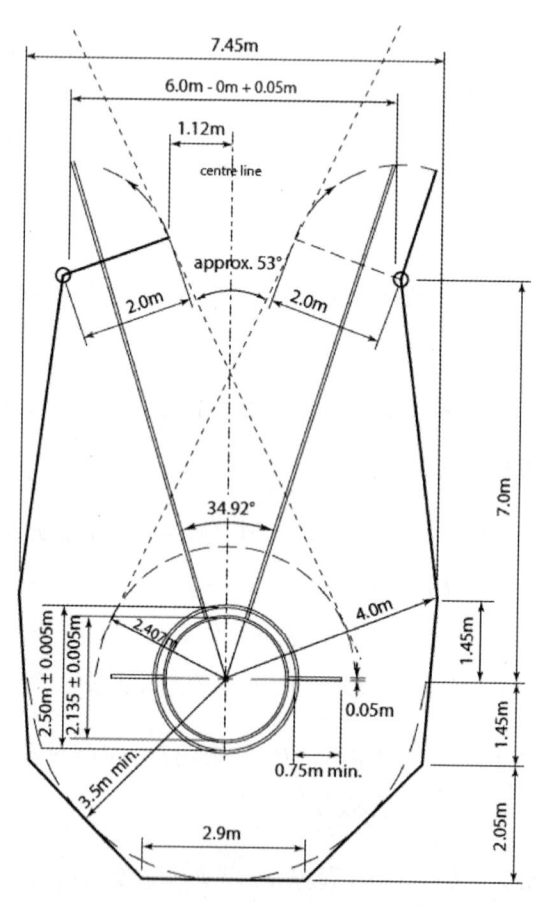

Figure (a) TR37 – Cage for Hammer and Discus Throw with concentric circles (Hammer Throw configuration for right-handed thrower with cage dimensions to netting)

注（iv）：活动挡网的结构和操作方式取决于护笼的整体设计，可为滑动式，或与水平轴或垂直轴铰接，或可以拆卸。对活动挡网的唯一坚固性要求是挡网能够完全挡住链球的冲击，不得有链球从固定挡网和活动挡网之间冲出去的任何危险。

注（v）：与传统设计的护笼相比，新设计的护笼只要能提供相同或者更好的保护能力，而且不增加危险区域，也可能得到世界田联的认证。

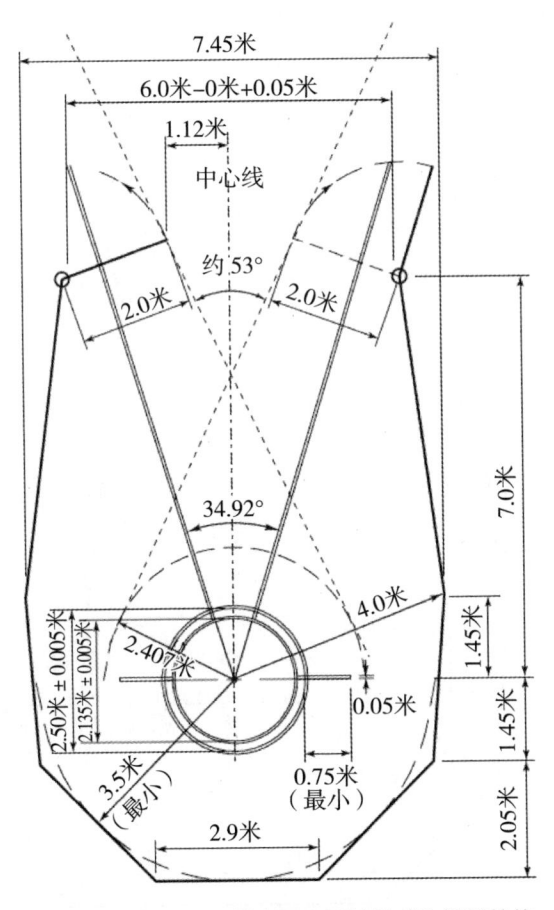

技术规则37条图（a） 带有同心圆的链球和铁饼护笼
（包含护笼尺寸和到挡网距离的右手投掷链球护笼布局）

37.5 The netting for the cage can be made from suitable natural or synthetic fibre cord or, alternatively, from mild or high tensile steel wire. The distance of adjacent mesh cord centres shall be a maximum of 45mm for cord netting and 50mm for steel wire netting.

Note: Further specifications for the netting and safety inspection procedures are set out in the World Athletics Track and Field Facilities Manual.

37.6 Where it is desired to use the same cage for Discus Throw, the installation can be adapted in two alternative ways. Most simply, a 2.135m/2.50m concentric circle may be fitted, but this involves using the same surface in the circle for Hammer Throw and Discus Throw. The hammer cage shall be used for Discus Throw by fixing the movable netting panels clear of the cage opening.

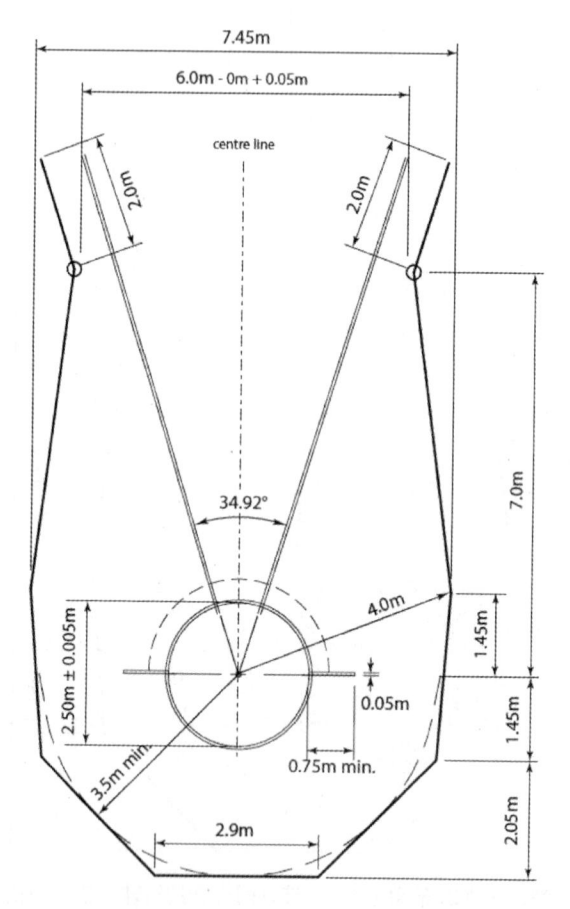

Figure (b) TR37 – Cage for Hammer and Discus Throw with concentric circles (Discus Throw configuration, with cage dimensions to netting)

37.5 制作护笼的挡网可采用合适的天然材料或合成纤维索,也可采用低碳钢丝或高抗张力钢丝。相邻的绳网最大中心距离为45毫米,相邻的钢丝网最大中心距离为50毫米。

注:有关挡网及挂网的规格及安全验查程序在《世界田联田径场地设施手册》中有详细规定。

37.6 如要使用同一护笼投掷铁饼,有两种安装方法可供选择。最简单的方法是安装一个直径分别为2.135米和2.50米的同心圆投掷圈,使链球投掷和铁饼投掷使用同一个圈内地面。在链球护笼内投掷铁饼时,应将活动挡网完全打开和固定。[技术规则37条图(b)]

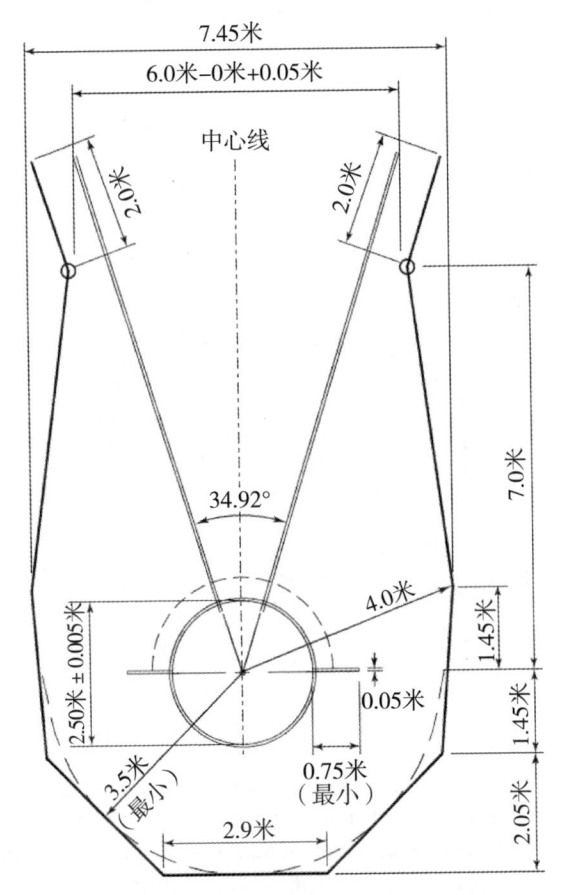

技术规则37条图(b) 带有同心圆的链球和铁饼护笼

(包含护笼尺寸和到挡网距离的铁饼护笼布局)

For separate circles for Hammer Throw and Discus Throw in the same cage, the two circles shall be placed one behind the other with the centres 2.37m apart on the centre line of the landing sector and with the discus circle at the front. In that case, the movable netting panels shall be used for Discus Throw in order to lengthen the cage sides.

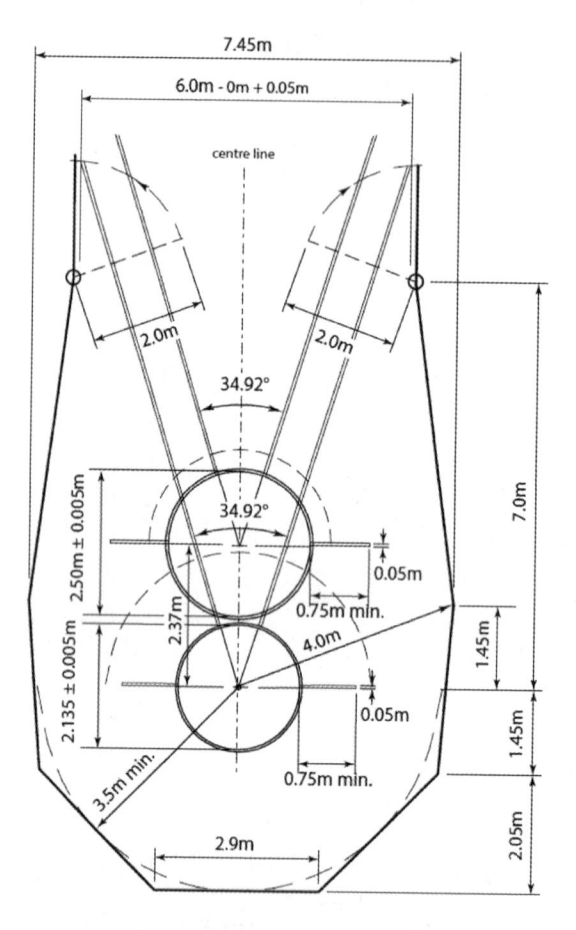

Figure (c) TR37 – Cage for Hammer and Discus Throw with separate circles (With cage dimensions to netting) [Only if the discus circle is in front of the hammer circle. For Hammer Throw, the gate should be as in Figure (a) TR37]

另一种方法是在同一个护笼内将掷链球圈和掷铁饼圈分开设置。两个投掷圈必须纵向排列在落地区中轴上。铁饼投掷圈圆心在链球投掷圈圆心前面2.37米处。在这种情况下，为了延长护笼两侧，活动挡网应用于铁饼项目。［技术规则37条图（c）］

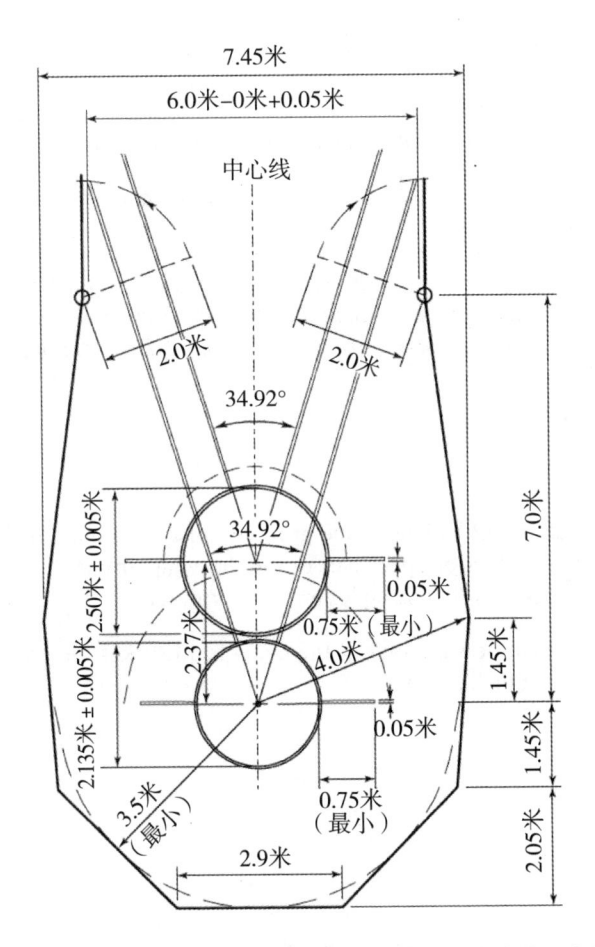

技术规则37条图（c）　带独立投掷圈的链球和铁饼护笼（包含护笼尺寸和到挡网距离）［仅当铁饼圈在链球圈前面时。对于链球比赛，开口应如技术规则37条图（a）所示］

Note: The arrangement of the rear panels/draped netting is not important provided the netting is a minimum of 3.50m away from the centre of concentric circles or the hammer circle in case of separate circles (or 3.00m for cages with separate circles built under the Rule in force before 2004 with the discus circle at the back) (see also Rule 37.4 of the Technical Rules).

37.7 The maximum danger sector for hammer throws from this cage is approximately 53°, when used by both right and left-handed throwers in the same competition (calculated by assuming that the hammer is released from a circumscribed circle of 2.407m radius). The position and alignment of the cage in the Field of Play is, therefore, critical for its safe use.

Note (i): The method used to determine the danger zone is illustrated in Figure (a) TR37.

Note (ii): At each competition site, a danger zone plan for display at the venue should be prepared that plots the danger zone for the location of each throwing cage considering its configuration and orientation.

38. Javelin Throw

Competition

38.1 The javelin shall be held at the grip with one hand only. It shall be thrown over the shoulder or upper part of the throwing arm and shall not be slung or hurled. Non-orthodox styles are not permitted.

38.2 A throw shall be valid only if the metal head strikes the ground before any other part of the javelin.

注：投掷圈后方如何安放挡网及挂网并不重要，但挂网至同心投掷圈圆心或分开设置的链球投掷圈圆心的距离至少有3.5米（或根据2004年前的规则，铁饼投掷圈在后，挂网至铁饼投掷圈圆心的距离至少3米）（另见技术规则37.4条）。

37.7 同场比赛中用左手和右手投掷的运动员，从这种护笼内投掷链球的最大危险区约为53°（通过假设链球从半径为2.407米的外接圆中掷出计算得出）。因此，护笼在比赛场地中的位置和方向对于安全使用极为重要。

注（ⅰ）：对危险区域的确定方法在技术规则37条图（a）中进行了展示。

注（ⅱ）：在每个比赛场地，都应准备一份用于展示场馆危险区的平面图，根据每个投掷护笼的配置和方向，绘制每个投掷护笼位置的危险区域。

38. 标枪

比赛

38.1 投掷标枪时应用单手握在把手处，从肩部或投掷臂上臂的上方掷出，不得抛甩。不得采用非传统姿势进行投掷。

38.2 只有标枪的金属枪头先于标枪的其他部位触地，试掷方为有效。

Previous references in the Rules to the "tip" of the javelin have been removed and are replaced by a generic reference to the head. This acknowledges that the shape of the head varies greatly, making it harder to separately define the tip. It means that Judges in determining whether the javelin has landed correctly in terms of Rule 32.16 of the Technical Rules and this Rule 38.2 and the reference point for measurement in terms of Rule 32.20.2 of the Technical Rules now have a bigger area with which to assess. But the principles remain as before and there must be some angle on landing, however small, for the throw to be valid. Flat or "tail-first" landings are still to be red flagged.

38.3 Until the javelin has been thrown, an athlete shall not at any time turn completely around, so that their back is towards the throwing arc.

Note: This Rule refers to the run-up and the act of throwing, not to an athlete walking back before starting their attempt or after having interrupted it.

38.4 If the javelin breaks during a throw or while in the air, it shall not count as a failure, provided the trial was otherwise made in accordance with this Rule. Nor shall it count as a failure if an athlete thereby loses their balance and as a result contravenes any part of this Rule. In both cases the athlete shall be awarded a replacement trial.

Javelin

38.5 The javelin shall consist of three main parts: a shaft, a head and a cord grip.

38.6 The shaft may be solid or hollow and shall be constructed of metal or other suitable material so as to constitute a fixed and integrated whole. The surface of the shaft shall have no dimples or pimples, grooves or ridges, holes or roughness, and the finish shall be smooth (see Rule 33.4 of the Technical Rules) and uniform throughout.

38.7 The shaft shall have fixed to it a metal head terminating in a sharp point. The head shall be constructed completely of metal. It may contain a reinforced tip of other metal alloy fixed to the front end of the head provided that the completed head is smooth (see Rule 33.4 of the Technical Rules) and uniform along the whole of its surface. The angle of the tip shall not exceed 40°.

Note: The metal head up to 3mm from the tip may be disregarded for the angle of the point, when the construction of the tip is made with safety measures implemented.

以前规则中对于"标枪头"的参考要求被删除了，目前对其只有一般性的参考要求。这表示对于形状差异较大的标枪头部，分别规定"标枪头"比较困难。这就要求裁判员根据技术规则32.16条、38.2条和关于测量要求的技术规则32.20.2条对标枪落地正确与否进行判罚评定。但是原则和以前一样，标枪落地必须具有一定的角度，哪怕是很小的角度，也可判为有效。标枪水平落地或尾部先落地仍然应该举起红旗。

38.3 运动员试掷时，在标枪出手以前的任何时间，身体不得完全转向背对投掷弧。

注：本规则指的是助跑和投掷动作中，而不是指运动员在投掷开始前或投掷中断后走回来的动作。

38.4 如果标枪在试掷时或在空中飞行时折断，只要该次试掷符合规则要求，不应判为试掷失败。如果运动员因此失去平衡而违反本规则的任何规定，也不应判作一次试掷失败。以上两种情况应允许运动员重新进行一次试掷。

标枪

38.5 标枪由3个主要部分组成，即枪身、枪头和缠绳把手。

38.6 枪身可为实心或空心，由金属或其他适宜的类似材料制成，以组成一个固定的整体。枪身表面不得有凹窝、凸起、沟槽、突脊、空洞、粗糙，枪尾必须自始至终平滑和均匀一致（见技术规则33.4条）。

38.7 枪头固定于枪身，末端尖形，应完全由金属制成。可在枪头前端焊接一个其他合金的加固枪尖，但整个枪头表面必须平滑和均匀一致（见技术规则33.4条）。枪尖张角不得大于40°。

注：出于安全考虑，在测量标枪尖端角度时，可以忽略距离尖端3毫米以内的金属头。

38.8　　The cord grip, which shall cover the centre of gravity, shall not exceed the average diameter of the shaft by more than 8mm. It may have a regular non-slip pattern surface but without thongs, notches or indentations of any kind. The grip shall be of uniform thickness.

38.9　　The cross-section shall be regularly circular throughout [see Note (ⅰ)]. The maximum diameter of the shaft shall be immediately in front of the grip. The central portion of the shaft, including the part under the grip, may be cylindrical or slightly tapered towards the rear but in no case may the reduction in diameter, from immediately in front of the grip to immediately behind, exceed 0.25mm. From the grip, the javelin shall taper regularly to the tip at the front and the tail at the rear. The longitudinal profile from the grip to the front tip and to the tail shall be straight or slightly convex [see Note (ⅱ)], and there shall be no abrupt alteration in the overall diameter, except immediately behind the head and at the front and rear of the grip, throughout the length of the javelin. At the rear of the head, the reduction in the diameter may not exceed 2.5mm.

Note (ⅰ): Whilst the cross section throughout should be circular, a maximum difference between the largest and the smallest diameter at any cross section of 2% is permitted. The mean value of these two diameters, at any nominated cross section, shall meet the specifications of a circular javelin in the tables hereunder.

Note (ⅱ): The shape of the longitudinal profile may be quickly and easily checked using a metal straight edge at least 500mm long and two feeler gauges 0.20mm and 1.25mm thick. For slightly convex sections of the profile, the straight edge will rock while being in firm contact with a short section of the javelin. For straight sections of the profile, with the straight edge held firmly against it, it must be impossible to insert the 0.20mm gauge between the javelin and the straight edge anywhere over the length of contact. This shall not apply immediately behind the joint between the head and the shaft. At this point it must be impossible to insert the 1.25mm gauge.

38.8 绳索把手须包绕标枪重心，其平均直径不得超过枪身直径8毫米。把手表面应为规则的不光滑型，但不得有任何种类的绳头、结节或呈锯齿形。把手的厚度应均匀。

38.9 标枪所有部位横断面应为规则的圆形［见注（ⅰ）］。枪身最大直径应在紧靠把手前端的地方。枪身中央部位，包括把手下面的部分，应为圆柱形或向枪尾方向稍微变细。但把手前后临近部位，枪身直径减小不得超过0.25毫米。从把手处起，标枪应有规律地向两端逐渐变细。从把手至标枪前后两端点的纵剖面应为直线或略有凸起［见注（ⅱ）］，除了在枪头与枪身的结合部位和把手前后两端，枪身任何部位的直径均不得有突然改变。枪头后部直径的减小不得超过2.5毫米。

注（ⅰ）：标枪整体横断面应呈圆形，任何部位最大直径和最小直径允许的误差不超过2%。两个直径的平均值必须符合圆形标枪的规格，并要符合以下表格的要求。

注（ⅱ）：使用长至少为500毫米的金属直规和两把厚度分别为0.20毫米和1.25毫米的塞尺，可以迅速、简便地检查标枪纵剖面的形状。对于纵剖面有稍稍凸起的部分，将直规紧贴这一小段，直规可有轻微晃动。对于纵剖面的直线部分，直规紧贴这一部分时，直规与标枪贴紧的部分，不能塞进0.20毫米的塞尺。在紧靠枪头与枪身结合处的后面这一部位，上述方法不适用，此处塞不进1.25毫米的塞尺。

38.10   The javelin shall conform to the following specifications:

Minimum weight and diameter limits for admission to competition and acceptance of a Record (inclusive of the cord grip) :				
	500g	600g	700g	800g
Overall length (L0) :				
Minimum	2000mm	2200mm	2400mm(2400mm*)	2600mm
Maximum	2100mm	2300mm	2500mm(2500mm*)	2700mm
Distance from tip of metal head to centre of gravity (L1) :				
Minimum	780mm	800mm	850mm(850mm*)	900mm
Maximum	880mm	920mm	990mm(990mm*)	1060mm
Distance from tail to centre of gravity (L2) :				
Minimum	1120mm	1280mm	1410mm(1410mm*)	1540mm
Maximum	1320mm	1500mm	1640mm(1650mm*)	1800mm
Length of metal head (L3) :				
Minimum	220mm	250mm	250mm	250mm
Maximum	270mm	330mm	330mm	330mm
Width of cord grip (L4) :				
Minimum	135mm	140mm	150mm	150mm
Maximum	145mm	150mm	160mm	160mm
Diameter of shaft at thickest point (in front of grip - D0) :				
Minimum	20mm	20mm	23mm	25mm
Maximum	24mm	25mm	28mm	30mm

* Amended in August 2023 and in force from 1 April 2025.

38.10　标枪应符合以下规格：

允许比赛和承认纪录的最小重量和直径范围（包括绳索把手）：				
	500克	600克	700克	800克
标枪全长（L0）：				
最小	2000毫米	2200毫米	2400毫米（2400毫米*）	2600毫米
最大	2100毫米	2300毫米	2500毫米（2500毫米*）	2700毫米
枪尖至重心距离（L1）：				
最小	780毫米	800毫米	850毫米（850毫米*）	900毫米
最大	880毫米	920毫米	990毫米（990毫米*）	1060毫米
枪尾至重心距离（L2）：				
最小	1120毫米	1280毫米	1410毫米（1410毫米*）	1540毫米
最大	1320毫米	1500毫米	1640毫米（1640毫米*）	1800毫米
金属枪头长度（L3）：				
最小	220毫米	250毫米	250毫米	250毫米
最大	270毫米	330毫米	330毫米	330毫米
把手宽度（L4）：				
最小	135毫米	140毫米	150毫米	150毫米
最大	145毫米	150毫米	160毫米	160毫米
枪身最粗处直径（在把手前-D0）：				
最小	20毫米	20毫米	23毫米	25毫米
最大	24毫米	25毫米	28毫米	30毫米

*2023年8月修订，自2025年4月1日起生效。

38.11　The javelin shall have no mobile parts or other apparatus, which during the throw could change its centre of gravity or throwing characteristics.

38.12　The tapering of the javelin to the tip of the metal head shall be such that the angle of the point shall be not more than 40°. The diameter, at a point 0.15m from the tip, shall not exceed 80% of the maximum diameter of the shaft. At the midpoint between the centre of gravity and the tip of the metal head, the diameter shall not exceed 90% of the maximum diameter of the shaft.

38.13　The tapering of the shaft to the tail at the rear shall be such that the diameter, at the midpoint between the centre of gravity and the tail, shall not be less than 90% of the maximum diameter of the shaft. At a point 0.15m from the tail, the diameter shall be not less than 40% of the maximum diameter of the shaft. The diameter of the shaft at the end of the tail shall not be less than 3.5mm.

Team of Officials

For a Javelin Throw event, it is recommended to allocate the available officials as follows:

a. The Chief Judge will watch over the whole of the event.

b. Two Judges checking whether the throw has been made correctly and measuring the trial. One must be provided with two flags - white to indicate if the trial is valid and red if it is a failure. When the throw has been measured, it is advised that the Judge stands on the runway holding the red flag, while the implement is returned and the landing area is cleared. A cone may be placed on the runway instead (In some competitions this position is assumed by the Chief Judge of the event).

Where EDM is not in use, the second Judge should pull through and hold the measuring tape in such a way that it passes through the 8m point marked on the runway.

c. one or two Judges immediately after the throw placing a marker indicating the point from which the trial is to be measured. If the implement lands outside the sector either this Judge or the one with the spike/prism (whichever is closer to the line) should indicate this by holding their arm outstretched. An appropriate indication is also required if these Judges determine that the implement has not landed "head first". It is recommended that some form of signal other than flags is used for this purpose. No indication is required for a valid trial.

38.11   标枪不得有可移动部分，或投掷时可以改变其重心或投掷性能的装置。

38.12   标枪头张角不得大于40°。距枪尖0.15米处，枪头直径不得大于枪身最大直径的80%。在重心至枪尖的中点处，枪身直径不得大于枪身最大直径的90%。（技术规则38条图）

38.13   在标枪重心至枪尾末端的中点处，枪身直径不得小于枪身最大直径的90%。在距枪尾末端0.15米处，枪身直径不得小于枪身最大直径的40%。枪尾末端直径不小于3.5毫米。

裁判员团队

标枪比赛，建议裁判员的配置如下：

a. 主裁判，负责管控整个比赛。

b. 旗示和落点裁判员，判断试掷是否有效并对成绩进行测量。旗示裁判必须携带两面旗子——白旗标示试掷成功，红旗标示试掷失败。测量成绩后，在标枪回送和整理落地区时，建议裁判手握红旗站在助跑道上。也可以将圆锥筒放在这个点来替代（在某些比赛中，该职责由该项目主裁判承担）。

如果不使用电子测距，另一名裁判员协助使用钢尺丈量，并保持尺子通过助跑道的8米标志点。

c. 1~2名落点裁判员，在试掷后立即插放一个标志，指示从该点进行测量。如果标枪落在落地区外，落点裁判员或负责插放铁钎/棱镜的裁判员（靠近标枪落点一侧边线者）应举手指向界外。在标枪没有以"枪头领先"的方式着地时也应做特定的手势。建议使用其他形式而不是用旗示进行此类沟通，成功的投掷不必再做提示。

d. Judge positioning the spike / prism at the point where the marker has been placed ensuring the tape is on the zero mark.

e. one or more Judges or assistants in charge of retrieving the implements and returning them to the implement stand or placing them in the return device. Where a tape is used for measurement, one of these Judges or assistants should ensure that the tape measure is taut in order to ensure a correct measurement.

f. Judge - a recorder scoring the results sheet and calling each athlete (and the one who is to follow).

g. Judge in charge of the scoreboard (trial-number-result).

h. Judge in charge of the clock indicating to the athletes that they have a certain time to take their trial.

i. Judge in charge of athletes.

j. Judge in charge of the implement stand.

Note (i): This is the traditional setting-up of the officials. In major competitions, where a data system and electronic scoreboards are available, specialised personnel are certainly required. To be clear in these cases, the progress and scoring of a Field Event is followed by both the recorder and by the data system.

Note (ii): Officials and equipment must be placed in such a way as not to obstruct the athlete's way nor impede the view of the spectators.

Note (iii): A space must be reserved for a wind-sock to indicate the wind direction and strength.

d. 丈量裁判员，将铁钎/棱镜插在以上标志的位置，确保零点对正标志。

e. 1名或多名器械回送裁判员或助手，取回器械，将其回送到器械架或通过回送设备送回。如果使用钢尺测量，落点裁判员或助手应确保卷尺拉紧，以保证准确测量。

f. 记录裁判员，记录成绩单，并通知每名运动员（和下一名运动员）试跳。

g. 成绩显示屏裁判员（试掷轮次—运动员号码—试掷成绩）。

h. 时限裁判员，负责向运动员显示某次试跳时限。

i. 管理裁判员，负责运动员的管理。

j. 器械管理裁判，负责投掷器械的放置与管理。

注（ⅰ）：这是裁判团队的常规设置。在大型比赛中，需要专业人员操作数据系统、电子显示牌。需要明确的是，记录裁判员和数据系统均要完成跟踪田赛项目的比赛进程和记录成绩。

注（ⅱ）：裁判员的站位和设备的摆放既不能妨碍运动员比赛，也不能阻挡观众的视线。

注（ⅲ）：须在合理位置放置风标，用于显示风向和风力。

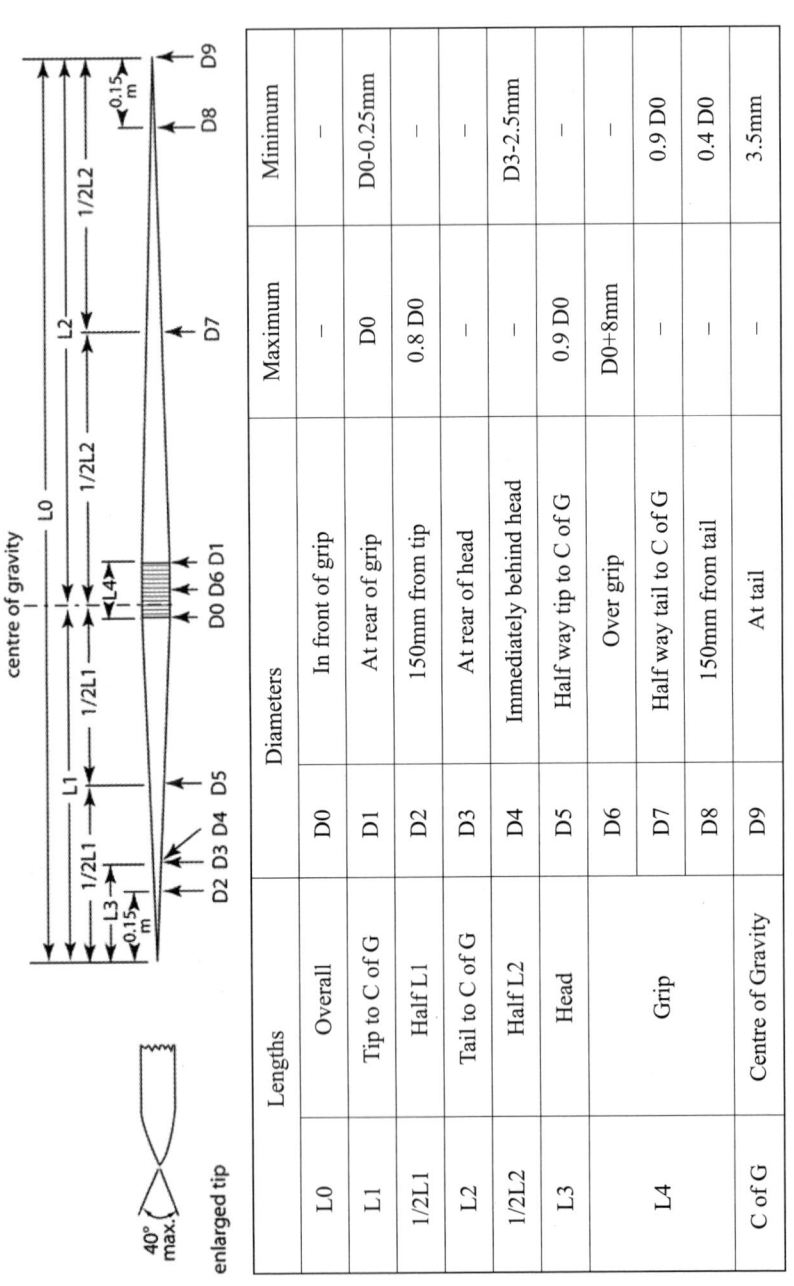

Lengths			Diameters		Maximum	Minimum
L0	Overall		D0	In front of grip	—	—
L1	Tip to C of G		D1	At rear of grip	D0	D0−0.25mm
1/2L1	Half L1		D2	150mm from tip	0.8 D0	—
L2	Tail to C of G		D3	At rear of head	—	—
1/2L2	Half L2		D4	Immediately behind head	—	D3−2.5mm
L3	Head		D5	Half way tip to C of G	0.9 D0	—
L4	Grip		D6	Over grip	D0+8mm	—
			D7	Half way tail to C of G	—	0.9 D0
			D8	150mm from tail	—	0.4 D0
C of G	Centre of Gravity		D9	At tail	—	3.5mm

Figure TR38 – International Javelin

Note: All measurements of diameters must be made with an uncertainty of not more than 0.1 mm.

长度		直径		最大	最小
L0	全长	D0	把手前端的枪身	—	—
L1	枪尖至重心	D1	把手后端的枪身	D0	D0−0.25毫米
1/2L1	L1的二分之一	D2	距枪尖150毫米处	0.8 D0	—
L2	枪尾至重心	D3	枪头后端	—	—
1/2L2	L2的二分之一	D4	紧接枪头后端处	—	D3−2.5毫米
L3	枪头	D5	枪尖至重心的中点	0.9 D0	—
L4	把手	D6	把手	D0+8毫米	—
		D7	枪尾至重心的中点	—	0.9 D0
		D8	距枪尾末端150毫米处	—	0.4 D0
C of G	重心	D9	枪尾末端	—	3.5毫米

技术规则38条图 用于国际比赛的标枪

注：所有参数的测量应该精确到0.1毫米。

208

PART IV COMBINED EVENTS COMPETITIONS

39. Combined Events Competitions

U18, U20 and Senior Men (Pentathlon and Decathlon)

39.1 The Pentathlon consists of five events which shall be held on one day in the following order: Long Jump; Javelin Throw; 200m; Discus Throw; 1500m.

39.2 The Men's Decathlon consists of ten events which shall be held on two consecutive 24-hour periods in the following order:

First day: 100m; Long Jump; Shot Put; High Jump; 400m.

Second day: 110m Hurdles; Discus Throw; Pole Vault; Javelin Throw; 1500m.

U20 and Senior Women (Heptathlon and Decathlon)

39.3 The Heptathlon consists of seven events which shall be held on two consecutive 24-hour periods in the following order:

First day: 100m Hurdles; High Jump; Shot Put; 200m.

Second day: Long Jump; Javelin Throw; 800m.

39.4 The Women's Decathlon consists of ten events which shall be held on two consecutive 24-hour periods in the order of Rule 39.2 or in the following order:

First day: 100m; Discus Throw; Pole Vault; Javelin Throw; 400m.

Second day: 100m Hurdles; Long Jump; Shot Put; High Jump; 1500m.

第四部分 全能项目比赛

39. 全能项目比赛

少年男子U18、青年男子U20和成年男子（五项和十项全能）

39.1 五项全能包括5个单项，须在同一天按下列顺序进行：跳远、标枪、200米、铁饼、1500米。

39.2 男子十项全能包括10个单项，须在连续的两个24小时内按下列顺序举行：

第一天：100米、跳远、铅球、跳高、400米。

第二天：110米栏、铁饼、撑竿跳高、标枪、1500米。

青年女子U20和成年女子（七项和十项全能）

39.3 七项全能包括7个单项，须在连续的两个24小时内按下列顺序举行：

第一天：100米栏、跳高、铅球、200米。

第二天：跳远、标枪、800米。

39.4 女子十项全能包括10个单项，须在连续的两个24小时内按技术规则39.2条的顺序或者下列顺序举行：

第一天：100米、铁饼、撑竿跳高、标枪、400米。

第二天：100米栏、跳远、铅球、跳高、1500米。

U18 Women (Heptathlon only)

39.5 The U18 Women's Heptathlon consists of seven events, which shall be held on two consecutive 24-hour periods in the following order:

First day: 100m Hurdles; High Jump; Shot Put; 200m.

Second day: Long Jump; Javelin Throw; 800m.

General

39.6 At the discretion of the Combined Events Referee, there shall, whenever possible, be an interval of at least 30 minutes between the time one event ends and the next event begins, for any individual athlete. If possible, the time between the finish of the last event on the first day and the start of the first event on the second day should be at least 10 hours.

The minimum period of 30 minutes is to be calculated as being the actual time between the end of the last race or trial for any athlete in the previous event to the start of the first race or trial in the next event. It is therefore possible and not uncommon for athletes to go directly from the conclusion of one event to the warm-up for the next so that the 30 minutes is in effect taken up by the movement from one site to another and the warm-up. Changes in the number of days over which a Combined Events competition is conducted are not allowed except for special cases (e.g. exceptional weather conditions). Such decisions are matters for the Technical Delegates and/or Referees in the particular circumstances of each case. However if, for any reason, the competition is held for a longer period than according to Rules 39 or 53 of the Technical Rules then a record in Combined Events (total number of points) cannot be ratified.

39.7 In each separate event, except the last, of a Combined Events competition, the heats and groups shall be arranged by the Technical Delegate(s) or Combined Events Referee, as applicable, so that the athletes with similar performances in each individual event during a predetermined period, shall be placed in the same heat or group. Preferably five or more, and never less than three, athletes shall be placed in each heat or group. When this cannot be achieved because of the timetable of events, the heats or groups for the next event should be arranged as and when athletes become available from the previous event.

In the last event of a Combined Events competition, the heats should be arranged so that the last one contains the leading athletes after the penultimate event.

青年女子U18七项全能（仅有七项全能）

39.5　少年女子U18七项全能包括7个单项，须在连续的两个24小时内按下列顺序举行：

第一天：100米栏、跳高、铅球、200米。

第二天：跳远、标枪、800米。

总则

39.6　在可能的情况下，全能裁判长有权决定给予任何运动员在上一项比赛结束后至下一项比赛开始前至少30分钟的休息时间。如有可能，在第一天的最后一项比赛结束到第二天第一项比赛开始应至少给运动员10小时的休息时间。

最少30分钟时间的计算是从任何一名运动员的前一项目比赛或试跳（掷）结束至下一项目比赛或试跳（掷）开始的实际时间。运动员在结束一个项目比赛后，直接进入下一个项目的热身是可能的，也是常见的。因此，30分钟实际上包括从一个比赛区域到下一个比赛地点及热身的时间。全能比赛在进行过程中不得改变比赛天数，除非由于某些特殊情况而改变（如极端天气条件等）。由技术代表和（或）裁判长根据各种特殊情况作出这种决定。但是，如果由于任何原因，比赛时间比根据技术规则39条或53条更长，则全能项目的纪录（项目总分）不予批准。

39.7　除最后一项外，全能比赛每个单项的分组要由技术代表或全能裁判长安排，如有可能，须将在预先规定的时间内每个单项成绩相近的运动员们分在同组。各组运动员人数最好为5人或5人以上，但不得少于3人。如由于竞赛日程不能实现以上要求，则可在前一项比赛结束后，对已满足比赛时间要求的运动员进行下一项分组。

全能比赛最后一项的分组，应将倒数第二项比赛后积分领先的运动员分在最后一组。

The Technical Delegate(s) or the Combined Events Referee shall have the authority to rearrange any group if, in their opinion, it is desirable.

39.8 The Rules for each event constituting the competition will apply with the following exceptions:

  39.8.1 in the Long Jump and each of the throwing events, each athlete shall be allowed three trials only.

  39.8.2 in case a Fully Automatic Timing and Photo Finish System is not available, each athlete's time shall be taken by three Timekeepers independently.

  39.8.3 in the Track Events, only one false start per race shall be allowed without the disqualification of the athlete(s) responsible for the false start. Any athlete(s) responsible for further false starts in the race shall be disqualified by the Starter (see also Rule 16.9 of the Technical Rules).

  39.8.4 in the Vertical Jumps, each increase of the bar shall be uniform throughout the competition: 3cm in the High Jump and 10cm in the Pole Vault.

  39.8.5 starting positions/lanes for last event of a Combined Events competition may be determined by the Technical Delegate(s) or the Combined Events Referee as they deem desirable. In the 200m and 400m events, after ranking the athletes according to Rule 20.3.1 of the Technical Rules, the lanes shall be drawn in accordance with Rule 20.4.4 and 20.4.5 of the Technical Rules, respectively. In all other events, they shall be drawn by lot.

39.9 Only one system of timing may be applied throughout each individual event. However, for Record purposes, times obtained from a Fully Automatic Timing and Photo Finish system shall be applied regardless of whether such times are available for other athletes in the event.

Two systems of timekeeping are recognised for this purpose - those set out in Rules 19.1.1 and 19.1.2 of the Technical Rules.

If for example there is a malfunction of Photo Finish being used for some but not all of the heats it will be impossible to compare directly the points scores in the two systems for the same time - one by Hand Time and the other automatic.

如果技术代表或全能裁判长认为这是合适的，则有权重新排列任何分组。

39.8　各单项的比赛规则均适用于全能各项目的比赛，但以下情况除外：

39.8.1　跳远及各投掷项目，每名运动员只能试跳（掷）3次。

39.8.2　当未使用全自动计时和终点摄影系统时，每名运动员要由3名手动计时员独立计取比赛时间。

39.8.3　在径赛项目中，每组比赛只允许一次起跑犯规而不取消该次犯规运动员的比赛资格，之后任何1名或多名运动员在比赛中再次起跑犯规将被发令员取消该项目的比赛资格（另见技术规则16.9条）。

39.8.4　在高度跳跃项目比赛中，横杆每次提升的高度自始至终应是固定的：跳高3厘米，撑竿跳高10厘米。

39.8.5　全能比赛最后一项的起跑位置或道次，可由技术代表或全能裁判长自行决定。在200米、400米项目中，按技术规则20.3.1条对运动员进行排名后，要按技术规则20.4.4条和20.4.5条分别抽签。在所有其他比赛项目中，要抽签决定。

39.9　全能各单项比赛只能始终使用一种计时方法。然而在承认纪录时，要使用全自动计时和终点摄影系统计取的成绩，不管这种计时成绩对该项目的其他运动员是否可用。

为此，执行技术规则19.1.1条和19.1.2条规定的两种计时方式均应该被承认。

例如，如果终点摄影计时系统发生故障，部分运动员采用了该计时方法，而并不是所有运动员都采用了该计时方法。因此，不可能将两个系统（手计时和自动计时系统）时间的得分直接进行对比。

Since under Rule 39.9 of the Technical Rules, only one system of timing may be applied throughout any single event in a competition, in such a case all athletes would have their points determined based on their manual times using the specific manual times table.

To be clear, if in other events all athletes have Photo Finish times, the electronic times table can be used for those events.

39.10　Any athlete failing to attempt to start or make a trial in one of the events shall not be allowed to take part in the subsequent events but shall be considered to have abandoned the competition. They shall not, therefore, figure in the final classification.

Any athlete deciding to withdraw from a Combined Events competition shall immediately inform the Combined Events Referee of their decision.

39.11　The scores, according to the current Combined Events Scoring Tables, shall be announced, separate for each event and as a cumulative total, to all athletes after the completion of each event.

The athletes shall be placed in order according to the total number of points obtained.

The same Scoring Tables are used for each event even if for the younger age groups the specifications for the hurdles or throwing implements differ from those used for senior competition.

The score for any performance in either a Track Event or a Field Event can be found in the appropriate table. In many events, not all possible times or distances are listed in the table. In such cases, the score for the nearest lesser performance shall be used.

Example: For the women's Javelin Throw there is no points score shown for a distance of 45.82m. The nearer shorter distance listed in the table is 45.78m for which there is a score of 779 points.

39.12　When it is decided to use the Gundersen (or similar) Method for the start of the last event of a Combined Events competition, the relevant competition regulations should specify any particular rules that should be applied and the method by which the races should be started and conducted.

39.13　If two or more athletes achieve an equal number of points for any place in the competition, it shall be determined as a tie.

由于根据技术规则39.9条，在比赛中，在任何单项中只能应用一种计时系统。在这种情况下，所有运动员可以使用特定的手动计时表格依据人工计时时间确定自己的得分。

需要明确的是，如果所有运动员在其他项目比赛中均使用了终点摄影计时系统，这些项目应对照电子计时评分表核查分数。

39.10　在任何一个单项比赛中，如果某运动员未能参加起跑或试跳（掷），则不能参加后续项目的比赛，按放弃比赛处理，不能计算总成绩。

任何决定退出全能比赛的运动员，要立即将其决定通知全能裁判长。

39.11　每一个单项比赛结束后，裁判员要根据世界田联现行全能项目评分表向全体运动员宣布该单项得分和各项的累积分。

运动员要按照获得的总分顺序排列。

每一个单项都应该使用同样的评分表，即使青少年组别的比赛栏架和投掷器械的规格不同于成年组别比赛。

径赛或田赛的比赛成绩均可在对应的评分表中核查得分。在很多项目中，并不是所有成绩的时间或距离都会在评分表中列出，在这种情况下，应计取最接近的较低成绩对应的积分。

示例：在女子标枪项目中没有45.82米成绩对应的积分，评分表中查到最接近的较低距离成绩是45.78米，对应的积分是779分。

39.12　当组织者决定在全能比赛最后一项中采用岗德森法（或类似的方法）起跑时，在相关竞赛规程中应对采用的起跑方法和特定规则作详细说明。

39.13　如果在比赛中2名或多名运动员，在任何名次上获得了相等的积分，应判定名次并列。

PART V 200M STANDARD OVAL TRACK STADIUM (SHORT TRACK) COMPETITIONS

40. Applicability of 400m Standard Oval Track Stadium Rules to Short Track Competitions

With the exceptions stated in the following Rules of this Part V and, in the case of performances made in an enclosed and covered facility, the requirement for wind measurement set out in Rules 17 and 29 of the Technical Rules, the Rules of Parts I to IV for 400m Standard Oval Track Stadium competitions shall apply to Short Track Competitions.

41. The Short Track Stadium

41.1 The stadium may be completely enclosed and covered. If enclosed and covered, lighting, heating and ventilation shall be provided to give satisfactory conditions for competition.

41.2 The Field of Play should include an oval track; a straight track for sprints and hurdles; runways and landing areas for jumping events. In addition, a circle and landing sector for the Shot Put should be provided, whether permanently or temporarily. All the facilities should conform to the specifications in the World Athletics Track and Field Facilities Manual.

41.3 All the tracks, runways or take-off surface areas shall be covered with a synthetic material that should preferably be able to accept 6mm spikes in running shoes (see also Regulation 11 of the Athletic Shoe Regulations). The track manufacturer or the stadium operator may allow the use of spikes of up to 9mm.

Short Track Athletics competitions under paragraphs 1. (a), (b), (c) and 2. (a), (b) of the World Rankings Competition definition should be held only on facilities that hold a World Athletics Short Track Athletics Facility Certificate. It is recommended that, when such facilities are available, competitions under paragraphs 1. (d), (e) and 2. (c), (d), (e) of the World Rankings Competition definition should also be held on these facilities.

第五部分　200米标准椭圆形跑道体育场（短道）比赛

40.　400米标准椭圆形跑道体育场规则对短道比赛的适用条款

除本部分（第五部分）另有规定的情况，以及在封闭和有顶棚的设施中比赛时需遵守技术规则17条和29条中风速测量的要求外，规则第一至第四部分的400米标准椭圆形跑道体育场比赛规则也适用于短道比赛。

41.　短道体育场

41.1　运动场馆可被完全封闭和覆盖。如果被封闭和覆盖，则要为比赛提供符合条件的照明、供暖和通风设备。

41.2　比赛场地应包括一个椭圆形跑道，一个用于短跑和跨栏的直道，以及用于跳跃项目的助跑道和落地区。此外，应提供铅球比赛使用的永久性或临时性的投掷圈和扇形落地区。所有的设施都要符合《世界田联田径场地设施手册》的要求。

41.3　所有跑道、助跑道和起跳区均要用人工合成材料覆盖，并适合使用长度为6毫米的钉鞋（另见运动鞋规程11）。跑道制造商或体育场运营商可允许使用最大9毫米的钉鞋。

举行世界排名比赛定义1.（a）（b）（c）和2.（a）（b）所述短道田径比赛，其场地设施应有世界田联短道田径场地设施证书。建议举行世界排名比赛定义1.（d）（e）和2.（c）（d）（e）所述比赛，如果有可能，也要在这样的场地上举行。

41.4 The foundation on which the synthetic surface of the tracks, runways and take-off areas is laid shall be either solid, e.g. concrete or, if of suspended construction (such as wooden boards or plywood sheets mounted on joists), without any special sprung sections and, as far as technically possible, each runway shall have a uniform resilience throughout. This shall be checked, for the take-off area for the jumps, before each competition.

Note: A "sprung section" is any deliberately engineered or constructed section designed to give extra assistance to an athlete.

Note (i): The World Athletics Track and Field Facilities Manual, which is available from the World Athletics Office, or may be downloaded from the World Athletics website, contains more detailed and defined specifications for planning and construction of Short Track stadia including diagrams for track measurement and marking.

Note (ii): The current standard forms required to be used for the certification application and measurement report as well as the Certification System Procedures are available from the World Athletics Office, or may be downloaded from the World Athletics website.

Lack of suitable lighting is a common problem for covered stadium competitions. A covered stadium must have a lighting which allows a correct and fair delivery of the events and if there is television coverage the illumination level may need to be higher. The finish line area(s) may require additional lighting for the Fully Automatic Timing.

42. The Straight Track

(See the Rules for 400m Standard Oval Track Stadium competitions and the World Athletics Track and Field Facilities Manual.)

43. The Oval Track and Lanes

Oval Track

43.1 The nominal length of a standard running track shall be 200m ("200m Standard Oval Track"). It shall consist of two parallel straights and two bends, which may be banked, and whose radii should be equal.

41.4　所有跑道、助跑道和起跳区合成材料覆盖的基层必须坚固，如混凝土等，如果是悬空结构（如木板或合成板托架），则不能有任何特殊的弹性部分，并在技术上要尽可能使每条助跑道各处的弹性保持一致。每次比赛前，须对起跳区的弹性进行检查。

注："弹性部分"是任何为运动员提供额外帮助而特意设计或建造的部分。

注（i）：《世界田联田径场地设施手册》中包含更多详细和明确的短道体育场馆的布局、结构的技术信息，包括跑道测量和画线的图表。《世界田联田径场地设施手册》可以从世界田联办公室获得，或从世界田联官方网站下载。

*注（ii）：*认证申请和测量报告所使用的现行标准表格以及认证系统程序，可向世界田联办公室索取或从世界田联官方网站下载。

缺乏适宜的照明是有顶棚的体育场馆比赛中普遍存在的问题。在有顶棚的体育场馆内比赛，必须有适宜的灯光照明，以确保比赛正确、公平地进行，如果有电视转播，则对照明水平可能有更高的要求。终点线区域需要额外的照明用于全自动计时。

42.　直道

（见400米标准椭圆形跑道体育场比赛规则和《世界田联田径场地设施手册》。）

43.　椭圆跑道和分道

椭圆跑道

43.1　标准跑道的长度为200米（"200米标准椭圆形跑道"）。它应由两个平行的直道和两个可呈斜坡状的弯道组成，弯道半径应相等。

The inside of the track shall be bordered either with a kerb of suitable material, approximately 50mm in height and width, or with a white line 50mm wide. The outside edge of this kerb or line forms the inside of lane 1. The inside edge of the kerb or line shall be horizontal throughout the length of the track. However, this kerb or line may be located on the banking slope such that the pivot line of the banking shall be horizontal throughout the length of the banking.

Note: All measurements shall be taken as indicated in Rule 14.2 of the Technical Rules.

Lanes

43.2　The track should have a minimum of four and a maximum of six lanes. The nominal width of the lanes shall be between 0.90m and 1.10m including the lane line on the right. All lanes shall be of the same nominal width with a tolerance of ± 0.01m to the selected width. The lanes shall be separated by white lines 50mm wide.

Banking

43.3　The angle of banking in all the lanes in the bend and, separately, in the straight, should be the same at any cross section of the track. The straight may be flat or have a maximum lateral inclination of 1 : 100 (1%) towards the inside lane.

In order to ease the change from the straight to the banked bend, the change may be made with a smooth gradual horizontal transition which may be extended into the straight. In addition, there should be a vertical transition.

Marking of the Inside Edge

43.4　Where the inside edge of the track is bordered with a white line, it shall be marked additionally with cones or flags on the bends and, optionally, on the straights. The cones shall be at least 0.15m high. The flags shall be approximately 0.25m × 0.20m in size, at least 0.45m high and set at an angle of 60° with the ground away from the track. The cones or flags shall be placed on the white line so that the edge of the base of the cone or flag pole coincides with the edge of the white line closest to the track. The cones or flags shall be placed at intervals not exceeding 1.5m on the bends and, if used, 10m on the straights.

跑道内沿要用适宜材料制成高、宽各50毫米的突沿，或用50毫米宽的白线标出。以突沿或白线的外沿作为第1分道的内侧边沿。跑道突沿或白线的内沿要始终与跑道保持在同一水平面上。然而，这一突沿或白线可位于斜坡上，这样，斜坡的枢轴线在斜坡长度内要始终保持在同一水平面上。

注：所有场地的测量应根据技术规则14.2条的相关要求执行。

分道

43.2　弯道上的分道应最少4条道，最多6条道。各分道宽度须相同，分道宽在0.90~1.10米，分道宽包括右侧分道线。各分道应该宽度相同，公差为±0.01米。各分道要用50毫米宽的白线分隔。

坡形跑道

43.3　在任意一处坡道横断面上，所有分道的倾斜角度应相同。直道部分可以是平坦的，或朝向内侧跑道的最大横向倾斜度为1∶100（1%）。

为使从直道进入坡形弯道的变化较为平缓，可通过一个平滑的逐渐水平过渡段实现，而这个过渡段可以延伸到直道上。此外，还应该有一个垂直过渡段。

内沿标记

43.4　如以白线作为跑道内沿，还须在弯道和需要的直道上另外用锥形物或小旗作为标记。锥形物高至少0.15米。小旗尺寸约为0.25米×0.20米，高至少0.45米，远离跑道与地面成60°。锥形物或小旗要放置在白线上，使锥形物或小旗的底部边沿与离跑道最近一侧的白线边沿重合。锥形物或小旗的安放间距在弯道上不要超过1.5米，如果在直道上使用不要超过10米。

Note: For all Short Track competitions directly under World Athletics, the use of an inside kerb is strongly recommended.

An oval Track may be longer than 200m but any records for 200m or longer races would not be ratified. To organise top level competitions, it will be useful to have a 6-lane track. The ideal width of the lanes of an oval Track should be 1m.

When positioning the flags or cones it must be taken into account that the white line on the inside edge of lane 1 does not belong to the athlete drawn in that lane. Cones are preferred and recommended for Short Track Competitions.

44. Start and Finish on the Oval Track

44.1 Technical information on the construction and marking of a standard banked Short Track oval is given in detail in the World Athletics Track and Field Facilities Manual. The basic principles to be adopted are given hereunder.

Basic Requirements

44.2 The start and finish of a race shall be denoted by white lines 50mm wide, at right angles to the lane lines for straight parts of the track and along a radius line for curved parts of the track.

44.3 The requirements for the finish line are that, if at all possible, there should be only one for all the different lengths of race, it shall be on a straight part of the track and as much of that straight as possible should be before the finish.

44.4 The essential requirement for all start lines, straight, staggered or curved, is that the distance for every athlete, when taking the shortest permitted route, shall be the same.

44.5 As far as possible, start lines (and takeover zone lines for Relay Races) should not be on the steepest part of the banking.

Conduct of the Races

44.6 Conduct of the Races, as follows:

    44.6.1 Races of up to, and including, 300m shall be run entirely in lanes.

    44.6.2 Races over 300m, and less than 800m shall start and continue in lanes up to the breakline marked at the end of the second bend.

注：所有由世界田联直接管辖的短道比赛，强烈建议使用内突沿。

椭圆跑道可以超过200米，但是200米或更长距离项目的任何纪录不会被承认。为了组织高水平的赛事，将采用6条分道。椭圆跑道理想的分道宽度为1米。

放置小旗或锥形物时，必须考虑到第1分道内沿的白线不属于在该跑道上的运动员。短道比赛首选和推荐使用锥形物。

44. 椭圆跑道上的起点和终点

44.1 《世界田联田径场地设施手册》中详细规定了标准倾斜短道椭圆形跑道建造和标记的技术信息。下面给出的是要采用的基本原则。

基本要求

44.2 比赛的起、终点线应用50毫米宽的白线标出，并与直道部分的分道线成直角，在弯道上的起、终点线应沿弯道半径方向标出。

44.3 对终点线的要求如下：在可能的情况下，所有不同距离的径赛应只设一个终点，终点必须设置在跑道的直段上，在终点之前应为尽可能多的直道。

44.4 对于所有直道上的、梯形的和弧形的起跑线的基本要求是，使每一位运动员沿允许的最短路线跑进时，跑的距离要完全相等。

44.5 起跑线（和接力区标志线）应尽可能不设在坡道的最陡处。

比赛的进行

44.6 对比赛进行的要求如下：

44.6.1 300米和300米以下的项目，须自始至终为分道跑。

44.6.2 300米以上和800米以下的项目，须分道起跑，并在分道内跑至第二个弯道末的抢道标志线。

44.6.3　For the start of races of 800m, each athlete may be assigned a separate lane, or up to two athletes may be assigned per lane, or a group start, as in Rule 17.5.2 of the Technical Rules preferably commencing in lanes 1 and 4, may be used. In these cases, athletes may leave their lane, or those running in the outer group may join the inner group, only after the breakline marked at the end of the first bend, or if the race is run with two bends in lanes, at the end of the second bend. A single curved start line may also be used.

Note (i): In competitions under paragraphs 1. (e) and 2. (e) of the World Rankings Competition definition, the participating teams may agree not to use lanes for the 800m event.

Note (ii): On tracks with less than six lanes, a group start may be used to allow six athletes to compete.

44.6.4　Races longer than 800m shall be run without lanes using an arced start line or group starts. If a group start is used, the breakline shall be at the end of either the first or second bend.

If an athlete does not follow this Rule, they shall be disqualified.

The breakline shall be an arced line marked after each bend, 50mm wide, across all lanes other than lane 1. To assist athletes identify the breakline, small cones, prisms or other suitable markers, 50mm × 50mm and no more than 0.15m high, preferably of different colour from the breakline and the lane lines, shall be placed on the lane lines immediately before the intersection of the lane lines and the breakline.

Start Line and Finish Line for a Track of 200m Nominal Length

44.7　The start line in lane 1 should be on the principal straight. Its position shall be determined so that the most advanced staggered start line in the outside lane (400m races) should be in a position where the angle of banking should not be more than 12°.

44.6.3　800米比赛时，运动员可被分配指定的分道起跑，或最多2名运动员共用1条分道，也可分组同时起跑，根据技术规则17.5.2条，分组起跑时最好使用第1分道和第4分道。在这些情况下，运动员可以在第一个弯道末的抢道线后选择并道，在外侧起跑的运动员可以并入内侧起跑组，或者如果比赛采用两个弯道分道跑，则运动员可在第二个弯道末的抢道线后离开各自分道。也可采用一条弧形起跑线。

注（i）：举办世界排名比赛定义1.（e）和2.（e）所述的比赛，参赛队可达成协议，800米比赛采用不分道跑。

注（ii）：当跑道的分道少于6条时，分组起跑可允许6名运动员一同参加比赛。

44.6.4　800米以上项目须采用弧形起跑线的不分道起跑，或分组同时起跑。如采用分组起跑，抢道线须在第一个或第二个弯道末。

如运动员不遵守此条规定，将被取消比赛资格。

抢道线应为一条弧线，宽50毫米，横跨除第1分道外的所有跑道。为了帮助运动员确认抢道线，可在各分道线与抢道线的交界处之前放置小的锥形物、棱柱体或其他适合的标志物（50毫米×50毫米），并且这些标志物最大高度为0.15米，要与抢道线和分道线的颜色不同。

200米标准跑道的起点和终点线

44.7　第1分道起跑线应在主要的直道上。确定它的位置时，应使最外道的梯形起跑线（400米赛跑）处于坡道倾斜角不超过12°的位置上。

The finish line for all races on the oval track shall be an extension of the start line in lane 1, right across the track and at right angles to the lane lines.

Colours to use for marking the track are indicated on the Track Marking Plan included in the World Athletics Track and Field Facilities Manual.

45. Seedings and Draw for Lanes in Track Events

45.1 The ranking and composition of heats shall be made in accordance with Rule 20.3 of the Technical Rules.

Note (i): Tables to determine the number of rounds and heats in each round to be held and the qualification procedure which may be used in the absence of any provision in applicable regulations or other determination by the Organisers are published on the World Athletics website.

Note (ii): The applicable regulations may specify how vacant positions due to withdrawals in semi- finals and finals may be filled in by athletes ranked next following the previous round after those qualified.

45.2 For all rounds in all events run wholly or partly in lanes around a bend, where there are successive rounds of a race, three draws for lanes will then be made:

    45.2.1 one for the two highest ranked athletes or teams to determine placings in the outer two lanes;

    45.2.2 another for the third and fourth ranked athletes or teams to determine placings in the next two lanes;

    45.2.3 another for the other athletes or teams to determine placings in any remaining inner lanes.

45.3 For all other races, the lane order shall be drawn in accordance with Rules 20.4.1, 20.4.2, 20.4.3 and 20.5 of the Technical Rules.

Where tracks have a different configuration of lanes, then the tables to be used should be adapted either in the specific Technical Regulations for the competition or if not by the Technical Delegate(s) or the Organisers.

46. [Intentionally Left Blank]

在椭圆跑道上，所有径赛的终点线应是第1分道起跑线的延长线，并与跑道垂直相交，与分道线成直角。

《世界田联田径场地设施手册》中"跑道标志的规划"注明了跑道使用标志线的颜色。

45. 径赛项目道次的排序和抽签

45.1　排名和分组须遵照技术规则20.3条的规定。

注（i）：如果在适用的竞赛规程中没有规定或者组织者没有作其他决定，可使用在世界田联官方网站上公布的晋级的赛次数、每赛次的组数，以及晋级方法的表格。

注（ii）：适用的规程可以规定，如何由晋级赛后排名靠后的运动员填补因半决赛和决赛有人退赛而产生的空缺位置。

45.2　跑弯道的全程或部分分道跑的所有赛次所有项目，如果有后续赛次比赛，应通过3次抽签决定道次。

　　　45.2.1　一是决定排前两名的运动员或队排在外侧两道。

　　　45.2.2　二是决定排第三和第四名的运动员或队排在中间两道。

　　　45.2.3　最后是决定其余的运动员或队排在剩下的内侧道。

45.3　其他各项比赛的运动员道次，应按技术规则20.4.1条、20.4.2条、20.4.3条和20.5条的规定抽签决定。

如果跑道的分道具有不同的布局，则比赛分道安排表应根据具体的技术规程制定，如果没有相关规定则由技术代表或组织者决定。

46.　［此处留空待续］

47. Hurdle Races

47.1   The standard distances shall be: 50m or 60m on the straight track.

47.2   Layout of the hurdles for races:

	U18 Men	U20 Men	Men	U18 Women	U20 Women / Women
Height of hurdle	0.914m	0.991m	1.067m	0.762m	0.838m
Distance	50m/60m				
Number of hurdles	4/5				
Start line to first hurdle	13.72m			13.00m	
Between hurdles	9.14m			8.50m	
Last hurdle to finish line	8.86m/9.72m			11.50m/13.00m	

48. Relay Races

Conduct of the Races

48.1   In the 4 × 200m race, all the first leg and the first bend of the second leg up to the nearer edge of the breakline described in Rule 44.6 of the Technical Rules, shall be run in lanes. Each takeover zone shall be 20m long and the second, third and fourth athlete shall start within this zone.

48.2   The 4 × 400m race shall be run according to Rule 44.6.2 of the Technical Rules.

48.3   The 4 × 800m race shall be run according to Rule 44.6.3 of the Technical Rules.

48.4   The waiting athletes in the third and fourth legs of the 4 × 200m race, in the second, third and fourth legs of the 4 × 400m and the 4 × 800m race shall, under the direction of a designated official, place themselves in their waiting position in the same order (inside to out) as the order of their respective team members as they enter the last bend. Once the incoming athletes have passed this point, the waiting athletes shall maintain their order, and shall not exchange positions at the beginning of the takeover zone. If an athlete does not follow this Rule, their team shall be disqualified.

47. 跨栏跑

47.1 跨栏跑的标准距离为50米或60米,在直道上进行。

47.2 比赛栏架的设置:

	少年男子(U18)	青年男子(U20)	成年男子	少年女子(U18)	青年女子(U20)、成年女子
栏架高度	0.914米	0.991米	1.067米	0.762米	0.838米
比赛距离	50米/60米				
栏架数量	4个/5个				
起跑线至第一栏	13.72米			13.00米	
栏间距离	9.14米			8.50米	
最后一栏距终点	8.86米/9.72米			11.50米/13.00米	

48. 接力跑

比赛的进行

48.1 在4×200米比赛中,第一棒的全程和第二棒第一个弯道,直至技术规则44.6条所述的抢道线后沿应为分道跑。每个接力区长20米,第二、三、四棒的运动员要在各自接力区内起跑。

48.2 4×400米比赛须根据技术规则44.6.2条进行。

48.3 4×800米比赛须根据技术规则44.6.3条进行。

48.4 4×200米比赛中第三、四棒,以及4×400米和4×800米比赛中的第二、三、四棒等待接棒的运动员,要在指定裁判员的指示下,按照各队进入最后一个弯道的先后顺序(由内向外)排列各自的接棒位置。一旦传棒运动员跑过此点,接棒运动员须保持其排列顺序,在接力区开始处不可交换位置。如果运动员不遵守本规则,将取消其接力队的比赛资格。

Note: Owing to the narrow lanes, Short Track Relay Races are much more liable to collisions and unintended obstruction than Relay Races on 400m Standard Oval Tracks. It is, therefore, recommended that, when possible, a spare lane should be left between each team.

49. High Jump

Runway and Take-Off Area

49.1 If portable mats are used, all references in the Rules to the level of the take-off area must be construed as referring to the level of the top surface of the mat.

49.2 An athlete may start their approach on the banking of the oval track provided that the last 15m of their run up is on a runway complying with Rules 27.3, 27.4 and 27.5 of the Technical Rules.

50. Pole Vault

Runway

An athlete may start their approach on the banking of the oval track provided that the last 40m of their run up is on a runway complying with Rules 28.6 and 28.7 of the Technical Rules.

51. Horizontal Jumps

Runway

An athlete may start their approach on the banking of the oval track provided that the last 40m of their run up is on a runway complying with Rules 29.1 and 29.2 of the Technical Rules.

52. Shot Put

Landing Sector

52.1 The landing sector shall consist of some suitable material on which the shot will make an imprint, but which will minimise any bounce.

注：由于分道狭窄，短道接力赛比400米标准椭圆形跑道接力赛更容易发生碰撞和意外的阻挡现象。因此，在条件允许时，建议相邻两队之间留出一条空道。

49. 跳高

助跑道和起跳区

49.1 如果使用可移动的垫子，规则中提及的所有起跳区平面都必须解释为垫子顶面的平面。

49.2 运动员可从椭圆跑道的坡道上开始助跑，但助跑的最后15米应在符合技术规则27.3条、27.4条和27.5条规定的助跑道上进行。

50. 撑竿跳高

助跑道

运动员可从椭圆跑道的坡道上开始助跑，但助跑的最后40米应在符合技术规则28.6和28.7条规定的助跑道上进行。

51. 水平跳跃

助跑道

运动员可从椭圆跑道的坡面上开始助跑，但助跑的最后40米应在符合技术规则29.1条和29.2条规定的助跑道上进行。

52. 铅球

铅球落地区

52.1 铅球落地区须用铅球落地时能留下痕迹并能使反弹减小到最低限度的适宜材料建成。

52.2　　Where necessary to ensure the safety of spectators, officials and athletes, the landing sector shall be enclosed at the far end and on the two sides by a stop barrier and/or protective netting, placed as close to the circle as required. The recommended minimum height of the netting should be 4m and sufficient to stop a shot, whether in flight or bouncing from the landing surface.

52.3　　If there is the limited space in the Field of Play, the area enclosed by the stop barrier may not be large enough to include a full 34.92° sector. The following conditions shall apply to any such restriction.

　　　　52.3.1　　The stop barrier at the far end shall be at least 0.50m beyond the current World Record in Shot Put for men or women.

　　　　52.3.2　　The sector lines on either side shall be symmetrical about the centre line of the 34.92° sector.

　　　　52.3.3　　The sector lines run radially from the centre of the Shot Put circle at an angle of 34.92°until the sector has a width of at least 9m. From there on they run parallel to the centre line of the landing sector.

It is recommended that the stop barrier/protective netting on either side should be extended towards the circle so that it starts within 8m of it and that, for the length of these extensions, the height of the netting should be at least 6m.

Construction of the Shot

52.4　　Depending on the type of landing area (see Rule 52.1 of the Technical Rules), the shot shall be either solid metal or metal cased or, alternatively, soft plastic or rubber casing with a suitable filling. Both types of shot may not be used in the same competition.

Solid Metal or Metal Cased Shot

52.5　　These shall comply with Rule 33.4 and 33.5 of the Technical Rules.

Plastic or Rubber Cased Shot

52.6　　The shot shall have a soft plastic or rubber case with a suitable filling such that no damage shall be caused when landing on a normal sports hall floor. It shall be spherical in shape and its surface finish shall be smooth.

52.2 为了确保观众、裁判员和运动员的安全，落地区远端和两侧要用挡网/防护网围起，设置的挡网可尽量靠近投掷圈，建议挡网的最低高度应为4米，以便能挡住正在飞行或从落地区表面反弹的铅球。

52.3 如果比赛场地空间有限，挡网包围的场地可能不足以容纳完整的34.92°的扇形落地区，下列条款适用于此类情况。

    52.3.1 在目前男子、女子铅球世界纪录位置之外至少0.50米的地方设置挡网。

    52.3.2 落地区两侧标志线必须和34.92°扇形落地区的中轴线对称。

    52.3.3 落地区标志线以34.92°的角度自铅球投掷圈圆心向外放射，直到落地区宽至少9米。从那里开始，它们与扇形落地区中心线平行。

建议两侧的挡网/防护网应向投掷圈延伸，使其在距投掷圈8米的范围内开始延伸，对于这些延伸的部分，挡网高度应至少为6米。

铅球的构造

52.4 根据落地区的类型（见技术规则52.1条），铅球既可为实心金属或是金属外壳，也可以是装有合适填充物并用软塑料或橡胶制作外壳。在同一场比赛中不得使用两种类型的铅球。

实心金属或金属外壳的铅球

52.5 这两种铅球应符合技术规则33.4条和33.5条中的规定。

塑料或橡胶外壳的铅球

52.6 当落地区为普通的运动地板时，铅球须为软塑料或橡胶外壳，并装有合适填充物，使铅球落地时不至于损坏地板。铅球外形须为球形，表面须光滑。

Information for manufacturers: to be smooth, the surface average height must be less than or equal to 1.6μm, i.e. a roughness number N7 or less.

52.7 The shot shall conform to the following specifications:

Minimum weight and diameter limits for admission to competition and acceptance of a Record:

Diameter	3.000kg	4.000kg	5.000kg	6.000kg	7.260kg
Minimum	85mm	95mm	100mm	105mm	110mm
Maximum	120mm	130mm	135mm	140mm	145mm

53. Combined Events Competitions

U18, U20 and Senior Men (Pentathlon)

53.1 The Pentathlon consists of five events, which shall be held on one day in the following order: 60m Hurdles; Long Jump; Shot Put; High Jump; 1000m.

U18, U20 and Senior Men (Heptathlon)

53.2 The Heptathlon consists of seven events which shall be held over two consecutive 24-hour periods in the following order:

First day: 60m; Long Jump; Shot Put; High Jump.

Second day: 60m Hurdles; Pole Vault; 1000m.

U18, U20 and Senior Women (Pentathlon)

53.3 The Pentathlon consists of five events and shall be held on one day in the following order: 60m Hurdles; High Jump; Shot Put; Long Jump; 800m.

Heats and Groups

53.4 Preferably four or more, and never less than three, athletes shall be placed in each heat or group.

制造商信息：为使表面光滑，球体表层平均起伏度应小于或等于1.6微米，即粗糙度为Ｎ7或更小。

52.7 这类铅球须符合下列规格：

比赛用和承认纪录的铅球的最小重量：

直径	3.000千克	4.000千克	5.000千克	6.000千克	7.260千克
最小	85毫米	95毫米	100毫米	105毫米	110毫米
最大	120毫米	130毫米	135毫米	140毫米	145毫米

53. 全能比赛

少年男子（U18）、青年男子（U20）和成年男子（五项全能）

53.1 五项全能包括5个单项，须在一天内按下列顺序举行：

60米栏、跳远、铅球、跳高、1000米。

少年男子（U18）、青年男子（U20）和成年男子（七项全能）

53.2 七项全能包括7个单项，须在连续的两个24小时内按下列顺序举行：

第一天：60米、跳远、铅球、跳高。

第二天：60米栏、撑竿跳高、1000米。

少年女子（U18）、青年女子（U20）和成年女子（五项全能）

53.3 五项全能由5个项目组成，按下列顺序在一天中完成：

60米栏、跳高、铅球、跳远、800米。

分组

53.4 每组运动员最好为4人或4人以上，不得少于3人。

PART VI RACE WALKING EVENTS

54. Race Walking

Distances

54.1 The standard distances on a Short Track shall be: 3000m, 5000m; on a 400m Standard Oval Track: 5000m, 10,000m, 20,000m, 35,000m, 50,000m; and on road courses: 10km, 20km, 35km, 50km.(In force from 1 January 2026: The standard distances on a Short Track shall be: 3000m, 5000m; on a 400m Standard Oval Track: 5000m, 10,000m, Half-Marathon, Marathon, 50,000m; and on road courses: 10km, Half Marathon, Marathon, 50km.)

Definition of Race Walking

54.2 Race Walking is a progression of steps so taken that the walker makes contact with the ground, so that no visible (to the human eye) loss of contact occurs. The advancing leg must be straightened (i.e. not bent at the knee) from the moment of first contact with the ground until the vertical upright position.

Judging

54.3 Judging, as follows:

    54.3.1 The appointed Judges of Race Walking shall elect a Chief Judge, if one has not been appointed previously.

    54.3.2 All the Judges shall act in an individual capacity and their judgements shall be based on observations made by the human eye.

    54.3.3 Where applicable, Judges shall be appointed in accordance with Rule 9 of the Competition Rules.

第六部分　竞走项目

54. 竞走

距离

54.1 短道项目的标准距离为：3000米、5000米；400米标准椭圆形跑道项目的标准距离为：5000米、10000米、20000米、35000米、50000米；公路赛道项目的标准距离为：10公里、20公里、35公里、50公里。（自2026年1月1日起生效：短道比赛的标准距离为：3000米、5000米；400米标准椭圆形跑道项目的标准距离为：5000米、10000米、半程马拉松、马拉松、50000米；公路赛道项目的标准距离为：10公里、半程马拉松、马拉松、50公里。）

竞走定义

54.2 竞走是运动员用双脚与地面保持接触，连续向前迈进的过程，没有（人眼）可见的腾空。前腿从脚触地瞬间至垂直部位必须伸直（即膝关节不得弯曲）。

执裁

54.3 执裁方法如下：

  54.3.1 如果事先没有指派竞走主裁判，要在指派的竞走裁判员中选出一人为主裁判。

  54.3.2 所有竞走裁判员均应独立行使其工作职责，要以眼睛观察为依据进行判罚。

  54.3.3 竞走裁判应按照竞赛规则9条的相关规定任命。

54.3.4 For Road Races, there should normally be a minimum of six to a maximum of nine Judges including the Chief Judge.

54.3.5 For Track Races, there should normally be six Judges including the Chief Judge.

54.3.6 In competitions held under paragraphs 1. (a) and (b) of the World Rankings Competition definition not more than one Judge (excluding the Chief Judge) affiliated with any one Member can officiate.

Note: The Member affiliation of each Judge is that properly stated on the current lists of World Athletics Gold, Silver or Bronze Level Race Walking Judges.

Chief Judge

54.4 Chief Judge, as follows:

54.4.1 In all World Rankings Competitions, the Chief Judge has the power to disqualify an athlete in the last 100m, when their mode of progression obviously fails to comply with Rule 54.2 of the Technical Rules regardless of the number of previous Red Cards the Chief Judge has received on that athlete. An athlete who is disqualified by the Chief Judge under these circumstances shall be allowed to finish the race. They shall be notified of this disqualification by the Chief Judge or a Chief Judge's Assistant by showing the athlete a red paddle at the earliest opportunity after the athlete has finished the race.

54.4.2 The Chief Judge shall act as the supervising official for the competition, and act as a Judge only in the special situation noted in Rule 54.4.1. In competitions held under paragraphs 1. (a), (b), (c) and 2. (a), (b) of the World Rankings Competition definition, two or more Chief Judge's Assistants shall be appointed. The Chief Judge's Assistant(s) are to assist with the notification of disqualifications only and shall not act as Race Walking Judges.

54.4.3 For all competitions held under paragraphs 1. (a), (b), (c) and 2. (a), (b) of the World Rankings Competition definition and where possible for other competitions, an official in charge of the Posting Board(s) and a Chief Judge's Recorder shall be appointed.

54.3.4 在公路比赛中，通常情况下，包括主裁判在内的裁判员最少为6人，最多为9人。

54.3.5 在场地竞走比赛中，通常情况下，包括主裁判在内的裁判员应为6人。

54.3.6 在举行世界排名比赛定义1.（a）和（b）所述比赛中，每个国家或地区最多只能有1名裁判员（主裁判除外）执裁。

注：在当前的世界田联金级、银级、铜级竞走裁判员名单中，要正确标明每位裁判员的协会隶属关系。

主裁判

54.4 主裁判，如下：

54.4.1 在所有世界排名比赛中，当运动员的行进方式明显违反了技术规则54.2条的定义时，不论该运动员此前已收到的红卡数量有几张，主裁判有权在比赛的最后100米取消该运动员的比赛资格。在这种情况下，被主裁判取消比赛资格的运动员允许完成本次比赛。主裁判或主裁判助理应在运动员完成比赛后尽早向该运动员出示红牌，以通知该运动员被取消比赛资格。

54.4.2 竞走主裁判应行使比赛监督官员的权力，并仅在出现规则54.4.1条所述的特殊情况下才能行使竞走裁判员的权力。在举行世界排名比赛定义1.（a）（b）（c）和2.（a）（b）所述比赛中，应指派2名或多于2名竞走主裁判助理。主裁判助理仅帮助通知被取消比赛资格的运动员，不能行使竞走裁判员的权力。

54.4.3 在举行世界排名比赛定义1.（a）（b）（c）和2.（a）（b）所述比赛和其他比赛中，如有可能，要指派1名负责红卡公告牌的裁判员和1名主裁判的记录员。

Yellow Paddle

54.5   When a Judge is not completely satisfied that an athlete is fully complying with Rule 54.2 of the Technical Rules, they should, where possible, show the athlete a yellow paddle with the symbol of the offence on each side.

An athlete cannot be shown a second yellow paddle by the same Judge for the same offence. Having shown a yellow paddle to an athlete, the Judge shall inform the Chief Judge of their action after the competition.

Red Cards

54.6   When a Judge observes an athlete failing to comply with Rule 54.2 of the Technical Rules by exhibiting visible loss of contact or a bent knee during any part of the competition, the Judge shall send a Red Card to the Chief Judge.

Disqualification

54.7   Disqualification, as follows:

54.7.1   Except as provided in Rule 54.7.3 of the Technical Rules, when three Red Cards from three different Judges have been sent to the Chief Judge on the same athlete, the athlete is disqualified and they shall be notified of this disqualification by the Chief Judge or a Chief Judge's Assistant by being shown a red paddle. The failure to give notification shall not result in the reinstatement of a disqualified athlete.

54.7.2   In competitions under paragraphs 1. (a), (b), (c) and (d) of the World Rankings Competition definition, in no circumstances shall the Red Cards of two Judges affiliated with the same Member have the power to disqualify.

Note: The Member affiliation of each Judge is that properly stated on the current lists of World Athletics Gold, Silver or Bronze Level Race Walking Judges.

黄牌

54.5 当竞走裁判员认为运动员的行进方式不完全符合技术规则54.2条的规定时，如有可能，该裁判员应向运动员出示两面都有犯规标志的黄牌予以警告。

同一名裁判员不能对同一名运动员相同的犯规出示第二次黄牌。对运动员出示黄牌后，该裁判员须在赛后向竞走主裁判报告该运动员的犯规行为。

红卡

54.6 当竞走裁判员在比赛的任何阶段观察到运动员的行进方式不符合技术规则54.2条的规定时，并表现出明显可见的腾空或膝关节弯曲，该裁判员须将一张红卡送交主裁判。

取消比赛资格

54.7 取消比赛资格：

54.7.1 除技术规则54.7.3条的规定外，当3名不同的竞走裁判员对同一名运动员发出的3张红卡送交主裁判时，该运动员将被取消比赛资格，并由主裁判或主裁判助理向该运动员出示红牌以通知运动员。如未能通知到，也不得恢复已被取消的比赛资格。

54.7.2 在世界排名比赛定义1.（a）（b）（c）和（d）所述比赛中，任何情况下，来自同一会员协会的2名裁判员的红卡无权取消运动员的比赛资格。

注：在当前的世界田联金级、银级或铜级竞走裁判员名单中，要正确标明每位裁判员的协会隶属关系。

54.7.3 A Penalty Zone shall be used for any race where the applicable regulations for the competition so provide and may be used for other races as determined by the relevant governing body or Organisers. In such cases, an athlete will be required to enter the Penalty Zone and remain there for the applicable period once they have received three Red Cards and are so advised by the Chief Judge or someone delegated by them.

The applicable period in the Penalty Zone shall be as follows:

Races up to and including	Time
5000m/5km	0.5 min
10,000m/10km	1 min
20,000m/20km	2 min
30,000m/30km	3 min
35,000m/35km	3.5 min
40,000m/40km	4 min
50,000m/50km	5 min

In force from 1 January 2026: The applicable period in the Penalty Zone shall be as follows:

Races up to and including	Time
5000m/5km	0.5 min
10,000m/10km	1 min
Half-Marathon	2 min
30,000m/30km	3 min
Marathon	4 min
50,000m/50km	5 min

54.7.3　如果适用的规程中有规定，任何比赛都可设立罚停区，罚停区可以用于由相关管理机构或组织者确定的其他比赛中。在比赛中使用此规则时，当某运动员接到3张红卡时，主裁判或其代表将告知该运动员需进入罚停区，并在此停留相应的时间。

在罚停区适用的停留时间如下：

项目距离	时间
5000米/5公里	0.5分钟
10000米/10公里	1分钟
20000米/20公里	2分钟
30000米/30公里	3分钟
35000米/35公里	3.5分钟
40000米/40公里	4分钟
50000米/50公里	5分钟

自2026年1月1日起生效，在罚停区适用的停留时间如下：

项目距离	时间
5000米/5公里	0.5分钟
10000米/10公里	1分钟
半程马拉松	2分钟
30000米/30公里	3分钟
马拉松	4分钟
50000米/50公里	5分钟

An athlete who fails to enter the Penalty Zone when required to do so, or remain there for the applicable period, shall be disqualified by the Referee.

54.7.4   If, under Rule 54.7.3 of the Technical Rules, an athlete receives a third Red Card and it is no longer practicable to direct them to enter the Penalty Zone before the end of the race, the Referee shall add the time they would have been required to spend in the Penalty Zone to their finishing time and adjust the finishing order as may be necessary.

54.7.5   If, at any time when Rule 54.7.3 of the Technical Rules applies, an athlete receives an additional Red Card from a Judge other than one of the three who had previously sent a Red Card, they shall be disqualified. They shall be notified of this disqualification by the Chief Judge or a Chief Judge's Assistant by being shown a red paddle. The failure to give notification shall not result in the reinstatement of a disqualified athlete.

54.7.6   In Track Races, an athlete who is disqualified shall immediately leave the track and, in Road Races, shall, immediately after being disqualified, remove the distinguishing bibs and leave the course. Any disqualified athlete who fails to leave the course or track or comply with directions given under Rule 54.7.3 of the Technical Rules to enter and remain for the required period in the Penalty Zone may be liable to further disciplinary action in accordance with Rules 7.1 and 7.3 of the Technical Rules.

54.7.7   One or more Posting Boards shall be placed on the course and near the finish to keep athletes informed about the number of Red Cards that have been sent to the Chief Judge for each athlete. The symbol of each offence should also be indicated on the Posting Board.

54.7.8   For all competitions falling under paragraphs 1. (a) and (b) of the World Rankings Competition definition, hand held computer devices with transmission capability must be used by the Judges to communicate all Red Cards to the Recorder and the Posting Board(s). In all other competitions, in which such a system is not used, the Chief Judge, immediately after the end of the event, shall report to the Referee the identification of all athletes disqualified under Rules 54.4.1, 54.7.1 or 54.7.5 of the Technical Rules by indicating the bib identification, the time of the notification and the offences; the same shall be done for all the athletes who received Red Cards.

任何拒绝进入罚停区或未停留规定时间的运动员，将被裁判长取消比赛资格。

54.7.4　在执行技术规则54.7.3条时，如果某运动员被判罚3张红卡，但在比赛结束前没能将其带入罚停区，裁判长应将相应的罚停时间计算到他完成比赛的成绩中，且如有必要，重新调整比赛名次。

54.7.5　在执行技术规则54.7.3条时，任何情况下，如果该运动员再接到另一张红卡，而该红卡并非由原先送交3张红卡的任何一名裁判员提交的，该运动员将被取消比赛资格。主裁判或主裁判助理要向他们出示红牌告知他们被取消比赛资格。如未能通知到，也不得恢复已被取消的比赛资格。

54.7.6　在场地竞走比赛时，运动员被取消比赛资格后，应立即离开跑道。在公路竞走比赛时，运动员被取消比赛资格后，应立即取下号码布，并离开赛道。如果被取消比赛资格的运动员不离开跑道或赛道，或不遵守技术规则54.7.3条的规定进入罚停区并停留规定的时间，可根据技术规则7.1条和7.3条的规定，受到进一步的纪律处罚。

54.7.7　应在赛道接近终点的地方设置1块或多块红卡公告牌，以便告知每名运动员已被送达竞走主裁判的红卡数量。红卡公告牌上应显示运动员每次犯规的符号。

54.7.8　在世界排名比赛定义1.（a）和（b）所述比赛中，竞走裁判员必须使用具有传输功能的掌上电脑，以便将红卡及时传送给记录员和红卡公告牌。在所有其他比赛中，如果没有使用此传输系统，竞走主裁判应根据技术规则54.4.1条、54.7.1条或54.7.5条的规定，在比赛结束后立即向裁判长报告取消比赛资格运动员的号码、通知时间和犯规性质，同时向所有接到红卡的运动员通告以上信息。

Start

54.8 The races shall be started by the firing of a gun, cannon, air horn or like device. The commands for races longer than 400m shall be used (Rule 16.2.2 of the Technical Rules). In races which include a large number of athletes, five-minute, three-minute and one-minute warnings before the start of the race should be given. On the command "On your marks", the athletes shall assemble on the start line in the manner determined by the organisers. The Starter shall ensure that no athlete has their foot (or any part of their body) touching the start line or the ground in front of it, and shall then start the race.

Safety

54.9 The Organisers of Race Walking Events shall ensure the safety of athletes and officials. In competitions held under paragraphs 1. (a), (b), (c) and 2. (a), (b) of the World Rankings Competition definition, the Organisers shall ensure that the roads used for the competition are closed to motorised traffic in all directions.

Drinking / Sponging and Refreshment Stations in Road Race Walking Events

54.10 Drinking/Sponging and Refreshment Stations in Road Race Walking Events, as follows:

    54.10.1 Water and other suitable refreshments shall be available at the start and finish of all races.

    54.10.2 For all events of 5km or longer up to and including 10km, water only drinking/sponging stations shall be provided at suitable intervals if weather conditions warrant such provision.

    Note: Mist stations may also be arranged, when considered appropriate under certain organisational and/or climatic conditions.

    54.10.3 For all events longer than 10km, refreshment stations shall be provided every lap. In addition, water only drinking/sponging stations shall be placed approximately midway between the refreshment stations or more frequently if weather conditions warrant such provision.

起跑

54.8 比赛须通过鸣枪、鸣炮、号角或相似设备开始起跑。发令须采用400米以上项目的起跑口令（技术规则16.2.2条）。当参赛运动员人数众多时，应在起跑前5分钟、3分钟和1分钟给予倒计时提示。"各就位"口令发出后，运动员须按照组织者决定的方式在起跑线上集合。发令员要确保任何运动员的脚（或身体的任何部分）没有触及起跑线或线前地面，方可发令开赛。

安全

54.9 竞走比赛的组织者应保证运动员和裁判员的安全。凡在世界排名比赛定义1.（a）（b）（c）和2.（a）（b）所述比赛中，赛事组织者须保证在比赛使用的道路上禁止所有方向的机动车通行。

公路竞走比赛饮水/用水（海绵）和补给站

54.10 公路竞走比赛饮水/用水（海绵）和补给站设置如下：

54.10.1 所有比赛的起、终点须备有饮水和其他适宜的补给品。

54.10.2 对于所有5公里至10公里（包括10公里）的竞走比赛，根据天气情况，以适当间隔设置仅提供饮水/用水的站点。

注：根据竞赛组织和/或天气情况，可以安排喷淋站。

54.10.3 10公里以上的竞走比赛，每圈都须设置补给站。此外，还可根据天气情况，在两个补给站之间设置1个或多个饮水/用水（海绵）站。

54.10.4　Refreshments, which may be provided by either the Organisers or the athlete, shall be placed at the stations so that they are easily accessible to, or may be put by authorised persons into the hands of, the athletes. Refreshments provided by the athletes shall be kept under the supervision of officials designated by the Organisers from the moment that the refreshments are delivered by the athletes or their representatives. Those officials shall ensure that the refreshments are not altered or tampered with in any way.

54.10.5　The Organisers shall delineate, by barriers, tables or markings on the ground, the area from which refreshments can be collected or received.

The authorised persons may hand the refreshment to the athlete either from behind, or from a position no more than one metre to the side, but not in front, of the table. They may not enter the course nor obstruct any athlete.

No official or authorised person shall, under any circumstances, move beside an athlete while they are taking refreshment or water.

54.10.6　In competitions held under paragraphs 1. (a), (b), (c) and 2. (a), (b) of the World Rankings Competition definition, a maximum of two officials per Member may be stationed at any one time behind the table.

Note: For an event in which a Member may be represented by more than three athletes, the Technical Regulations may allow additional officials at the refreshment tables.

54.10.7　An athlete may, at any time, carry water or refreshment by hand or attached to their body provided it was carried from the start or collected or received at an official station.

54.10.8　An athlete who receives or collects refreshment or water from a place other than the official stations, except where provided for medical reasons from or under the direction of race officials, or takes the refreshment of another athlete, should, for a first such offence, be warned by the Referee normally by showing a yellow card. For a second offence, the Referee shall disqualify the athlete, normally by showing a red card. The athlete shall then immediately leave the course.

54.10.4 补给品（饮料、食品）可由组织者提供或由运动员自备，须放在便于运动员拿取的地方或经授权人员递到运动员手中。运动员的自备补给品，从运动员或其代表提交之时起，须始终在组织者指派的工作人员监管之下，并要确保提交的补给品不能有任何改变或篡改。

54.10.5 比赛组织者须在赛道适当的位置用栅栏、桌子或地面标记划定可以接收或拿取补给品的区域。

经授权人员可以从饮料桌后或桌子两侧不超过1米的位置给运动员递送补给品，但不能在桌前递送。他们不得进入赛道，也不得阻挡任何运动员。

无论在什么情况下，当运动员取水或补给品时，任何裁判员或授权人员都不能在运动员身边伴随移动。

54.10.6 在举行世界排名比赛定义1.（a）（b）（c）和2.（a）（b）所述比赛中，在自备饮料桌的后面，每个国家或地区每次最多可站2名官员。

注：当一个国家超过3名运动员参加同一项目比赛时，技术规程可允许在补给站安排额外的官员。

54.10.7 只要是从起点或官方供应站拿取，运动员可以在任何时候手持或随身携带该水或补给。

54.10.8 除医疗原因或有竞赛官员的指示外，运动员如在官方供应站以外的地方接收或者拿取补给或水，或从其他运动员处获取，第一次出现这种犯规，裁判长通常将出示黄牌警告，第二次出现犯规，裁判长将出示红牌取消其比赛资格。该运动员须立即离开赛道。

Note: An athlete may receive from or pass to another athlete refreshment, water or sponges provided it was carried from the start or collected or received at an official station. However, any continuous support from an athlete to one or more others in such a way may be regarded as unfair assistance and warnings and/or disqualifications as outlined above may be applied.

Generally, where it is logical and in accordance with practice, there is uniformity of the provisions within Rules 54, 55 and 56 of the Technical Rules pertaining to outside events. It should be noted, however, that Rule 54.10.5 of the Technical Rules is intentionally different from Rule 55.8.5 of the Technical Rules in that in Race Walking Events, the team officials are not permitted in front of the tables.

Road Courses

54.11   Road courses, as follows:

    54.11.1   The circuit shall be no shorter than 1km and no longer than 2km. For events that start and finish in the stadium, the circuit should be located as close as possible to the stadium.

    54.11.2   Road courses shall be measured in accordance with Rule 55.3 of the Technical Rules.

Race Conduct

54.12   An athlete may leave the marked course with the permission and under the supervision of an official, provided that by going off course they do not shorten the distance to be covered.

54.13   If the Referee is satisfied on the report of a Judge or Umpire or otherwise that an athlete has left the marked course thereby shortening the distance to be covered, they shall be disqualified.

54.14   In the case of Race Walking Events not covered by this Rule, the applicable regulations should specify any particular rules that should be applied and the method by which the event should be conducted.

> 注：运动员可以相互接收或传递由起点或沿途官方供应站提供的补给、水或海绵块，但由一名运动员连续向另一名或多名运动员递送上述物品时，可被视为不公平帮助，可使用上述方法予以警告和/或取消其比赛资格。

通常，针对场外比赛，技术规则54条、55条和56条具有一致性。但应该注意的是，技术规则54.10.5条有意与技术规则55.8.5条区别，因为在竞走项目中，运动队官员不允许站在桌前。

公路赛道

54.11 公路赛道：

  54.11.1 环形赛道的长度，每圈最长为2公里，最短为1公里。起、终点设在体育场内的公路竞走比赛，环形路线应尽可能设在距体育场较近的地方。

  54.11.2 赛道须根据技术规则55.3条的规定进行测量。

比赛行为

54.12 在得到裁判员的许可并在1名裁判员的监督下，运动员可离开标定的赛道，但不得因此而缩短比赛距离。

54.13 如果裁判长认可裁判员或检查员的报告，或通过其他方式确认，运动员离开了标定的赛道而缩短了比赛距离，将取消运动员的比赛资格。

54.14 本规则未涵盖的竞走项目，规程应明确该项目适用的特定规则及实施的方法。

PART Ⅶ ROAD RACES

55. Road Races

Distances

55.1　The standard distances shall be: Road Mile(1609.344m), 5km, 10km, 15km, 10Miles, 20km, Half-Marathon, 25km, 30km, Marathon (42.195km), 50km, 100km and Road Relay.

Note: It is recommended that the Road Relay race be run over the Marathon distance, ideally over a 5km loop course, with stages of 5km, 10km, 5km, 10km, 5km, 7.195km. For an U20 Road Relay, the recommended distance is a Half-Marathon with stages of 5km, 5km, 5km, 6.098km.

Course

55.2　The races shall be run on made-up roads. However, when traffic or similar circumstances make it unsuitable, the course, duly marked, may be on a bicycle path or footpath alongside the road, but not on soft ground such as grass verges or the like. The start and finish may be within an athletic Field of Play.

Note (i): It is recommended that, for Road Races staged over standard distances, the start and finish points, measured along a theoretical straight line between them should not be further apart than 50% of the race distance. For approval of Records, see Rule 31.21.2 of the Competition Rules.

Note (ii): It is acceptable for the start, finish and other segments of the race to be conducted on grass or other non-paved surfaces. These segments shall be kept to a minimum.

55.3　The course shall be measured along the shortest possible route that an athlete could follow within the section of the road permitted for use in the race.

第七部分　路跑比赛

55. 路跑比赛

距离

55.1 标准比赛距离为：1英里路跑（1609.344米）、5公里、10公里、10英里、15公里、20公里、半程马拉松、25公里、30公里、马拉松（42.195公里）、100公里和公路接力赛跑。

注：建议公路接力赛跑的距离与马拉松相同，理想的赛道应为一条5公里的环形赛道，各段距离为 5 公里、10公里、5公里、10公里、5公里、7.195公里。青年（U20）公路接力赛跑，建议距离为半程马拉松，各段距离为5公里、5公里、5公里、6.098公里。

赛道

55.2 此类赛跑应在铺装路面上进行。然而，如果交通或类似环境不允许，比赛路线可设在路旁的自行车道或人行道上，并适当标记，但不得通过路旁草地等柔软地段。比赛起、终点可设在田径场内。

注（i）：建议按标准距离举行路跑比赛时，起、终点之间的直线距离不应超过比赛距离的50%。如果要申报纪录，见竞赛规则31.21.2条。

注（ii）：比赛的起、终点和其他部分赛段可以在草地或其他非铺装的地面上进行，但应尽量避免。

55.3 赛道应沿着运动员所允许跑过的最短路线进行丈量。

In all competitions under paragraphs 1. (a) and (b) and, where possible, 1. (c) and 2. (a), (b) of the World Rankings Competition definition, the measurement line should be marked along the course in a distinctive colour that cannot be mistaken for other markings.

The length of the course shall not be less than the official distance for the event. At all World Rankings Competitions, the uncertainty in the measurement shall not exceed 0.1% (i.e., 42m for the Marathon) and the length of the course shall have been measured and certified in advance by an International Road Course Measurer.

Note (i): For measurement, the "Calibrated Bicycle Method" shall be used.

Note (ii): To prevent a course from being found to be shorter than the official race distance on future re-measurement, it is recommended that a "short course prevention factor" be built in when laying out the course. For bicycle measurements this factor should be 0.1% which means that each km on the course will have a "measured length" of 1001m.

Note (iii): If it is intended that parts of the course on race day will be defined by the use of non-permanent equipment such as cones, barricades, etc. their positioning shall be decided not later than the time of the measurement and the documentation of such decisions shall be included in the measurement report.

Note (iv): It is recommended that for Road Races staged over standard distances, the overall decrease in elevation between the start and finish should not exceed 1:1000, i.e. 1m per km (0.1%). For approval of Records, see Rule 31.21.3 of the Competition Rules.

Note (v): A course measurement certificate is valid for 5 years, after which the course shall be re- measured even when there are no obvious changes to it.

55.4　The distance in kilometres on the route shall be displayed to all athletes.

在世界排名比赛定义1.（a）和（b）所述的比赛中，如有可能也包括世界排名比赛定义1.（c）和2.（a）（b）所述的比赛，应用区别于赛道上其他标志的醒目颜色沿赛道标出丈量线。

路线长度不得短于该项目的正式距离。在所有世界排名比赛中，路线的丈量误差不得超过0.1%（如马拉松为42米），该路线的距离在赛前要经过一名国际公路赛道丈量员测量和认证。

注（ⅰ）：应采用"经过标定的自行车丈量法"进行赛道丈量。

注（ⅱ）：为防止在以后丈量时发生路线长度不足的问题，建议设计路线时加入一个"防止路线缩短的系数"，使用"经过标定的自行车丈量法"时，该系数应为0.1%，意味着每1公里的路线要有1001米的"丈量长度"。

注（ⅲ）：如计划在比赛当天使用临时性设备，如锥形物、栅栏等来标明部分路线的界线，则此类设备安放的位置最迟须在丈量路线时确定下来，并且要在丈量报告中进行说明。

注（ⅳ）：建议按标准距离举行路跑比赛时，起、终点之间海拔高度下降不超过1∶1000，即每公里下降不超过1米（0.1%）。如果批准纪录，见竞赛规则31.21.3条。

注（ⅴ）：赛道丈量认证有效期为5年，此限期后，即使该赛道无明显改变，也需重新测量。

55.4 须以公里为单位，在赛道上向所有运动员显示赛程的距离。

55.5　　For Road Relays, lines 50mm wide shall be drawn across the course to mark the start of each stage distance (scratch line). Similar lines shall be drawn 10m before and 10m after the scratch line to denote the takeover zone. For all takeovers, athletes are not permitted to begin running outside their takeover zones, and shall start within the zone. All takeover procedures, which, unless otherwise specified by the organisers, shall comprise a physical contact between the incoming and outgoing athletes, shall be completed within this zone. If an athlete does not follow this Rule, their team shall be disqualified.

Start

55.6　　The races shall be started by the firing of a gun, cannon, air horn or like device. The commands for races longer than 400m shall be used (Rule 16.2.2 of the Technical Rules). In races which include a large number of athletes, five-minute, three-minute and one-minute warnings before the start of the race should be given. On the command "On your marks", the athletes shall assemble on the start line in the manner determined by the organisers. The Starter shall ensure that no athlete has their foot (or any part of their body) touching the start line or the ground in front of it, and shall then start the race.

As for middle and long distance Track Events, it is emphasised for events held outside the stadium that Starters and Referees should avoid being over-zealous in the application of the false start rules to such events. Recalling starts in road races and other outside events can be difficult, and in large fields impractical, in any case. However, where there is a clear and wilful breach, the Referee should not hesitate to consider appropriate action in respect of an individual either during or after the race. However, in major events, where the start mechanism malfunctions and it is clear or possible that the timing system may not have started a recall where practical might be the best option.

Safety

55.7　　Organisers of Road Races shall ensure the safety of athletes and officials. In competitions held under paragraphs 1. (a), (b), (c) and 2. (a), (b) of the World Rankings Competition definition, the Organisers shall ensure that the roads used for the competition are closed to motorised traffic in all directions.

55.5 举行公路接力跑，应在所跑公路上画出50毫米宽的横线标明各棒次之间的距离和接力区标志线（scratch line）。运动员不得在接力区以外起跑，必须从接力区内起跑。在标志线前、后10米处各画一条50毫米宽的横线作为接力区。除非组织者另有规定，交接棒的程序是交、接棒运动员须有身体接触，并必须在接力区内完成。如果运动员不遵守本规则，将取消其接力队的比赛资格。

起跑

55.6 比赛须通过鸣枪、鸣炮、号角或相似设备发令开始起跑。发令要采用400米以上项目的起跑口令（技术规则16.2.2条）。当参赛运动员人数众多时，应在起跑前5分钟、3分钟、1分钟给予倒计时提示。"各就位"口令发出后，运动员须按照组织者决定的方式在起跑线上集合。发令员要确保任何运动员的脚（或者身体任何部分）没有接触起跑线或起跑线前的地面，然后发令开赛。

对于中长距离的径赛项目，需要强调的是，如果是在体育场外进行的比赛，发令员和裁判长应避免过度使用规则判罚起跑犯规。在很大的场地上，路跑比赛或其他室外比赛起跑召回非常困难，无论如何也不切合实际。但是，对于明显故意犯规的情形，裁判长应毫不犹豫地在赛中或赛后给予相关人员适宜的判罚。然而，在大型赛事中，如果起跑发令系统发生故障，并且计时系统确定或可能没有启动，执行召回可能是最佳的选择。

安全

55.7 路跑比赛的组织者须保证运动员和裁判员的安全。凡举行世界排名比赛定义1.（a）（b）（c）和2.（a）（b）所述的比赛，比赛组织者须保证在比赛所使用的道路上禁止任何方向的机动车辆通行。

Drinking / Sponging and Refreshment Stations in Road Races

55.8 Drinking/Sponging and Refreshment Stations in Road Races, as follows:

55.8.1 Water and other suitable refreshments shall be available at the start and finish of all races.

55.8.2 For all events, water shall be available at suitable intervals of approximately 5km. For events longer than 10km, refreshments other than water may be made available at these points.

Note (i): Where conditions warrant, taking into account the nature of the event, the weather conditions and the state of fitness of the majority of the competitors, water and/or refreshments may be placed at more regular intervals along the route.

Note (ii): Mist stations may also be arranged, when considered appropriate under certain organisational and/or climatic conditions.

55.8.3 Refreshments may include drinks, energy supplements, foodstuffs or any other item other than water. The Organisers will determine which refreshments it will provide based on prevailing conditions.

55.8.4 Refreshments will normally be provided by the Organisers but it may permit athletes to provide their own, in which case the athlete shall nominate at which stations they shall be made available to them. Refreshments provided by the athletes shall be kept under the supervision of officials designated by the Organisers from the time that the refreshments are lodged by the athletes or their representatives. Those officials shall ensure that the refreshments are not altered or tampered with in any way.

55.8.5 The Organisers shall delineate, by barriers, tables or markings on the ground, the area from which refreshments can be collected or received. It should not be directly in the line of the measured route. Refreshments shall be placed so that they are easily accessible to, or may be put by authorised persons into the hands of, the athletes. Such persons shall remain inside the designated area and not enter the course nor obstruct any athlete. No official or authorised person shall, under any circumstances, move beside an athlete while they are taking refreshment or water.

路跑比赛饮用/用水（海绵）和补给站

55.8 路跑比赛饮水/用水（海绵）和补给站设置如下：

55.8.1 所有比赛的起、终点要提供饮水和其他适宜的补给品。

55.8.2 所有项目，要以大约5公里的适当间隔提供饮水。超过10公里的项目，除提供饮水外，这些站点还应提供补给品。

注（i）：在条件允许的情况下，应考虑到比赛性质、天气情况和大多数参赛者身体状况等的需要，可以在赛道沿途以多于常规间隔提供饮水和/或补给。

注（ii）：组织者也可根据需要和/或天气情况，设置喷淋站。

55.8.3 补给品可包括饮料、能量补充品、食品或除水以外的任何食物。组织者将根据现有条件确定提供何种补给品。

55.8.4 通常情况下，补给品由组织者提供，也可允许运动员自备。当运动员自备补给品时，须指定放置的站点。由运动员提供的自备补给品，自运动员或其代表上交之时起，要始终处于组织者指派裁判员的监督之下。这些裁判员须确保这些补给品不以任何方式被改变或篡改。

55.8.5 比赛组织者须在赛道适当的位置用栅栏、桌子或地面标记划定可以拿取或接收补给品的区域。补给品不应该直接摆放在测量赛道的线上。补给品要摆放在运动员便于拿取的地方，或由授权人员将其递到运动员手中。此类人员须停留在指定区域内，不得进入赛道，也不得阻挡任何运动员。无论在什么情况下，当运动员取水或补给品时，任何裁判员或授权人员都不能在运动员身边伴随移动。

55.8.6　　In competitions held under paragraphs 1. (a), (b), (c) and 2. (a), (b) of the World Rankings Competition definition, a maximum of two officials per Member may be stationed at any one time inside the area designated for them.

Note: For an event in which a Member may be represented by more than three athletes, the Technical Regulations may allow additional officials at the refreshment tables.

55.8.7　　An athlete may, at any time, carry water or refreshment by hand or attached to their body provided it was carried from the start or collected or received at an official station.

55.8.8　　An athlete who receives or collects refreshment or water from a place other than the official stations, except where provided for medical reasons from or under the direction of race officials, or takes the refreshment of another athlete, should, for a first such offence, be warned by the Referee normally by showing a yellow card. For a second offence, the Referee shall disqualify the athlete, normally by showing a red card. The athlete shall then immediately leave the course.

Note: An athlete may receive from or pass to another athlete refreshment, water or sponges provided it was carried from the start or collected or received at an official station. However, any continuous support from an athlete to one or more others in such a way may be regarded as unfair assistance and warnings and/or disqualifications as outlined above may be applied.

Race Conduct

55.9　　An athlete may leave the marked course with the permission and under the supervision of an official, provided that by going off course they do not shorten the distance to be covered.

55.10　　If the Referee is satisfied on the report of a Judge or Umpire or otherwise that an athlete has left the marked course thereby shortening the distance to be covered, they shall be disqualified.

55.11　　Umpires should be placed at regular intervals and at each key point. Other umpires should move along the course during the race.

55.8.6 在举办世界排名比赛定义1.（a）（b）（c）和2.（a）（b）所述的比赛中，在指定区域后面，每个国家或地区每次最多可站2名官员。

注：若一个国家超过3名运动员参加同一项比赛，技术规程可允许增加进入补给站的人员。

55.8.7 只要是从起点或官方供应站拿取，运动员可在任何时候手持或随身携带水或补给品。

55.8.8 除医疗原因或有竞赛官员的指示外，运动员如在官方供应站以外的地方接收或者拿取补给或水，或从其他运动员处获取，第一次出现这种犯规，裁判长通常将出示黄牌警告，第二次出现犯规，裁判长要出示红牌取消其比赛资格。该运动员须立即离开赛道。

注：运动员可以相互接收或传递由起点或沿途官方供应站提供的补给品、水或海绵块，但由一名运动员连续向另一名或多名运动员递送上述物品时，可被视为不公平的帮助，可使用上述方法予以警告和/或取消比赛资格。

比赛行为

55.9 在路跑中，在得到裁判员的许可并在1名裁判员的监督下，运动员方可离开标定的赛道，但不得因此而缩短比赛距离。

55.10 如果裁判长认可裁判员或检查员的报告，或通过其他方式确认，运动员离开了标定的赛道而缩短了比赛距离，将取消运动员的比赛资格。

55.11 检查员应有规律地间隔分布在赛道和每个关键点上，另一些检查员应在比赛中沿赛道移动。

It is acknowledged that following the practice of first giving a warning when applying relevant aspects of Rule 55 of the Technical Rules and where applicable Rules 6.2 and 6.3 of the Technical Rules will create difficulties in implementation but where the opportunity arises, the Referee should do so. It is suggested that one option might be that course or refreshment station umpires be designated as assistant Referees and that they be in communication with the Referee and each other to ensure the effective co-ordination of warnings and disqualifications. But there remains the possibility as per the Note to Rule 6.2 of the Technical Rules that in some circumstances, disqualification can, and should, occur without a warning being given.

When a Transponder Timing System is not in use, or where an additional back-up recording system is desired, it is recommended that a funnel system such as that described for Cross Country Races in the green text on Rule 56 of the Technical Rules be used.

在执行技术规则55条和技术规则6.2条、6.3条的相关条款时，即在第一次给予警告后，可能会导致执行困难，但是一旦发生违反规则的情形，裁判长应作出裁决。建议的做法是指派在赛道上或补给站的检查员作为裁判长助理，他们可以与裁判长进行及时沟通和配合，确保有效地给予警告和取消比赛资格。但根据技术规则6.2条注释的规定，有一种可能是在某些情况下可以不用警告，而直接给予运动员取消比赛资格的判罚。

如果没有使用芯片计时系统，或需要额外的备份计时，建议采用分流的方法，如技术规则56条绿色文字中越野跑的相应做法。

PART VIII CROSS COUNTRY, MOUNTAIN AND TRAIL RACES

There are extreme variations in conditions in which Cross Country Running, Mountain Running and Trail Running are practised throughout the world and it is difficult to legislate international standardisation of these events. It must be accepted that the difference between very successful and unsuccessful events often lies in the natural characteristics of the venue and the abilities of the course designer. The following Rules are intended as a guide and incentive to assist Members to develop Cross Country Running, Mountain Running and Trail Running.

56. Cross Country Races

Distances

56.1 Distances at World Athletics Cross Country Championships should be approximately:

Senior Men:	10km	Senior Women:	10km
U20 Men:	8km	U20 Women:	6km

The distances recommended for U18 competitions should be approximately:

U18 Men:	6km	U18 Women:	4km

It is recommended that similar distances be used for other International and National competitions.

Course

56.2 Cross Country course rules, as follows:

    56.2.1 The course must be designed on an open or woodland area, covered as far as possible by grass, with natural obstacles, which can be used by the course designer to build a challenging and interesting race course.

    56.2.2 The area must be wide enough to accommodate not only the course but also all the necessary facilities.

第八部分 越野跑、山地跑和野外跑

在世界各地举行越野跑、山地跑和野外跑的条件差异极大,很难通过立法制定这些项目的国际标准。必须承认的是,赛事的成功与失败往往取决于比赛地点自然环境的特点和路线设计者的能力。下列规则旨在指导和鼓励各会员协会开展越野跑、山地跑和野外跑运动。

56. 越野跑

距离

56.1 世界田联越野锦标赛距离应约为:

成年男子: 10公里 成年女子: 10公里

青年男子U20: 8公里 青年女子U20: 6公里

建议少年U18比赛距离应约为:

少年男子U18: 6公里 少年女子U18: 4公里

建议其他国际和国内比赛也采用类似的比赛距离。

赛道

56.2 越野跑赛道规则如下:

  56.2.1 越野跑的赛道必须设计在空旷的田野或林地,尽可能被草坪覆盖,并带有自然障碍,使赛道设计者设计出一条具有挑战性和趣味性的比赛路线。

  56.2.2 该区域必须有足够的宽度,不仅可以安排赛道,还可容纳其他所需设施。

56.3 For Championships and international events and, wherever possible, for other competitions:

56.3.1 A loop course must be designed and it should measure between 1500m and 2000m. If necessary, a small loop can be added in order to adjust the distances to the required overall distances of the various events, in which case the small loop must be run in the early stages of the event. It is recommended that each long loop should have a total ascent of at least 10m.

56.3.2 Existing natural obstacles shall be used if possible. However, very high obstacles should be avoided, as should deep ditches, dangerous ascents/descents, thick undergrowth and, in general, any obstacle which would constitute a difficulty beyond the aim of the competition. It is preferable that artificial obstacles should not be used but if such use is unavoidable, they should be made to simulate natural obstacles met within open country. In races where there are large numbers of athletes, narrow gaps or other hindrances which would deny the athletes an unhampered run shall be avoided for the first 300m.

56.3.3 The crossing of roads or any kind of macadamised surfaces shall be avoided or at least kept to a minimum. When it is impossible to avoid such conditions in one or two areas of the course, the areas must be covered by grass, earth or mats.

56.3.4 Apart from the start and finish areas, the course must not contain any other long straight. A "natural", undulating course with smooth curves and short straights, is the most suitable.

56.4 Course markings, as follows:

56.4.1 The course shall be clearly marked with tape on both sides. It is recommended that all along one side of the course a 1m wide corridor, heavily fenced from the outside of the course, shall be installed for the use of organisation officials and media. Crucial areas must be heavily fenced; in particular the start area (including the Warm-up Area and the Call Room) and finish area (including any Mixed Zone). Only accredited people will be allowed access to these areas.

56.3 举办世界锦标赛、国际比赛或其他比赛时，如有可能，都应按下列要求设计路线：

    56.3.1 比赛路线必须设计成环形赛道，它测量长度应为1500～2000米。如有必要，可加上一个小的环形赛道，以便将距离调整为不同项目所需要的总距离，在这种情况下，比赛时应先跑小圈。建议每个大圈的总爬升高度至少为10米。

    56.3.2 如有可能，可采用已存在的自然障碍物，但要避免过高的障碍物，如深坑、危险的上下坡、茂密的灌木丛等。总之，应避免一切会给比赛带来困难而违背比赛宗旨的障碍物。不宜设置人造障碍物，如不能避免，应模拟在开阔区域遇到的自然障碍物。在运动员参加人数较多的比赛中，前300米要避免狭窄空间或其他妨碍运动员顺利奔跑的障碍物。

    56.3.3 应避免穿过公路或任何形式的碎石路面，或将其减少至最低限度。如果在比赛路线中不可避免地遇到1～2处类似路面，则须在该区域覆盖草、泥土或垫子。

    56.3.4 除起、终点区域外，赛道不得包含任何长的直道。一条"自然"起伏的路线，带有平缓的弯道和较短直道是最理想的。

56.4 赛道标志，如下：

    56.4.1 在赛道的两边须用带子做出明显的标志。建议在整个赛道的一侧设置一条1米宽的通道，在赛道外部用加固的栅栏围起来，仅供比赛工作人员或媒体人员出入。在重要区域必须设立加固的栅栏，特别是在起点区域（包括热身场地和检录处）和终点区域（包括混合区）。只有持有效证件的人员方可进入这些区域。

56.4.2　The general public should only be allowed to cross the course at well organised cross- over points, marshalled by stewards.

56.4.3　It is recommended that, apart from the start and finish areas, the course be a width of 5 metres, including the obstacle areas.

56.5　For Cross Country Relays, lines 300mm wide 20m apart shall be drawn across the course to denote the takeover zone. For all takeovers, athletes are not permitted to begin running outside their takeover zone, and shall start within the zone. All takeover procedures, which, unless otherwise specified by the organisers, shall comprise a physical contact between the incoming and outgoing athletes, shall be completed within this zone. If an athlete does not follow this Rule, their team shall be disqualified.

Note: 1m × 1m flags, mounted at least 2m high, should be placed at the beginning and end of the takeover zone. Green flags for the beginning of the zone and red flags for the end of the zone.

Start

56.6　The races shall be started by the firing of a gun, cannon, air horn or like device. The commands for races longer than 400m shall be used (Rule 16.2.2 of the Technical Rules).

In races which include a large number of athletes, five-minute, three-minute and one-minute warnings should be given.

Wherever possible departure boxes should be provided for teams races with the members of each team to be lined up behind each other at the start of the race. In other races, the athletes shall be lined up in the manner determined by the organisers. On the command "On your marks", the starter shall ensure that no athlete has their foot (or any part of their body) touching the start line or the ground in front of it, and shall then start the race.

Safety

56.7　Organisers of Cross Country Races shall ensure the safety of athletes and officials.

田径技术规则

56.4.2 观众只允许在管理人员的指挥下，在事先规定的交叉路口有组织地横越赛道。

56.4.3 建议除起、终点区域外，包括障碍区域在内的赛道宽度为5米。

56.5 在越野跑接力比赛中，应用两条相距20米、横过赛道300毫米宽的线标出接力区。所有接棒运动员都应在接力区内开始跑动，不得在接力区外开始。除组织者另有特别说明外，接力的程序要包括交、接运动员的身体接触，且须在接力区内完成。如果某运动员没有遵守此条规则，该队将被取消比赛资格。

注：在接力区的起始处应设置1米×1米的旗子，高度不低于2米。绿色旗子设在接力区的开始处，红色旗子设在接力区的结束处。

起跑

56.6 比赛须通过鸣枪、鸣炮、号角或类似设备开始起跑，发令须采用400米以上项目的起跑口令（技术规则16.2.2条）。

当参赛运动员人数众多时，应在起跑前5分钟、3分钟、1分钟时给予倒计时的提示。

比赛出发时，尽可能为各队提供一个出发区域，各队队员在各自的出发区域内排成一路纵队。在其他比赛中，运动员须按照组织者确定的方式在起跑线集合。"各就位"口令发出后，发令员应确保运动员的脚（或身体任何部分）没有触及起跑线或起跑线前的地面，方可发令开赛。

安全

56.7 越野跑组织者要确保运动员和裁判员的安全。

Drinking / Sponging and Refreshment Stations in Cross Country Races

56.8 Water and other suitable refreshments shall be available at the start and finish of all races. For all events, a drinking/sponging station shall be provided every lap, if weather conditions warrant such provision.

Note: Where conditions warrant, taking into account the nature of the event, the weather conditions and the state of fitness of the majority of the competitors, water and sponges may be placed at more regular intervals along the route.

Race Conduct

56.9 If the Referee is satisfied on the report of a Judge or Umpire or otherwise that an athlete has left the marked course thereby shortening the distance to be covered, they shall be disqualified.

The finish area shall be wide enough to enable several runners to sprint side by side and long enough to separate them at the finish.

Unless a Transponder Timing System is being used together with a backup system (such as a video recording) to check finishing orders, finish lanes ("funnels") should be set up some 8 to 10 metres after the finish line with a maximum width of 0.70-0.80m. Once in the funnels, the athletes must not be able to overtake one another. The funnels should be 35-40m long into which the athletes will be directed as they cross the finish line.

At the end of each funnel, officials will note the athletes' numbers/names and if applicable recover their Transponder Timing chips.

The funnels should have moveable ropes at the end at which the athletes enter, so that when one lane is full, the next rope can be drawn across behind the last athlete, to enable the next finisher to enter the new finish lane, and so on.

Judges and Timekeepers will additionally be placed on either side of the finish line and it is recommended that, in order to follow up any protest or appeal relative to the finishing order, an official with video recording equipment (if possible with a timing clock in sight) shall be assigned and placed a few metres after the finish line in order to record the order in which the athletes cross the line.

越野赛饮水/用水（海绵）和补给站

56.8　在所有比赛的起、终点要备有饮水和其他适当的补给品。对于所有项目的比赛，根据天气情况，每圈都应设置饮水/用水站。

注：在条件允许的情况下，可根据比赛性质、天气情况和大多数参赛者的身体状况，在赛道沿途更规律地间隔设置饮水、用水和/或补给站。

比赛行为

56.9　如果裁判长认可裁判员或检查员的报告，或通过其他方式确认，运动员离开了标定的赛道而缩短了比赛距离，将取消运动员的比赛资格。

终点区域要有足够的宽度，以确保多名冲刺运动员能并排跑进，还要有足够的长度，从而在终点处能够分开运动员。

除非同时使用芯片计时系统和备份系统（如视频录像）核查运动员通过终点的名次，否则应在终点线后的8~10米处，设置最大宽度为0.70~0.80米的终点（分流）通道。一旦运动员进入分流通道，运动员不得相互超越。分流漏斗长度应为35~40米，运动员在越过终点线时将被引导进入漏斗。

在每个分流漏斗通道出口，裁判员应记录每个运动员的号码和姓名，同时回收计时芯片。

在运动员进入分流漏斗的末端应设置可移动的围绳，这样当一条通道已满时，可以在最后一名运动员的身后拉上围绳，以使下一位完赛者能够进入新的终点通道，依此类推。

裁判员和计时员被安排在终点线的两侧，以跟进与比赛名次相关的任何抗议与申诉，并且建议安排一名视频录像裁判员在终点线后数米进行拍摄（如有可能，镜头里可以看到时钟），以便记录运动员冲线的顺序。

57. Mountain and Trail Races

Part One: General Rules

Course

57.1 General rules for the course, as follows:

57.1.1 The discipline of Mountain and Trail Running takes place on various types of natural terrain (sand, dirt roads, forest paths, single track footpaths, snow trails etc), and in various kinds of environment (mountains, forests, plains, deserts etc).

57.1.2 Races take place mostly on off-road surfaces, however sections of paved surfaces (e.g. asphalt, concrete, macadam etc.) are acceptable as a way to reach or link the trails of the course but should be kept to a minimum. Preferably existing roads and trails should be used.

57.1.3 For Mountain Races only, some special exceptions do exist where races are held on a paved surface but are only acceptable when there are large elevation changes on the course.

57.1.4 The course must be marked in such a way that no navigation skills will be required from the athletes. Trail races have no limits to distance or altitude gain or loss and the course must represent the logical discovery of a region.

57.1.5 Mountain Races are traditionally divided into "uphill" and "up and down" races. The average altitude gain or loss can vary from approx. 50 – 250 metres per kilometre, and the distances up to 42.2km.

Start

57.2 Mountain and Trail Races typically have mass starts. Runners can also start separated by gender or age-related categories.

57. 山地跑和野外跑

第一部分：通则

赛道

57.1 赛道通则，如下：

    57.1.1 一般情况下，山地跑和野外跑是在野外各种自然地形（如沙地、土路、林间小路、单向人行道、雪道等）和各种环境（如山地、森林、平原、沙漠等）中进行。

    57.1.2 比赛主要在越野路面上进行，但部分铺砌的路面（如沥青、混凝土、碎石等）可以作为到达或连接赛道的一种方式，应保持在最低限度。最好使用现有的道路和山间小径。

    57.1.3 仅在山地跑中，确实存在一些特殊情况，即只有当赛道上出现较大的海拔变化时才可以接受比赛在人工铺设的路面上进行。

    57.1.4 赛道须以运动员不需要导航技能的方式标记。野外跑对距离或海拔高度的增减没有限制，但赛道必须代表一个地区的地貌特点。

    57.1.5 山地跑按惯例被分为"上坡跑"和"上下坡跑"两种。赛道的平均海拔升高或降低可能有所不同，每公里50~250米，距离可达到42.2公里。

起跑

57.2 山地跑和越野跑通常有大规模的起跑，运动员可以按性别或年龄分类起跑。

Safety, Environment

57.3　Organising Committees shall ensure the safety of athletes and officials. Specific conditions, such as high altitude, changing weather conditions and available infrastructure should be respected. The event organiser is responsible for taking care for the environment when planning the course, during and after the competition.

Equipment

57.4　Mountain and Trail Races do not imply the use of a particular technique, alpine or other, or the use of specific equipment, such as mountaineering equipment. The use of hiking poles could be permitted at the discretion of the Race organisation. The Race Organiser may recommend or impose mandatory equipment due to the conditions expected to be encountered during the race, which will allow the athlete to avoid a situation of distress or, in the case of an accident, to give the alert and wait in safety for the arrival of help.

Race Organisation

57.5　The Organiser shall, prior to the race, publish specific regulations of the race including at minimum:

   57.5.1　Details of the organiser responsible (name, contact details)

   57.5.2　Programme of the event

   57.5.3　Detailed information about the technical characteristics of the race: total distance, total ascent/descent, description of the main difficulties of the track

   57.5.4　A detailed map of the course

   57.5.5　A detailed profile of the course

   57.5.6　Course marking criteria

   57.5.7　Location of the control posts and medical/aid stations (if applicable)

   57.5.8　Allowed, recommended or mandatory equipment (if applicable)

安全与环境

57.3 组织者要确保运动员和裁判员的安全，高度重视山地跑和越野跑的特殊条件和环境，如高海拔、变化无常的天气和可用的基础设施等。赛事组织者在规划赛道、比赛期间及比赛后都应注意保护环境。

比赛装备

57.4 山地跑和野外跑并不需要特定的高山或其他技术，或者使用特定的装备，如登山装备。比赛组织者可酌情决定是否允许使用登山杖。比赛组织者可根据比赛期间可能遇到的情况强制或建议使用强制性设备，这将使运动员避免遇险，或在发生事故时及时报警并安全地等待救援人员。

赛事组织

57.5 组织者要在比赛前公布比赛的详细安排，至少包括：

57.5.1 组织者负责人的详细信息（姓名、详细的联系方式）。

57.5.2 比赛活动安排。

57.5.3 有关比赛技术特点的详细信息：如总距离、上下坡的总量及对主要难度较大路段的描述。

57.5.4 赛道的详细地图。

57.5.5 赛道的详细介绍。

57.5.6 赛道的评估标准。

57.5.7 赛后控制中心和医疗/援助站的具体位置（如果适用）。

57.5.8 允许、建议或者强制性装备（如果适用）。

57.5.9 Safety rules to be followed

57.5.10 Penalties and disqualification rules

57.5.11 Time limit and cut-off barriers (if applicable)

Part Two: International Technical Rules

Scope of Application

57.6 While strongly recommended for all international championships, the application of the following technical rules is mandatory only in World Championships. For all Mountain and Trail Running Events other than World Championships, the specific event rules and/or the national rules shall have precedence. If a Mountain and Trail Running competition is held under "International Technical Rules", it must be specified in the event regulations. In all other cases, if a referee is appointed by a Member, an Area Association or the authority that oversees the competition, this person must ensure compliance with the general rules of Athletics but shall not enforce the following International Technical Rules.

Start

57.7 The commands for races longer than 400m shall be used (Rule 16.2.2 of the Technical Rules). In races which include a large number of athletes, five-minute, three-minute and one-minute warnings before the start of the race should be given. A 10s countdown to the start can also be given.

Race conduct

57.8 If the Referee is satisfied on the report of a judge, or Umpire, or otherwise, that an athlete:

57.8.1 has left the marked course thereby shortening the distance to be covered; or

57.8.2 receives any form of assistance such as pacing, or refreshments outside of the official aid stations; or

田径技术规则

57.5.9 应遵守的安全规则。

57.5.10 处罚和取消比赛资格的规则。

57.5.11 时间限制和使用阻拦运动员跑进的栅栏（如果适用）。

第二部分：国际技术规则

适用范围

57.6 虽然强烈建议在所有国际锦标赛中使用以下技术规则，但该技术规则仅在世界锦标赛中强制使用。对于除世界锦标赛外的所有山地跑和野外跑赛事，具体赛事规则和/或各国家相关协会的规则应优先采用。如果按照"国际技术规则"举办山地跑、野外跑的比赛，则须在竞赛规程中明确规定。在所有其他情况下，如果裁判长是由会员协会、地区协会或监督比赛的相关部门指派的，该裁判长必须遵守田径运动的一般规则，但不得强迫执行以下国际技术规则。

起跑

57.7 发令采用400米以上项目比赛的起跑口令（技术规则16.2.2条）。当参赛运动员人数众多时，应在起跑前5分钟、3分钟和1分钟给予倒计时提示。还可以进行10秒倒计时。

比赛行为

57.8 如果裁判长认可裁判员、检查员的报告或通过其他方式确认，运动员：

57.8.1 离开标定路线而缩短了比赛距离；或

57.8.2 接受任何形式的帮助，如速度分配，或在官方援助站以外的地方拿取补给品；或

57.8.3　　does not comply to any of the specific race regulations;

they shall be disqualified or get the penalty stated by the specific race regulations.

Specific Provisions for Trail Races

57.9　　Specific provisions for Trail Races, as follows:

　　57.9.1　　Sections of paved surfaces shall not exceed 25% of the total course.

　　57.9.2　　Races are classified by "km-effort"; the km-effort measure is the sum of the distance expressed in kilometres and a hundredth of the vertical gain expressed in meters, rounded to the nearest whole number (for example, the km-effort of a race of 65km and 3500m ascent is: 65 + 3500/100 = 100); accordingly races will be classified as follows:

Category	Km-effort
XXS	0 – 24
XS	25 – 44
S	45 – 74
M	75 – 114
L	115 – 154
XL	155 – 209
XXL	210 +

　　57.9.3　　World Championships races shall be based on the Short (S) and the Long (L) categories:

　　　　a.　　in the Short Race the distance must be between 35km and 45km and the minimum vertical gain 1500m or more;

　　　　b.　　in the Long Race the distance must be between 75km and 85km.

57.8.3 不遵守任何特定比赛规则；

他们将被取消比赛资格或接受具体竞赛规程规定的处罚。

野外跑的具体规定

57.9 野外跑的具体规定如下：

57.9.1 人工铺设路面部分不能超过比赛路线总距离的25%。

57.9.2 比赛按照"公里难度"进行分类；"公里难度"是以"公里"表示的距离和以"米"表示的百分之一的垂直爬升的总和，四舍五入到最接近的整数（如一场距离为65公里和爬坡高度为3500米的比赛为：65 + 3500/100 = 100）。因此，将比赛分类如下：

分类	公里难度参数
XXS（极短）	0 ~ 24
XS（超短）	25 ~ 44
S（短）	45 ~ 74
M（中）	75 ~ 114
L（长）	115 ~ 154
XL（超长）	155 ~ 209
XXL（极长）	210+

57.9.3 世界锦标赛将根据短距离（S）和长距离（L）进行分类：

a. 短距离比赛的距离必须为35 ~ 45公里，最小垂直爬升的增量为1500米或1500米以上。

b. 长距离比赛必须为75 ~ 85公里。

57.9.4　Competitions shall be based on the concept of self-sufficiency, meaning that the athletes will have to be autonomous between aid stations in terms of gear, communications, food and drink.

57.9.5　A survival blanket (140cm × 200cm minimum size), a whistle and a mobile phone are the minimum items the athletes have to carry at all times. However, the LOC may impose additional mandatory items due to the conditions expected to be encountered during the race.

57.9.6　Aid stations at official competitions shall be sufficiently spaced out so as to respect the "principle of self-sufficiency". The maximum total number of aid stations, excluding start and finish line, including water points, shall be no more than the km-effort points of the race divided by 15, rounded to the lower integer (example of a race with a km-effort of 58: 58/15=3.86, which means no more than 3 aid stations, excluding start and finish, are allowed).

Note (i): In a maximum of half of the above aid stations, rounded to the lower integer, food, drinks and personal assistance may be given (e.g. maximum total number of aid stations 3, 3/2=1.5, maximum number of aid stations where food and personal assistance may be given is 1); at the remaining aid stations only drinks, but no food nor personal assistance, may be given.

Note (ii): aid stations layout, where personal assistance is allowed, shall be organised in a way that allows each country to have an individual table or allocated space, identified with the flag of the Country (or Territory) and where their official staff will give assistance to the athletes. Tables shall be organised by alphabetical order, and each team is allowed to have a maximum of 2 officials per table.

Note (iii): Assistance to the athletes may only be given at complete (food and drinks) aid stations as defined above.

57.9.7　A finishing position resulting in a tie is permissible when clearly evident by the athletes' intention.

57.9.4　比赛基于自给自足的理念，运动员应在援助站之间自主安排其装备、通信、食品和饮料。

57.9.5　救生毯（最小尺寸为140厘米×200厘米）、口哨和手机是运动员必须始终携带的最低限度的物品。然而，根据比赛中可能遇到的特殊情况，当地组委会可能强制要求运动员携带其他额外物品。

57.9.6　正式比赛的援助站要有足够的间距，以遵守"自给自足原则"。除起、终点外，援助站的总数量，包括水站在内，不得超过公里难度参数除以15，取较小的整数为站点数目（以难度参数58为例，即58/15 = 3.86。意味着除了起、终点的援助站外，在赛道上设置的援助站不得超过3个）。

注（i）：在上述最多一半的援助站中，取较小的整数，可提供食物、饮料及自备补给（如援助站的最高总数为3，则3/2 = 1.5，取整数为站点数目。即可提供食物和自备补给的援助站最多为1个）；在剩下的援助站中，只能提供饮料，不得提供食物，也不得提供自备补给。

注（ii）：在允许自备补给的情况下，援助站应允许每个国家提供单独的桌子或分配适当的空间，并标有各个国家的国旗，以及官方的工作人员为运动员提供协助。桌子须按字母顺序依次摆放，每队每桌最多可允许2名官员。

注（iii）：对运动员的帮助只能由上述定义的完整的（有食品和饮料）援助站提供。

57.9.7　当运动员已清楚地表明其意图时，则允许在终点的位置名次并列。

Specific provisions for Mountain Races

57.10 Mountain Races are classified as follows:

    57.10.1 "Classic Uphill"

    57.10.2 "Classic Up and Down"

    57.10.3 "Vertical"

    57.10.4 "Long Distance"

    57.10.5 "Relays"

57.11 In all categories other than Vertical, the average incline should be between 5% (or 50m per km) and 25% (or 250m per km). The most preferable average incline is approximately 10%-15% provided that the course remains runnable. These limits do not apply to the Vertical category, where the incline shall be not less than 25%.

57.12 World Championships races shall be based on the following categories and distances:

    57.12.1 "Classic Uphill": 5km to 6km for U20 Men and U20 Women; 10km to 12km for Senior Men and Senior Women

    57.12.2 "Classic Up and Down": 5km to 6km for U20 Men and U20 Women; 10km to 12km for Senior Men and Senior Women

    57.12.3 "Vertical": it should have at least 1000m of positive vertical elevation and be measured in a certified manner to an accuracy of +/−10m.

    57.12.4 "Long Distance": the race distance should not exceed 42.2km and the nature of the course maybe mainly uphill or up and down. The total amount of ascent in the race should exceed 2000m. The men's winning time should be between two and four hours and less than 20% of the distance should be paved surfaces.

山地跑分类的具体规定

57.10　山地跑分类如下：

  57.10.1　"经典上坡跑"。

  57.10.2　"经典上下坡跑"。

  57.10.3　"垂直跑"。

  57.10.4　"长距离跑"。

  57.10.5　"接力跑"。

57.11　在除垂直山地跑外的所有类别中，赛道的平均坡度应在5%（或每公里50米）和25%（或每公里250米）之间。如果确保赛道能正常使用，最理想的平均坡度为10%~15%。另外，这些限制并不适用于垂直山地跑类别的赛道，在垂直山地跑赛道中，爬升坡度应不低于25%。

57.12　世界锦标赛须按照以下类别和距离进行：

  57.12.1　"经典上坡跑"：U20（男女）5~6公里；成年（男女）10~12公里。

  57.12.2　"经典上下坡跑"：U20（男女）5~6公里；成年（男女）10~12公里。

  57.12.3　"垂直山地跑"：应具有至少1000米的垂直标高，并以经认证的方式测量，精度为+/-10米。

  57.12.4　"长距离跑"：比赛距离不应超过42.2公里，自然赛道主要包括上坡或上下坡。赛道爬升的总高度应超过2000米。男子夺冠的时间应为2~4小时，人工铺设路面不得超过比赛距离的20%。

57.12.5 "Relays": Any course or team combinations, included mixed gender/age group, are possible as long as they are defined and communicated in advance. Distance and elevation gain of each individual leg should respect the parameters of the "Classic" categories.

Note: "Classic Uphill" and "Classic Up and Down" events traditionally alternate at each edition of the World Athletics Championships.

57.13 Water and other suitable refreshments shall be available at the start and finish of all races. Additional drinking/sponging stations should be provided at suitable places along the course.

57.12.5 "接力跑"：任何赛道和接力队的组合，包括混合性别或年龄组，只要赛前定义和沟通都是可能的。每棒的距离和爬坡高度的增加，应符合"经典"类别中参数的规定。

注："经典上坡跑"和"经典上下坡跑"赛事，通常在每一届世界锦标赛中交替进行。

57.13 在所有比赛的起、终点，都须为运动员提供饮水和其他适宜的补给。比赛过程中，应在沿途适当的地方设置另外的饮水/用水站。

WORLD ATHLETICS

ATHLETIC SHOE
REGULATION

运动鞋规程

Specific Definitions

The words and phrases used in these Regulations that are defined terms (denoted by initial capital letters) will have the meanings specified in the Constitution and the Generally Applicable Definitions, or (in respect of the following words and phrases) the following meanings:

"Applicable Competition" means a competition that holds a permit issued by either World Athletics, an Area Association or a National Federation where all relevant World Athletics' Rules and Regulations are complied with and consequently at which World Ranking Points(see: https://www.worldathletics.org/world-rankings/introduction and https://www.worldathletics.org/world-ranking-rules/basics) are obtained. For competitions holding a permit issued by their National Federation, in addition the National Federation must endorse the competition as being valid for World Athletics' statistical and results purposes.

"Applicable Persons" means the persons described in Rule 1 of the Integrity Code of Conduct.

"Athletes" means, unless specified otherwise in these Regulations, any Person who is entered for, or participating in, an Athletics event or competition of World Athletics, its Member federation or Area Associations by virtue of their agreement, membership, affiliation, authorisation, accreditation, entry or participation.

"Athlete Support Personnel" means, unless specified otherwise, any coach, trainer, manager, authorised Athlete Representative, agent, team staff, official, medical or para-medical personnel, parent or any other Person working with, treating or assisting an Athlete participating in, or preparing for, an Athletics event or competition.

"Athletic Shoe" means, unless otherwise specified, road, cross-country and/or track and field shoes.

"Available for Purchase" means an Athletic Shoe that satisfies the availability requirements and process set out in Appendix 4 (as amended from time to time).

"Bespoke Shoe" means an Athletic Shoe that is one-off made to order (i.e. that are only one of its kind) specifically for a single Athlete and is not Available for Purchase. Customised Shoes and/or Development Shoes are not Bespoke Shoes for the purposes of these Regulations.

专门定义

本规程中使用的定义术语（以首字母大写表示）具有章程和一般适用定义中规定的含义，或（就下列词语和短语而言）具有以下含义：

"适用的比赛"是指举办由世界田联、地区协会或国家联合会颁发许可证的比赛，并遵守所有相关世界田联规则和规程的比赛，从而获得世界排名积分（见https://www.worldathletics.org/world-rankings/introduction和https://www.worldathletics.org/world-ranking-rules/basics）。此外，对于举行其国家联合会颁发的许可证的比赛，国家联合会必须认可该比赛作为世界田联统计和成绩的有效依据。

"适用人员"是指诚信行为准则规则1条所述的人员。

"运动员"，除本规程另有规定外，是指凭借协议、会员资格、从属关系、授权、认证，报名或参与世界田联、其会员或地区协会、某项田径赛事或竞赛的任何人。

"运动员支持人员"，除非另有规定，是指任何教练员、训练师、经理、授权运动员代表、经纪人、团队工作人员、官员、医疗或准医疗人员、父母或任何其他与参加或准备体育赛事或比赛的运动员一起工作、为他们提供治疗或协助他们的人。

"运动鞋"，除非另有说明，是指路跑、越野和/或田径鞋。

"可供购买"是指满足附录4（不时修订）中规定的可用性要求和流程的运动鞋。

"全定制鞋"是指专门为一名运动员一次性定制的运动鞋（即只有一种），不提供购买。定制鞋和/或开发鞋并非本规程所指的全定制鞋。

"Call Room" means the room(s) at the event where Athletes gather immediately prior to their competition and entering the Field of Play.

"Chief Executive Officer (or their nominee)" means the chief executive officer of World Athletics or their Staff nominee.

"Customised Shoe" means an Existing Shoe or New Shoe that is Available for Purchase which has been adapted in accordance with Regulation 7 of these Regulations.

"Development Shoe" means an Athletic Shoe which has never been Available for Purchase and which a sports manufacturer is developing to bring to market and would like to conduct tests with their sponsored and/or supported Athletes (who agree to test the shoe) on issues for safety and performance before the shoe is Available for Purchase.

"Existing Shoe" means an Athletic Shoe that has been approved by the Chief Executive Officer (or their nominee) under Technical Rule 5 in force prior these Regulations coming into force or was worn before 1 January 2016, which is deemed to meet the requirements of these Regulations unless specified otherwise in these Regulations or by the Chief Executive Officer (or their nominee).

"Field of Play" means the area in which the Athlete participates and/or competes in their Competition (which for non-stadium events means the course) including the post event area and, if the Athlete wins a podium place, the area leading to the podium, the mixed zone, press conference areas and where a medal ceremony or victory laps take place.

"Independent Expert" means a biomechanical or other suitably qualified expert appointed by the Chief Executive Officer (or their nominee) from time to time to apply the technical requirements and protocols for the approval of Athletic Shoes set out in these Regulations.

"New Shoe" means an athletics shoe that meets the requirements of these Regulations and will be worn for the first time by an Athlete at an Applicable Competition and is not a Development Shoe.

"Orthotics" means a prescription medical device inserted in an Athletic Shoe to correct a biomechanical foot or other medical issue of an Athlete.

"Shoe Control" means the procedure by which an Athletic Shoe is checked pursuant to Regulation 14.5 of these Regulations.

"Shoe Control Officer" means a referee, judge or other competition official or a volunteer or member of Staff appointed to ensure that an Athletic Shoe is checked during Shoe Control.

"检录处"是指运动员在比赛开始前聚集并由此进入比赛场地的房间。

"首席执行官（或其指定人）"是指世界田联的首席执行官或其指定的工作人员。

"定制鞋"是指根据本规程7条进行改装的现有鞋或可供购买的新鞋。

"开发鞋"是指从未可供购买的运动鞋，但运动品制造商正在开发以推向市场，并希望在鞋可供购买之前与其赞助和/或支持的运动员（同意测试鞋的运动员）就安全性和性能问题进行测试。

"现有鞋"是指在本规程生效前已由首席执行官（或其指定人）根据有效的技术规则5条批准的运动鞋，或在2016年1月1日前穿的运动鞋，被视为符合本条例的要求，除非本条例另有规定或首席执行官（或其指定人）另有规定。

"比赛场地"是指运动员参加和/或比赛的区域（对于非体育场项目则意味着赛道），包括赛后区域，如果运动员获得领奖的名次，则包括通往领奖台的区域、混合区、新闻发布会区域以及举行颁奖仪式或获胜绕圈的区域。

"独立专家"是指由首席执行官（或其指定人）不时任命的生物力学或其他具有相关资格的专家，以适用本规程中规定的运动鞋批准的技术要求和协议。

"新鞋"是指符合本规程要求并将由运动员在适用的比赛中首次穿着的运动鞋，而不是开发鞋。

"矫形器"是指插入运动鞋中的处方医疗设备，用于矫正运动员足部的生物力学或其他医学方面的问题。

"运动鞋控制"是指根据本规程14.5条对运动鞋进行检查的程序。

"运动鞋控制官员"指裁判长、裁判或其他竞赛官员、志愿者或工作人员，被任命在运动鞋控制期间确保运动鞋得到检查。

"Staff" means any person employed or engaged by World Athletics to undertake work for it, or on its behalf (including those employed or engaged to work with the Integrity Unit, unless specified otherwise).

"Warm-Up Area" means the area where Athlete may warm up, train and prepare themselves prior to competing.

"World Athletics Series Event" or "WAS Event" means the World Athletics Championships, the World Indoor Championships, the World Athletics Relays, the World Athletics U20 Championships, the World Athletics Road Running Championships, the World Athletics Race Walking Team Championships and the World Athletics Cross-Country Championships.

1. Overview

1.1 These Regulations seek to implement the objects of Articles 4.1 (a), (c), (d) and (e) of the Constitution and Rule 5.2 of the Technical Rules by establishing the requirements and procedures by which Athletic Shoes to be worn in Applicable Competitions are submitted for approval to World Athletics.

1.2 Without prejudice to the specific limitations and requirements of these Regulations, these Regulations seek to balance the following principles:

   1.2.1 fairness within the sport of Athletics;

   1.2.2 measures that support health & safety (including injury prevention) of Athletes upon whom high levels of physical and mental demands are placed;

   1.2.3 performances (including records) in Athletics are achieved through the primacy of human endeavour over technology in Athletic Shoes and advances in the same (e.g. to allow for meaningful competition); and

   1.2.4 acknowledging that Athletes wish to compete in 'high quality', 'innovative' and 'leading' Athletic Shoes.

1.3 The implications of the principles referred to in Regulation 1.2 above are reflected in these Regulations and arise from World Athletics' review of Athletic Shoes only. These Regulations will continue to be reviewed and amended from to time to reflect the constantly changing nature of technological and other developments in Athletic Shoes.

"工作人员"是指世界田联雇用或聘用为其从事工作或代表其从事工作的任何人员（包括雇用或聘用为诚信部门的人员，除非另有规定）。

"热身场地"是指运动员在比赛前热身、训练和准备的区域。

"世界田径系列赛"或"WAS赛"是指世界田径锦标赛、世界田径室内锦标赛、世界田径接力赛、世界田径U20锦标赛、世界田径路跑锦标赛、世界田径竞走团体锦标赛和世界田径越野锦标赛。

1. **概述**

1.1 本规程旨在通过规定在适用的比赛中针对所穿运动鞋向世界田联提交批准的要求和程序，实现章程4.1（a）（c）（d）和（e）及技术规则5.2条的目标。

1.2 在无损于本规程的具体限制和要求的前提下，本规程力求平衡以下原则：

    1.2.1 田径运动中的公平；

    1.2.2 支持有高水平身心需求的运动员的健康和安全（包括伤害预防）措施；

    1.2.3 田径运动中的成绩（包括纪录）是通过人类努力在运动鞋技术上的进步（如允许有意义的竞争）实现的；和

    1.2.4 承认运动员希望穿着"高质量""创新"和"领先"的运动鞋参加比赛。

1.3 上述规程1.2条提到的原则的含义反映在这些规程中，并且仅来自世界田联对运动鞋的审查。这些规程将不时地继续审查和修订，以反映运动鞋技术和其他发展的、不断变化的性质。

2. Purpose

2.1 The purpose of these Regulations is to:

    2.1.1 establish a transparent, objective, feasible, and fair set of requirements and procedures;

    2.1.2 identify the actions, timescales, criteria, and the application and decision- making processes and procedures for approving Athletic Shoes in Applicable Competitions; and

    2.1.3 ensure that all Applicable Persons involved in such processes and procedures comply with the Integrity Code of Conduct.

3. Application

3.1 These Regulations apply to:

    3.1.1 all Applicable Competitions;

    3.1.2 all Athletes competing in Applicable Competitions; and

    3.1.3 all Applicable Persons, including World Athletics Officials, Area Officials, and Staff.

3.2 Without limiting the above:

    3.2.1 Athletes competing in Applicable Competitions will comply with and respect these Regulations; and

    3.2.2 each Member Federation is responsible for the activities and conduct of Athletes throughout the application and decision-making process; and

    3.2.3 where appointed by an Athlete or Member Federation to submit information, approval requests, or do any act under these Regulations, their representatives (including sports manufacturers who either support or sponsor them) must also comply with these Regulations. However, appointing a representative shall not avoid the Athletes' or Member Federations' obligations to comply with these Regulations and the Athlete shall procure that its representatives (including sports manufacturers who either support of sponsor them) comply with these Regulations.

2. **目的**

2.1 本规程的目的是：

  2.1.1 建立一套透明、客观、可行和公平的要求和程序；

  2.1.2 确定在适用的比赛中批准运动鞋的行动、时间表、标准以及申请和决策过程与程序；和

  2.1.3 确保参与此类流程和程序的所有适用人员均遵守诚信行为准则。

3. **适用**

3.1 本规程适用于：

  3.1.1 所有适用的比赛；

  3.1.2 所有参加适用比赛的运动员；和

  3.1.3 所有适用人员，包括世界田联官员、地区官员和工作人员。

3.2 在不限制以上内容的情况下：

  3.2.1 参加适用比赛的运动员将遵守并尊重本规程；和

  3.2.2 每个会员协会负责运动员在整个申请和决策过程中的活动和行为；和

  3.2.3 如果运动员或会员协会指定代表提交信息、批准要求或根据本规程做任何行动，他们（包括资助或赞助他们的运动用品制造商）也必须遵守本规程。但是，指定代表不得免除运动员或会员协会遵守这些规程的义务，运动员应促使其代表（包括资助或赞助他们的运动用品制造商）遵守这些规程。

4. Bare Foot and Athletic Shoes

4.1 Where an Athlete competes in Athletic Shoes, their primary purposes are to give protection and stability to the feet and a grip on the ground.

4.2 Unless otherwise stated, all Athletic Shoes must meet the limits and requirements set out in these Regulations.

5. Existing Shoes

5.1 Unless requested by the Chief Executive Officer (or their nominee), an Existing Shoe does not need to be submitted to World Athletics for approval under these Regulations and be deemed approved by World Athletics.

5.2 If an Existing Shoe is customised, then it must comply with Regulation 7.

5.3 From 1 November 2024, an Existing Shoe with a sole greater than the maximum thicknesses set out in the new sole thickness table in Appendix 3, and in force from the same date, is no longer approved and cannot be worn in Applicable Competitions.

6. New Shoes

6.1 All New Shoes prior to being worn by an Athlete for the first time in an Applicable Competition must be approved by World Athletics in accordance with the process set out in Appendix 1.

6.2 If a New Shoe is customised, then it must comply with Regulation 7.

7. Customised Shoes, Inserts and Additions

7.1 Customised Shoes are permitted to be worn in Applicable Competitions provided that:

7.1.1 any proposal to customise an Existing Shoe or New Shoe needs to be submitted to World Athletics for approval in accordance with the process set out in Appendix 1; and

7.1.2 within the proposal, the reason(s) for the customisation of the Existing Shoe or New Shoe must also be submitted.

7.2 Subject always to approval of the Chief Executive Officer (or their nominee) under Regulation 7.1, the following customisations for medical and/or safety

4. 赤脚和运动鞋

4.1　当运动员穿着运动鞋参加比赛时，主要目的是为脚提供保护和稳定性以及在地面上的抓地力。

4.2　除非另有说明，否则所有运动鞋必须符合本规程规定的限制和要求。

5. 现有的鞋子

5.1　除非首席执行官（或其指定人）提出要求，现有鞋不需要根据本规则提交给世界田联审批，并被视为世界田联批准。

5.2　如果现有鞋是定制的，那么它必须符合规程7条。

5.3　从2024年11月1日起，鞋底超过附录3新鞋底厚度表中规定的最大厚度的现有鞋将不再被批准，并且不能在适用的比赛中穿着。

6. 新鞋

6.1　运动员第一次在适用的比赛中穿的所有新鞋必须根据附录1中规定的程序获得世界田联的批准。

6.2　如果新鞋是定制的，那么它必须符合规程7条。

7. 定制鞋、填充物和附加物

7.1　在适用的比赛中允许穿定制鞋，但条件是：

  7.1.1　任何定制现有鞋或新鞋的建议都需要按照附录1中规定的流程提交世界田联批准；和

  7.1.2　在建议书内，必须提交现有鞋或新鞋的定制理由。

7.2　根据规程7.1条，须经首席执行官（或其指定人）批准，出于医疗和/或安全原因，允许进行以下定制：

reasons are permissible:

- 7.2.1 changes to the construction of the sole and/or maximum thickness of the sole provided always that the maximum thickness does not go beyond the limits set out in Appendix 3;

- 7.2.2 customising a non-spike shoe into a spike shoe can only be made to an Existing Shoe or New Shoe;

- 7.2.3 changing an upper of an Existing Shoe or New Shoe with an upper from another Existing Shoe or New Shoe or adding a new upper;

- 7.2.4 adding inner soles, other insertions and additions to an Athletic Shoe but only in the following circumstances:

    a. the additional inner sole or insertion is a removable Orthotic (i.e. it cannot be permanently fixed inside the shoe); or

    b. the addition is a heel raise or heel cap (e.g. to jumping shoes) or a brace or strap (e.g. to thrower shoes);

- 7.2.5 for the avoidance of doubt, the use of an Orthotic, a heel raise or heel cap pursuant to Regulation 7.2.4 above does not fall within the maximum thickness for soles set out in the table in Appendix 3, with the intent that any other type of additional inner soles, insertions or additions are not permitted.

7.3 For the avoidance, of doubt, changes to the colour and/or the look of an Existing Shoe or New Shoe or an Athlete taping their shoe (for example taping the outside of a throwing shoe) are not customisations, are permitted and do not require approval.

7.4 Customised Shoes are not required to be made Available for Purchase in accordance with Regulation 13 of these Regulations because, as required by these Regulations, the underlying standard model must be Available for Purchase.

8. Development Shoes

8.1 A Development Shoe cannot be worn by an Athlete in an Applicable

7.2.1 更改鞋底结构和/或鞋底最大厚度，但最大厚度不得超过附录3规定的限制；

7.2.2 将无钉鞋定制为钉鞋只能用于现有鞋或新鞋；

7.2.3 用另一个现有鞋或新鞋的鞋面替换现有鞋或新鞋的鞋面，或添加新的鞋面；

7.2.4 在运动鞋中添加内底、其他填充物和附加物，但仅限在以下情况：

    a. 所述附加内底或填充物为可拆卸的矫形器（如不能永久固定在鞋内）；或

    b. 填充物是提高鞋跟、鞋后套（如跳鞋）、支撑或绑带（如投掷鞋）。

7.2.5 为避免疑问，根据上述规程7.2.4条，矫形器、提高鞋跟或鞋后套不属于附录3表中鞋底最大厚度范围。意图是说明任何其他类型的附加内底、填充物或附加物都是不被允许的。

7.3 为避免疑问，现有鞋或新鞋的颜色和/或外观发生变化，或者运动员在鞋上贴上胶带，而不是定制（如贴在投掷鞋的外面），是允许的，不需要批准。

7.4 根据本规程13条，定制鞋不要求可供购买，因为根据本规程的要求，基础标准型号必须可供购买。

8. 开发鞋

8.1 未经世界田联根据附录1和附录2事先书面批准，运动员不得在适用的比赛中穿开发鞋。

8.2 If approved, a Development Shoe may be worn by an Athlete for a maximum period of 12 months starting from the date when an Athlete proposes to wear the Development Shoe for the first time in an Applicable Competition. The Development Shoe can only be worn within this 12-month period.

8.3 Development Shoes are:

    8.3.1 not required to be made Available for Purchase in accordance with Regulation 13; and

    8.3.2 not permitted to be worn at the World Athletics Series Events and the Olympic Games.

9. Bespoke Shoes

9.1 Bespoke Shoes are not permitted to be worn in any Applicable Competition.

10. Technical Requirements for Athletic Shoes

10.1 Unless specifically agreed by the Chief Executive Officer (or their nominee) in writing, any Athletic Shoe worn in Applicable Competitions must, at the points set out in Regulations 10.3 and 10.4 below, have a sole with a maximum thickness as set out in the table in Appendix 3. For the avoidance of doubt, the maximum thickness of the soles excludes the thickness of an additional inner sole, other insertion or addition that are inserted in accordance with Regulation 7.

10.2 The sole of the shoe (including the part beneath the heel of the Athletic Shoe) may have grooves, ridges, indentations or protuberances, provided these features are constructed of the same or similar material to the basic sole itself.

10.3 The thickness of the sole will be measured at the centre of the forefoot and the centre heel of the Athletic Shoe as the distance between the inside top

Figure (a) – Measuring the thickness of the sole

8.2　如果获得批准，运动员可以穿着开发鞋最长12个月，从运动员提议在适用的比赛中首次穿着开发鞋之日起算。开发鞋只能在这12个月内穿着。

8.3　开发鞋是：

8.3.1　无须根据本规程13条规定可供购买；和

8.3.2　不允许在世界田联系列赛和奥运会上穿着。

9.　全定制鞋

9.1　不允许在任何适用的比赛中穿着全定制鞋。

10.　运动鞋的技术要求

10.1　除非得到首席执行官（或其指定人）的书面特别同意，在相关的比赛中所穿的任何运动鞋，必须按照规程10.3条和10.4条的规定，具有附录3表中所列的最大鞋底厚度。为避免产生疑问，鞋底的最大厚度不包括附加内鞋底的厚度、根据规程7条插入的其他填充物或附加物的厚度。

10.2　鞋底（包括运动鞋后跟以下的部分）可以有凹槽、隆起、凹痕或突起，只要这些是由与主要的鞋底本身相同或类似的材料构成的。

10.3　鞋底的厚度将在运动鞋的前脚掌中心和后跟中心分别测量，分别为前脚掌中心和后跟中心的内侧顶面与外侧底面平面之间的距离。该测量包括上述特征。如图（a）：

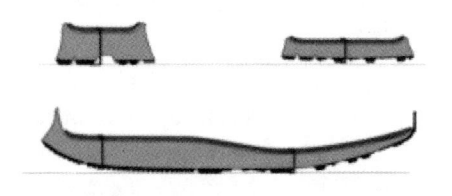

运动鞋规程10条图（a）　测量鞋底厚度

side and the plane of the outside under side at the centre of the forefoot and heel respectively. This measurement includes the above-mentioned features. See Figure (a) below:

10.4 The centre of the forefoot of the Athletic Shoe is the centre point of the shoe at 75% of its internal length. The centre of the heel of the Athletic Shoe is the centre point of the hoe at 12% of its internal length. See Figure (b), below. For a standard sample unisex size 42 (EUR), the centre of the forefoot of the Athletic Shoe will be the centre point of the shoe approximately 203mm from the inside back of the shoe, and the centre of the heel of the Athletic Shoe will be the centre point of the shoe approximately 32mm from the inside back of the shoe. The thickness of the sole outside of these points is not relevant for the purposes of meeting the technical requirements of these Regulations.

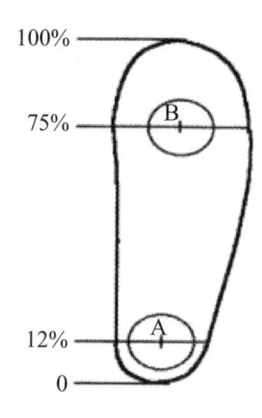

Figure (b) – Location for measurement of the centre of the forefoot and heel

10.5 World Athletics acknowledges that an Athletic Shoe above that standard sample size might contain a marginally thicker sole than that of a standard sample size shoe of the same make and model, which marginal increase in sole thickness is only attributable to the larger size of the shoe. Such marginal increases will be disregarded for the purposes of confirming compliance with these Rules.

10.6 Until further notice, unless in exceptional circumstances and specifically agreed by the Competition Commission in writing, any Athletic Shoe used in Applicable Competitions:

  10.6.1 (except where Regulation 10.6.3 applies) must not contain more than one rigid structure (e.g. plate, blade etc.) whether that structure runs the full length of the shoe or only part of the length of the shoe;

  10.6.2 the one rigid structure referred to in Regulation 10.6.1 may be in more than one part, but those parts must be located in one plane (i.e. must not be stacked above each other, must not overlap);

  10.6.3 may contain one additional rigid structure or other mechanism (e.g. plate, blade etc.) only where used solely to attach spikes to

10.4　运动鞋前脚掌的中心是鞋内长度75%的中心点。运动鞋鞋跟的中心是鞋内长度12%的中心点。如图（b）。对于42码（欧码）男女通用的标准样品，运动鞋前脚掌的中心距离鞋后内侧约203毫米，运动鞋后跟的中心点距离鞋后内侧约32毫米。这些点之外的鞋底厚度与满足本规程的技术要求无关。

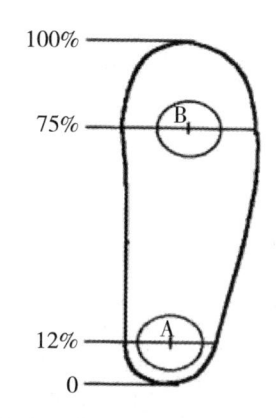

运动鞋规程10条图（b）　测量前脚掌和脚后跟中心的位置

10.5　世界田联承认，高于该标准样本尺码的运动鞋鞋底可能比相同品牌和型号的标准样本尺码鞋的鞋底稍厚，鞋底厚度的边际增加仅是因为鞋码较大。出于确认遵守本规程的目的，将忽略此类边际增加。

10.6　在进一步通知之前，除非有特殊情况并得到竞赛委员会的书面明确同意，在适用的比赛中使用的任何运动鞋：

　　10.6.1　（除非适用规程10.6.3条）不得包含一个以上的刚性结构（如板、薄片等），无论该结构是贯穿鞋的整个长度还是只贯穿鞋的部分长度；

　　10.6.2　规程10.6.1条中提到的一个刚性结构可以有多个部分，但这些部分必须位于一个平面上（即不得相互堆叠及重叠）；

　　10.6.3　可能包含一个额外的刚性结构或其他装置（如板、薄片等），仅用于将鞋钉连接到鞋的外底面的情况。为避免疑问，用于连接鞋钉的附加刚性结构不能是规程10.6.1条中提及的刚性结构的延续；

the outer underside of the shoe. For the avoidance of doubt, the additional rigid structure to attach spikes cannot be a continuation of the rigid structure referred to in Regulation 10.6.1;

10.6.4　must not contain any embedded 'sensing or intelligent' technology whatsoever. This does not prevent heart rate or speed distance monitors or stride sensors carried or worn personally by an Athlete pursuant to Technical Rule 6.4.4;

10.6.5　must have a sole with a maximum thickness as set out in the table in Appendix 3.

11. Athletic Shoes: Spikes

11.1　The sole of the shoe (including the part beneath the heel of the Athletic Shoe) may be so constructed as to provide for the use of up to 11 spikes.

11.2　Any number of spikes up to 11 may be used, but the number of spike positions must not exceed 11.

11.3　That part of each spike which projects from the sole or the heel will not exceed 9mm (for indoor 6mm) except in the High Jump and Javelin Throw, where it must not exceed 12mm. The spike must be so constructed that it will, at least for the half of its length closest to the tip, fit through a square sided 4mm gauge. If the track manufacturer or the stadium operator mandates a lesser maximum, or prohibits the use of certain shaped spikes, this will be applied and the Athletes notified accordingly. The surface (outdoor or indoor) must be suitable for accepting the spikes permitted under this Regulation 11.

11.4　For Cross-Country competitions, the specific regulations or the Technical Delegates may allow an increased length of the sizes of the spikes of the shoes depending on the surface (s) of the course.

12. Independent Expert

12.1　Subject to these Regulations, the Independent Expert will have the following responsibilities and authority:

10.6.4 不得包含任何嵌入式"传感或智能"技术。这并不妨碍运动员根据技术规则6.4.4条个人携带或佩戴的心率监测仪、速度距离监测器或步幅传感器；

10.6.5 必须具有附录3表格中规定的鞋底的最大厚度。

11. 运动鞋：鞋钉

11.1 鞋底（包括运动鞋后跟下方的部分）的构造可以供多达11个鞋钉的使用。

11.2 可以使用不超过11枚的任何数量的鞋钉，但鞋钉钉座不得超过11个。

11.3 每个鞋钉从鞋底或鞋跟突出的部分不得超过9毫米（室内为6毫米），但在跳高和标枪项目中不得超过12毫米。鞋钉的构造必须使其至少在最靠近尖端的一半长度上能够穿过4毫米的方形量规。如果跑道制造商或体育场运营商规定了较低的鞋钉长度最大值，或禁止使用某些形状的鞋钉，此规定将被应用并相应地通知运动员。场地层面（室外或室内）必须适合接受本规程11条允许的鞋钉。

11.4 对于越野比赛，具体规程或技术代表可能会根据赛道层面允许增加鞋钉的长度。

12. 独立专家

12.1 在遵守本规程的前提下，独立专家将具有以下职责和权利：

12.1.1 检查运动鞋实物是否符合本规程的技术要求（如有必要，包括对运动鞋进行切割）；

12.1.1 to check if the physical Athletic Shoe complies with the technical requirements of these Regulations (which includes, if necessary, cutting up the Athletic Shoe);

12.1.2 to review and evaluate physical Existing Shoes, New Shoes, Development Shoes or Customised Shoe and/or their specifications against the criteria and requirements set out in these Regulations;

12.1.3 to liaise with and seek input from the Chief Executive Officer (or their nominee) concerning their tasks;

12.1.4 to present the results of their reviews and evaluations to the Chief Executive Officer (or their nominee); and

12.1.5 to carry out such other tasks as instructed by the Chief Executive Officer (or their nominee) from time to time.

13. Availability Scheme

13.1 Existing Shoes and New Shoes must be Available for Purchase by any Athletes participating in Applicable Competitions.

13.2 Where an Athlete proposes to wear a New Shoe at an Applicable Competition, if approved by World Athletics in accordance with these Regulations, the New Shoe must be made Available for Purchase by the relevant sport manufacturer no later than one month prior to the start date of the first Applicable Competition at which the Athlete proposes to wear the New Shoe unless otherwise agreed in writing by the Chief Executive Officer (or their nominee).

13.3 In accordance with Regulation 13.2 above, the Chief Executive Officer (or their nominee) must be notified where and how the New Shoe is or will be made Available for Purchase at the time of seeking approval in accordance with Regulation 6 above and Appendix 1 below.

13.4 The Chief Executive Officer (or their nominee) may, on written request, require evidence from the sports manufacturer that the New Shoe is or will be Available for Purchase.

13.5 The procedure for the Availability Scheme is set out in Appendix 4.

14. Compliance

14.1 Athletes may be subject to Shoe Control at any time before, during or after an Applicable Competition and immediately before or immediately after

12.1.2 根据本规程的标准和要求，审查及评估现有实物鞋、新鞋、开发鞋或定制鞋和/或其规格；

12.1.3 就其工作事宜与首席执行官（或其指定人）联络，并征询他们的意见；

12.1.4 向首席执行官（或其指定人）提交审查及评估的结果；和

12.1.5 执行首席执行官（或其指定人）不时指示的其他任务。

13. 可用性方案

13.1 现有鞋和新鞋必须可供参加适用的比赛的任何运动员购买。

13.2 如果运动员计划在适用的比赛中穿新鞋，世界田联根据本规程批准，除非首席执行官（或其指定人）另有书面同意，新鞋必须在运动员计划穿的第一场适用的比赛开始日期前不迟于一个月由相关运动用品制造商提供给运动员购买。

13.3 根据规程13.2条规定，在根据规程6条和附录1寻求批准时，必须通知首席执行官（或其指定人）在何处及将如何购买新鞋。

13.4 首席执行官（或其指定人）可以书面请求，要求运动鞋制造商提供新鞋现在或将来可供购买的证据。

13.5 可用性方案的程序见附录4。

14. 合规

14.1 运动员在适用的比赛之前、期间或之后的任何时间，以及比赛之前或之后的任何时间，都可能接受运动鞋检查，具体由赛事组织者和/或首席执行官（或其指定人）自行决定。首席执行官（或其指定人）可以发布与这些法规一致的进一步的运动鞋控制程序。

competing at the discretion of the event organiser and/or Chief Executive Officer (or their nominee). The Chief Executive Officer (or their nominee) may publish further Shoe Control procedures that are consistent with these Regulations.

14.2 An Athlete subject to Shoe Control:

> 14.2.1 must comply with the reasonable directions given by the Shoe Control Officer or other authorised person conducting Shoe Control;
>
> 14.2.2 may be required at any time;
>
> > a. to confirm the Athletic Shoe they are wearing;
> >
> > b. to give their Athletic Shoes to the Shoe Control Officer for the purpose of checking (e.g. photographing, measuring etc.) the information which will be sent to World Athletics for verification; and
>
> 14.2.3 where they have finished competing, give their Athletic Shoe to the Referee or Chief Executive Officer (or their nominee) for further examination and investigation (which includes, if necessary, cutting up the Athletic Shoe). The Athletic Shoe will be shipped to the Independent Expert and returned (if practicable) to the Athlete in accordance with Regulation 14.9.4.

14.3 Where an Athlete achieves a World Record (as referred to at Rules 31 to 35 of the Competition Rules) the Athlete will be subject to the procedure at Regulation 14.2.

14.4 Unless an Athlete is directed by the Referee to give them their Athletic Shoe in accordance with Regulations 14.5 to 14.7, Athletes must always keep their Athletic Shoe in their possession in the Warm-up Area, Call Room and Field of Play, and must not give their shoes to any Athlete Support Personnel or throw their Athletic Shoes into the crowd at any time. For the avoidance of doubt, this includes after the Athlete has finished competing but is still to

14.2 受运动鞋控制约束的运动员：

  14.2.1 必须遵守运动鞋控制官员或其他进行运动鞋控制授权人员发出的合理指示；

  14.2.2 可在任何时候被要求：

    a. 确认他们所穿的运动鞋；

    b. 将运动鞋交给运动鞋控制官员以核对（如拍照、测量等）资料，并将资料送交世界田联核对；和

  14.2.3 运动员结束比赛后，将运动鞋交给裁判长或首席执行官（或其指定人）进一步检查和调查（如有必要，包括切开运动鞋）。运动鞋将被运送给独立专家，并根据规程14.9.4条退还（如果可行的话）给运动员。

14.3 如果运动员创造了世界纪录（如竞赛规则31—35条所述），该运动员需要遵守规程14.2条的程序。

14.4 除非裁判长根据规程14.5—14.7条的规定指示运动员将运动鞋交给他们，否则运动员在热身区、检录室和比赛场地必须始终保管运动鞋，并且不得将鞋交给任何运动员支持人员或在任何时候将运动鞋扔进人群。为免生疑问，这包括在运动员结束比赛后仍需完成的任何赛后流程。

14.5 当裁判长有理由认为运动鞋或特定技术可能不符合本规程的文字或精神时，裁判长可以按照规程14.6条和14.7条的规定执行。

	complete any post competition procedures.
14.5	Where the Referee has reason to believe that an Athletic Shoe or specific technology may not comply with the letter or spirit of these Regulations, they may act in accordance with Regulations 14.6 and 14.7.
14.6	If either before or at an Applicable Competition, the status of an Athletic Shoe is not established or is otherwise unclear, the Referee may, in their discretion, permit the Athlete to compete, but after competing the Athletic Shoe must be given to the Referee pursuant to Regulation 14.7 for further examination and investigation by an Independent Expert. Where the Referee has permitted the Athlete to compete pursuant to this Regulation 14.6, the Athlete's result will be classified as "Uncertified" ("UNC TR5.2"). However, where it has already been declared that an Athletic Shoe does not comply with the letter or spirit of these Regulations, the relevant Referee will act as soon as reasonably practical in accordance with Regulation 15.1.
14.7	Pursuant to Regulation 14.5, the Referee may request the Athlete immediately to hand over the shoe to the Referee at the conclusion of the event for further examination and investigation by an Independent Expert. Pending further examination and investigation pursuant to this Regulation 14.7 the use of that Athletic Shoe or technology in Applicable Competitions is prohibited.
14.8	Where a Referee exercises their discretion under Regulation 14.6 and permits the Athlete to compete, but the Athlete intends to subsequently compete in later rounds of the same event or in other events during the same competition, the Referee will ensure the Athletic Shoe is available to the Athlete to use in each such subsequent event. How, when and on what conditions the shoe is made available to the athlete during the competition are at the Referees' discretion.
14.9	For the avoidance of doubt and in addition to the powers set out above, the Chief Executive Officer (or their nominee), acting reasonably, reserves the right:

    14.9.1   to issue a written direction to the Referee to act in accordance with Regulations 14.5, 14.6 and/or 14.7;

    14.9.2   to instruct at any time that the Athlete give their Athletic Shoe to the Referee and/or for further examination and investigation;

14.6 如果在适用的比赛前或比赛中，运动鞋的状况尚未确定或不清楚，裁判长可以自行决定允许运动员参赛，但在比赛后，运动鞋必须根据规程14.7条的规定交给裁判长，由独立专家进行进一步审查和调查。如果裁判长允许运动员根据本规程14.6条进行比赛，运动员的成绩将被列为"未经认证"（"UNC TR5.2"）。然而，如果运动鞋已经被宣布不符合本规程的文字或精神，相关裁判长在合理可行的情况下，将根据规程15.1条采取行动。

14.7 根据规程14.5条的规定，裁判长可要求运动员在比赛结束后立即将鞋交给裁判长，由独立专家进行进一步审查和调查。在根据本规程14.7条进行进一步审查和调查之前，禁止在适用的比赛中使用该运动鞋或技术。

14.8 如果裁判长根据规程14.6条行使其自由裁量权，允许运动员参加比赛，但该运动员打算随后参加同一项目的后续比赛或同一比赛期间的其他项目，裁判长应确保该运动员在后续的每个项目中都能使用该运动鞋。比赛期间如何、何时以及在何种条件下向运动员提供鞋子由裁判长决定。

14.9 为避免疑问，除上述权利外，首席执行官（或其指定人）在合理行事的情况下，保留以下权利：

14.9.1 向裁判长发出书面指示，要求其按照规程 14.5条、14.6条和/或14.7条执行；

14.9.2 在任何时候指示运动员将运动鞋交给裁判长和/或进行进一步审查与调查；

14.9.3 如运动鞋尚未移交，或尚未接受进一步审查及调查，则要求运动员将运动鞋移交首席执行官（或其指定人）进行进一步审查及调查；和

14.9.3　where the Athletic Shoe has not already been handed over for, or has not already been subject to further examination and investigation, to request the Athlete to hand over to the Chief Executive Officer (or their nominee) their Athletic Shoe for further examination and investigation; and

14.9.4　the costs of shipping the Athletic Shoe for further examination and investigation to World Athletics or the Independent Expert must be borne by the event organiser who will send them immediately to the address notified by the Chief Executive Officer (or their nominee) and provide a copy of the shipping documents and tracking number. Once the examination and investigation has been completed World Athletics will, if practicable, arrange for the return of the Athletic Shoe to Athlete.

15. Breaches and Sanctions

15.1　If an Athlete:

15.1.1　is found by either the Referee or Shoe Control Officer to be wearing an Athletic Shoe that does not comply with these Regulations; or

15.1.2　does not comply with any direction or instruction of the Referee under these Regulations; or

15.1.3　does not present themselves to Shoe Control when requested;

the Athlete may be disqualified.

15.2　If an Athlete disqualified pursuant to Regulation 15.1 has already competed, then such disqualification has all resulting consequences for the Athlete, including but not limited to declaring the Athlete's performance as invalid for non-compliance with these Regulations, the forfeiture of all titles, awards, medals, points and prize and appearance money.

15.3　In addition to any disqualification of the Athlete by a Referee, or if at any time it is found that either an Athlete or their representatives (including sports manufacturers who support or sponsor them) and/or Member Federation has been acting or, has acted against the letter or spirit of these Regulations (including Technical Rule 5 in force prior to these Regulations coming into force or any Rules thereover), then the Chief Executive Officer (or their

14.9.4 将运动鞋运送给世界田联或独立专家进行进一步审查和调查的费用必须由赛事组织者承担，他们需要立即将运动鞋发送到首席执行官（或其指定人）通知的地址，并提供邮寄文件副本和跟踪号码。一旦审查和调查完成，世界田联将在可行的情况下安排将运动鞋退还给运动员。

15. 违规行为和制裁

15.1 如果运动员：

15.1.1 被裁判长或运动鞋控制人员发现所穿的运动鞋不符合本规程；或

15.1.2 不遵守裁判长根据本规程作出的任何指导或指示；或

15.1.3 未按要求到运动鞋控制处报到；

运动员可能被取消比赛资格。

15.2 如果根据规程15.1条被取消比赛资格的运动员已经参加比赛，则该取消资格将对运动员产生所有后果，包括但不限于宣布运动员的成绩因不遵守这些规程而无效，取消所有名次及没收所有奖励、奖牌、积分、奖金和出场费。

15.3 除了裁判员取消运动员比赛资格，在任何时候发现运动员或其代表（包括资助或赞助他们的运动用品制造商）和/或会员协会一直在采取行动或采取行动违反了本规程的文字或精神（包括在这些规程生效之前生效的技术规则5条或任何相关规则），则首席执行官（或其指定人）保留实施一系列制裁的权利，包括但不限于：

15.3.1 向运动员和/或会员协会发出警告；

15.3.2 对运动员和/或其会员协会处以罚款；

nominee) reserves the right to apply a range of sanctions including but not limited to:

15.3.1 issuing a warning to the Athlete and/or Member Federation;

15.3.2 imposing a fine on the Athlete and/or their Member Federation;

15.3.3 disqualifying the Athlete and declaring the Athlete's performance as invalid for non-compliance with these Regulations with all resulting consequences for the Athlete, including the forfeiture of all titles, awards, medals, points and prize and appearance money;

15.3.4 declaring an Existing Shoe, New Shoe, Development Shoe or Customised Shoe as being non-compliant;

15.3.5 removing an Existing Shoe, New Shoe or Development Shoe from the list of shoes which have been approved by World Athletics; and

15.3.6 withholding, for a reasonable time, approval of subsequent requests for an Existing Shoe, New Shoe, Development Shoe or Customised Shoe from a particular shoe manufacture.

15.4 The Chief Executive Officer (or their nominee) may, if it considers it appropriate, announce, publish or otherwise communicate the reasons for any sanction applied pursuant to this Regulation 15.

15.5 The Chief Executive Officer (or their nominee) may in addition to taking action under these Regulations refer any potential breach of these Regulations, by Applicable Persons, to the Athletics Integrity Unit.

15.6 Any potential breach of these Regulations by Applicable Persons may amount to a breach of the Integrity Code of Conduct and, in addition to any action taken under Regulation 14 and/or Regulation 15.3, may be subject to investigation and prosecution by the Athletics Integrity Unit under the Athletics Integrity Unit Reporting, Investigation and Prosecution Rules (Non-Doping) and possible proceedings under the Disciplinary Tribunal Rules.

15.3.3 取消运动员的比赛资格，宣布运动员的成绩无效，并对运动员产生所有后果，包括取消所有名次、奖励、奖牌、积分、奖金和出场费；

15.3.4 声明现有鞋、新鞋、开发鞋或定制鞋不符合规定；

15.3.5 将现有鞋、新鞋或开发鞋从世界田联批准清单中删除；和

15.3.6 在合理的时间内，拒绝批准特定运动制造商的现有鞋、新鞋、开发鞋或定制鞋的后续请求。

15.4 首席执行官（或其指定人）如果认为适当，可以宣布、公布或以其他方式传达根据本规程 15 条实施的任何制裁的理由。

15.5 除根据本规程采取行动外，首席执行官（或其指定人）还可以将适用人员可能违反本规程的任何行为提交给田径诚信部门。

15.6 适用人员任何可能违反本规程的行为都可能构成违反诚信行为准则，并且除了根据规程14条和/或15.3条采取的任何行动，还可能被田径诚信部门根据《田径诚信部门报告、调查和起诉规则（非兴奋剂）》调查和起诉，并可能根据纪律法庭规则提起诉讼。

APPENDIX

APPENDIX 1　NEW SHOES, DEVELOPMENT SHOE OR CUSTOMISED SHOES APPROVAL PROCESS

1. Where a New Shoe, Development Shoe[1] or Customised Shoe[2] is proposed to be worn in an Applicable Competition, an Athletic Shoe specification form must be completed by the relevant sports manufacturer, or where applicable by the Athlete (i.e. where an Athlete arranges for a Customised Shoe themselves and with no involvement of a sports manufacturer), and submitted to World Athletics containing the following information:

1.1　sports manufacturer's brand name and shoe/model name;

1.2　size, dimensions, sole thickness, structure [including number and construction of plates, technology (including if it contains any smart, responsive, adaptive technology)], date of availability, photograph, diagrams;

1.3　confirmation if the shoe is a New Shoe, Development Shoe or Customised Shoe; and

1.4　if the request relates to a Customised Shoe pursuant to Regulation 7.2, then the relevant medical information relating to the athlete's condition and the medical advice, report or information setting out the reasons why the customisation is necessary.

2. If requested by World Athletics, a sample of the New Shoe or Development Shoe or, if applicable, the Customised Shoe will be submitted by either the Athlete[3] or the sports manufacturer for further examination by an Independent Expert.

1　For Development Shoes, in addition, process and information set out in Appendix 2 must be followed.

2　Where an Athlete arranges for the customization of their Athletic Shoe without the involvement of a sports manufacturer the Athlete shall be responsible pursuant to Regulation 7 for obtaining approval from World Athletics for that customization.

3　See footnote 2.

附录

附录1　新鞋、开发鞋或定制鞋的审批流程

1. 如果建议在适用的比赛中穿着新鞋、开发鞋[1]或定制鞋[2]，运动鞋规格表必须由相关运动用品制造商填写，或在适用情况下由运动员填写（即运动员自己安排定制鞋，并且没有运动用品制造商的参与），并提交给世界田联，其中包含以下信息：

1.1　运动用品制造商的品牌名称及鞋/型号名称；

1.2　大小、尺寸、鞋底厚度、结构［包括板的数量和结构、技术（包括是否包含任何智能、响应性、适应性技术）］，以及可用日期、照片、图表；

1.3　确认鞋子是否为新鞋、开发鞋或定制鞋；和

1.4　如果要求的是根据规程7.2条规定的定制鞋，则应提供与运动员身体状况有关的医疗信息，以及说明需要定制原因的医疗建议、报告或信息。

2. 如果世界田联要求，在可行的情况下，运动员[3]或运动用品制造商将提交新鞋、开发鞋或定制鞋的样品，由独立专家进行进一步检查。

---

1. 此外，对于开发鞋，必须遵循附录2中规定的流程和信息。
2. 如果运动员在没有运动用品制造商参与的情况下自行定制运动鞋，应根据规程7条规定负责获得世界田联的批准。
3. 见脚注2。

3. World Athletics will use reasonable efforts to complete its examination as soon as practicable (if possible, within 30 days of receipt of the New Shoe by the Independent Expert).

4. If approved, then World Athletics will publish the New Shoe or Development Shoe on the list of approved Athletic Shoes. Customised Shoes will not be published, as customisations are made to an Existing Shoe which are deemed approved or New Shoe that has been approved, see Regulation 7 of these Regulations.

5. Except for Development Shoes, as soon as a New Shoe appears on World Athletics' published list, the New Shoe can be worn in Applicable Competitions and not before. For the period when a Development Shoe can be worn, see Appendix 2.

6. World Athletics reserves the right to implement such measures concerning the practical implementation of the approval procedure as it sees fit, including the use of technology (e.g. unique codes, certification mark etc.) compliance with which shall form part of these Regulations.

7. World Athletics reserves the right to remove an approved Athletic Shoe from its published list at any time, if it no longer complies with these Regulations.

3. 世界田联将尽合理努力尽快完成检查（如果可能，在独立专家收到新鞋后 30 天内）。

4. 如果获得批准，世界田联将在批准的运动鞋清单上公布新鞋或开发鞋。定制鞋将不会被发布，因为定制是对已批准的现有鞋或已批准的新鞋进行的，参见本规程7条。

5. 除开发鞋外，一旦新鞋出现在世界田联公布的清单中，新鞋就可以在适用的比赛中穿着，而在此之前不能穿。关于开发鞋可以穿的时间，请参见附录2。

6. 世界田联保留在其认为合适的情况下采取与批准程序的实际实施有关的措施的权利，包括技术的使用（如唯一代码、认证标志等），遵守这些技术将构成本规程的一部分。

7. 如果某款运动鞋不再符合本规程，世界田联有权随时将其从公布的运动鞋清单中删除。

APPENDIX 2 DEVELOPMENT SHOE

1. For Development Shoes, at the same time as submitting the specification under Appendix 1, the sports manufacturer must complete and submit the template development shoe form with the following information:

1.1 sports manufacturer brand and shoe/model name or number;

1.2 a list containing the dates and names of the first and all subsequent competitions at which the sponsored or supported Athlete proposes to wear a Development Shoe within the 12-month period starting from date of the first use of the Development Shoe;

1.3 a readable code (i.e. it can be scanned or be a link) that is unique to the Development Shoe, which can either be inserted in a visible location in or on the Development Shoe or provided to the Athlete in paper form or on a phone to show to the event officials. The code is to host either the Development Shoe form or the information contained within it;

1.4 confirmation of the latest date upon which the sports manufacturer will make the final version of the Development Shoe Available for Purchase (i.e. when it is intended that the Development will become a New Shoe), see paragraph 5 below.

2. Any changes to the list of competitions stated in the Development Shoe Form must be notified to World Athletics in writing with an updated Development Shoe Form.

3. If approved, World Athletics will publish on its website a list of approved Development Shoes stating the date starting from which the Development Shoe can be worn and the expiry date for approval. No technical or proprietary information belonging to a sports manufacturer will be published.

4. After the expiry date or if use of the Development Shoe ends before the expiry date, the Athletic Shoe no longer qualifies as a Development Shoe and can only continue to be worn if under paragraph 5.2 below the sports manufacturer decides to propose the Development Shoe to be a New Shoe. The Development Shoe will be removed from the approved list after its expiry date or the date when it is no longer in use.

附录2　开发鞋

1. 对于开发鞋，在提交附录1规范的同时，运动品制造商必须填写并提交模板开发鞋表格，其中包含以下信息：

1.1 运动用品制造商品牌及鞋/型号名称或编号；

1.2 首次使用开发鞋起12个月内，赞助或受资助运动员拟穿开发鞋参加的第一场及其后所有比赛的日期及名称；

1.3 开发鞋独有的可读代码（即它可以被扫描或成为链接），可以将其插入开发鞋中或其上的可见位置，或者以纸质形式或通过电话提供给运动员以向赛事官员展示。该代码将承载开发鞋表格或其中包含的信息；

1.4 确认运动用品制造商可供购买开发鞋最终版本的最晚日期（即开发将成为新鞋的预期时间），请参见下文第5段。

2. 开发鞋表格中列出的比赛清单如有任何变化，必须以书面形式通知世界田联，并附上最新的开发鞋表。

3. 如果获得批准，世界田联将在其网站上公布批准的开发鞋清单，说明开发鞋可穿的起始日期和批准有效期。任何属于运动用品制造商的技术或专有信息都不会被公布。

4. 在开发鞋可穿到期日之后，或者如果开发鞋在到期日之前停止使用，运动鞋不再具有开发鞋的资格，只有在运动用品制造商根据下面5.2中决定将开发鞋作为新鞋的情况下，运动鞋才能继续穿着。开发鞋在其有效期满或不再使用后，将从批准清单中删除。

5. If the sports manufacturer decides:

5.1 not to continue with the Development Shoe, so it is not either made Available for Purchase or complies with requirements of the Availability Scheme, then World Athletics reserves the right to request from the sports manufacturers further information concerning the discontinuance of the Development Shoe;

5.2 to proceed to produce a final version of the Development Shoe (i.e. it passes its performance and safety tests, etc.), then the Development Shoe will be deemed a New Shoe and will need to require written approval from World Athletics in accordance with Regulation 6 of these Regulations (i.e. that the final version of the Development Shoe complies with the requirements set out in these Regulations) highlighting any changes or confirming that no changes have been made to the Development Shoe.

6. World Athletics reserves the right to implement such measures concerning the practical implementation of the approval procedure as it sees fit including the use of technology (e.g. unique codes, certification mark etc.) compliance with which shall form part of these Regulations.

运动鞋规程

5. 如果运动用品制造商决定：

5.1 不再继续生产开发鞋，因此该鞋既不能供购买，也不符合可用性方案的要求，那么世界田联保留要求运动用品制造商提供关于停止生产开发鞋的进一步信息的权利；

5.2 继续生产开发鞋的最终版本（即通过性能和安全测试等），则开发鞋将被视为新鞋，需要获得世界田联根据规程6条的书面批准（即开发鞋的最终版本符合本规程中规定的要求），强调任何更改或确认没有对开发鞋进行任何更改。

6. 世界田联保留在其认为合适的情况下采取与批准程序的实际实施有关的措施的权利，包括技术的使用（如唯一代码、认证标志等），遵守这些技术将构成本规程的一部分。

APPENDIX 3   ATHLETIC SHOE SOLE THICKNESS TABLE

Shoe Sole Thickness Table – in force until 31 October 2024

Event	Maximum thickness of the sole (as per Regulation 10.6)	Further Requirement/Note
Field Events (except Triple Jump)	20mm	Applies to all Throwing Events, and Jumping Events, except the Triple Jump. For all Field Events, the sole at the centre of the athlete's forefoot must not be higher than the sole at centre of the athlete's heel referred to at Regulations 10.3 and 10.4 (i.e. at centre point of the shoe at 12% and 75% of the shoes internal length).
Triple Jump	25mm	The sole at the centre of the athlete's forefoot must not be higher than the sole at centre of the athlete's heel referred to at Regulations 10.3 and 10.4 (i.e. at centre point of the shoe at 12% and 75% of the shoes internal length).
Track Events (including hurdle events) up to but not including 800m	20mm	For relays, the rule applies to the distance of the leg being run by each athlete.
Track Events from 800m and above (including steeplechase events)	25mm	For relays, the rule applies to the distance of the leg being run by each athlete. For Track Race Walking Events, the maximum thickness of the sole is the same as that for Road Events.

附录3 运动鞋鞋底厚度表

鞋底厚度表——生效至2024年10月31日

项目	鞋底的最大厚度（根据规程10.6条）	进一步要求/注意事项
田赛（除了三级跳远）	20毫米	适用于所有投掷项目和跳跃项目，但三级跳远项目除外。 在所有田赛项目中，运动员前脚掌中心的鞋底不得高于规程10.3条和10.4条所述的运动员脚后跟中心的鞋底（即鞋的中心点在鞋内长度的12%和75%处）
三级跳远	25毫米	运动员前脚掌中心的鞋底不得高于规程10.3条和10.4条所述的运动员脚后跟中心的鞋底（即鞋的中心点在鞋内长度的12%和75%处）
径赛（包括跨栏项目）800米以下项目，不含800米	20毫米	对于接力赛，此规程适用于每位运动员所跑的每棒距离
径赛800米以上项目（包括障碍项目）	25毫米	对于接力赛，此规则适用于每位运动员所跑的每棒距离。 场地竞走项目的鞋底最大厚度与路跑项目相同

continued

Event	Maximum thickness of the sole (as per Regulation 10.6)	Further Requirement/Note
Cross-Country	25mm spike shoe or 40mm non-spike shoe	Athletes may wear spikes or non-spike shoes (i.e. road shoes). If wearing spike shoes the maximum thickness of the sole must not exceed 25mm. If wearing non-spike shoes the maximum thickness of the sole must not exceed 40mm.
Road Events (Running and Race Walking Events)	40mm	—
Mountain and Trail Races	Any Thickness	—

New Sole Thickness Table – in force from 1 November 2024

Event	Maximum thickness of the sole (as per Regulation 10.6)	Further Requirement/Note
Track Events (including hurdle and steeplechase events)	20mm spike shoe or non- spike shoe	For relays, the rule applies to the distance of the leg being run by each athlete. For Track Race Walking Events, the maximum thickness of the sole is the same as that for Road Events.
Field Events	20mm spike shoe or non- spike shoe	For all Jumping Events, the sole at the centre of the athlete's forefoot must not be higher than the sole at centre of the athlete's heel referred to at Regulations 10.3 and 10.4 (i.e. at centre point of the shoe at 12% and 75% of the shoes internal length).
Road Events (Running and Race Walking Events)	40mm	—

（续表）

项目	鞋底的最大厚度（根据规程10.6条）	进一步要求/注意事项
越野赛跑	25毫米钉鞋或40毫米无钉鞋	运动员可以穿钉鞋或无钉鞋（即路跑鞋）。如果穿钉鞋，鞋底的最大厚度不能超过25毫米。如果穿无钉鞋，鞋底的最大厚度不得超过40毫米
路跑项目（跑和竞走项目）	40毫米	—
山地跑和野地跑	任何厚度	—

新的鞋底厚度表——2024年11月1日起生效

项目	鞋底的最大厚度（根据规程10.6条）	进一步要求/注意事项
径赛项目（包括跨栏和障碍项目）	20毫米钉鞋或无钉鞋	对于接力赛，此规则适用于每位运动员所跑的每棒距离。对于场地竞走项目，鞋底的最大厚度与路跑项目相同
田赛项目	20毫米钉鞋或无钉鞋	对于所有跳跃项目，运动员前脚掌中心的鞋底不得高于规程10.3条和10.4条所述的运动员脚后跟中心的鞋底（即鞋的中心点在鞋内长度的12%和75%处）
路跑项目（跑和竞走项目）	40毫米	—

continued

Event	Maximum thickness of the sole (as per Regulation 10.6)	Further Requirement/Note
Cross-Country	20mm spike shoes or 40mm non-spike shoes	Athletes may wear spikes or non-spike shoes (i.e. road shoes). If wearing spike shoes the maximum thickness of the sole must not exceed 20mm. If wearing non-spike shoes the maximum thickness of the sole must not exceed 40mm.
Mountain and Trail Races	Any Thickness	—

Important notice: Pursuant to Regulation 5.3, from 1 November 2024 an Existing Shoe whose sole is greater than the maximum thicknesses set out in the above table is no longer approved and cannot be worn in Applicable Competitions.

（续表）

项目	鞋底的最大厚度（根据规程10.6条）	进一步要求/注意事项
越野赛跑	20毫米钉鞋或40毫米无钉鞋	运动员可以穿钉鞋或无钉鞋（即路跑鞋）。如果穿钉鞋，鞋底的最大厚度不得超过20毫米。如果穿无钉鞋，鞋底的最大厚度不得超过40毫米
山地跑和野地跑	任何厚度	—

重要通知：根据规程5.3条，从2024年11月1日起，鞋底超过上表所列最大厚度的现有鞋将不再被批准，并且不能在适用的比赛中穿着。

APPENDIX 4   ATHLETIC SHOE AVAILABILITY PROCESS

1. An Athletic Shoe can be purchased through a sports manufacturer's sales channel(s) which includes retail (brick and mortar), brand websites or apps and e-commerce (including pre-order periods which must be for at least one month).

2. Whilst Existing Shoes are deemed to or already comply with the requirement to be Available for Purchase, evidence of their availability may be requested by World Athletics from a sports manufacturer.

3. When seeking approval for a New Shoe, the sports manufacturer must provide information about the Athletic Shoe's availability (i.e. where and how they can be purchased) the time limit for which must be at least one month before an Applicable Competition.

4. If the requested information is not provided, then the shoe will not be approved and not be entered on the approved list. The New Shoe cannot be worn, unless it is on the approved list.

5. New Shoes that are Available for Purchase are subject to stock (including size ranges), supply chains and manufacturing timelines. There is no obligation on a shoe manufacturer to re-stock an Athletic Shoe that has been Available for Purchase and is sold out.

6. If a New Shoe is no longer Available for Purchase (e.g. if it is sold out awaiting restocking, the line has ended, there are supply chain issues affecting manufacturer or delivery issues etc.), then the Athlete wishing to purchase the New Shoe may, depending on the ability of the sports manufacturer concerned to provide new stock of the New Shoe, wish to wait for the New Shoe to be restocked or purchase an alternative Existing Shoe or New Shoe that is Available for Purchase.

7. World Athletics will conduct checks by requesting sports manufacturers to provide evidence that the Athletic Shoe is/was Available to Purchase.

8. If evidence is provided that the Athletic Shoe is/was Available to Purchase, then no further action will be necessary.

附录4　运动鞋供应流程

1. 运动鞋可以通过运动用品制造商的销售渠道购买，包括零售（实体店）、品牌网站或应用程序和电子商务（包括至少1个月的预购期）。

2. 当现有的鞋被认为或已经符合可供购买的要求时，世界田联可能会要求运动用品制造商提供其可用性的证据。

3. 在申请新鞋的批准时，运动用品制造商必须提供运动鞋的可用性信息（即在哪里以及如何购买），时间限制为必须至少在适用的比赛前一个月。

4. 如果没有提供要求的信息，那么该鞋将不会被批准，也不会进入批准清单。除非新鞋在批准的清单上，否则不能穿。

5. 可供购买的新鞋受库存（包括尺寸范围）、供应链和制造时间表的影响。运动鞋制造商没有义务重新储备可供购买且已售罄的运动鞋。

6. 如果新鞋不再可供购买（例如，如果已售完等待补货、生产线已关闭、存在影响制造商的供应链问题或交付问题等），则希望购买新鞋的运动员可能会等待新鞋补货或购买可供购买的替代现有鞋或新鞋，具体取决于相关运动用品制造商提供新鞋新库存的能力。

7. 世界田联将进行检查，要求运动鞋制造商提供运动鞋可以/曾经可以购买的证据。

8. 如果有证据表明该运动鞋可以/曾经可以购买，则无须采取进一步行动。

9. If no evidence is provided, then the Athletic Shoe is not compliant, and then:

   a. the Athletic Shoe is removed from the approved list;

   b. this action is notified to Member Federations/Athletes; and

   c. the Athlete(s)', who wore the shoe, results will be marked accordingly "UNC TR5.2" (uncertified).

10. If a sports manufacturer is unable provide evidence of a New Shoes' availability, World Athletics may withdraw the New Shoe's approval until such a time as the sports manufacturer can provide the requested evidence showing the New Shoe is Available to Purchase.

11. The World Athletics Chief Executive Officer (or their nominee) may, on the written request of the World Federation of the Sporting Goods Industry, temporarily waive any or all of the requirements set out in this Appendix 4 in circumstances beyond the reasonable control of the sports goods manufacturer industry that make a sports goods manufacturing industry unable to make the New Shoe Available for Purchase in accordance with this Appendix 4, provided that the sports manufacturers have made reasonable efforts, to the satisfaction of the World Athletics Chief Executive Officer (or their nominee), to do so.

9. 如果没有提供证据，那么运动鞋是不合规的，然后：

   a. 该运动鞋将从批准清单中删除；

   b. 通知各会员协会/运动员；和

   c. 穿着这双鞋的运动员，其成绩将被相应地标记为"UNC TR5.2"（未经认证）。

10. 如果运动用品制造商无法提供新鞋可供购买的证据，世界田联可以撤销新鞋的批准，直到运动用品制造商能够提供所需的证据证明新鞋可供购买。

11. 应世界体育用品工业联合会的书面请求，世界田径运动首席执行官（或其指定人）可在超出体育用品制造业合理控制范围的情况下，暂时放弃本附录4条规定的任何或所有要求，使体育用品制造业无法根据本附录4条提供新鞋可供购买，前提是运动用品制造商已做出合理努力，令世界田联首席执行官（或其指定人）满意。